D0824773

PEOPLE PLACES

PEOPLE PLACES

Design Guidelines for Urban Open Space

Edited by

Clare Cooper Marcus

and

Carolyn Francis

Departments of Architecture and Landscape Architecture
University of California, Berkeley

Drawings by
Su Sin Tang and Yun Flora Yeh

VNR VAN NOSTRAND REINHOLD
_____ New York

Library of Congress Catalog Card Number 89-28505
ISBN 0-442-31929-0

Printed in the United States of America

Van Nostrand Reinhold
115 Fifth Avenue
New York, New York 10003

Van Nostrand Reinhold International Company Limited
11 New Fetter Lane
London EC4P 4EE, England

Van Nostrand Reinhold
480 La Trobe Street
Melbourne, Victoria 3000, Australia

Nelson Canada
1120 Birchmount Road
Scarborough, Ontario M1K 5G4, Canada

16 15 14 13 12 11 10 9 8 7 6 5 4 3 2 1

Library of Congress Cataloging-in-Publication Data

People places: design guidelines for urban open space/edited by Clare
  Cooper Marcus, Carolyn A. Francis.
    p.   cm.
  ISBN 0-442-31929-0
  1. Plazas—United States. 2. Open spaces—United States. 3. City
planning—United States—History—20th Century. I. Marcus, Clare
Cooper.   II. Francis, Carolyn A., 1956–
NA9070.P45   1990
711′.4—dc20   89-28505
                                                            CIP

To our children, Jason and Lucy,
Michael and Kate,

and

To the profession of landscape
architecture, whose role it is to create
and nurture outdoor environments, and in
celebration of the seventh-fifth anniversary of the
Department of Landscape Architecture of
the University of California at Berkeley

CONTENTS

PREFACE   xi
ABOUT THE EDITORS   xiii
CONTRIBUTORS   xvii
INTRODUCTION   1

1. URBAN PLAZAS   9
*Clare Cooper Marcus, with Carolyn Francis and
    Robert Russell*
Is There a Role for the Urban Plaza?   9
Definition   10
Literature on Plazas   10
Plazas in the Contemporary U.S. Scene   12
A Typology of Downtown Plazas   15
Design Recommendations   18
Case Studies   46
References   63
Design Review Checklist   65

2. NEIGHBORHOOD PARKS   69
*Clare Cooper Marcus, with Clare Miller Watsky,
    Elliot Insley, and Carolyn Francis*
History of American Parks   69
Future of Neighborhood Parks   70
Literature on Urban Parks   71
Design Recommendations   71
Special User Group Needs   74
Typical Activities   82
Park Typology and Case Studies   90
References   113
Design Review Checklist   115

3. MINIPARKS AND VEST-POCKET
   PARKS   119
*Clare Cooper Marcus, with Nanine Hilliard
    Greene*
Design Recommendations   120

Case Studies   135
References   140
Design Review Checklist   141

4. CAMPUS OUTDOOR SPACES   143
Clare Cooper Marcus, with Trudy Wischemann
Literature on Campus Open Spaces   143
Design Recommendations   144
Case Studies   163
References   167
Design Review Checklist   169

5. HOUSING AND OUTDOOR SPACES
   FOR THE ELDERLY   171
Diane Y. Carstens
Design and the Aging Process   171
Housing for the Elderly   173
Literature on Design and Aging   173
Guidelines for Site Planning, Design, and
    Detailing   174
Guidelines Based on Older People's Social and
    Psychological Needs   176
Case Studies   197
References   208
Design Review Checklist   210

6. DAY CARE OUTDOOR SPACES   215
Carolyn Francis
Importance of the Environment   216
The Literature   218
Play and Development in the Day Care Setting   219
Design Recommendations   221
Case Studies   246
References   257
Design Review Checklist   259

7. HOSPITAL OUTDOOR SPACES   263
Robert Paine and Carolyn Francis
The Evolution of Hospital Design and Medical
   Theory   263
The Literature   266
General Findings   267
Design Recommendations   272
Case Studies   282
References   287
Design Review Checklist   289

INDEX   291

PREFACE

This book has had a rather long history. The idea for it began to take shape during the early years of my teaching career at the University of California at Berkeley. In 1969 I offered a course entitled "Social and Psychological Factors in Open Space Design" in the Department of Landscape Architecture. Two years later, when this course was required for all graduate and undergraduate students in that department, I introduced two demanding fieldwork assignments. First, the students had to observe and compare environment–behavior interactions in two downtown San Francisco plazas. Then, later in the semester, they conducted a detailed postoccupancy evaluation of a neighborhood park of their choice.

In the fall of 1975, this class concentrated on miniparks. The Berkeley Parks Department hired a former student (Gary Mason) in this class to make a detailed evaluation of six miniparks, to which the course's current students made a major fieldwork contribution.[1] In addition, two former students, Rolf Diamant and Greg Moore, were hired by the National Park Service to help plan the Golden Gate National Recreation Area. In 1975, at their suggestion, all of my current students conducted user studies of beaches on the Pacific Ocean and San Francisco Bay.

These students' evaluations were often very good, and I kept the best reports. As I read more and more of these studies, I noticed patterns of use and misuse. A graduate seminar in landscape architecture in 1974 and 1975 reviewed these studies and the relevant published literature and drew up preliminary design guidelines for various kinds of outdoor spaces. In 1976, two under-

graduates who had become interested in this work, Linda Johnson and Cindy Rice, volunteered to do the layout and illustrations of a monograph entitled *People Places,* published in 1976 by the University of California's Department of Landscape Architecture, with support from the Beatrix Farrand Fund and including chapters on urban plazas by graduate students Tom Farrell, Maureen McVann, and myself; on neighborhood parks by Rolf Diamant, Marta Huck, Joel Summerhill, and Lesley Turner; on street parks by Sheila Brady; and on miniparks by Gary Mason and myself. This monograph then became the core of the present book.

In the years since then, I collected more papers from my courses; evaluation reports of parks and plazas were published by Project for Public Spaces in New York; and books appeared on user needs in neighborhood spaces,[2] neighborhood parks,[3] and urban plazas.[4]

In 1980, debates on the planning of the Berkeley Campus prompted me to have all the students in LA 140 (approximately 80) study how outdoor spaces on campus were used and what students felt about them. Subsequent to this, one graduate landscape student— Trudy Wischemann—and I wrote a lengthy report on the analysis of this material.[5]

---

[1] Gary Mason, Alex Forrester, and Robin Hermann, *Berkeley Park Use Study* (Berkeley, Calif.: City of Berkeley Park Department, 1975).

[2] Randolph Hester, *Neighborhood space* (Stroudberg, Pa.: Dowden, Hutchinson & Ross, 1975).

[3] Albert J. Rutledge, *Anatomy of a park* (New York: McGraw-Hill, 1971); and Albert J. Rutledge, *A visual approach to park design* (New York: Garland STPM Press, 1981).

[4] William Whyte, *The social life of small urban spaces* (Washington, D.C.: Conservative Foundation, 1980).

[5] Clare Cooper Marcus, and Trudy Wischemann, Campus open space: An underutilized potential (mimeo, Department of Landscape Architecture, University of California, Berkeley, 1983).

The possibility of summarizing all these studies as design guidelines looked more promising. But there still were noticeable gaps: Outdoor areas in housing for the elderly for recreation, gardening, and socializing had received scant attention; the courtyards and gardens of hospitals were being designed and built with no apparent attempts at evaluation; and although there were a few insightful studies of the outdoor play areas of day care centers,[6] and at least two master's theses had reported on postoccupancy evaluations of specific settings,[7] no definitive summary of this work on day care design had yet appeared.

Gradually these gaps began to be filled. A graduate student, Robert Paine, in landscape architecture at Berkeley wrote on hospital outdoor spaces for his M.L.A. thesis;[8] at the University of Illinois at Champaign-Urbana, Diane Carstens wrote her M.L.A. thesis on the design of outdoor space for elderly housing.[9] I invited both of them to summarize their theses for chapters in this book. Carolyn Francis, a Ph.D. candidate at Berkeley, helped me edit and organize this book. In fact, her work and suggestions were so important that she became its coeditor. My coeditor Carolyn Francis and I believe strongly in our field of study and the importance of considering the human use of designed spaces. First, we have assumed that the providers and designers of the kinds of spaces we describe in this book care about people and want to create places that are socially appropriate. Second, we have assumed that most such decision makers do not have time to do extensive reading or empirical research of their own. Third, we have assumed that to varying degrees, the physical environment does indeed affect behavior. Although we have not taken a strict determinist viewpoint, we do believe that certain environmental arrangements encourage certain activities, that other environments discourage certain activities, and that still others are seemingly neutral. Along with C. M.

Deasy, we believe that "the purpose of planning or design is not to create a physical artifact, but a setting for human behavior."[10]

Finally, we realize that to use human behavior or social activities to inform and shape the designed environment is not the approach of some designers or the approach of most studio teachers. But we feel strongly that this needs to be the approach. An approach based almost exclusively on visual form leads either to the reproduction of previously used "solutions" or to the proliferation of artistic statements that pertain more to current design fashion than to the needs of the public. We believe that aesthetic goals need to be balanced and merged with ecological needs, contextual issues, and user preferences. We also recognize that

there are many economic, technical and aesthetic considerations, that shape the buildings we know; they in turn shape the behavior patterns of people who use them. To reverse this relationship, to start from an understanding of human motivation and let this concern shape the form, will require a profound alteration in the basic approach to design.[11]

We hope that this book will join others in the same genre in offering designers the information they need, in a format that is useful, so that this "profound alteration in the basic approach to design" can begin to take shape.

C. C. M.

HOW TO USE THIS BOOK

Each chapter of this book is similarly arranged, starting with an introduction to and definition of the type of open space being discussed. This is followed by a review of the literature on this spatial form, covering studies of both the formal aspects and the user's needs. The bulk of the chapter is devoted to the design guidelines, followed by several short case studies. Each case study is accompanied by a site plan, a brief description of the site's use, and a summary of successful and less successful aspects of the site plan. The reason for these case studies is to present actual settings and to describe how they function in relation to the issues raised in this book. These are intended as real examples of varying success, rather than "best case" examples of the most up-to-date design responses. Each is presented in terms of how it was—physically and socially—at the time the evaluative study (or studies) was done; in some cases, spaces we have presented here have been

[6] Sybil Kritchevsky and Elizabeth Prescott, with Lee Walling, *Planning environments for young children: Physical space* (Washington, D.C.: National Association for the Education of Young Children, 1969); Fred Linn Osmon, *Patterns for designing children's centers* (New York: Educational Facilities Laboratories, 1971); and Gary T. Moore, C. Lane, A. Hill, V. Cohen, and T. McGinty, *Recommendations for child care centers* (Milwaukee: University of Wisconsin, Center for Architecture and Urban Planning Research, 1979).

[7] Maureen Simmons, "Children's play areas: Designing for developmental play needs" (M.L.A. thesis, University of California at Berkeley, 1974); and Amita Sinha, "Continuity and branching in preschool playgrounds" (M. Arch. thesis, Virginia Polytechnic Institute, 1984).

[8] Robert Paine, "Design guidelines for hospital outdoor spaces: Case studies of three hospitals" (M.L.A. thesis, University of California at Berkeley, 1984).

[9] Diane Y. Carstens, "Design guidelines for exterior spaces: Mid- to high-rise housing for older people" (M.L.A. thesis, University of Illinois at Champaign-Urbana, 1982).

[10] C. M. Deasy, *Design for human affairs* (Cambridge, Mass.: Schenkman, 1974), p. 40.

[11] Ibid.

subsequently redesigned.

Thus, this book might be used in a number of ways. Apart from reading through sequentially, perusing all the literature reviews would give the reader a good overview of what has, and has not, been covered in studies of designed open space use. Similarly, reviewing the case studies in various chapters would suggest some of the ways existing places work—and don't-work—for people.

It should be noted, too, that some of the material may be relevant to more than one chapter, and type of space. Most of the connections are quite self-evident: elderly people may share some conditions with, or represent a substantial portion of, hospital patients—therefore, material found in both chapters may be helpful in designing either for elderly housing *or* for hospitals. Likewise, children play at day care centers, as well as in parks and miniparks, as well as when they are hospitalized. Hence, relevant information may be gleaned from these chapters and applied to a particular project setting. Making these types of connections while using the book will allow the most complete review of pertinent material.

We imagined the readers of this book as being from the following groups:

1. Professional designers—architects, landscape architects, urban designers, city planners—who might use the guidelines first as an overview of issues in a particular type of setting and later as a checklist to evaluate a preliminary or final design solution from a user's perspective.

2. Students of landscape architecture, architecture, urban design, and urban planning who might use this as an educative resource. For example, when developing a program for a new or redesigned park, the guidelines in Chapter 2 may be a useful source; or in reading through each chapter's literature reviews, topics to study more deeply in a thesis or term paper should become apparent.

3. Open space providers, such as the staff of a parks department or the space-planning division of a corporation or hospital. These fee-paying clients might use the guidelines as a base from which to plan a specific design program. In addition, the guidelines should be useful when an existing space does not work; they could be used as a checklist for determining what features might need to be added, modified, or eliminated.

4. Environmental managers, such as the staff of a day care center or a housing scheme for the elderly. These are the people who will organize the use of outdoor space. The educational philosophy of a day care center, for example, should inform the design of the play space or identify a mismatch between the desired activities and the

provided facilities.

5. City officials who might use a particular set of guidelines in local policy regarding building or design regulations. For example, a city planning department might use these guidelines to implement a recommended or mandatory plaza design code.

6. Design award jurors or local government officials who might use a particular set of guidelines as an evaluative checklist to appraise and compare various designs. For example, the judges of a design competition for a new central plaza on a college campus might compare the entries with the appropriate design guidelines in order to rank them in terms of social appropriateness.

7. Future residents in, or users of, a particular designed setting who might use the guidelines to inform their discussion with the fee-paying client, the designers, or government officials. For example, a group of older people planning to create and build a housing co-op for their retirement might use the chapter on elderly outdoor space design as a base of information from which to develop their own design program.

8. An advocacy group or organization that is lobbying for more facilities, such as employer-based day care, who might use the guidelines to draw up their own sets of priorities to ensure that significant aspects of the environment—such as outdoor play spaces—are not overlooked or are poorly planned.

9. Social scientists and environment–behavior researchers who could use these guidelines as hypotheses to be tested and clarified in future empirical studies.

ABOUT THE EDITORS

CAROLYN FRANCIS

My interest in people and environments dates back as far as I can remember, to the home of my great grand-aunts, Effie and Lucy, in Port Hueneme, California, with the kitchen floor that sloped down, big glass jars of candy, and a barn full of bric-a-brac. My mother, and her mother too, played here as a child. Since then, the garden and house underwent many changes, and the ocean slowly devoured the land behind the house: When I was three, the backyard was largely sand, and before my children were born, the house was gone.

I have since lived in more places than I can readily recall—my father worked in heavy construction and my family moved often. I grew up in various locations in the United States, Australia, Pakistan, and many places in between. My immersion in such a rich stew of different peoples and environments during what they call the formative years, has left me with a keen sense of the value and meaning of *places* in our human experience.

When I went to the University of Chicago, I began studying people, in a social psychology program called "Human Behavior and Institutions," and found it interesting but not completely fulfilling. One day while waiting in line at the bookstore, I noticed a book, *With Man in Mind,* by Constance Perin (1970). I picked it up and thumbed through it, finding the combination of people and environments very provocative. The book was required for a geography class, along with five or six others, which I felt somehow compelled to buy; in turn, I felt compelled to take the course itself. From geography I moved to environmental design, and I have spent the last fifteen years reading, writing, observing, analyzing, discussing, and arguing the issues raised by the interface of human beings and their environments.

Along the way there have been a few diversions, perhaps the most rewarding being the birth of my two children. Through them I have been politicized regarding our society's priorities, especially the use of space, from the danger of cars in residential neighborhoods, to day care centers in basements with no outdoor play areas, to parks with hot, ugly, and boring play equipment, to asphalt school yards. Children usually manage to find an empty lot, back alley, or drainage ditch where they can interact with the environment, maybe find an insect, and develop an affirmative relationship with a place. But I hope that designed places will—if informed by an understanding of what children really do and enjoy—assume the quality of these "found" places.

Places can, and should, be responsive to our pragmatic needs: If we need to see out, there should be a window; if we need to use both hands, there should be a ledge for our packages. Places also can and should allow us to express who we are: with a window box to plant as we like or a porch that can be left open or easily enclosed and furnished to our taste. And places can and must express and affirm the value of each individual and our collective place in balance with the natural forces and other living species of the planet.

Places root us—to the earth, to our own history and memories, to our families and larger community. With our sensory perceptors and flexibility of movement, we are truly "designed" to fully experience and appreciate the qualities of place—and likewise are very sensitive to settings which don't live up to our needs and expectations.

CLARE COOPER MARCUS

My deep interest in the outdoor environment stems from my childhood during World War II when I was evacuated from London to the relative calm of the English countryside. There, in the woods, farmland, and overgrown ornamental gardens of the Rothschild estate, I spent my formative years exploring, building tree houses, growing vegetables, and raising chickens and rabbits. Because there was little danger from vehicular traffic (due to gasoline rationing), I was permitted a huge territorial range. The demands of the blackout and the elimination of all signs indicating direction or location (to fool the enemy, should the expected invasion occur) helped develop a keen visual sense of observation and orientation. I became fascinated with the minutiae of the landscape; it was small wonder that when I entered the University of London as an undergraduate, it was to major in cultural and historical geography.

Fieldwork as an undergraduate in England and later as a graduate student in geography at the University of Nebraska sharpened my skills of observation. After working for several years as a city planner in London, I returned to the United States, completed a second master's degree (in city and regional planning at Berkeley), and focused on the designed environment.

My interest in urban open space has its roots in four sources: graduate study in city planning, teaching landscape architecture, raising two children in an urban setting, and personal enjoyment of the public realm.

As a graduate student in city planning at Berkeley in the 1960s, I became interested in subsidized housing and how the users' needs meshed—or did not mesh—with the designer's goals. As I began conducting case studies of particular housing schemes and reading other such studies from North America and Britain that appeared in the early 1970s, I noticed that it was often the site plan and the detailing of outdoor spaces between buildings that were pivotal to a scheme's success. In 1969, I started teaching at Berkeley in the Department of Landscape Architecture. Of necessity, my courses focused on the kinds of outdoor spaces that landscape architects might be asked to design—neighborhood parks, downtown plazas, and the like.

A third source of interest evolved from raising two children in an urban setting. When they attended day care and afterschool care and asked to be taken to playgrounds and parks, my interest in those types of outdoor spaces was inevitably aroused. I observed my own children and other users and began to refine my understanding of why some parks seemed to "work" whereas others did not; why children were fascinated with some playgrounds but quickly became bored in others.

Now that my children are beyond the playground stage, I find myself drawn to gatherings in public spaces, such as art shows in the park, rallies in downtown plazas, and informal musical events on campus. I like being part of a crowd and enjoy the heightened state of awareness that such an experience seems to engender. I am drawn to informally observing people in public, in my daily life, on consulting or research jobs, while visiting other campuses on lecturing visits, and while traveling in foreign countries. My preferred locale for writing is also in the (semi) public realm: Indeed, most of my contributions to this book were written in Berkeley cafés tolerant of "resident scholars." I enjoy the ebb and flow of writing at a café table and then looking up to daydream or fantasize about the other café patrons. Although gardening quietly alone is my favorite recreational activity, sitting in a café near other people is certainly my second favorite; in such a setting, writing about outdoor space use has been more recreation than work.

ACKNOWLEDGMENTS

We would like to take this opportunity to express our gratitude to those who contributed to the various stages of development of *People Places*. The first to be acknowledged are all the students at Berkeley who took Landscape Architecture 140, "Social and Psychological Factors in Open Space Design" and whose work was the seed of all that followed. The contributors to our early monograph (*People Places* 1976) were the first to pull together the existing material on parks and plazas: Tom Farrell, Maureen McVann, Rolf Diamant, Marta Huck, Joel Summerhill, Lesley Turner, Sheila Brady, Gary Mason, Linda Johnson, and Cindy Rice.

As chapters covering more types of outdoor space were added and newly published material was incorporated into the manuscript, many students at the College of Environmental Design helped with library research, editing, and writing short pieces. We are especially indebted to Cathy Higdon, Amita Sinha, Virginia Warheit, Kimberley Moses, Elliot Insley, Teresa Clarke, Hitesh Mehta, Laura Hall, and Dan dePolo. Of particular note are those students whose master's theses we used in the chapters on day care outdoor spaces (Maureen Simmons, Amita Sinha) and in the chapter on outdoor spaces for housing for the elderly (Marian Wolfe). Two master's theses, by Robert Paine and Diane Carstens, appear in modified form as complete chapters in this book. To all of the above, we are immensely grateful.

We also found helpful and instructive the comments by the publisher's reviewers—David Chapin, Sue

Weidemann, Robin Moore, and Roger Trancik—and adjusted the manuscript accordingly. We especially appreciate the review comments on Chapter 6, by landscape architect Keila Fields (whose extensive visiting of day care centers informed her comments and provided many photo illustrations), and Sharon Stine, past director of Pacific Oaks College Children's School (now an environmental designer herself), who commented on child development as well as generously provided the case study and photos of Pacific Oaks.

In any book dealing with design, the illustrations are as important as the text. Hence, we are indebted to those who contributed illustrations for the book. Chapter authors Diane Carstens and Robert Paine gave photos as well as text; other photos were taken by Robert Russell, Jenni Webber, Anthony Poon, Nanine Hilliard Greene, Amita Sinha, Sharon Stine, and Keila Fields. We are grateful to five professional photographers who graciously allowed us to publish their work: Felice Frankel, Robert Laufman, Jane Lidz, Michael McKinley, and Gerald Ratto. The balance of the photos were taken by the editors, the bulk of them by Cooper Marcus. We also are grateful to the graphic artists who provided all the site plans and line drawings, Su Sin Tang and Yun Flora Yeh, who began their work as students in the Department of Landscape Architecture at Berkeley and are now professional landscape architects.

The indispensable and highly appreciated word-processing talents of Jane Dobson and Patricia McCulley of the Department of Landscape Architecture, Arleda Jean Martinez of the Institute of Urban and Regional Development, Betty King of the Department of Architecture, and Kaye Bock of the Department of City and Regional Planning—all at the University of California at Berkeley—can receive no praise too high. We were constantly rewarded with clean, up-to-date drafts in return for our often illegible, probably incomprehensibly annotated scrawl. Without their support, the manuscript would still be in a hopeless tangle.

A word also must be added regarding the ever-elusive financial support of work in progress. Because we were disappointed in our attempts to secure funding, from several major foundations, to support development of the manuscript, we are even more grateful for the funding received from the Beatrix Farrand Fund of the Department of Landscape Architecture, and the Committee on Research at the University of California at Berkeley.

We would also like to acknowledge the contribution of Wendy Sarkissian, whose work with Cooper Marcus on *Housing As If People Mattered* (1986) clarified many issues and concerns regarding the development of design guidelines. Having a clear idea of how we wanted to present this material allowed us to move forward confidently.

Finally are those to whom we are personally indebted, for encouragement, good humor, and help in fixing dinner. Carolyn gives her heartfelt thanks to Steve, children Mike and Kate, and her mother Donna. Clare gives her sincere thanks and appreciation to her children Jason and Lucy for understanding their often overcommitted and distracted mother and for the many times we enjoyed outdoor places together, the places that form the subject matter of this book.

CONTRIBUTORS

Diane Y. Carstens
Vice President, Planning and Design, Gerontological Services Inc., Santa Monica, California

Carolyn Francis
Ph.D. candidate, Department of Architecture, University of California, Berkeley

Nanine Hilliard Greene
Writer, Berkeley, California

Elliot Insley
Landscape Architect, Berkeley, California

Clare Cooper Marcus
Professor, Department of Architecture and Landscape Architecture, University of California, Berkeley

Robert Paine
Landscape Architect, RPA Designs, El Sobrante, California

Robert Russell
Landscape Architect, Quincy, California

Clare Miller Watsky
Landscape Architect, San Francisco, California

Trudy Wischemann
Researcher, Applied Behavioral Sciences, University of California, Davis

INTRODUCTION: PUBLIC PLACES AND DESIGN GUIDELINES

The medieval town square, or piazza, was often the heart of a city: its outdoor living and meeting place; a site for markets, celebrations, and executions; and the place where one went to hear the news, buy food, collect water, talk politics, or watch the world go by. Indeed, it is doubtful that the medieval city could have functioned without its piazza or town square. It is important to note that virtually every momentous demonstration for political change in eastern Europe, the Baltic republics, and China in 1989–1990 took place in the main square of the capital city. In some countries, public open space is still a very significant setting for a display of the strength of numbers behind a movement for political change.

In North America, some observers have argued that the contemporary privatization of life—the streamlining and decentralization of services—has made obsolete the piazza's function (Chidister 1988). What remains are the scattered, unconnected urban plazas used predominantly by one segment of the population (office workers), and only on weekdays during their lunch hour. Chidister contends that the use of such spaces does not constitute a recurring interest in public life, that plaza use is just an "event" in the well-established private life of most of the users (the ironic exception being the homeless, who often live in such spaces). But others believe that the enthusiastic use of such places as Faneuil Hall Market Place in Boston and Harbor Place in Baltimore are indications of a lively interest in public life (see, for example, Crowhurst-Lennard and Lennard 1987).

Whereas the importance of considering historic precedents has been established in the study and theory of urban form, much less attention has been paid to the historic precedents of urban functions, or the interplay between form and function. True, most of us no longer go to one central open-air market for our food, to a common pump for water, or to a central place to hear the town crier declare the news. We socialize in the privacy of our homes, where everything from water and electricity to news, mail, advertising, and even computer-based work is piped in to us. For that very reason, we believe, many people yearn for a public life, albeit perhaps only in a brief downtown lunch hour. The office-district plaza is certainly not the hub of city life that the piazza once was, but does that make it any less important to contemporary life?

Just as most of the activities that used to occur in the home (work, education, and marriage, birth, and death rituals) have been moved to special-purpose places, so the public activities of the central piazza (purchases, performances, sports, meetings) also have been moved to other special-purpose places (shopping malls, amphitheaters, stadiums, hotel and conference centers, neighborhood parks, and school yards). Public life has not so much disappeared as it has reconstituted. Although we might complain that public and semipublic spaces have now become the special territories of different age groups (the school yard, teen hangout, college campus, tennis club, senior citizen housing) or of different ethnic or cultural groups (the Latino playground, the yuppie shopping mall, the park used mainly by gays), this function–user specialization (some would say fragmentation) is a fact of contemporary life in urban North America. The medieval town square or Italian piazza cannot provide models of function to emulate, although it may offer important lessons in form, such as height-to-width ratio, sense of enclosure, and furnishing to enhance use. San Francisco is not Siena, and it is foolish to evoke historic forms in the hope that they will generate in the contemporary decentralized urban agglomeration the rich diversity of public life generated in the dense, highly centralized medieval city.

Public events now occur in a variety of places, which tend to be situated in a particular geographic context (central city, old suburb, new suburb) and to serve a particular segment of the population (families with children, older persons, office employees, college students). Likewise, the designs for their uses also have become more particular and complex. It is not enough to emulate historic forms, as some contemporary architectural theorists have proposed (Krier 1979; Rossi 1982). Our cities are replete with architectural statements that have little meaning to adjacent populations who might have become enthusiastic users but who—quite sensibly—avoid places that evoke in them feelings of alienation or discomfort. In the contemporary, changing, pluralist city, it is essential to consider the interplay of form and use in different geographic and socioeconomic contexts.

In our public places, commercial clients are replacing public or governmental agencies in sponsoring highly successful "festival market places." Beginning with Ghirardelli Square in San Francisco, in cities all over North America (and more recently in Europe) a new kind of semipublic space is emerging with its accompanying boutiques, cafés, and specialty stores. Some urban observers have opposed this trend, arguing that such places are accessible only to those with money to spend; closer to the truth is the fact that many users do not spend (much) money but come only to window-shop or to sit and watch the crowds. There

is no doubt that such places have enlivened whole sections of cities, for example, Baltimore's Harbor Place, Manhattan's South Street Seaport, Boston's Faneuil Hall, and London's Covent Garden. For city teenagers, these lively marketplaces have become at least as appealing as the shopping mall. Perhaps these are the modern equivalent of the street market. Though not public space in a legal sense, these marketplaces certainly are accessible to, and popular with, a large cross section of the public.

In downtown office districts, too, private developers (usually corporations) are replacing financially strapped public agencies as the providers of plazas. This move, largely prompted by bonuses to allow increased building height, has given our cities outdoor spaces in districts where employees need just a place to sit. Although corporate ownership has meant that some plazas are locked on the weekends (e.g., the Trans-America Redwood Park in San Francisco) and that others were designed to discourage use (e.g., CitiCorp Plaza in San Francisco), for the most part such spaces are actively used and appreciated. Though the first such spaces discouraged use because they lacked furnishings and amenities, tighter design guidelines in cities such as New York, San Francisco, Los Angeles, Seattle, Cleveland, and Chicago now ensure that there are places to sit, buy food, and relax in the sun at lunchtime.

A recent move is for the plaza to "move indoors." With Portman's Hyatt Hotels and the Ford Foundation's building setting a design trend for indoor foyers and atria to feel like an outdoor place, corporations in some cities are now locating the "public space" they are required to provide under height-bonus agreements inside the building's foyer.

Contemporary North Americans respond enthusiastically to opportunities to eat, browse, and mingle in public places: food concessions at an open-air arts and crafts fair, Live Oak Park, Berkeley, California.

Downtown plaza designs of the 1950s and 1960s provided few places to sit and were seldom concerned with human comfort. (Photo: Robert Russell)

The private indoor atrium has become almost a standard feature of new corporate office buildings, especially in New York City. The main criticism of these spaces is that they are not truly public, and thus not accessible or usable. . . . In Toronto and other Canadian cities, the lack of atrium publicness has become a major policy issue, with various interest groups initiating lawsuits to make these places more accessible. (Francis 1988, p.57).

Clearly, the issue of what is public and who is excluded from privately owned, publicly accessible places is important. But we should not assume too quickly that it is a totally negative trend. For example, for some people, such as the elderly residents of downtown areas, the semipublic atrium has become an attractive, temperature-controlled, secure social setting that is more appealing than an outdoor space. Rather, problems arise when such a place becomes so popular that one group—for example, low-spending elderly—become the dominant user, and management decides that it is time to move them out, by removing the seating. This occurred at the Crystal Court in Minneapolis when—after years of using this attractive, downtown atrium as a "sitting room"—elderly people were forced

out by a new management company that removed all the seating. With little clout in the corporate arena, older people's protests are largely ignored.

Public ownership per se, however, does not preclude similar policies. Just because an urban space is legally public land does not prevent the same kind of harassment from taking place as on some corporate plazas. In 1969, Sommer and Becker wrote about the redesign of a Sacramento park that deliberately made it unappealing to the elderly men and winos who used it (Sommer and Becker 1969). Upper middle–class commuters driving by had put pressure on the city's parks department to make these changes. Unfortunately, this trend has continued; in the late 1980s, it has often been the homeless who are expected to leave redesigned problematic spaces, such as Pershing Square in Los Angeles and Civic Center Park in San Francisco.

As in the past, public parks are being used as free "living rooms" by those who have no homes or who live alone in frugal circumstances. Depending on the park's location, this use is either accepted or discouraged. Thus Byerts's study of MacArthur Park in a residential district of Los Angeles portrayed a public space used by many local elderly people as a daylong "living room" (Byerts 1970). But the redesign of Pershing Square in Los Angeles was prompted in part by a need to make the homeless and elderly users less visible. Some parks situated in less prominent places now offer services to the homeless that earlier might have been

With the "graying" of the population, more concern needs to be focused on where and how older people can use the public realm: elderly woman enjoying a summer afternoon in a Stockholm park.

frowned on in a public park. For example, in People's Park, Berkeley, the Catholic Workers Association every morning hands out free coffee and sandwiches to a long line of homeless recipients; similarly in La-Fayette Square, Oakland, "Mother" Wright every Saturday serves a hot lunch to anyone who needs it. The city park and its functions have clearly expanded considerably since Frederick Olmsted's day. Although for some, the park is still a place for sports, recreation, play, and contemplation, for others it has become an important meeting place and social setting; for still others who are hungry and destitute, it is a place to eat, sleep, and call home.

Thus although the range of social and economic activities taking place in urban outdoor areas may be more limited than it was in medieval times, that range is considerably greater today than it was in, say, 1950. At the same time, new forms of open space are emerging, sponsored by both the public and the private sectors. For example, long-distance hiking or biking trails are being created in urban settings, such as the proposed Bay-Side Trail and Bay-Ridge Trail in the San Francisco Bay area. Community gardens in which individuals have small plots for growing vegetables have been created by groups of neighbors on land leased from private or public owners; they also are sometimes provided by corporations in office parks for their employees. Popular jogging tracks and bicycle trails have been developed—usually by the public sector—along former railroad rights-of-way or underneath elevated train lines. School yards have been transformed from the traditional blacktop into school parks with lawns, picnic areas, and trees and into environmental yards with native plants and water features. Streets have been closed to through traffic or—in northern Europe—transformed into "pedestrian precincts" (Woonerf) where pedestrians and cars share the space as equals, or into "walking streets" where vehicles or deliveries are banned after 9:00 A.M. and the shopping street becomes an outdoor mall. Public parking lots, empty on the weekends, have been transformed into popular flea markets. From all over the United States, the media report an upswing in small-town festivals, farmers' markets, craft shows, marathons, bike-a-thons, art fairs, ethnic festivals, and street performers.

Not only are public places being used in an era of home videos, computer games, and private pursuits, but a whole new category of outdoor space is assuming importance. This is what we might term *communal space,* or space shared by a specific group who uses a nearby special-purpose building: for example, landscaped areas for walking, sitting, and play interspersed in housing for the elderly; courtyards and gardens for the use of hospital visitors, patients, and employees; areas of outdoor play, learning, and exercise in day care centers; and spaces between buildings used for relaxation, social life, and study on the campuses of

schools and universities. None of these is technically public space; yet all contribute to a sense of public life, allowing one to meet, view, and converse with those other than one's own immediate family. In this era of high mobility, heterogeneous backgrounds, and fast-paced living, many prefer the relative predictability of social life in their neighborhood park, campus courtyard, or office-building plaza to the strangeness of the town square.

In this book, therefore, we address a variety of outdoor social spaces, including those that are publicly owned and publicly accessible (neighborhood parks, miniparks, some plaza spaces), those that are often privately owned and managed but accessible to the public (corporate plazas, college campuses), and those that are privately owned and accessible only to a particular group of users (residents and staff in elderly housing; children and staff in day care centers; and patients, staff, and visitors in hospitals). Clearly, there are many kinds of space in these three categories that we might have covered but did not, such as community gardens, playgrounds, streets, high schools, family housing, and office parks. We omitted them either because there is little research-based information on people's use of such space—for example, the office park or high school campus—or because there is already ample information in the form of books of design guidelines—for example, family housing (Cooper Marcus and Sarkissian 1986), play areas (*Play for All* 1986), community gardens (Francis, Cashdan, and Paxson 1981), and streets (Appleyard 1981; Gehl 1987; Vernez-Moudon 1987). For those types of open space we do discuss in this book, we offer the following definitions:

Neighborhood park: predominantly soft landscape of grass, trees, and planting areas, usually located in a residential setting and detailed and furnished for a variety of active (sports, play, walking) and passive (sitting, sunbathing, resting) uses. The details of use vary with the density and location of the neighborhood.

Miniparks: small, one to three house-lot–sized parks (sometimes known as vest-pocket parks), principally for local, pedestrian-oriented use. They are used primarily by children and teens.

Urban plazas: predominantly hard-surfaced outdoor space in a downtown area, generally developed as part of a new high-rise building. Such plazas are often privately owned and managed but generally accessible to the public.

Campus outdoor space: the hard and soft components of the campus landscape that can be used to walk through or to be in, for study, relaxation, and social encounters.

Elderly housing outdoor space: landscaped outdoor space for walking, sitting, viewing, gardening, and the like, attached to—and for the exclusive use of—the residents of a housing scheme for elderly people.

Day care open space: the outdoor play area of a day

It is predicted that by the last decade of the century, three fourths of the mothers of preschool children will be employed: Spaces for creative outdoor play are an essential component of day care center design. (Photo: Carolyn Francis)

care center, usually including hard and soft surfaces and some fixed and movable play equipment. The primary focus is on preschool-aged children (three to five years), but spaces for infants, toddlers, and school-aged children are sometimes provided.

Hospital outdoor space: courtyards, gardens, patios, or parks that are part of a hospital development. Such spaces are most often provided for use by patients, visitors, staff, and occasionally also the general public. They have important social and therapeutic uses and are a visual amenity. They may have predominantly hard or soft surfaces or a combination, depending on their location and intended use. They may also include hospital play areas for pediatric patients.

This book assumes, first, that public life is thriving in the contemporary industrialized city; second, that an important measure of the success of public open space is its use; third, that the use and popularity of a space depend greatly on its location and the details of its design; and last, that we must communicate what is currently known about the linkages between design, location, and use. This book is an attempt to convey such knowledge as it pertains to the seven types of urban open spaces just described.

This book is a contribution to the growing literature on design guidelines, a systematic attempt to compile what has emerged from the burgeoning field of environmental and behavioral research, and to present the

research in a form that is understandable and usable by the clients, users, designers, and managers of designed open space. We see these recommendations as informed suggestions, as reminders of what seems to have worked and not worked, what appears to be appreciated and not appreciated, by the users of existing spaces. The guidelines are worded so as to be performance-related, rather than prescriptive. For example, rather than prescribe a specific piece of play equipment, we have reminded the reader what children most like to do and which activities seem essential for their healthy development. The problem is not that designers are lacking for creative ideas, but rather that they are frequently hampered by not having the time to search out appropriate people-based research; this is what the authors of this book *have* had the time and inclination to do.

We believe there is a danger of those responsible for sponsoring or designing a particular type of environment, to say, "I've done a few of these [parks, child-care centers, plazas, and so on] before so I know what the issues are." Unfortunately, having designed one or two before, does not guarantee that they are flawless; few clients, designers, or managers have the time or money to engage in the kind of detailed postoccupancy evaluations that form the basis of this book.

We hope that this book will be useful not only for the design of new open spaces but also for the redesign of parks, plazas, and the like that no longer serve the needs of their potential users, because of either chang-

As new housing is being built and older housing is renovated in this neighborhood of Göteborg, Sweden, a temporary play park provides a needed facility for children and their parents. All the equipment is movable and will eventually be placed on a permanent site.

ing trends in the use of outdoor spaces or the changing demographic makeup of the surrounding neighborhood. Indeed, with the limited budgets and spiraling land costs of many cities, the redesign of urban spaces may soon become as significant to landscape architects and urban designers as is the design of such spaces on vacant sites.

Most of the design literature we have reviewed—if it refers to users at all—assumes that they all are able-bodied, relatively young, and male. The assumption of this book, however, is that public spaces should be accessible to all people, that no one—because of physical ability, gender, or cultural or ethnic background—should be excluded because of some aspect of design.

To take this idea a step further: Research-based recommendations cannot substitute for public participation, the input of those people who will actually be using the designed (or redesigned) space. Thus we see this book as informing the participation process rather than as replacing it. When the eventual users are known and can be involved in the creation of a design program (and this is not always the case), the appropriate chapter in this book may be used as a starting point for debate. It is often easier to start with a generic program, to discuss what a particular neighborhood or day care staff agree or disagree with, than to start from scratch.

Finally, as proponents of research-based and performanced-based guidelines, we address what we believe is the most thought-provoking criticism of the guideline format. Some critics have argued that by presenting guidelines geared to improving existing spaces or facilities we may be inadvertently or inappropriately supporting the status quo. We emphatically agree that some environments, often institutional, are essentially inhumane and would best be completely revamped. However, in our view, a designer or design researcher must consider both the larger societal changes and the creation of better, more supportive environments for people's daily lives. We believe that thoughtful design takes into account existing knowledge and provides a chance for people to express themselves, be effective, and feel empowered.

After reviewing all the user studies we could find that dealt with the seven types of open space covered in this book, we established a set of criteria for successful "people places." We believe that when possible, a people place should

- Be located where it is easily accessible to and can be seen by potential users.
- Clearly convey the message that the place is available for use and is meant to be used.
- Be beautiful and engaging on both the outside and the inside.
- Be furnished to support the most likely and desirable activities.

Many younger people in cities are looking for excitement and challenge in the public realm—but rarely find it: Teenagers exploring a participatory fountain in Seattle's Freeway Park.

- Provide a feeling of security and safety to would-be users.
- Where appropriate, offer relief from urban stress and enhance the health and emotional well-being of its users.
- Be geared to the needs of the user group most likely to use the space.
- Encourage use by different subgroups of the likely user population, without any one group's activities disrupting the other's enjoyment.
- Offer an environment that is physiologically comfortable at peak use times, in regard to sun and shade, windiness, and the like.
- Be accessible to children and disabled people.
- Support the philosophical program espoused by the managers of the space, for example, the educational program of a day care center or the therapeutic program of the hospital.
- Incorporate components that the users can manipulate or change (e.g., sand play in day care, raised garden beds in housing for the elderly, interactive sculpture and fountains in urban plazas).
- Allow users the option—either as individuals or as members of a group—of becoming "attached" to the place and caring for it, through involvement in its design, construction, or maintenance; by using it for special events; or by temporarily claiming personal spaces within the setting.
- Be easily and economically maintained, within the limits of what is normally expected in a particular

type of space (e.g., a concrete park might be easy to maintain but is not what a park is expected to be).
- Be designed with equal attention paid to place as an expression of visual art and place as social setting. Too much attention focused on one approach at the expense of the other may result in an unbalanced or unhealthy place.

In conclusion, we repeat that we are less concerned with the debate as to whether public life is or is not on the decline in North America than we are with the need to enhance the use of those outdoor spaces that do exist and that serve an important role in many people's lives. We offer these recommendations as a means to inform the clients, the designers, and the potential users of tomorrow's urban spaces, so that these settings may provide pleasing, comfortable, supportive and beautiful people places.

REFERENCES

Appleyard, Donald. 1981. *Livable streets.* Berkeley and Los Angeles: University of California Press.

Byerts, Thomas. 1970. Design of the urban park environment as an influence on the behavior and social interaction of the elderly. M. Arch. thesis, University of Southern California.

Chidister, Mark. 1988. Reconsidering the piazza. *Landscape Architecture* 78 (1): 40–43.

Cooper Marcus, Clare, and Wendy Sarkissian. 1986. *Housing as if people mattered: Site design guidelines for medium-density family housing.* Berkeley and Los Angeles: University of California Press.

Crowhurst-Lennard, Suzanne H., and Henry L. Lennard. 1987. *Livable cities.* Southampton, N.Y.: Gondolier Press.

Francis, Mark. 1988. Changing values for public spaces. *Landscape Architecture* 78 (1): 54–59.

———, Lisa Cashdan, and Lynn Paxson. 1984. *Community open spaces.* Washington, D.C.: Island Press.

Gehl, Jan. 1987. *Life between buildings: Using public space.* New York: Van Nostrand Reinhold.

Krier, Rob. 1979. *Urban space.* New York: Rizzoli.

Moore, Iacofano, Goltsman. 1987. *Play for all: Guidelines for the planning, design and management of outdoor play settings for all children.* Berkeley, Calif.: Moore, Iacofano, Goltsman.

Rossi, Aldo. 1982. *The architecture of the city.* Cambridge, Mass.: MIT Press.

Sommer, Robert, and Franklin D. Becker. 1969. The old men in Plaza Park. *Landscape Architecture*, January, pp. 111–113.

Vernez-Moudon, Anne, ed. 1987. *Public streets for public use.* New York: Van Nostrand Reinhold.

1

URBAN PLAZAS

Clare Cooper Marcus, with
Carolyn Francis and
Rob Russell

IS THERE A ROLE FOR THE URBAN PLAZA?

In "Dreaming of Urban Plazas," Robert Jensen points out that we are frequently disappointed in the urban places we create, because we imagine that they will be like the quintessential urban spaces of Siena or Barcelona.

It is indicative that we call them plazas or sometimes piazzas. Our own English word "place" won't do. "Place" is derived from the Latin word "platea"—meaning an open space or broadened street—as in the Spanish "plaza" and the Italian "piazza.". . . The word is at once too common and too diverse in its meaning to designate what we want in an urban center downtown. So we turn to Spanish and Italian. That is what we want. (Jensen 1979, p. 52)

But not necessarily what we get.

The modern plaza is not the piazza of days gone by; yet it does have some relevant contextual and functional parallels. Is it farfetched to consider the corporate skyscraper the modern equivalent of the medieval cathedral, each symbolizing, for its era, the seat of power? The public outdoor space next to each is, or was, crowded at certain times of the day because that particular building function attracted people. In each case, the primary people generator (cathedral and corporate office tower) has, or had, a vested interest in the appearance of the space and in how it is used. What is undoubtedly different is that the contemporary office plaza has a very limited range of uses compared with those of the medieval piazza. Indeed, according to observation studies of modern plaza use, sitting, standing, walking, and their combination with eating, reading, watching, and listening account for more than 90

percent of all use.

It is not surprising that many Americans spend their vacations in Europe. Part of the attraction is that the hearts of many European cities are dedicated to pedestrian movement. To a resident of Los Angeles—where a planning report referred to the pedestrian as "the largest single obstacle to free traffic movement" (Rudofsky 1969, p. 106)—strolling through the streets and plazas of a French, German, or Italian city must indeed seem like being in another world.

Rudofsky suggested in *Streets for People* that just as we look back in amazement to an era when people were willing to share the streets with trains, so "future generations will marvel at the obtuseness of people who thought nothing of sharing the street with motor cars" (Rudofsky 1969, p. 341). Although Americans have less of a tradition than do Europeans for strolling, promenading, or frequenting outdoor cafés, studies of street life in U.S. cities indicate that more and more people are recreating in downtown outdoor space. Whyte found a 30 percent increase between 1972 and 1973 in the number of people sitting in plazas and small parks in Manhattan; he found between 1973 and 1974 an additional 20 percent increase. Whyte concluded that more people are getting into the habit of sitting in plazas and that with each new plaza the clientele grows (Whyte 1974, p. 27). Outdoor eating has also become more popular: "There is more picnicking in the parks and plazas and on the library steps at lunch, and throughout the day so much street-corner munching of hot dogs and knishes it is a wonder every New Yorker is not fat" (Whyte 1974, p. 28). Also on the increase are public displays of affection, smiling, street entertainment, crazy characters, shmoozing

Town square, Malmö, Sweden.

(groups engaged in sidewalk gossiping), and impromptu sidewalk "conferences" among businesspersons.

Gehl reported that as the total area of pedestrian streets and squares in Copenhagen tripled between 1968 and 1986, the number of people standing or sitting in those areas tripled also, while the total city population remained the same. Thus, even in northern Europe—with no particular tradition for street life— public outdoor activities are on the rise (Gehl 1987).

Studies of the U.S. West Coast confirm the same trends in San Francisco and Seattle. Enhancing these trends are the economic situation, encouraging more people to bring lunches from home; demographic trends, more people living alone, who may seek relaxed conversations and companionship during the lunch hour; and the stress of office environments.

Downtown open spaces are also being used more by the people who live there, not just by the lunch-hour crowd. In San Francisco, Union Square is an outdoor living room for elderly people who live in downtown hotels, a place for lunch-hour relaxation for nearby shop and office workers, and a weekend neighborhood park for Chinatown residents.

DEFINITION

According to J. B. Jackson, a plaza is an urban form that draws people together for passive enjoyment (Jackson 1985). Kevin Lynch suggested that "the plaza is intended as an activity focus, at the heart of some intensive urban area. Typically, it will be paved, enclosed by high-density structures, and surrounded by streets, or in contact with them. It contains features meant to attract groups of people and to facilitate meetings . . ." (Lynch 1981, p. 443).

For our purposes, a plaza is defined as a mostly hard-surfaced, outdoor public space from which cars are excluded. Its main function is as a place for strolling, sitting, eating, and watching the world go by. Unlike a sidewalk, it is a place in its own right rather than a space to pass through. Although there may be trees, flowers, or ground cover in evidence, the predominant ground surface is hard; if grass and planted areas exceed the amount of hard surface, we have defined the space as a park rather than a plaza.

This book is concerned with plazas from which traffic is permanently excluded. Although some piazzas in Europe are closed to traffic just in the afternoon (e.g., Perugia's Corso Vanucci) or on special occasions (e.g., Siena) and some U.S. cities (e.g., San Francisco) are experimenting with excluding traffic during lunchtime from some office-district streets, this is not a common occurrence.

LITERATURE ON PLAZAS

Camillo Sitte's classic *The Art of Building Cities* (written in the late 1800s but first published in English in 1945) voices some very real concerns about the use of public squares by city dwellers, which still are relevant today. Interestingly, this study of medieval and baroque squares was prompted by the creation of new streets and public places in Sitte's native Vienna, which he regarded as inhuman in scale.

In the more recent literature on the design of urban plazas, we found virtually nothing on the behavioral aspects of plaza use, let alone their psychological or symbolic implications. Standard texts such as Gibberd's *Town Design* deal primarily with the sculptural arrangements of buildings and space, with almost no reference to their actual day-to-day use, except on a visual or aesthetic level. Eckbo's *Urban Landscape Design* comments on existing designed spaces, with descriptions and critiques again based on pure design and little direct reference to behavioral or attitudinal responses. Cullen's *Townscape,* which considers both large- and small-scale features in the urban landscape, has an almost exclusive emphasis on visual design.

There is clearly a gap between some of these standard texts and the more pragmatic, such as the *Architects Journal's Handbook of Urban Landscape.* A collection of information on construction details, current standards, materials, and the like, this book considers user behavior in some forms of open space (e.g., playgrounds, housing sites) but ignores it in others (e.g., urban plazas, miniparks). Rudofsky's *Streets for People: A Primer for Americans* is an interesting, though predictable, text on "Aren't European streets wonderful—why can't we do the same?" but with little practical guidance.

A book much discussed by architects and designers is Rowe and Koetter's *Collage City.* This highly metaphoric book discusses the larger philosophical issues of buildings and open space, the tensions inherent in city design and development, and issues of figure and ground, space definition versus occupation, and so on. Whatever the book's basic points are, they are so disguised by rambling and ostentatious rhetoric as to be essentially invisible. Unfortunately, this type of almost breathless, revelatory writing seems to influence many designers, particularly design students, who become so caught up in discussions of the "solid-void dialectic" and the desirability of an environment in which "buildings *and* spaces exist in an equality of sustained debate" (Rowe and Koetter 1978, p. 83) that they forget to take into account the more mundane but essential issues of people's use of, and interaction with, the environment—such as places to sit and shade from the sun. Although the authors express some concern for human activity, interaction, control, and values, they include no direct study of people's use (or nonuse) of specific spaces or plazas.

Similarly, the works of both Rob and Leon Krier (see, for example, *Urban Space* and *Rational Architecture*) have created excitement and debate in the design community. Although they mention the issues of human scale or the desirability of twenty-four-hour activity in urban open spaces, they mainly dwell on the spatial and aesthetic qualities of various building forms and the areas enclosed by them. *Urban Space* discusses a "morphological classification of urban spaces" in which "the three basic shapes (square, circle and triangle) are affected by . . . modulating factors: angling; segmentation; addition; merging; overlapping or amalgamation of elements, and distortion." It then provides a staggering array of shapes and configurations based on this scheme—many of which are existing places—but

does not clearly explain the relationship of these spaces to the activities and experiences they might support. This book is at least coherently written but provides very little concrete connection between people's desires and needs and the built environment. Concluding with some drawings by his seven-year-old daughter, the author states, "She has included people in her drawings, as if to remind her father that the whole abstract game-playing has no meaning without people. She is right, and I'm ashamed at so much 'useless messing around'" (R. Krier 1979, p. 91).

Another book currently enjoying the attention of the design community, in which we searched for clear environment–behavior connections, is Rossi's *The Architecture of the City.* Like the preceding books, it offers a substantial historical grounding, followed by a methodology for studying and describing cities. Rossi discusses the importance of real estate structure and economics and social–historical influences, among other concerns. Although he clearly believes architecture to be inseparable from its social–cultural context, he does not describe the human use of designed spaces.

On the whole, those books that serve as inspirational and self-defining material for designers of the urban environment are theoretical, concerned more with developing universal axioms and meaningful methods for analyzing form than with exploring the more concrete issues of casual use of real spaces by ordinary people. Certainly these larger issues are valid and important, but it is our fear that they often are the only inspirational source, to the detriment of the population affected by the resulting designed spaces.

Fortunately, another form of literature exists. A well-documented volume put out by the Organization for Economic Cooperation and Development, entitled *Streets for People,* is an excellent, detailed documentation of the pedestrianization of many European inner cities. Its accent is more on policy, planning, and managerial guides than on design, though the photographic illustrations are a good source of design ideas.

A number of more recent studies deal with pedestrian movement, using many of the same methods formerly applied to traffic movement. The first of these, Gehl's "Mennisker til fods" (People on foot), appeared in the Danish journal *Arkitekten* in 1968. A study largely conducted by architecture students, it focuses on pedestrian behavior in one of the earliest and most famous European street closures, Strøget in Copenhagen. This study documents some amazing facts: For example, during the first year after Strøget was converted to a walking street, the number of pedestrians increased by 35 percent, the number of baby carriages by 400 percent (Gehl 1987, p. 136).

In 1971, a major American study, Fruin's *Pedestrian Planning and Design,* was published. This is a detailed and statistical look at pedestrian traffic capacities in streets, subways, elevators, escalators, and the like. In addition, a report for the New York Regional Plan Association, *Urban Space for Pedestrians*, by Pushkarev and Zupan (1975), is a sophisticated analysis of pedestrian behavior on streets and plazas. Finally, *On Streets*, a collection of articles edited by Anderson (1978), is concerned with the design and social significance of streets. Because the various authors support the notion of streets acting as courtyards, or supporting uses that are generally consigned to plazas or private spaces, this book offers some insights useful to plaza design, especially to the plaza/street interface and to long strip plazas or "widened sidewalks."

From the mid-1970s on, several behavioral studies of plazas were published, principally of those in cities on the West and East coasts. In New York City, the Street Life Project (initially funded by the Rockefeller Foundation and directed by William H. Whyte) undertook a great series of plaza studies, using stop-frame filming and behavioral observation. This work, which continued for many years, was reported in an excellent small book by Whyte, entitled *The Social Life of Small Urban Spaces* (1980). The work of the Street Life Project was continued by Project for Public Spaces (directed by Fred Kent III), a consulting firm hired by many cities to study problematic streets and plazas. The results of these studies are available in written and film formats.

Students also conducted important case studies. In "Emotional and Behavioral Responses of People to Urban Plazas: A Case Study of Downtown Vancouver" (1978), Joardar and Neill used time-lapse photography to record some six thousand users of ten public plazas in Vancouver. Two university departments of landscape architecture had their students evaluate plazas in Chicago and San Francisco. Rutledge and his graduate students at the University of Illinois at Champaign-Urbana produced in 1975 what probably is still the most detailed study of a single plaza, the First National Bank Plaza, Chicago. Besides interviewing both the designer and the users, the students also tracked and mapped the use of the plaza. Their study remains a model of what can be achieved on a small budget and in a very short time (Department of Landscape Architecture 1975).

Finally, at the University of California at Berkeley, students in a class I teach on behavioral issues in open space design have conducted detailed evaluations of more than a dozen San Francisco plazas. Many of these have been examined by different students in different years, and so we were able to look at the stability, or change, in the plazas' uses over time. Our methods were mainly behavior mapping and informal interviews. These studies are the principal source material for this chapter, with summaries of several of them forming the case studies (Cooper Marcus 1975–1988).

Several, more recent books have addressed the issue of people's use of city spaces. Two volumes by Crowhurst-Lennard and Lennard (*Public Life in Urban Places:*

Architectural Characteristics Conducive to Public Life in European Cities and *Livable Cities—People and Places: Social and Design Principles for the Future of the City*) discuss the theory and practice of humanizing the environment and highlight presentations by (largely) European planners and urban designers at a number of international conferences organized by the authors on "making cities livable."

Finally, a revised English translation of Gehl's *Life Between Buildings: Using Public Space* (originally published in Danish in 1971) appeared in 1987. This book —simply written and handsomely illustrated—is not about special occasions (festivals, carnivals, street markets) but about "ordinary days and the multitude of outdoor spaces that surround us. It is a book about everyday activities and their specific demands on the man-made environment" (Gehl 1987, p. 9). At last, an architect (not a social scientist) has produced a highly readable book about the simple activities of walking, standing, and sitting in the spaces between buildings.

An excellent source of ideas and information on the management and programming of downtown public spaces (including private, corporate-owned plazas) is *Managing Downtown Public Spaces*, by the Project for Public Spaces, Inc. This handbook summarizes the results of a study of two hundred downtown organizations and offers useful guidelines on how the private sector— and the public and private sectors working together— can enhance the viability, safety, liveliness, and maintenance of downtown outdoor spaces used by the public. The authors warn that the programming of performances, vending, farmers' markets, and so on, in one downtown may not necessarily work in another. Each chapter ends with a set of questions to consider before planning programs. The authors note, however, that there as yet have been few attempts to evaluate programs systematically.

It is both interesting and heartening to note that as the public use of urban open space has increased and the city has regained its popularity as a place to live, some of the clients of urban spaces have sponsored evaluative studies of how these spaces work. In the early 1970s, for example, it was not unusual to find plazas that actively discouraged people from using them, sometimes by guards employed by the owner to move people on. But now, for example, the Public Building Service of the General Services Administration has constructed federal buildings with exterior outdoor spaces specifically designed to encourage use. It has also sponsored studies of such spaces to see how well they serve the public and to generate guidelines for future buildings.

PLAZAS IN THE CONTEMPORARY U.S. SCENE

In their exhaustive study of pedestrian needs in Manhattan, *Urban Space for Pedestrians*, Pushkarev and

Zupan pointed out some of the historic trends in the provision of pedestrian space in urban centers:

Planning for pedestrians in urban centers has been badly neglected. Nineteenth Century street layouts frequently allocated as much as half the urban right-of-way to walkways, which was ample when very few buildings were more than 3 stories high. But when buildings in downtown areas started to get taller—and to attract more pedestrian trips—no effort was made to set them back further from the building line. On the contrary, real estate pressures forced closer encroachment. When the motor vehicle arrived on the scene, roadways began to be widened, likewise at the expense of walkway space. Thus, in downtown areas, the pedestrian was squeezed into leftover space between the traffic and building walls. . . . Virtually the only attention paid to pedestrians was with respect to their physical safety, not to their comfort and amenity. (Pushkarev and Zupan 1975, p. 15)

Just how much the pedestrian in our cities is squeezed out by the automobile is nicely, though shockingly, illustrated in an observation by William Whyte in Manhattan.

The center sidewalk of Lexington Avenue between 57th and 58th streets [is] quite possibly the most congested one anywhere in the world. The sidewalk width has been cut down to 12 feet, and of this only about 6 feet is negotiable. The rest is obstructed by a complex of wastebaskets, sign stanchions, gratings, floral displays, beggars, leather-belt vendors, and cops arresting leather-belt vendors. For the pedestrian it is a fight all the way, and tracking studies of people dodging and feinting, accelerating and decelerating, make one awestruck at what extraordinary transportation units human beings can be. An astonishing number run the gauntlet. We made a count on an average weekday: between 8:00 A.M. and 8:00 P.M., some 38,000 people passed by.
   Now consider the adjacent channel—the vehicular lane next to the curb. It is 9½ feet wide. During the same period it was occupied by 12 parked cars carrying a total of 15 persons. (Whyte 1974, p. 32)

In the late 1950s and early 1960s, the plight of the harassed urban pedestrian began to be noticed. A number of well-publicized new office buildings in Manhattan sacrificed legally permissible building space to create some of the first modern U.S. pedestrian plazas, for example, the Lever House (Gordon Bunshaft 1951), the Seagram Building (Mies van der Rohe 1957), the Time–Life Building (Harrison and Abramovitz 1959), and the Chase Manhattan Bank (Skidmore, Owings, and Merrill 1961).

In 1961, a new zoning law in New York City (patterned on that in Chicago, which preceded it by a few years) pioneered the idea of making higher densities an incentive for providing ground-level pedestrian plazas and arcades. For example, in the highest-density districts of Manhattan, a developer who provided one unit of open space at or near the sidewalk level could build, in return for giving up this ground-floor space, ten extra units of floor area at the top.

As soon as the new law came into effect, almost every new major building in Manhattan took advantage of the plaza bonus. By 1970, in the central square mile of midtown Manhattan alone, there were over eleven acres of public pedestrian plazas on private land and over two acres of ornamental space, consisting of landscaping and fountains (Pushkarev and Zupan 1975, p. 18).

Unfortunately, the designers of these new plazas, having few U.S. precedents on which to draw, fell into the trap of "if open space is good, more open space is better." Monumental plazas thus were built, completely overdesigned for human use and often devoid of human activity. Perhaps the culmination of these was Minoru Yamasaki's World Trade Center plaza, whose five acres remain virtually empty, whereas the adjacent—though visually and structurally separate—sidewalks and subway approaches are heavily congested. Similarly, Marcel Breuer's HUD Building in Washington, D.C. (1969), has a large front plaza traversed by fourteen thousand people a day; yet no one stops, and there is no place to sit down (Project for Public Spaces 1979). An evaluative study in 1979 reported that a survey of the building's employees yielded not one favorable comment about this space (Project for Public Spaces 1979).

Plazas built during the 1950s and 1960s more often resembled stage sets than places for people to enjoy.

In San Francisco, as in Manhattan, the bonus specifications were vague enough that some plazas offered
only limited use to the public. In fact, bonuses could
be awarded, though at a lesser rate, to ground-level
open space that was not actually accessible for use, if it
provided street-level visual amenity "consistent with
the purposes of the bonus system." Writing in 1977,
Dornbusch noted that of eighty-six buildings of over
fifteen stories in the downtown area of San Francisco,
only eighteen, or 21 percent, provided plazas that were
accessible to the general public (Dornbusch and Gelb
1977, p. 129). Although many of these plazas are quite
large, generally they are neither very green nor very
sunny, features in great demand by plaza users. At
noon in the fall, seven are totally in shade; six are 50
percent or more in shade; and ten are partially or totally in the sun.

As the bonus system came into effect and city planners demanded the provision of urban open space by
high-rise developers, the building–outdoor space interface acquired a number of forms. Before the bonus system, most high-rise urban buildings filled their site, the
street-level facade abutting directly onto the sidewalk.
Later came the high rise on a podium, the roof of the
podium sometimes being open to use but its separation
from the street limiting real accessibility. Next came
the tower in the park, the building taking up only a
portion of the site. Variations in the detailing of this
form have transformed the urban plaza from an empty
stage set to an animated outdoor lunchroom. Finally,
some cities' bonus legislation allows publicly accessible
indoor space (foyer, atrium, galleria) to substitute for
outdoor space. The success of many (e.g., the IBM
atrium in Manhattan, the Galleria in San Francisco)
indicates that this may be one appropriate solution
where the climate precludes public outdoor space use
for much of the year. However, such spaces should be
seen only as an adjunct to public outdoor space since
certain segments of the public are often excluded from
using them.

One could perhaps argue that plazas and pedestrian
malls will not be popular in U.S. cities because there is
no cultural tradition for promenading or walking for
pleasure in the city. The error of this thinking is amply
illustrated in William Whyte's and Pushkarev's and
Zupan's studies of Manhattan, where every new plaza
consciously designed to encourage use was quickly inhabited by hoards of sitters, strollers, brown baggers,
and "schmoozers." A study in northern and central Europe similarly indicates that exclusively pedestrian environments greatly change typical urban middle-class
behavior:

The tendency is everywhere for leisure activity to increase
. . . seventeen cities report an increase in promenading, an
activity which seemed restricted in the past to Mediterranean
countries. Communication between strangers also appears to
occur more often in foot-streets than in those burdened with
traffic. . . . In contrast to people in cars who tend to be cut
off from their surroundings and behave aggressively, people in
pedestrian areas are said to be more considerate of their fel-
lows. (OECD 1974, pp. 67–68)

The disadvantages of the bonus systems as originally
formulated were, first, that compliance was not mandatory and, second, that additions to urban open space
frequently took the form of isolated and unrelated plazas, with no coherent pedestrian system. Fruin suggested that "the successful implementation of a bonus
program that provides system-wide, rather than isolated
spot benefits, is dependent on a well-planned and administered 'carrot-and-stick' policy by local government" (Fruin 1971, p. 144). His book describes in
some detail the popular elevated systems of Montreal
and Toronto. Descriptions and illustrations of many
successful European schemes for integrating plazas,
street closures, elevated walkways, and the like can be
found in the OECD publication *Streets for People*
(1974).

In San Francisco, after many years of experience
with a bonus system for creating downtown open space,

*Zellerbach Plaza, the first of San
Francisco's postwar office
plazas, has none of the features
that make a successful plaza: It
is below street level, with few
entry points, no seating, and no
place to buy a snack. Note the
heavy use of boundary wall for
sitting and watching the
passersby. (Photo: Robert
Russell)*

the city adopted in 1985 a far-reaching "downtown plan," described by architectural critic Paul Goldberger as "the most carefully-worked-out downtown plan in the United States." Under the old regulations, downtown open spaces could earn bonus building allowances even if they were almost totally shaded in the lunch hour (Giannini Plaza), were grudgingly open to the public for walking through (Citicorp Plaza), or were totally closed to public access (Chevron Garden). Under the new plan, however, one square foot of accessible open space must be dedicated for public use for every fifty square feet of new office space. No fewer than thirteen types of downtown space are identified (including urban parks, sun terraces, hard plazas, and galleria), and for each type there is a set of guidelines covering dimension, textures, seating, planting, water features, sun access, food, and so on. Though not legally regulated (as in a building code) the competition for permission to build high in downtown is such that only those developments carefully following the suggested guidelines are likely to receive permission. Particularly significant—in view of Fruin's remarks—is the fact that every attempt is to be made to connect new and existing plazas via pedestrian streets and access ways, so that the end result will be a pedestrian system rather than isolated oases.

Parallel with developments in New York and San Francisco, Cleveland, Chicago, and Los Angeles now require developers to indicate how a proposed new plaza will contribute to the downtown's vitality, before the design will be approved (Francis 1987, p. 81).

A TYPOLOGY OF DOWNTOWN PLAZAS

The purpose of the following typology is to make some sense of the varied categories of downtown open space in U.S. cities. Although this typology was developed in San Francisco, we believe it can be applied to most cities. It may be used as a basis (1) for understanding the variety of spaces described in this chapter as "urban plazas," (2) for categorizing plaza spaces in a specific city, and (3) for developing local guidelines for specific plaza types.

One could categorize downtown spaces in many ways: by size, use, relationship to street, style, predominant function, architectural form, location, and so on. But because this book is concerned with the interplay of form and use, our classification is based on a mix of form and use, moving from the smallest to the largest in size. We describe five broad categories of plazas plus subcategories of each, with illustrations and examples named. (Unless otherwise noted, all the examples are located in San Francisco.)

The Street Plaza

A street plaza is a small portion of public open space immediately adjacent to the sidewalk and closely connected to the street. It sometimes is a widening of the sidewalk proper or an extension of it under an arcade. Such spaces are generally used for brief periods of sitting, waiting, and watching, and they tend to be used more by men than by women.

The seating edge: A seating height wall or stepped edge to a sidewalk.

The widened sidewalk: A widened portion of the sidewalk that is furnished with seating blocks, steps, or bollards. Used primarily for viewing passersby (see Case Study 1).

The bus-waiting place: A portion of the sidewalk at a bus stop, sometimes furnished with a bench, shelter, kiosk, or litter container.

The seating edge. A seating wall facing Sansome Street, San Francisco, often used by construction workers and bicycle messengers. The wall bounds the seldom-used Zellerbach Plaza. (Photo: Robert Russell)

The widened sidewalk. Crocker Plaza, one of the most highly used plazas in San Francisco, is little more than sets of steps looking onto adjacent sidewalks. (Photo: Michael McKinley)

The pedestrian link: An outdoor passage or alley that connects two blocks or, sometimes, two plazas. Sometimes it is wide enough for planting; other times it is just a passageway between buildings. It is used almost exclusively for walking.

The corner sun pocket: A building footprint that is designed to open up a small plaza where two streets meet and where there is access to sun during the peak lunchtime period. It is used for sitting, viewing, eating lunch, and the like.

The arcade plaza: A sidewalk that is widened by means of an extension under a building overhang. It is sometimes furnished with chairs or benches.

The Corporate Foyer

The corporate foyer is part of a new, generally high-rise building complex. Its main function is to provide an elegant entry and image for its corporate sponsor. It is usually privately owned but accessible to the public. It is sometimes locked after business hours.

The decorative porch: A small decorative entry, sometimes planted or supplied with seating or a water feature. It often is too narrow or shaded to encourage much use.

The impressive forecourt: A larger entry plaza, often finished in expensive materials (marble, travertine) and sometimes designed to discourage any use but passing through.

The stage set: A very large corporate plaza flanked by an impressive tall building that it helps frame. The plaza often is detailed so as to discourage use by "undesirables" or to minimize its use for sitting or eating. It is primarily a stage set with building as a backdrop (see Case Study 4).

The Urban Oasis

The urban oasis is a type of plaza that is more heavily planted, has a garden or park image, and is partially secluded from the street. Its location and design deliberately set this place apart from the noise and activity of the city. It is often popular for lunchtime eating, reading, socializing, and it is the one category that tends to attract more women than men or, at least, equal proportions of each. The urban oasis has a quiet, reflective quality.

The outdoor lunch plaza: A plaza separated from the street by a level change or a pierced wall and furnished for comfortable lunchtime use. It is often attractively planted, provided with more than adequate seating, and sometimes incorporating a café or take-out restaurant.

The garden oasis: A small plaza, often enclosed and secluded from the street, whose high density and variety of planting conveys a garden image. The garden oasis sometimes includes flower planters and a water feature and usually supplies a variety of seating possibilities. It is popular for lunchtime use and as a quiet respite from city activities (see Case Study 5).

The roof garden: A rooftop area developed as a garden setting for sitting, walking, and viewing. Its access is sometimes poorly signed, perhaps to discourage heavy use.

The Transit Foyer

The transit foyer is a type of plaza space created for easy access in and out of heavily used public transit terminals. Although the detailing may not encourage any activities but passing through, the captive audience of transit users sometimes draws street entertainers, vendors, and people watchers.

The subway entry place: A place for passing through, waiting, meeting, and watching. It sometimes becomes a favorite hangout for a particular group (e.g., teens) who can reach this place by public transit (see Case Study 6).

The bus terminal: Where many city bus lines converge and many commuters arrive and leave the city

The impressive forecourt. The Federal Office Building, Seattle, has a plaza intended primarily as a walking route to an important building, with trees, sculpture, but few places to sit.

The stage set. The First Federal Bank Plaza, Minneapolis, seems to be a stage set for a play that never happens. Tubular seating discourages its use, but weekend skateboarders love it.

The garden oasis. The TransAmerica Redwood Park, San Francisco, is a small through-block space with trees, lawn, fountain, and ample seating that is often used very much for lunch-hour relaxation. (Photo: Robert Russell)

center each day. It is primarily a space to move through, but it sometimes attracts vendors of newspapers, flowers, light snacks, and the like.

The Grand Public Place

The grand public place comes closest to our image of the old-world town square or piazza. When located near a diversity of land uses (office, retail, warehouse, transit) it tends to attract users from a greater distance and in greater variety (by age, gender, ethnicity) than do other plazas. Such an area is often big and flexible enough to "host" brown-bag lunch crowds; outdoor cafés; passers through; and occasional concerts, art shows, exhibits, and rallies. It is usually publicly owned and is often considered the "heart" of the city—the place where an annual Christmas tree might be erected or guests are taken for a visit.

The city plaza: An area predominantly hard surfaced, centrally located, and highly visible. It is often the setting for programmed events such as concerts, performances, and political rallies (see Case Study 7).

The city square: A centrally located, often historic place where major thoroughfares intersect. Unlike many other kinds of plazas, it is not attached to a particular building; rather, it often encompasses one or more complete city blocks and is usually bounded by streets on all four sides. Hardscape and planting are often finely balanced, so that this place could be considered midway between a plaza and a park. Sometimes it contains a major monument, statue, or fountain. It attracts a variety of users and activities. However, sometimes because of its central location and high land value, the city square has been redesigned to incorporate underground parking (see Case Study 8).

This typology is not necessarily exhaustive; rather, it is presented as a starting point for thinking about downtown plaza spaces. The following guidelines can apply to any or all of these types. Some cities (for example, San Francisco) have developed their own categories or guidelines for each. We have not attempted to do this, because we hope that the recommendations which follow can be utilized/modified for settings that differ by region, climate, and culture.

DESIGN RECOMMENDATIONS

Location

The best locations are those that attract a variety of users. Located in a mixed hotel/luxury apartment/office district, Justin Herman Plaza in San Francisco, for example, attracts workers, tourists, and families on outings, which in turn draw a variety of craft vendors and outdoor cafés. In Manhattan, the same is true for the area around Pulitzer Fountain and Grand Army Plaza.

A study of the effect of context on the use of five downtown Minneapolis plazas found that the most frequently used plaza was in the area of greatest land use diversity, where office and retail districts overlapped (Chidister 1986a).

In determining whether or not a new plaza would be an asset in its proposed location, designer and client should ask themselves the following questions:

- Does an analysis of nearby public open space indicate that the new space would be welcomed and used, or would it be redundant? A large empty space created just to show off the building or to gain additional floor area ratio under incentive zoning is not necessarily a net gain in a dense urban setting.
- Assuming a "catchment area" of approximately nine hundred feet (determined in San Francisco to be the maximum distance that most people will walk to a downtown open space), does the proposed plaza serve a currently unserved population? And does the presence of a large number of employees in the catchment area ensure a lunchtime clientele?
- Is the proposed plaza located so that a variety of people might use it? Is it close to retail stores, hotels, offices, and restaurants?
- Does the location of the plaza tie in to an existing or proposed pedestrian system for downtown? If a recessed plaza with a passage or arcade at the back would facilitate mid-block pedestrian movement, it should be encouraged. If a large recessed plaza would seriously interrupt retail frontage on the adjacent street, the provision of the plaza should be seriously questioned, or a continuous shopping facade around the plaza, extending the retail frontage on the street, should be considered.
- Does the local climate warrant providing a plaza? People enjoy using plazas in reasonably comfortable weather; the temperature seems to matter more than the presence or absence of sunshine. In regions where an outdoor space can be used for less than three months of the year—because of extreme heat, cold, or wetness—its provision should be seriously questioned, and an alternative indoor public space considered.

The location of a plaza on the block also can influence the type of space it will become.

- A corner location where two adjacent streets are at approximately the same grade will enable the plaza to become an active meeting place, a place to pass through, and a place to watch passersby (sidewalk as well as plaza users). It will have the highest use potential of any of the five locations discussed here if it receives lunchtime sun.

- A corner location where there is a considerable grade change between one street and the other (e.g., Giannini Plaza, San Francisco) will not be used as a passing-through space and therefore will not generate so much activity and people watching.
- A mid-block location where the plaza extends right through the block (e.g., TransAmerica Redwood Park, San Francisco) will generate passing-through traffic and may also become an oasis space or quiet sitting area, depending on its size and design.
- A mid-block location where the plaza does not extend through the block but forms a cul-de-sac may result in a verdant, human-scale oasis, such as Paley Park, or a cold entry "slot," such as 345 California Street, San Francisco, depending on orientation, the ratio of width to depth and height, and on the detailing of the space.
- A widened sidewalk forming a partial setback for a building, circulation, and sitting space can be a highly successful people place or a problematic one, depending on design details. A basic conflict in this form is that between encouraging use by passing sidewalk pedestrians (therefore keeping the plaza open to access at many points) and creating an oasis space to encourage sitting (e.g., Wells Fargo Plaza, Oakland).

Size

It is difficult to make recommendations regarding size, as every location and context is different. However, Kevin Lynch suggested that dimensions of 40 feet appear intimate in scale; up to 80 feet is still a pleasant

human scale; and that most of the successful enclosed squares of the past have not exceeded 450 feet in the smaller dimension (Lynch 1971). Gehl proposed a maximum dimension of 70 to 100 meters (230 to 330 ft.), as this is the maximum distance for being able to see events. This might be combined with the maximum distance for being able to see facial expressions (20 to 25 meters, or 65 to 80 ft.).

Visual Complexity

In a study of reactions to ten downtown plazas in Vancouver, Canada, Joardar and Neill noted that on those plazas receiving high scores, the subjects' comments pertained to the form, color, and texture of various landscape elements: trees, shrubs, fountains and sculptures, variously shaped artifacts, space articulations, nooks, corners, and changes in level. Conversely, for low-scoring plazas, people referred to " 'barrenness' or 'obviousness' in the landscape, redundancy in material color or texture, 'excessive cement/concrete paving', 'lack of color contrast', 'lack of green' . . . and monotony of space organization, i.e. 'clutter of elements of the same type' and 'no focal point.' Both density and variety as opposed to sparseness and repetition appeared to be perceptually important"(Joardar and Neill 1978, p. 488).

Observations in New York City and in San Francisco confirm these findings; plazas with higher intensities of use are those with greater variety of color, textures, sitting places, landscape elements, and so on.

For those people working all day in standard office environments in which forms, colors, temperatures, neighbors, and so on all are predictable, a lunch hour spent in an environment of pleasing sensory complex-

The best-used plazas are often those that are easily accessible to a variety of people. Justin Herman Plaza in San Francisco is within easy walking distance of corporate office buildings, downtown stores and housing, and tourist and convention hotels. (Photo: Jennifer Webber)

Although visual complexity is a significant component of well-liked and well-used plazas, a visually complex plaza will not often be used unless it is located in an area of high demand. The Plaza d'Italia in New Orleans is not.

ity is a welcome relief. This complexity usually needs to be created within the plaza and so is an important design component.

Sometimes a complex view from the plaza is a significant attraction, and in such cases the designer's role is to create a setting that capitalizes on that visual asset. Thus, in the Vancouver study, waterfront plazas with views of distant mountains and marine activities were rated as more pleasant than were most other spaces (Joardar and Neill 1978). In San Francisco, a simple set of steps and planters at Crocker Plaza has been successful, largely because a continuous parade of passersby on Market Street creates a constantly changing display (see Case Study 1).

Uses and Activities

In this book, *users* are defined as those people who pass through or linger in a plaza space, as distinguished from those who just glance in as they walk or drive by. Although we would define a successful plaza as one that encourages people to remain in it, we would not exclude the passers through as users.

Passers Through and Lingerers

Behavioral studies of Manhattan plazas indicate that as long as the plaza is flush with the sidewalk, 30 to 60 percent of the pedestrians entering the block will walk through it and avail themselves of the space (Pushkarev and Zupan 1975, p. 162). The higher percentages occur on the wider plazas and on those that help cut a corner; the lower percentages occur on the narrower plazas, on those that have a physical obstruction between the sidewalk and the plaza, and on those that do not act as thoroughfares. Thus, of those entering the block adjacent to New York City's Burroughs Plaza (a wide plaza running the length of the block and flush with the sidewalk), 53 percent walk through or linger in the plaza. During the same midday period, of those entering the block on which the CBS Building Plaza is located, only 18 percent enter the plaza, which is somewhat lower than the sidewalk and separated by a barrier (Pushkarev and Zupan 1975, p. 163). Even isolated barriers—planting boxes in the case of the block-long plaza at 1411 Broadway—will decrease the number of passers through, and a continuous barrier (CBS Building Plaza) will limit them to virtually only the building occupants (Pushkarev and Zupan 1975, p. 165).

A New York study indicated that the proportion of plaza users who do not use the adjacent buildings ranges from 76 percent at the Lever House to a mere 3 percent at the CBS Building. The width of the plaza, the absence of a grade change between the plaza and the sidewalk, and the absence of a strong barrier all seem to influence this percentage (Pushkarev and Zupan 1975, p. 165).

Pushkarev's and Zupan's work indicates that it is those plazas that do not act primarily as thoroughfares that cause users to stay the longest (see Table 1.1). The Lever House, which largely attracts passers through who do not use the adjacent buildings, has relatively few sitters. The Time-Life Plaza (an expanded sidewalk with fountains and substantial sitting areas) attracts more sitters and lingerers. Of the few who enter the CBS Building Plaza, most come to sit down.

Pushkarev and Zupan concluded that the functions of a plaza as a circulation facility and a sitting oasis are, if not incompatible, then at least distinct (Pushkarev and Zupan 1975, p. 165). That is, if both uses are to be accommodated, they should be relegated to distinct subareas of the plaza or at least have a transition space between them: No short cutters with a brief lunch hour want to weave their way through the fountain lingerers; conversely, the brown baggers and people watchers will not feel comfortable with a continuous stream of pedestrians passing a few feet in front of them.

In order to encourage people to linger in a plaza space, it needs to have something to persuade them to

TABLE 1.1 PEDESTRIANS' BEHAVIOR IN PLAZAS

	Number of Pedestrians*	Percentage of Sitters	Percentage of Pedestrians Not Using Bldg.	Percentage of Users Not Destined for Building Who		
				Walk Through	Linger	Sit Down
Lever Bldg.	na	na	76	58	13	29
Time–Life Bldg.	144	72	49	24	35	41
CBS Bldg.	12	100	4	20	28	52

* Midday occupancy on random weekday determined by aerial photography.

Source: Compiled from Pushkarev and Zupan 1975.

stay. People look for visual complexity in their surroundings and for "anchors" to which they can attach themselves, either physically (sitting, leaning against) or symbolically (standing near, looking at). In a time-lapse study of six thousand users in ten Vancouver plazas Joardar and Neill found that, amazingly, less than 1 percent carried out activities in the open pavement away from any physical artifacts.

We found that "busy" open spaces were effectively utilized. They had dense furnishings, attractive focal elements and defined edges. Their pedestrian circulation channels were effectively used. This was in contrast to non-articulated expansive plazas with dispersed facilities. The latter were found to be mere concourses for random pedestrian movement. (Joardar and Neill 1978, p. 489)

Male and Female Users

Males tend to dominate the use of most urban open spaces, especially the use of downtown plazas (Dornbusch and Gelb 1977, p. 208). Women who use plazas are more likely, than are men, to come in groups or as one of a couple. Despite our society's changing values, the cultural bias against women being seen alone in parks still prevails, carrying over to some plaza spaces. Notable exceptions are plazas where food is served and part of the space is an outdoor cafe (e.g., Paley Park, Manhattan; Australia Tower Square, Sydney); sitting at a table eating take-out food seems to allow those hesitant about using a plaza to be there with a legitimate reason.

Whyte concluded in his study of Manhattan plazas that the most-used plazas are also the most sociable. That is, they have higher than average proportions of people in twos and threes and more women:

Women are more discriminating than men as to where they will sit, more sensitive to annoyances, and women spend more time casting the various possibilities. If a plaza has a markedly lower than average proportion of women, something is wrong. Where there is a higher than average proportion of women the plaza is probably a good one and has been chosen as such. (Whyte 1980, p. 18)

However, this may be a New York phenomenon or particular to the time at which Whyte did his studies. A Seattle study found that in the one well-used portion of an underused bank plaza, 90 percent of the use

Walking and sitting are two activities accommodated in this plaza in the French Quarter of New Orleans.

(brown bagging and sunning) was by women. This may be an example of a phenomenon observed elsewhere, a particular age, sex, or ethnic group taking over a portion of public open space and the tradition becoming so entrenched that others are reluctant to intrude.

Another difference between male and female plaza users that Whyte noted is that men favor front locations, whereas women—who nearly always come in pairs or groups—favor the rear. (This has obvious implications for the location of group seating.) This conclusion was confirmed by our studies in San Francisco: Men predominated in all kinds of upfront, street plazas, whereas women were more likely to use the secluded sections of the street plazas and—in more significant numbers—what we have defined as urban oases. One thing seems to be clear. The more a plaza is used, the greater the variety of users' ages and the more evenly the sexes are balanced (Project for Public Spaces 1978; Cooper Marcus 1975–1988).

In a study of men's and women's uses of San Francisco downtown plazas, Mozingo (1984) compared Crocker Plaza (a busy, noisy street plaza) and Trans-America Redwood Park (a quiet green urban oasis). She used behavioral mapping and a questionnaire survey of users and nonusers. Not only did she find that women overwhelmingly preferred and used the oasis over the street plaza but also that men and women plaza users differed on other dimensions as well. Women use downtown public space less often than men; they are more sensitive to "environmental negatives" (pollution, noise, dirt, excessive concrete); they walk shorter distances to use a plaza (and their lunch hours are generally shorter than those of their male colleagues). Women generally do not want to be on display and thus when possible avoid places like Crocker Plaza. Mozingo observed that when seated in a

plaza, a woman's personal space was intruded on twice as often as a man's space was. She concluded that men and women have wholly different concepts of downtown open space and what they seek from it. That is, women are looking for a relief from urban stress and the office environment; they prefer to spend time in natural environments and to seek spaces that filter out urban stimuli and are secure. Men, on the other hand, perceive downtown public space as a place for human interaction; they expect to be intruded on and are more tolerant of such interruptions. In short, women seek "backyard" experiences (comfort, relief, security, control, relaxation); whereas men seek "front yard" experiences (publicness, social interaction, involvement). Mozingo stressed that we need to see these as part of a continuum, not necessarily as two separate kinds of space. The challenge for a designer is to integrate both uses into one plaza setting. The importance of Mozingo's study is that it contradicts some of Whyte's conclusions, particularly that the most successful plazas are those at the "100 percent corner," which capitalizes on social interaction and front yard behavior; that is, these may be the most successful areas for men but are not necessarily so for women.

Another important issue concerning women's use of downtown public spaces was discussed in a 1984 survey of users of nine such spaces in San Francisco, six of which were indoor galleries and atrium spaces open to the public for eating, sitting, passing through, and so on (Cranz 1984). The indoor spaces, which were flanked by retail stores, were the only downtown spaces where the women consistently outnumbered the men, supporting what common sense would suggest, that working women are more likely to be doing lunch-hour shopping than are men and therefore are more likely to use the public open spaces adjacent to retail stores.

Men tend to predominate in upfront, on-display locations in urban plazas. (Photo: Jennifer Webber)

Women tend to prefer backstage, quiet, and natural settings. (Photo: Robert Russell)

What Do People Do in Urban Spaces?

A detailed user evaluation of a large, highly used downtown plaza—First National Bank Plaza, Chicago (Department of Landscape Architecture 1975)—documented the following as typical behaviors in an observation day:

Walking through	52%	
Walking and watching	7	
Walking and talking	6	
All walking		65%
Stand and watch	11	
Stand and talk	4	
Stand only	1	
All standing		16
Sit and watch	6	
Sit and talk	5	
Sit and eat	2	
Sit and read	2	
Sit and ———	1	
All sitting		16
Other	3	3
	100%	100%

Approximately two thirds of the users were male, and one third was female. Interestingly, the male pre-

dominance, noticeable in the morning and noon hours, gave way during the afternoon, and by 5 P.M., women predominated. This was the only time, too, that the proportion of white-collar office workers to shoppers was roughly equal; during most of the day, white-collar males were the principal users. These users of the First National Bank Plaza made the following observations:

What Do You Like?	
Entertainment	26%
Fountain	19
Watching people	12
Atmosphere	11
Opposite sex	10
Isolation	8
Appearance	6
Sun	5
Location	3
	100%

Sixty percent of these responses refer to design changes, and when a comparable question was asked about a Seattle plaza, the results were similar (Project for Public Spaces 1979b):

What Do You Usually Do Here?*

Watch	34%
Listen	16
Eat	13
Sit	11
Relax	7
Walk	5
Sun	5
Read	5
Talk	4
Stand	3
Smoke	3

* Respondents could check more than one activity; therefore the total does not add up to 100 percent.

How Would You Modify or Change This Plaza?

More seats	21%
More programs	21
More greenery	15
Better acoustics	7
Drinking fountains	5
Safer stairs	3
Place to buy soft drinks	3
Cheaper food	3
Colored lights in fountain	3
Lower planters for visibility	3
More music	1
Miscellaneous	15
	100%

What Would Encourage You to Use the Plaza in Nice Weather?

More concerts and events	33%
Tables and umbrellas	20
Seasonal flowers	14
Food concession	8
Cafeteria with take-out food	6
Longer lunch break	4
Movable chairs	3
	88%

In 1976 a study was conducted in Sydney, Australia, of the users of three plazas and one small urban park, to discover what they did there, what they liked and disliked, and what characteristics they desired in a public urban open space (Purcell and Thorne n.d.). Most of the respondents were young (80 percent under thirty years old) clerical workers who answered the questionnaires distributed through their work places (close to one of the studied plazas). Of the respondents, 86 percent left the building during their lunch hour, and 55 percent used open spaces. When asked about their activities in the open spaces, the majority responded with relaxation (62 percent), followed by eating (22 percent), and walking (10 percent). Proximity to workplace was by far the most common reason (69 percent) for the choice of a particular place, followed by "trees and grass" and "lack of crowds." The extra facilities that an overwhelming majority of open space users wanted included more outdoor restaurants, coffee shops, and refreshment stalls; an open air theater; concerts; and more seating. Of those respondents who did not use downtown open spaces, their main reasons were that they were too busy or that the spaces were too crowded; they also voiced a concern over dirtiness, sense of confinement, and types of people found there.

A 1984 study of three downtown San Francisco public spaces revealed some interesting differences in use between a space in our category of city plaza (Justin Herman Plaza) and one in the category of urban oasis (TransAmerica Redwood Park) (Cranz 1984) (see Table 1.2). Because of its visibility, proximity to workplaces, tourist hotels, and shops, Justin Herman Plaza is more likely to attract a variety of people (in age, race, and reason for being downtown) and people who are first-time or infrequent users. Ironically, when these people were asked whether there was anything they disliked about this space, it was the other people. TransAmerica Redwood Park, the urban oasis, attracts a large number of frequent users who work nearby and who go there to eat their lunch and enjoy the out-

TABLE 1.2 REASONS FOR USING AN URBAN SPACE

Can You Tell Me Why You Come To . . . ?	City Plaza: Justin Herman	Urban Oasis: TransAmerica Redwood Park
Eat lunch	23%	23%
Pass through	14	15
Spend time/sit	14	6
Meet someone/wait	14	6
Work nearby	9	21
Curiosity	7	10
Outdoor/fresh air	5	19
Like physical space	2	8
Comes to site "often"	52	79
Feels comfortable being there alone	89	98
Works in downtown San Francisco	59	85

doors. A higher proportion felt comfortable there alone, and no one complained about the other people in the space.

Justin Herman Plaza may be closer in its variety of uses and users to the historic town square; 28 percent of its users, for example, went there to "wait for someone" or just to "sit and take a break," but only 12 percent cited these reasons for being at TransAmerica. At TransAmerica, by contrast, 41 percent said they liked the place because of its "greenery and landscaping" (versus only 4 percent at Justin Herman); 12 percent liked the urban oasis for "relaxing away from work," a reason cited by no one at Justin Herman Plaza.

Vandalism and "Undesirables"

Plazas that are frequently used are less likely to be troubled by crime, vandalism, or a preponderance of what managements term *undesirables* (e.g., winos, old unemployed men, the homeless). This fact was reported in Whyte's studies in Manhattan and confirmed by studies in Chicago (Department of Landscape Architecture 1975) and in San Francisco (Cooper Marcus 1975–1988). Therefore, from a long-term management point of view, a plaza design that invites heavy use has distinct advantages, even though this may mean more wear and tear and more littering. Whyte observed that plazas whose managements adopt a live-and-let-live attitude seem to encourage a lively and popular plaza scene, such as that at Seagram Plaza, Exxon Plaza, and 77 Water Street, New York City. Any so-called undesirables blend with the crowd.

Potential Service Area

When planning a new downtown plaza, its general use should be considered first, followed by an investigation of who the actual users of a specific site might be. This should include knowing where the potential users will come from and how far they will travel to use a plaza.

A catchment area study in San Francisco found that the users of eight downtown open spaces had traveled an average of nine hundred feet (2¼ city blocks, or a four-minute walk), excluding special cases of longer distances (e.g., to meet a specific person) (Lieberman 1984). The authors of a study in Sydney, Australia, reached similar general conclusions regarding the service area of open spaces: "In very general terms it seems that extreme proximity has a marked bearing on the decision to use a space, whether it is park-like or a reasonably comfortable hard paved plaza, but once there is a greater distance to all spaces, there is a tendency for those who use them at lunch time to choose the park-like ones" (Purcell and Thorne n.d., p. 31).

Another San Francisco study considered the possible impacts of high-rise development on the use of parks and plazas in or near downtown (Dornbusch and Gelb 1977). Interviews with the users of four downtown plazas produced some unexpected findings that will either be confirmed or questioned by further research. These findings were that

1. The visibility of a neighborhood park or plaza is a significant factor in its use by the surrounding community. People who cannot see a park or plaza from home or work tend to visit it comparatively infrequently.
2. Plazas that are relatively small and have low visibility (e.g., are sunken or separated from adjacent thoroughfares) tend to have smaller service areas than are theoretically possible. For example, the majority of users of Crown Zellerbach Plaza in San Francisco (amid tall buildings, below street level, low visibility) originated from very close by whereas such a plaza if not sunken could expect to draw from a much wider area.
3. A plaza with high visibility tends to have a much larger service area, though it still rarely reaches the proportions of its potential service area. Many of the users of Justin Herman Plaza in San Francisco walk four or five blocks to get there. It has high visibility, not only because of its large size, but also because a major downtown elevated freeway runs along one of its sides. It became regionally prominent when newspapers carried stories about its controversial Vaillancourt Fountain (thought by some to resemble a wrecked portion of the nearby elevated freeway) and about the battles of local young artists to sell their wares in the plaza space. A diagram of weekend use in the Dornbusch and Gelb study shows a local, walking clientele much smaller than that on weekdays, but a great number of visitors arriving by car or bus, from all over San Francisco (Dornbusch and Gelb 1977).

Microclimate

Sunlight

Every plaza designed for stationary use (standing, sitting) should have as much area as possible falling within the "comfort zone"—a range of weather conditions physically pleasing to a person who is in shade and in casual clothes. The principal factors affecting outdoor comfort are temperature, sun, humidity, and wind.

A plaza should be located so as to receive as much sunlight as its surrounding environment will permit. The seasonal movement of the sun and the existing and proposed structures all must be taken into account so that the plaza will receive the maximum amount of summer and winter sunshine. In those parts of the country with very hot summers, summer shade in at least part of the plaza is desirable and can be achieved by planting or shade from nearby buildings.

A study conducted by Eva Lieberman of the San Francisco Planning Department—on which several of the provisions of that city's new and well-publicized downtown plan were based—contained comments on the users' responses to eight open spaces. According to this study, which covered four plazas, three parks, and one urban garden, users cited access to the sun as their main concern (25 percent) in choosing a particular space. The second most common response was proximity to the respondent's workplace (19 percent), followed by a combination of aesthetics and comfort (13 percent) and the social aspect of parks and plazas (11 percent) (Lieberman 1984).

Ideally, building height and mass would be controlled to permit sunlight to reach all public open spaces. Unfortunately, however, in most cities the needs of the buildings' clients are frequently placed before those of the potential plaza users. And so we have cases such as Giannini Plaza outside the Bank of America Building in San Francisco, where the bank's need for a prestigious California street address, for the building to be seen while approaching it downhill on that street, and for the new massive building not to block the view of an adjacent attractive older building all combined to create a situation in which the Bank of America Building shades its own plaza throughout most of the day. Apart from access to the building entrances, the main plaza is rarely used, though two subspaces and a sidewalk wall that do catch the sun are heavily used.

A 1977 study of San Francisco plazas found that 47 percent of downtown plaza space at that time was shaded by buildings during the fall season noon hour. Ironically, most were shaded by the building that they were intended to serve, and so one cannot blame prior construction for their dilemma (Dornbusch and Gelb 1977, p. 171). Designers should consider using "borrowed" sunlight, reflected off nearby steel, glass, or marble buildings, to brighten and warm a plaza space that has little direct sun exposure.

Temperature

Studies in Manhattan and Copenhagen confirmed that when the temperature was above about 55° F there is a considerable increase in the amount of pleasure walking, standing, and sitting in urban malls and plazas (Gehl 1987; Pushkarev and Zupan 1975). Therefore, when predicting locations for popular noon-hour seating areas, sun–shade patterns should be calculated for those months when the average noon temperature is 55° F or higher. Where summer temperatures are uncomfortably hot (75° for some people, higher for others), some shaded areas should be provided. The

elderly, especially, require protection from direct sun and glare, and many younger people, as well, are sensitive to the sun.

Glare

The problem of glare is another aspect of the microclimate that must be considered. Because by definition, plazas are predominantly hard surfaced and are usually surrounded by highly reflective building surfaces, glare on sunny days can be a serious problem. One Chicago plaza evaluation reported: "While the streetside temperature lingered in the 70s, significantly higher levels were reached in the sunken area; the disparity aggravated by the glare rebounding from the unyielding reaches of white granite" (Department of Landscape Architecture 1975, p. 46). Dark surfaces, by contrast, can be gloomy and depressing in a region where many days are wet or overcast, such as in the Pacific Northwest.

Wind

It is now common knowledge among designers that many high-rise buildings deflect winds downward, multiplying their force and making walking or sitting on their windward side a problem. Table 1.3 shows the effect on pedestrians of different wind speeds. "More than sixty years ago, a guidebook called attention to New York's Flatiron Building (a mere dwarf by today's standards) with its curious effect in increasing the violence of the winds at its apex, so that, during a storm, people are sometimes whirled off the sidewalks. . . . Since then, air turbulences in the city's canyons have been magnified" (Rudofsky 1969, p. 338). Wind conditions known as *cornerflows, downwashes,* and *wakes* are the strongest and most problematic wind effects, with the most effective mitigating strategy being to redesign the building envelope itself or, when possible, to orchestrate the relationship of the sizes and shapes of the buildings near the effected area.

TABLE 1.3 EFFECT OF WIND ON PEDESTRIANS

Wind Speed	Pedestrian Discomfort
Up to 4 mph	No noticeable effect is felt.
4 to 8 mph	Wind is felt on the face.
8 to 13 mph	Wind disturbs hair, flaps clothing, and extends a light flag mounted on a pole.
13 to 19 mph	Wind raises dust, dry soil, and loose paper and disarranges hair.
19 to 26 mph	The force of the wind is felt on the body.
26 to 34 mph	Umbrellas are used with difficulty; hair is blown straight; and pedestrians have difficulty in walking steadily.

Overall Comfort

In his work in San Francisco and in the Environmental Simulation Laboratory of the College of Environmental Design at Berkeley, Peter Bosselmann did his pioneering work on climate and comfort issues in downtown settings (see, for example, Bosselmann et al. 1984). Through careful analysis and modeling, he determined direct relationships among the width of streets, height and bulk of buildings, footprint dimensions of buildings, and comfortable climatic conditions for pedestrians.

Public and professional concern for retaining access to sunshine in public open spaces has become quite strong in recent years; in 1984 San Francisco voters approved an ordinance prohibiting new construction that would shade a public open space at any time. Bosselmann's group devised a system of solar fans with which to determine necessary building cutoff angles to achieve the desired sun access. The San Francisco Downtown Plan and its accompanying Zoning Ordinance of 1984 list specific requirements to maximize sun access to sidewalks and other public spaces. At a minimum, buildings should be controlled to enable sunshine to enter public open spaces between 11 A.M. and 2 P.M. (12 noon and 3 P.M. daylight time) throughout the year.

The negative impact of wind in San Francisco has been thoroughly analyzed; the numerous complicated airflows resulting from modern high rises and their neighbors have been described and quantified; and some new zoning requirements have been approved. In the downtown office districts, for example, new buildings and additions to existing buildings shall be shaped, or other wind baffling measures shall be adopted, so that the development will not cause ground level wind currents to exceed—more than 10% of the time, year round, between 7 am and 6 pm—the comfort level of 11 m.p.h. equivalent wind speed in areas of substantial pedestrian use and 7 m.p.h. equivalent wind speed in public seating areas. (City of San Francisco 1984, p. 26)

Because an uncomfortable plaza will be an under- or unused plaza, any building or plaza designer should seriously consider sun and wind effects. Bosselmann and his colleagues point out that landscaping, though helpful, is less effective than modification to the buildings (Bosselmann et al. 1984). Because of the complexity of the interrelating elements, they strongly suggested that designers work with wind experts.

Designers who must create a usable plaza within the constraints of existing buildings should prepare a solar access analysis of the site, to determine which areas will have sun and when. This information will in turn aid design decisions about where to locate various features and will suggest ways both to enhance what is available (e.g., via "borrowed" sun) and to ameliorate any undesirable effects.

Boundaries and Transitions

A plaza must be perceived as a distinct place, and yet it must be visible and functionally accessible to passersby. In fact, exposure to adjacent sidewalks is essential; a successful plaza has one or preferably two sides exposed to public rights-of-way. The more readily that passersby

A plaza, such as that at 101 California Street, San Francisco, should be perceived as a distinct place, yet be easily accessible to passersby. (Photo: Jennifer Webber)

perceive the plaza as being an extension of that right-of-way, the more likely that they are to feel invited into it; thus, an extension of plaza planting onto the sidewalk may imply to passersby that they are already in the plaza. On the other hand, even a minor barrier or level change can considerably reduce the number of passersby who enter and use a plaza (Pushkarev and Zupan 1975).

The transition from sidewalk to plaza is one of the most important aspects of plaza design, as it can either encourage or discourage the plaza's use. Street plazas generally have no boundary of any sort: The adjacent sidewalk is more or less widened and furnished on its inner (building frontage) side with a seating wall, steps, or a seating island. There, people sit almost on the sidewalk; users are more likely to be men than women and are likely to include more blue-collar workers (construction workers, bicycle messengers) than at other types of plazas. Street plazas—barely distinct from the adjacent sidewalk—are popular because they provide easy access, a passing parade of people to watch, and a sense of surveillance and security.

The corporate foyer uses transitions that fall into one of four types:

1. In the narrow, mid-block plaza the narrowness of the entry and the imposing corporate front door straight ahead seem to be an adequate announcement of transition. No boundary per se is needed.
2. At the opposite extreme is the stage set, a huge corporate expanse, often on a semipodium level with few furnishings to tempt people to linger. Accordingly, a boundary is not needed, as few are invited in beyond those coming and going to the building (e.g., Seagram's Plaza, New York City; First Federal Bank Plaza, Minneapolis; Giannini Plaza, San Francisco).
3. A corner location often indicates a transition, by changes in surface and planters or seating islands (or "ziggurats") marking the outer boundary of the plaza, which has multiple entries and exits. One is invited to take a shortcut through it or to linger in the space. When one is in it, one is aware of being "inside" and of the persons walking by on the sidewalk as being "outside." This kind of boundary is best for encouraging use.
4. Another kind of boundary is formed by an arched wall or arcade that marks the outer edge of the plaza, so that entering the space feels a little like going inside a building. This announcement, plus an imposing, unfurnished interior with strong management presence, may have the effect of rejecting most potential users. An example is Citicorp Plaza in San Francisco: Cold marble surfaces abound, and even taking photographs is discouraged by a uniformed guard. This is a public place virtually reclaimed as corporate territory by the adjacent building.

But it is important to note that it is not the boundary alone that creates this mixed message. At 5 Fremont Place Plaza in San Francisco, an arched-wall boundary similar to that at Citicorp Plaza does not discourage use, because inside one can see sunny planting beds, trees, benches, seating walls, people sitting or passing through, and even an attractive McDonalds on the far side of the plaza. Once in the space, the "wall" provides a pleasing sense of enclosure and separation from traffic on the adjacent street.

The facade of the Citicorp Atrium is imposing and seemingly closed, but in fact, there are entries to a semioutdoor plaza between the columns. (Photo: Michael McKinley)

If the plaza is enclosed on two or three sides by adjacent buildings, the transition between plaza and building also should be considered. For example, if windows face on the plaza at grade and people at restaurant tables or office desks are sitting immediately inside those windows, plaza users should not be permitted to come too close, or the building and plaza users will infringe on each other's personal space and feel uncomfortable. Planting (inside or outside), level changes, or reflective glass are possible solutions.

The functions of building spaces and the plaza perimeter are important determinants of plaza activity. Blank walls of office buildings or banks tend to deaden the space; retail stores and cafés attract people into the space and thus enliven it. Whyte suggested that at least 50 percent of the total frontage of an urban open space be allocated to retail or service establishments (Whyte 1980). The 1984 San Francisco Downtown Plan allows up to 20 percent of a plaza to be restaurant outdoor seating. Outdoor café seating offers a visual cue to passersby that use of the plaza is encouraged. Indeed, the addition of umbrella-covered outdoor seating on a Seattle plaza measurably increased the use of a plaza next to a cafeteria (Project for Public Spaces, 1979b).

Because people universally tend to sit on the edges of spaces, rather than in the middle of them, the edges or boundaries of a plaza should, where possible, be planned for seating and viewing. A straight edge accommodates fewer uses than does an edge, which has many "ins and outs."

Subspaces

With the exception of plazas specifically designed for large public gatherings, markets, or rallies, large plazas should be divided into subspaces to encourage their use. A large open space devoid of planting, street furniture, or people is intimidating to most people, who prefer to be "enclosed" rather than "exposed"; accordingly, they will tend to pass through quickly or stick to the sides.

The least-used portion of Giannini Plaza in San Francisco is a large, shaded, dark-surfaced entry plaza; well-used sections include a smaller sunken garden and planters in a narrow side plaza that catches the sun (see Case Study 4). In a Seattle plaza, many users named the wide-open east plaza as their least favorite place; their favorite section was the South Cascade, a complex arrangement of steps and semiprivate courts that caught the sun and provided shelter and seclusion (Project for Public Spaces 1979). Subdivision into smaller spaces by means of changes of level, planting, construction, seating, and the like not only creates a more pleasing visual appearance when there are few people present to "fill up" the space but also encourages people to find their own enclosed niche and linger for a while.

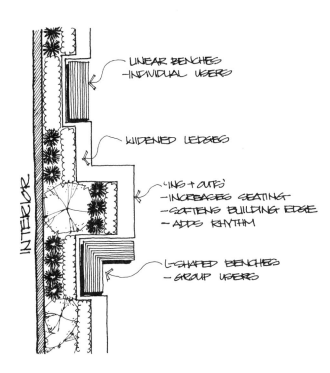

The more articulated the edge of a plaza is, the more edge sitters can sit on it.

Users of the Federal Office Building Plaza in Seattle much prefer the "south cascade" of steps and semiprivate courts to the wide-open East Plaza.

Boundaries of Subspaces

The spatial subdivision should be clear but subtle, or a person may feel segregated into a particular area. Examples of how and how not to do it appear in the Alcoa Plaza, San Francisco. A successful subspace in the northeast and southeast corners offers seating around a central circular planter, looking out over enclosing eye-level planters that square off the space, which is about twenty feet square. Not far away are two slightly larger subspaces enclosed by five-foot-high iron railings, with the points angled inwards. One enters through a narrow entrance to a paved sunken miniplaza banked by low plantings. Wherever one sits on the steps of the sunken area, one's view out is through a bleak iron railing. The feeling is of being in a prison. Needless to say, the first subspace is always more heavily used than is the second.

Size of Subspaces

The size of the whole plaza, or of a subspace within it, must never be so small that one feels one is entering a private room and intruding on the privacy of someone who may already be there. Nor should it be so large that one feels intimidated or alienated sitting there alone or with a few others present. This is the case in lower Sproul Plaza on the Berkeley campus; in the little-used monumental plaza outside the Lawrence Hall of Science in the Berkeley hills; and in the spacious, often wind-swept expanse of Giannini Plaza in San Francisco's financial district.

Circulation

The extent to which downtowners wish to walk, if a pleasant place is provided, is illustrated by many statistics on the effects of street closures in U.S. and European cities, quoted in Streets for People.

In the center of Vienna where nine city blocks were closed to traffic over Christmas 1971, the 30-day experiment received 80 percent support by pedestrians with the result that the ban is now permanent. . . . Copenhagen's Strøget, one year after traffic was removed, had an increase in pedestrian volume of 20–48 percent. . . . Also of interest are figures from the experimental closing of New York's Madison Avenue where pedestrian numbers more than doubled without any decrease in the number using the neighboring, and more popular, Fifth Avenue. This possibly indicated that people who otherwise may not leave their offices can be attracted to walk, if the environment is made conducive to walking. (OECD 1974, p. 10)

Pedestrian Planning and Health

The potential improvement in physical health from walking is only one benefit from the provision of more downtown plazas. More areas of the inner city reserved for pedestrians also mean less pollution, less noise, and fewer accidents. An unpopular and temporary ban on cars in downtown Athens was imposed in the spring of 1982 because pollution levels had reached alarming levels. A traffic ban in Tokyo's Ginza district for two days a week reduced the carbon monoxide level from 14.2 ppm to 2.9 ppm. A ban on cars in inner Vienna is reported to have lowered pollution levels by 70 percent. In Göteborg, Sweden, a traffic-restraint scheme reduced the overall mean carbon dioxide level from 30 ppm to 5 ppm. A Southampton, England, closure of 160 meters of a main shopping street resulted in the noise level's dropping from 80 dbA to 70 dbA (OECD 1974, pp. 19, 20, 42).

These benefits can be enhanced if plazas are linked by pedestrian walkways, malls, street closures, and the like. For an excellent account of many successful U.S. and European plans to "pedestrianize" city cores and parts of them, see the Organization for Economic Co-operation and Development's Streets for People (1974).

Circulation Patterns

The principal use of many plazas is by pedestrians entering and leaving nearby buildings. Regardless of local weather, the aesthetics of the plaza, or anything else, people will take the shortest and straightest route between the sidewalk (bus stop, car drop-off, intersection) and the nearest building entry. A basic decision in plaza design is thus predicting the route by which people will flow in and out of a building, thereby ensuring an unimpeded path for their movement. A study of a major Seattle plaza, for example, indicated that the designer had misjudged the volume of pedestrians entering from the southeast corner and thus squeezed a narrow stairway between a high ventilation shaft and a large Henry Moore sculpture, both of which blocked views, resulting in many near collisions as people rounded the corner to or from the plaza. An evaluation study recommended moving the sculpture and widening the stairway, a costly solution to a problem that the designer should have foreseen (Project for Public Spaces 1977).

Besides the peak rush-hour flows to and from building entries, most plazas must be able to accommodate three other forms of circulation:

1. passing through: people using the plaza as a shortcut or a pleasant walking-through space.
2. access to a café, bank, or other retail use peripheral to the plaza.
3. access to seating or viewing areas: people entering the plaza in order to sit in the sun, eat a bag lunch, view an exhibit, or listen to a concert.

People in the first two categories seem to prefer an open walkway area. According to a German study, they objected to such things as display cases breaking up the flows (OECD 1974, p. 60); according to an evaluation of the Sacramento Mall (Becker 1973, p. 105), users objected to the dominance of large, sculptured concrete forms (symbolic, to the designers, of nearby Sierra Nevada mountain forms).

In regard to walkway sizes, if the designer wishes to attain a relatively unimpeded traffic flow at peak times, Pushkarev and Zupan recommend a minimum of two people per minute per foot of walkway width. These standards, they pointed out, are at sharp variance with those used by transit operating agencies in Chicago, London, and New York, where values of twenty-eight, twenty-seven, and twenty-five persons per minute per foot of subway passage width are considered maximum capacity. Obviously, strolling for pleasure in an outdoor plaza has very different standards than does rush-hour subway traffic.

In regard to guiding pedestrian flow, Pushkarev and Zupan made an interesting observation from their studies in Manhattan, that "pedestrians totally disregard any color patterns on the walkway, be they different shades of brick or concrete, or painted lines. . . . [However] pedestrians respect physical barriers and strong changes in texture" (Pushkarev and Zupan 1975, p. 156). Our own observation in San Francisco confirmed this. Therefore, if the intention is to guide pedestrians in a certain direction, this message must be clearly conveyed in physical form through the location of walls, planters, bollards, or change of level or texture (pedestrians avoid cobblestones, gravel, and ventilation gratings).

There seems to be a tendency for a moving pedestrian flow to remain in the center of a space or flight of stairs and for eddies of sitters, watchers, and talkers to gravitate to the edges. This phenomenon was described in regard to a Chicago plaza.

On the stair flights where one might have expected the greatest conflicts between travellers and sitters, an interesting phenomenon to the contrary occurred. As cued by the density maps and confirmed by the 35 mm slides, sitters clustered on the edges, not only leaning against the wing walls, but also nestling along the handrails which dissected the staircases. Thereby, for the most part, through channels were maintained in the middle. Gravitation to edges with a resulting maintenance of mid-channels repeated itself with equal regularity among those standing about on the lower level. (Department of Landscape Architecture 1975, p. 50)

This phenomenon was also observed in many San Francisco plazas, although William Whyte's Manhattan study found the opposite reaction. Referring to street conversations lasting one minute or more, he noted, "People didn't move out of the main pedestrian flow. They stayed in it or moved into it, and the great bulk of the conversations were smack in the center of the flow—the 100% location, to use the real-estate term" (Whyte 1980, p. 21). This may imply that New Yorkers have different patterns of behavior in public spaces, or as Whyte concluded, in "mid-flow" one could choose to break off or to continue, as one would at a cocktail party.

A final note regarding circulation: Ramps must always be parallel—or be provided in conjunction—with stairs where changes of level occur. The whole plaza should be equally accessible to disabled persons, the elderly, parents with strollers, and vendors with display carts.

Seating

Even when zoning regulations encourage the provision of more downtown public open space, there is not necessarily a parallel increase in places to sit. For example, the original 1961 ordinance in New York City permit-

Some of the most popular public seating places are steps and walls alongside busy streets and sidewalks, as here, in Cambridge, Massachusetts.

ted street furniture such as flag poles, fountains, planters, and statuary but did not list as a permitted use either benches or outdoor cafés. These regulations were revised in the 1975 zoning amendments to encourage providing seating and food kiosks. However, steps, walls, planting boxes, and fountain edges still represent the basic seating facilities in most downtown public spaces.

Perhaps the most detailed evaluation of outdoor seating behavior, William Whyte's study of Manhattan plazas, reported: "After 3 months of checking out various factors—such as sun angles, size of spaces, nearness to transit—we came to a spectacular conclusion: people sit most where there are places to sit. Other things matter too—food, fountains, tables, sunlight, shade, trees—but this simplest of amenities, a place to sit, is far and away the most important element in plaza use" (Whyte 1974, p. 30). The main reason for a lack of benches in plazas is not only that bonus requirements have not, until recently, required them but also that the management of many buildings have

an obsessive fear of "undesirables." This is why they tell architects to put spikes on ledges. This is why benches are made short. If you made them long, a wino might sleep on them. This is why the Madison Avenue Mall was fought so bitterly by many merchants. Open it up and we'll be overrun by hippies, students, and other undesirables. (Our time-lapse study of the two-week test closing in 1971 shows that the crowd was overwhelmingly an office-worker and shopper crowd. No matter, merchants swore they saw hippies everywhere). (Whyte 1974, p. 30)

A time-lapse study of ten Vancouver plazas found patterns comparable to those in New York City. People gathered on artifacts of various shapes and sizes (benches, steps, planting edges) around and close to focal elements; they were attracted to fountains and sculptures; and they gathered along edges and close to where other people were. Therefore, for plazas to be used for stationary activities, and not just as pedestrian

walkways, many kinds of sitting, leaning, and resting places need to be provided.

Who Are the Sitters?

There are at least five varieties of sitters in urban plazas, in regard to where they want to sit:

1. Those waiting briefly for a bus or taxi.
2. Passersby who want to sit on the edge of the plaza looking out at the passing traffic and sidewalk action (fence sitters, in terms of plaza use, but still to be accommodated). These users are predominantly men.
3. Users who want only to dip their toes in and to sit just inside the plaza looking in. All of these three categories are more likely to be single users rather than groups, and therefore seating should be arranged so that people can sit side by side, instead of in more intimate arrangements, such as opposite to or at right angles.
4. Most of the users (if this is a well-used plaza) tend to sit not too close to traffic and sidewalk and not too close to building entries. These can be both groups and people alone. Both types tend to gravitate first to edge or island seating, just as restaurant users gravitate first to tables along the walls or edges of a room. The amount of edge seating can be increased by articulating the perimeter of the space, which at the same time can create subspaces for small groups.
5. A small but important group of users is likely to be couples and lovers seeking out secluded, intimate places to be alone, and pairs or groups of women, who tend to favor inner, less exposed locations. An unheralded but significant use of plazas and downtown parks is as a setting for courtship and secluded liaisons (the plaza as trysting place). Seating for this group might be the back of the plaza (if it has a back) or in a dead-

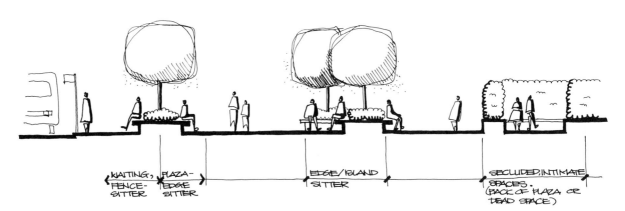

People vary in where they want to sit: on the edge looking out, on the edge looking in, around plaza edges, on "islands," or in secluded alcoves.

end space, where intrusions from passersby are at a minimum. At the opposite extreme, those who fall into the category of "young love on display" tend to sit in the most exposed locations.

People Watching

Faced with the task of locating seating, the designer should be aware that for much of the year (except in the hottest weather) people will seek a sunny spot. Therefore, sunny locations between 11:30 A.M. and 2:30 P.M. should receive the most attention.

However, when considerable space is likely to receive sunlight in good weather, people will be drawn to a location where other people are passing by. A study of Chase Manhattan Plaza in New York, for example, found that it had two distinct subareas: the Pine–Liberty area, adjacent to activity and bustle and always filled to capacity with people watchers, and the Nassau–Liberty area, out of the way and considerably less frequently used (Project for Public Spaces 1975). Thus, prior analysis of likely pedestrian movement should reveal which subarea will be the busiest, and the most seating should be located within view of this activity.

Primary and Secondary Seating

Although this chapter has emphasized the use of plazas during peak hours, some users (tourists, students, shoppers) use plazas before or after the prime-time office lunch hours. Large expanses of hard open space, or row upon row of benches can seem intimidating and unwelcome when only a few people are present. In this respect, a plaza that offers plenty of places to sit that are not all benches does not appear so empty when people

are not present. So-called secondary seating—mounds of grass, steps with a view, seating walls, and retaining walls that allow seating—can appear as part of the sculptural effect of the design and need not look lonely when devoid of people. A New York–based consulting firm that has evaluated many plazas recommends that secondary seating comprise a maximum of 50 percent of the total seating on a plaza. To be usable, this form of seating should be between sixteen and thirty inches in height (Project for Public Spaces 1978).

Styles of Seating

Different people want to sit in different ways, and given enough choice, each will seek out the setting best suited to him or her. Thus, to serve a variety of users, every plaza should provide a variety of seating, not only in location, but also in differing forms of seating posture. A Vancouver study reported that variety in the shape, size, and arrangement of seating or leaning facilities significantly affected the public use potential of downtown plazas (Joardar and Neill 1978, p. 489).

Benches. A study of the Federal Building Plaza in Seattle found that people overwhelmingly preferred wooden benches, followed by steps, planters, and (low on the list) stone seats and the ground (Project for Public Space 1978).

A three-by-six-foot wooden, backless bench—two backsides deep—offers a versatile form of seating, allowing for a variety of social groupings and sight lines. Two people can sit comfortably with plenty of room for sandwiches and cold drinks between them. If a third or fourth person joins them, the bench becomes a seat

Casual or "secondary" seating on steps, walls, mounds, and planters does not appear empty when people are not present. (Photo: Robert Russell)

Different people need different forms of seating: a young office worker in Justin Herman Plaza, San Francisco, relaxing on a waveshaped concrete ledge. (Photo: Jennifer Webber)

An elderly man waiting on a comfortable wooden bench in New Orleans's French Quarter.

and table combined. Up to four unattached people at a time can also comfortably use such a bench without infringing too much on one another's privacy. The bench enables one to sit facing in any one of four directions, according to sun, shade, desired view, or whatever. A three-by-three-foot version of this same wooden bench enables one to have a private seat but still sit with a friend if there are no other places. Whereas both orientation and back (or lack of back) design should be varied to accommodate different users' needs, seat height should conform to average body measurements, as documented in such manuals as *Architecture Graphic Standards.* These height standards must also be followed with regard to the heights of planters and retaining walls, for these also will be used

by some people, at some times, for seating. Whyte recommended a seating height of seventeen inches. A Chicago plaza study described a typical problem:

The planter on the lower level in front of the restaurant is the most ill-suited of all for sitting purposes of any sort. It measures approximately a foot in height thereby thrusting a sitter's knees into his chest. Apparently, the planter was built low so as to allow a view of the fountain from within the restaurant. As irony would have it, however discomforting, scores of people do perch all around the planter during the main eating hour, their torsos serving nicely to block the view. Those sitting on the backside of the planter can stare directly into the eating facility which, to complete the irony, may be the reason why the restauranteur has now screened off his windows. (Department of Landscape Architecture 1975, p. 46)

A three-by-six-feet wooden backless bench provides many seating opportunities.

Steps and Ledges. The best places to sit are often the simplest. People (especially younger men) will cluster on steps and ledges if they are wide enough. On steps, people can sort themselves out into an infinite variety of groupings, more so than on fixed benches. However, for groups of more than two, linear steps and ledges do not prove comfortable. An evaluation of a Chicago plaza, typical of many, discovered:

Seating is accommodated primarily by way of steps and planters. While their orientation to the fountain and congregations of people services "watching," their linear design is not well-suited for conversation. Conversationalists were constantly observed in uncomfortably angled postures, all that the design allowed toward bringing about eye contact with an adjacent neighbor. Indeed, many simply stood to gain a face-to-face position rather than occupy an available space on a planter. (Department of Landscape Architecture, 1975, p. 46)

A Vancouver study noted that the corners of raised pools and planters were much more frequently used than were their straight middle sections. Along boundary railings, too, sitting density was significantly higher in the corners than in the straight sections (Joardar and Neill 1978, p. 489). Thus the more articulated the edges and ledges are, the more they will probably be used.

Table Seating. With limited lunch hours and crowded downtown restaurants, more and more people are bringing their own lunch to work. Although it is possible to eat while sitting on a bench, people in groups find it more comfortable to sit at a table. There are some good examples of table seating for public use: On the plazas and wide passageways of the Embarcadero Center in San Francisco, for example, attractive white metal "garden" furniture is liberally distributed and used. It is unobtrusively bolted to the ground and by no means gives the same message as do the tables in state or national parks, which are chained to a post. Under the shaded arcades of the AT & T Building in New York, however, similar garden chairs and tables are not bolted down, thus allowing users to move them around into convenient groupings. If tables are meant exclusively for the use of a particular café or restaurant, they should be subtly separated from public rights-of-way by means of planters.

The addition of umbrellas to outdoor tables can be advantageous: (1) The roof canopy can provide a sense of spatial enclosure and intimacy for table users; (2) in hot regions, umbrellas can offer needed shade; (3) umbrellas can give some protection from down drafts caused by high-rise buildings; and (4) they can offer an important visual cue to passing pedestrians that seating and lunching are encouraged. In a Seattle plaza study, the addition of tables with umbrellas outside a cafeteria greatly increased the use of that part of the plaza; indeed, on one sunny day when the umbrellas were inadvertently not put out, the use of the tables fell dramatically (Project for Public Spaces, 1977).

Sitting Alone and in Groups

To accommodate those who come alone to a plaza and want to sit near—but not within eye contact of —other users, one of two arrangements is recommended. First, steps, ledges, or straight benches permit natural spacing between people and do not force unwanted eye contact, as would benches set at right angles or opposite each other. Second, a circular bench around a planter (for trees or flowers) enables several unattached users to sit fairly close but to maintain their privacy by looking out in different directions (known as sociofugal seating).

To accommodate groups of three or more, the following arrangements are recommended: wide, backless benches, benches forming right angles at corners, or benches curving inward. Movable chairs and tables (garden design) might also be provided. In the highly used Paley and Greenacre parks in Manhattan (very small, expensively designed plazas with water, greenery, and food service), not one of the movable chairs has ever been stolen. (It should be noted, however, that these plazas are closed at night.)

Orientation of Seating

A variety of orientations is important as well. This includes variety in what is seen while seated, for people differ in their need to watch passersby, water, foliage, distant views, nearby programs, and the like; and also variety in sun and shade, as not only do people want more or less sun depending on the season but people need more or less according to their own circumstances.

A Vancouver study found that in Granville Square, "clusters of small seats providing orientational variety held a greater diversity of population and a wider mix of age, sex, posture or activity than typical linear configurations" (Joardar and Neill 1978, p. 489). Another successful plaza, in Kings Cross, Sydney, Australia, is a triangular space at a busy street intersection with an eye-catching fountain at its apex. The benches are wide and narrow, backed and backless, private and exposed, looking in and looking out, and in sun and shade. Hardly any seating need has not been met.

Seating Materials

Materials for seating should not be particularly responsive to temperature. Wood is a warm and comfortable material for public seating, other materials are much colder and harder, but could be effective for secondary seating. Such materials include concrete, metal, tile, and stone. Unfortunately, the client's desire to prevent

vandalism often persuades the designer to use such materials, whereas vandalism could just as easily be avoided by a design that encourages continued use and by the presence of a full-time gardener/manager during daylight hours.

Materials such as rough unfinished wood or concrete aggregates should also be avoided if they even look as though they might damage clothes.

Amount of Seating

After studying many plazas in New York and elsewhere, the Project for Public Spaces recommended one linear foot of seating for each thirty square feet of plaza space (Miles, Cook, and Roberts, 1978). The requirement in the 1986 Downtown Plan for San Francisco is one linear foot of seating for each linear foot of plaza perimeter. If the plaza is located in a potentially high-use area and is designed to attract people, probably all the seating that can be provided will be used. Whyte's studies of five of the most intensively used sitting places in New York found a range of thirty-three to thirty-eight people per one hundred linear feet of sitting space. He therefore suggested a rough rule of thumb for estimating the average number of people using the prime sitting space at peak periods: Divide by three the number of linear feet provided.

Planting

The variety and quality of textural, color, massing, aural, and olfactory effects created by a careful planting plan can add immeasurably to a plaza's use. In a study of ten downtown plazas in Vancouver, Joardar and Neill found that people were attracted to plazas that offered visual variety and complexity, with trees, un-

Privacy while sitting: A simple bench allows these men in Chinatown, San Francisco, to create their own private places. (Photo: Anthony Poon)

Privacy while sitting: Flower-filled planters on a seating ziggurat at 101 California Street, San Francisco, permit singles or pairs of people to find semiprivate niches. (Photo: Jennifer Webber)

common shrubs, and colorful annuals being especially important (Joardar and Neill 1978). Not only may they initially attract passersby into a plaza, but once there, they will enormously enhance their experience. For, as Fruin noted: "When the pedestrian is assured of his primary concern for orientation and direction, his level of receptivity to sensory gradients, such as changes in color, light, ground slope, smells, sounds, and textures is increased" (Fruin 1971, p. 120).

A survey of the spaces around the HUD Building in Washington, D.C., reported urgent requests from employees for more grass, trees, and benches (Project for Public Spaces 1979a). Largely surrounded by busy streets and bleak concrete plazas, one of the most heavily used open spaces was a small sitting garden with grass, trees, and benches. At its peak use, each person had only two feet, seven inches of sitting space; yet the larger half of the garden (over a loading dock) could not be used at all, as it had no seating. For greenery to be enjoyed, therefore, there must clearly be places to sit, or lawns so positioned and designed as to be conducive to casual sitting.

Planting Variety

It is important in the relatively small area of most plazas to have a variety of planting for visual interest while sitting there or passing through. Most people are drawn to stay in a plaza for its oasis effect and so need something visually pleasing to attract their attention, especially (1) if they are alone, (2) if they are without behavioral props (such as lunch, book, or paper), or (3) if there are few passersby to watch. In San Francisco, St. Mary's Square is particularly successful in this regard. Its planting includes Lombardy poplars, pittosporum, birch, stone pine, flowering plum, and agapan-

thus in planters at the base of trees, offering a pleasing variety of color, texture, height, and degree of shade.

The smaller (or more sunken) the plaza is, the more feathery-leaved, quasi-open trees should be selected, so that users can see through them to different portions of the plaza. Such trees also allow the high winds associated with high buildings to blow through them with less potential damage than thick or large-leaved species do.

Height of Planting

The eventual height and mass of planting should not cut off the view of an activity or performance area for some plaza users. In a Chicago example, the height of plantings along the edge of the intermediate level of a three-level plaza cuts off the view of a fountain and major circulation space below. Worse still,

the sight lines become fully blocked during peak hours by the torsos of those sitting on the planter edges. Sitters are obliged to position themselves with backs to the lower level or twist aside into uncomfortable postures in order to survey the scene below. A full view is obtainable only if one stands smack against a wall, or as was repeatedly observed, immediately in front of a supposedly relaxing sitter. (Department of Landscape Architecture 1975, p. 54)

If a plaza has to be sunken, trees should be planted in it that will soon grow above sidewalk level, so that their foliage will add to a pleasing street experience, even if the plaza is rarely used except to pass through. A good example of this is Crocker Plaza in San Francisco, where tall honey locust trees reach from the sunken plaza to well above sidewalk level and blend in with the same species used as street trees.

Boundary Planting

If one or more sides of a plaza are bounded by buildings that cannot be accessed from the plaza, their walls might be screened by trees. If the plaza-bounding building has few windows for which light or views need to be considered, densely growing trees might be selected (e.g. redwoods in the TransAmerica Redwood Park in San Francisco). If the building needs to be screened for the aesthetic enjoyment of the plaza users but the building users need light and views, a more open, feathery species might be selected. A good example is the screening of old brick Chinatown buildings by a row of tall Lombardy poplars at the back of St. Mary's Square, San Francisco. This species has the added advantage of having a small horizontal spread, consequently taking up little usable space in the plaza. Lower, bushy planting beneath them makes up for the fact that poplars do not typically branch and leaf below twelve to fifteen feet.

Importance of Color and Fragrance

Color is an important element of the users' enjoyment of plazas. The trees and shrubs may be of various colors, and brightly colored annuals or perennials in planters and flowering shrubs may be used as well. Along with color, fragrance should also be considered; it is pleasant, for example, to sit in Hallidie Plaza, San Francisco and smell the unexpected fragrance of lavender.

Many city dwellers live in apartments without gardens or balconies and may spend eight hours a day in an environment decorated with plastic house plants. In cities with no bright colors, public flower gardens are especially welcome. Tubs with seasonal annuals can provide attractive splashes of color without creating

too much of a maintenance problem. But if a public garden is for looking at only and cannot be entered and sat in, is it justified? Such a case is Chevron's Garden Plaza at 555 Market Street, San Francisco. A beautiful geometric arrangement of granite blocks, falling water, flower beds, grass, and Japanese maples, this plaza can be seen only from a fenced viewing platform. Although it was granted as a bonus for building higher, entry to this garden was made impossible in order to reduce maintenance costs and keep the space in pristine condition. Under the new downtown open space guidelines, however, this would no longer be permitted as a public open space.

Protection of Planting

If there are not enough benches, steps and so on for sitting in a plaza, any horizontal surface will be used, including the narrow edges of planters and the walls or ledges behind the planting (resulting in trampled planting). At Crocker Plaza in San Francisco, unattractive cylinders of chicken wire had to be added to circular planters to protect the plants from sitters. And at Hallidie Plaza in San Francisco, a low wall with ivy growing up and over it has been screened by chicken wire on a frame to prevent people sitting on it. Unfortunately, the same screen frame now partially obscures the bench sitters' view of the pedestrian parade on Market Street.

Provision of Lawn Areas

A sloped lawn area lining one or more sides of the main circulation and seating space of a plaza can provide aesthetic relief from concrete and wood; allow users to sit, sprawl, or sunbathe in a more casual fash-

Redwood trees in this small San Francisco plaza park (TransAmerica Redwood Park) surrounded by skyscrapers help screen out adjacent buildings and create an oasislike setting. (Photo: Robert Russell)

ion than benches will normally allow; and permit lawn users to have a slightly elevated view of the passersby and plaza activity.

An excellent example of a small but intensively used lawn area is that in the TransAmerica Redwood Park in San Francisco (see Case Study 5). The presence of a lawn backed by about twenty forty-foot redwood trees evidently inspired the creators of the TransAmerica Redwood Park to term this space a park rather than a plaza. (But by our definition, it is still a plaza, as hard surfaces predominate). During the noon hour, people have been seen to smoke marijuana quite openly while seated on this lawn; rarely do people do this on the plaza benches. That is, this lawn is perceived to be both more casual and more private than the rest of the plaza is, despite its visibility and relatively small size. The trees successfully screen out the three- and four-story buildings bordering the plaza on its east side. The lawn is fully in sun (as indeed, the whole plaza is) at the noon hour. Elevated portions allow near views of plaza sitters, a fountain, and planters and far views of Coit Tower, Telegraph Hill, and Nob Hill. The back edge of the lawn is subtly articulated to form enclaves that people can claim as semi-private sitting areas. This lawn is heavily used for picnics, sleeping, reading, sunbathing, people watching, or just sprawling.

The design and location of a lawn space determine whether or not it will be used. Contrast the highly used lawn at the TransAmerica Redwood Park with the rarely used lawn in the Alcoa Plaza, San Francisco. The latter is large, flat, square, and surrounded on all four sides by walkways. People avoid "prairie" expanses, whether in parks, plazas, housing developments, or inside buildings.

Level Changes

Aesthetic and Psychological Effects

Changes of level can have important visual, functional, and psychological consequences. For most observers, a plazascape that includes some modest but observable changes in level is preferable aesthetically to one that is absolutely flat. There are also some important functional advantages: For example, seating and circulation spaces can be separated by slight changes in level; an upper level can function as a temporary "stage" or platform for speeches or performances (for example, the Sproul Hall steps on the Berkeley campus); and a very large plaza can be subdivided into more human-scale "outdoor rooms" by the differing levels.

There is a peculiar human satisfaction in standing on a vantage point, preferably leaning against some comforting prop such as a wall or railing and looking down at the people below. The natural fascination of people watching is thus enhanced by the provision of an elevated vantage point. Cullen suggested that height in

the townscape equals privilege; depth equals intimacy; and depending on one's psychological need, a plaza incorporating level changes provides locales for both these moods (Cullen 1961, pp. 175–177). However, the use of differing levels should be handled with care so that disabled users are not precluded from access to any of the spaces. Wherever possible, a ramped slope should parallel or substitute for the steps between different plaza levels.

Perils of Sunken Plazas

Dramatic changes of level between the sidewalk and the plaza should be avoided whenever possible (Fruin 1971, p. 17). In their study of Manhattan plazas, Pushkarev and Zupan showed that plazas with below-average use generally have significant differences in elevation, up or down, architectural barriers, and an absence of seating (Pushkarev and Zupan 1975, p. 165). San Francisco's examples of low-use plazas include Giannini Plaza, which from one direction is attainable only after a significant climb from California Street; Zellerbach Plaza, which is not only sunken below sidewalk level but also has ambiguous entry points and is totally devoid of seating (see Case Study 3); and Hallidie Plaza, which is accessible by escalator, as it is also a below-grade access to BART (Bay Area Rapid Transit) but is often hot and visually displeasing. A space too far above street level loses visual contact with the street. A small space too far below street level is uncomfortable for its occupants and is suitable only as a place of movement or access.

Where there are subtle changes of level, it is important to maintain a visual connection between levels to enhance a specific experience. For example, a space slightly above street level gives a sense of overlook and advantage to its occupants, while the passersby retain visual connection and interest. Or, a space slightly below street level gives a sense of intimacy and enclosure to its occupants, as well as a sense of overlook and advantage for the passersby on the sidewalk.

People Attractors in Sunken Plazas

If a plaza has to be designed below grade, an eye-catching feature may draw people in; the farther down the plaza is, the larger the "draw" has to be. For example, a medium-sized metal fountain sculpture (whose water is rarely turned on) functions poorly in this regard in Zellerbach Plaza, San Francisco (only six to eight steps down from sidewalk level); a massive fountain pool with high jets acts as a positive attractor in the very much larger sunken plaza of the First National Bank Plaza, Chicago (over thirty steps down). But having drawn people down, there must be places to sit and enjoy the ambience.

If the inducement to go down to a plaza is nothing more than a subway entrance, there will be little rea-

The West Plaza of Seattle's Federal Office Building, just above street level, provides a sense of overlook but not access for disabled people.

son to stay, even if seating is provided. At Hallidie Plaza in San Francisco, there is little to look at beyond a large expanse of brick paving, glaring granite walls (on a hot day it is like an oven), small trees that offer no shade, and colorless planters. During rush hours, the spasmodic flow of BART users provides people to look at; but on weekends, when the rapid transit system is less heavily used, not even this diversion is present. It is little wonder that the seats at the intermediate and upper levels, where passersby and traffic on Market Street create some interest, are always more heavily used than are those in the sunken plaza areas.

Raised Plazas

Conversely, sitting in a raised plaza, as long as it is visually obvious from the street (through planting) and not too many steps up, can be a pleasing experience. There is something psychologically and physiologically pleasing about being above the noise and smell of car traffic and beyond the view of passing pedestrians. At St. Mary's Square in San Francisco, mature trees announce the presence of something interesting and draw many intrigued tourists up the half-dozen steps from Grant and California streets. Where a raised plaza is not visible from the street but forms part of a complex of interrelated plazas and walkways, as at San Francisco's Golden Gateway (Alcoa Plaza), there must be sufficient reason to be there (shops, building entrances, restaurants) to draw people up in the first place.

Public Art

The authors of *Livable Cities* propose some excellent criteria for evaluating art in public places that they feel "should make a positive contribution to the life of the city, and to the well being of its inhabitants . . . [it] should generously give the public some positive benefit —delight, amenity, fantasy, joy, sociability—in a word, a sense of well-being" (Crowhurst-Lennard and Lennard 1987, pp. 89, 90). Among the criteria they suggest are that art in a public place should

1. Create a sense of joy, delight, and wonder at the life of the city.
2. Stimulate play, creativity, and imagination by drawing on legend, metaphor, mythology, or history and/or by creating a form that can be manipulated, sat on, walked under, or whatever. Sculptures or fountains that intrigue children generally also intrigue adults.
3. Promote contact and communication. A sculpture or fountain that is highly visible and near well-traveled paths may encourage people to stop, perhaps to sit nearby or strike up a conversation. This is a theme also emphasized by Whyte in his studies of Manhattan plazas: He called it *triangulation* and encouraged performance or public art as a potential bridge between adjacent strangers in public places.
4. Provide comfort and amenity by incorporating steps, ledges, or railings for sitting or leaning

A café may draw people to a plaza above street level. This one at the First Interstate Bank Center in Seattle offers access by stairs and by escalator.

In European cities, as here in Malmö, Sweden, statues of monarchs and heroes were traditionally placed on a high plinth in the center of the city square.

The contemporary street sculpture in Malmö, Sweden, brings art to a level where people can touch and enjoy it.

within or close to the work of art. Sensory experiences—the texture of a "touch-me" sculpture, the sound and feel of a fountain—may offer brief but pleasing encounters.

5. Encourage interaction and cast people as actors rather than audience. Lawrence Halprin's fountain in Portland, Oregon's Lovejoy Plaza was designed, for example, with people's participation as a major design criterion: Children and young people delight in playing in the water and climbing over the forms to an extent perhaps not true of any other public work of art. On a smaller scale, German artist Bonifatius Stirnberg's sculpture fountains in many German cities celebrate local identity and history with simple, understandable figures, of which many are bronze "puppet sculptures" that the viewer can move and reposition (Crowhurst-Lennard and Lennard 1987). Contrast Halprin's and Stirnberg's work with that of Serra, for example, whose massive, rusted steel beam (Tilted Arc) across a New York plaza was so disliked that employees in the adjacent office building petitioned to have it removed. It fulfilled none of the preceding criteria, except insofar as it promoted communication among those who resented its presence (Storr 1985).

Although establishing performance criteria for public art may raise some eyebrows, we agree with the authors of *Livable Cities* that

a work of art in a private collection, or in a collection open to the public, can appropriately be a personal expression of the artist, a private joke, a statement of an inner psychological state, an aesthetic combination of colors, textures, shapes, etc. They are works of art that may be extremely relevant to a few individuals, and can be visited and appreciated by those

to whom they do speak. A public work of art may be expected to fulfill any or all of the above criteria, but in addition it should be expected to speak profoundly to a larger percentage of the population who will inevitably use the public space in which it is located. (Crowhurst-Lennard and Lennard 1987, p. 90)

Some hundred years earlier, Camillo Sitte, in his remarkable book *The Art of Building Cities*, reminded us:

It must be remembered that art has a legitimate and vital place in civic arrangement, for it is this kind of art alone that daily and hourly influences the great mass of people, while the influence of the theatre and concert hall is generally confined to a relatively small segment of the population. (Sitte 1889/1945, p.72)

Sitte advised against placing a sculpture at the geometric center of a square, for this may suggest that the square is there solely for the sculpture rather than for the people; thus an off-center location is preferable, close to the main pedestrian routes (Sitte 1889/1945). Where sight lines are important, for example, between a building lobby and a car or taxi pickup or around an entry corner, a sculpture should be positioned carefully so as not to block views.

Fountains

The visual and aural attraction of moving water is universal. A "noisy" fountain located close to seating may successfully screen out surrounding traffic noises and help immeasurably in creating a pleasant ambience. A Vancouver study noted that a fountain programmed to produce complex patterns of water movement generated public use of Courthouse Square all day, whereas two comparable plazas without fountains a block away were used only as places to pass through quickly (Joardar and Neill 1978, p. 489).

Lawrence Halprin's fountain in a Portland, Oregon, plaza encourages interaction with the water.

One also should not underestimate the stress-reducing effects of the sound of falling water. In a dense urban setting, a fountain should be designed so that the sound of falling water is as noisy as possible and the seating is arranged so that as many users as possible can sit within earshot. A fountain needs to be in scale with its setting. In the large open space of Justin Herman Plaza, San Francisco, the Vaillancourt Fountain's massive structure is not out of place. In contrast, a small fountain in the TransAmerica Redwood Park consists of seven simple jets at varying heights in a pebble-lined pool; the soothing sounds are within earshot of all those using the benches and lawn nearby (see Case Study 5).

A problem may be created when fountains are located in high-rise office districts. High-rise buildings are notorious for creating turbulent local winds that can blow spray from fountain jets over a wide area, rendering portions of the plaza unusable. For instance, a fountain at Giannini Plaza in San Francisco had to be removed for this reason and replaced by a less offensive planter: a costly mistake. One solution may be to employ a full-time gardener or plaza manager who can control the fountain and moderate jet heights according to wind velocity.

Though fountains and water features are a true amenity for any plaza, the costs of their operation and maintenance should be considered before they are constructed. Indeed, a beautiful large cascade fountain provided in San Francisco's PG&E plaza had to be turned off at one period owing to the energy costs of operating it.

Paving

After only a brief observation of people in public places, it soon becomes apparent that people will seek to move from A to B in as direct a line as possible. All major circulation routes must accommodate this principle, or people will take shortcuts across lawns or even planting to get to where they want to go, as quickly as possible. Surfaces that most people avoid (and so can be used to channel movement) are large-sized gravel and cobbles. Women are more likely to avoid them than are men.

A change in surface that is readily apparent to the feet and eyes, such as the transition from sidewalk paving to brick, can define a plaza as a separate place without discouraging entry. A small plaza at the Berkeley BART station that is little more than a widened sidewalk creates a sense of place by the use of brick paving throughout; with the same brick extended up into the semienclosing, curvilinear walls.

Food

William Whyte's observation about Manhattan is that a plaza with a food kiosk or outdoor restaurant is much more likely to attract users than is one without such features. Not only will the plaza attract more users and be more lively, but the food concessions will do a good business. Why is the United States so far behind Europe in recognizing this? Rudofsky in *Streets for People* offered a suggestion: "Psychologists have likened the act of eating in public to the indecent exposure of the body . . . eating in full view of non-eaters is often felt to be improper, if not altogether offensive. . . . 'The great fundamental function of eating,' asserted Havelock Ellis, 'is almost as conspicuous as that of loving'" (Rudofsky 1969, pp. 320–321).

Apparently, the U.S. public is becoming liberated. Asked to do something about an unused minipark near the Exxon Building in Manhattan, Whyte and his 'Street Life Project' staff moved in a food cart, cable

Sculpture for different moods in Seattle: a Zen-like composition in a bank plaza by Isamu Noguchi.

spools, and planters; the park's use rose remarkably.

One way to increase the liveliness and activity (and hence leave little room for "undesirables" or potential vandals) is to provide a food kiosk or be tolerant of pushcart food vendors.

If you want to seed a place with activity, put out food. In New York, at every plaza or set of steps with a lively social life, you will almost invariably find a food vendor at the corner and a knot of people around him—eating, shmoozing, or just standing. . . . Food attracts people who attract more people. (Whyte 1980, pp. 51, 52)

A survey of employees at the Seattle Federal Building found that more than three-fourths ate their lunch indoors, even during nice weather. Most said they would eat outside more often if there were take-out food available at the cafeteria or a food concession on the plaza. Table 1.4 compares where employees at the Seattle Federal Building eat their lunch.

The higher proportion of men eating at the cafeteria and the higher proportion of women eating on the plaza can be partly accounted for by the continued discrepancy between men's and women's wages. As long as women earn less for similar jobs, they are more likely to bring lunch from home and eat outside. The provision of food vendors and outdoor eating places will thus disproportionately benefit women, a small enough reward for the disadvantage of lower wages.

All plazas, but especially large ones where food can be purchased, should offer all those facilities for human comfort that we take for granted in a restaurant, particularly drinking fountains, restrooms, and telephones. In addition, trash containers should be distributed around the plaza, as people will not go far out of their way from bench or exit point to dispose of garbage.

TABLE 1.4 WHERE PEOPLE EAT THEIR LUNCH

	Men	Women
Ate lunch:		
In cafeteria	41%	22%
At desk	24	26
In restaurant	19	21
On plaza	11	24

Source: Project for Public Spaces 1979b.

Programs

Designers customarily "sign off" the design process when the construction has been completed. But in the case of urban plazas, as in most other designed spaces, the subsequent management of that space is crucial to its success or demise. The provision of food in a plaza is one crucial element in its success; another is the provision of programs.

Programs in plazas include those offered by a single corporation in one plaza, for example, summer performances in the First National Bank Plaza in Chicago; seasonal festivals in many downtown locations, such as the five-week Cityfest program organized each fall by the Dallas Central Business District Association; the Greater Cleveland Association's Party in the Park program; summer evening concerts to keep people downtown after work; and street performers who have been auditioned and licensed to entertain passersby in major city squares and marketplaces, such as Ghirardelli Square in San Francisco and Faneuil Hall in Boston. Perhaps the most ambitious and successful program of plaza events is Seattle's Out to Lunch program which provides music, dance, or theater every day of the summer between June and September, at fourteen different downtown parks and plazas. Supported by contribu-

Eating at outdoor cafés is universally popular in the summer months. In Vancouver, Canada, the glassed-in structure to the left offers a unique facility —public indoor seating with tables for brown baggers who want to eat inside.

tions from downtown businesses, the city of Seattle, the federal General Services Administration, and the American Federation of Musicians, the Out to Lunch program provides monthly flyers and maps of its activities, tethers a large yellow Out to Lunch blimp at the site of each event, and attracts an estimated seventy thousand people annually.

A survey of four different events in different locations revealed that 87 percent of the attendants had been introduced to areas they had never visited before, and 73 percent said they had patronized a business on the way to the event. Thus, programs in urban plazas may not only enliven and animate space but also educate people about downtown and be good for business (Project for Public Spaces 1984, p.28).

A designer of a new or redeveloped plaza could facilitate the future development of programmed events by (1) persuading the client/manager of the plaza that this is an important use of the space, (2) providing a permanent or temporary stage location where onlookers can be comfortable (with some seating not looking directly into noon sun) and where their presence does not interfere with normal plaza circulation, and (3) ensuring that a stage, if provided, can be used for sitting, eating lunch, and so on when a concert is not being held.

If a stage for occasional performances is provided, its location should be carefully planned. A plaza study in downtown Chicago found considerable disruption of

normal cross-plaza traffic when a portable stage was erected in a pivotal location. Although it served its entertainment function well, the location also became a major traffic impediment (Department of Landscape Architecture 1975, p. 50).

A study comparing plaza use at the Seattle Federal Building on an "event" and on a "nonevent" day found a dramatic increase in use when a concert was held. In addition, detailed observations of plaza behaviour on that day yielded some interesting and useful guidelines for plaza design regarding concerts or large-audience events:

1. The event should be located so that the normal circulation flow to and from the building is not seriously interrupted.
2. Light-weight folding chairs should be provided, with the first row put in place to define the distance between the audience and the performers.
3. Amplification should not be too loud, or the crowd will stand far away and less space will be available for an audience.
4. Events must be timed to coincide with typical lunch breaks.
5. Temporary food concessions on event days will ensure that the plaza will be highly used.
6. A highly visible sign should publicize coming events (Project for Public Spaces, 1979b).

Vending

Small items have been sold from stalls, wagons, handcarts, and kiosks in city plazas since cities first evolved. But when retail districts developed and especially since department stores sprang up, vending began to be viewed as detrimental to commercial districts. Merchants saw it as unfair competition; city officials worried about health codes and congestion.

But since the 1960s, there has been a remarkable reversal of this attitude in many downtown areas. Merchants began to see that vending certain types of goods in particular locations can increase the popularity of retail areas, enliven the environment of a plaza or a sidewalk, and provide security. Successful vending programs have been established in Berkeley, San Francisco, Boston, Chicago, and Eugene and Portland (Oregon). New vending regulations in each of these cities specify the location, size and design of carts; type of goods sold; and permit fees (Project for Public Spaces 1984, p. 33). The items sold tend to be those not usually offered in downtown stores, such as fruit, vegetables, flowers, crafts, and take-out food.

The most appropriate locations are those plazas already popular for lunchtime relaxation, plazas that are poorly used and where the addition of a food vendor and a few movable chairs and tables might make a significant difference, and sidewalk and transit plazas

Mime on a skateboard, Justin Herman Plaza, San Francisco. (Photo: Jennifer Webber)

where there are guaranteed customers. Design details in regard to actual vending locations include sidewalk width, pedestrian flows, building entrances, visibility, accessibility, street furniture, bus stops, and nearby display windows.

Farmers' markets are a form of vending that is rapidly gaining in popularity as customers become more conscious of the health benefits of fresh produce. While some comprise just a place where farmers can pull up their trucks in a parking lot or beside the street, others are specially designed stalls set up in a downtown plaza. A survey of market patrons in Hartford, Connecticut, showed that one third made a special trip downtown specifically to go to the market. One market in Baltimore serves up to ten thousand people a day and has over one hundred farmers; it introduced so many people to an area that they had previously avoided that nearby empty warehouses began to be converted into stores (Project for Public Spaces 1984, p. 40). A smaller market on the United Nations Plaza in San Francisco is held twice a week, providing fresh produce for low-income residents of nearby hotels and for office workers shopping in the lunch hour. A downtown location close to likely customers is critical. Other important considerations are a relatively congested atmosphere (reminiscent of European street markets) and food concessions.

A lone "egg man" on an unused entry plaza at the HUD Building in Washington, D.C., was reported to sell an average of three thousand eggs every day! An evaluative study of this plaza proposed the addition of a vendors' and farmers' market. Another interesting proposed feature, which could be adopted elsewhere, was a fabric structure or roof for the market which would

1. add color and vitality to the plaza.
2. provide shelter and shade.
3. contrast with the scale of the surrounding environment.
4. improve the visibility of building entrances.
5. help the plaza not look "empty" during winter or off-peak hours.

Information and Signs

Although permanent employees in any building soon find their way about even if there are no directional signs, the occasional visitor or new employee may become disoriented without this information. A particular disaster in this regard is the HUD Building in Washington, D.C., a structure that one might have expected to be a model of urban redevelopment. It was designed by Marcel Breuer, completed in 1969, and supposed to symbolize the new commitment to federal support for urban revitalization. But an evaluative study in 1979 reported:

The lack of welcome [displayed by the bleak front plaza] extends into the building lobbies, where there is a need for information of nearly every kind. . . . There are no public maps; outdoor directional signs are too few and too small; the Metro signposts are so discreet they are hard to find . . . there is no indication of where visitors should enter; the entrances are hard to find . . . the main reception desk is in the south lobby, though more people enter through the north; information boards are not where people look for them; house phones are not clearly labelled; cafeteria entrances and the HUD information center are hidden. Finally, the lobbies themselves are so dimly lit—especially in contrast to the glaring front plaza—that this, too, adds to the confusion. (Project for Public Spaces 1979a, p. 13)

Clearly, for an agency that is supposed to be serving the public and promoting good urban design, this is a disgrace.

At the very least, the name of the building should be clearly displayed and well lit after dark and the main entrance should be obvious. On entering a building that frequently has visitors, there should be immediate and obvious signs to an information desk as well as signs to elevators, restrooms, telephones, and a cafeteria or coffee shop, if there is one. Finally, for those leaving the building, there should be clear directional signs to public transit stops, taxi stands, and nearby streets; simple, clear maps of the neighborhood would be a welcome addition. The cost of installing these necessary but often overlooked details is certainly less than paying a receptionist or doorman to supply people with this information.

Maintenance and Amenities

Finally, in any public space, people will care for an environment if they see that management cares. Planters filled with dead flowers, inadequate litter containers, and poorly maintained lawns not only give the adjacent building a bad image but also indicate to people that their use of the place is not welcome. Watering the lawns at lunchtime is another not-so-subtle message that the public should stay away.

Litter containers seem to be a detail that is often overlooked by the designer but that is essential to the successful functioning of an outdoor space. In San Francisco, for example, a highly used downtown park (Walton Square) had few or no litter containers, with the result that ugly dumpsters have to be wheeled into the park to cope with the daily lunchtime rubbish. A small garden adjacent to the HUD Building in Washington, D.C., is so heavily used that its two trash containers are overflowing long before lunch is over.

CASE STUDIES

The case studies which follow illustrate in specific settings many points raised in this chapter. Referring back to the "Typology of Downtown Plazas" earlier in this chapter, these cases are representative of the following types of plazas.

1. Crocker Plaza: Street Plaza—the Widened Sidewalk
2. Mechanics Plaza: Street Plaza—Corner Sun Pocket
3. Zellerbach Plaza: Corporate Foyer—the Impressive Forecourt
4. Giannini Plaza: Corporate Foyer—the Stage Set
5. TransAmerica Redwood Park: Urban Oasis—the Garden Oasis
6. Berkeley BART Plaza: Transit Foyer—Subway Entry Place
7. Justin Herman Plaza: Grand Public Place—the City Plaza
8. Union Square: Grand Public Place—the City Square

1. Crocker Plaza: Street Plaza—the Widened Sidewalk [1]

Location and Context

Crocker Plaza is located at one of the busiest vehicular and pedestrian intersections in downtown San Francisco, at the approximate meeting point of the financial district, the department store/retail district, and the fast-developing South-of-Market area. It consists of

[1] Compiled from reports written by students Dana Banks (1988), Gustavo Gonzalez (1988), and Michael McKinley (1988).

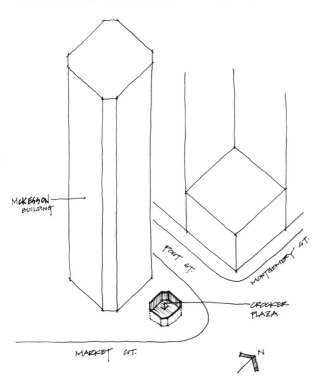

Location of Crocker Plaza, San Francisco.

a main street level plaza and a secondary sunken plaza which form the entrance to the Montgomery Street BART (Bay Area Rapid Transit) station. This somewhat triangular site is oriented toward the activity on the adjacent sidewalks. Exposure to the sun for much of the day plus expansive vistas down the "urban canyon" street corridors enhance this plaza's sense of openness. Nearby street-level building frontage consists of a mix of retail shops, restaurants, and financial services.

Description

The physical structure of Crocker Plaza has an apparent simplicity: From a distance, it is not even obvious that it is a plaza—merely a widened sidewalk and an entrance to the Montgomery Street BART station. Basically, it is an octagon-shaped hole in the ground; from below, people leave the subway stop, cross a small sunken plaza, and exit up some steps to the street. At the lower level, the octagon shape is repeated in two levels of stepped-up platforms; the space is bordered by a physical fitness center, a small café, and a flower shop.

At street level, the octagon shape has been elaborated into a series of granite step ledges, used for sitting and backed by an iron fence surrounding the pit of the lower plaza. Two concrete cubes placed among small shrubs in planters create a more secluded seating area in a triangle between the octagon and Market Street.

Several honey locust trees planted in the lower plaza have grown tall enough to create a feathery canopy over both plaza levels and add to the greenery created by the several street-level trees. A view of these trees down Market Street suggests that something "different" is happening at this intersection.

Main Uses and Users

The lower plaza is used almost exclusively as a pass-through route to the transit facilities below. As a place to linger or sit, it feels secluded, dank, and cut off from the life above. Even at the lunch-hour peak, the number of users (generally solitary readers) rarely exceeds four or five.

The main plaza is heavily used during the lunch period, with between 90 and 150 people sitting there at any given time. The majority of users are adults in their twenties and thirties. Users include office workers, construction workers, shoppers, and the apparently unemployed. Some fairly distinct user patterns can be observed: The most densely used area is the stair seating facing the intersection of Montgomery and Market streets. This is used predominantly by men, most of whom have come alone to eat their brown-bag lunch and/or to watch the passing street parade on the wide brick sidewalks of Market Street. Casual interaction between apparent strangers occurred most frequently in

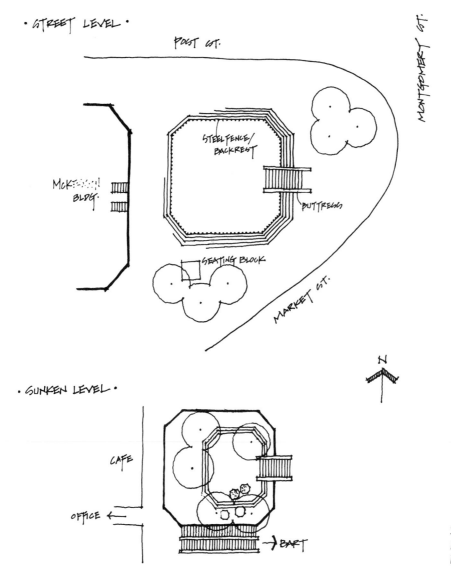

· STREET LEVEL ·

POST ST.

MONTGOMERY ST.

STEEL FENCE/
BACKREST

McKESSON
BLDG.

BUTTRESS

SEATING BLOCK

MARKET ST.

N

· SUNKEN LEVEL ·

CAFE

OFFICE ←

→ BART

Site plan of Crocker Plaza, San Francisco, upper and lower levels.

this subarea. The step seating facing Post Street is dominated by male and female office workers who arrive in couples or small groups. Stair and block seating facing south overlooking Market Street is used by white women and an ethnic mix of males who generally arrive alone. Women prefer to use the quieter portions of the plaza facing Post Street and the McKesson Building. The ratio of male to female users is about three to one. Eating, reading, and people watching are the dominant user activities. A food truck, vendors, and entertainers occupy the sidewalk on a daily basis. In the fall of 1988, a man doing ten-minute neck and shoulder massages was doing a brisk business at Crocker Plaza. This is one of the most successful plazas in San Francisco: It is in a highly visible location, is sunny during the lunch hour, has food available, has a variety of seating locations, and offers a passing parade of pedestrians and traffic. Users seem to enjoy the combination of being both spectators and on display.

Successful Features

· Located at busy intersection
· Sunny location
· Diverse use zones
· Abundant seating with diverse orientations
· Tree canopy linkage between upper and lower plaza
· Vendors and entertainers encouraged by presence of audience
· Outward focus of upper plaza to passing parade
· Casual nature of seating—steps permit plaza not to appear "empty" when unused

Unsuccessful Features

· Lower plaza too enclosed and pitlike
· Street level planters might have been designed to double as seating places
· Inadequate provision for those who want more formal seating

People watching people watching people at Crocker Plaza. Simple steps provide a casual seating arena; a masseur brings his own chair for head and shoulder massages. (Photo: Michael McKinley)

- Uncomfortably noisy main plaza
- Noticeable litter and dirt

2. Mechanics Plaza: Street Plaza—Corner Sun Pocket[2]

Location and Context

Located at the intersection of Market and Battery streets in downtown San Francisco, Mechanics Plaza is a small, three-sided street plaza. Its design is simple, consisting of three rows of benches, oversized bollards, and the Mechanics statue. Unrestricted access to the plaza is provided from both street sidewalks. The third side of the plaza is the Imperial Bank building.

Description

Mechanics Plaza is open to view, receives good sun and reflected light, and is designed as one open area. Although the plaza can be easily entered along Market

[2] Compiled from reports written by students Holly Duback (1980) and Sandra Wendel (1980).

Location of Mechanics Plaza, San Francisco.

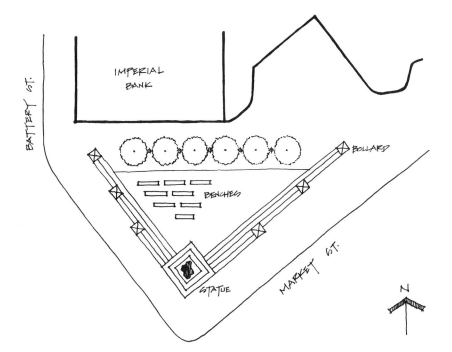

Site plan of Mechanics Plaza, San Francisco.

Mechanics Plaza near the end of lunch hour on a warm spring day. (Photo: Robert Russell)

and Battery streets, it is physically defined as a distinct area by a minor step-down level change and a variation in paving materials on the plaza floor. In addition, several large bollards along the plaza edge define the sidewalk/plaza boundary without blocking the users' views of the street activity. A drinking fountain is located on the Market Street sidewalk. Within the plaza are several parallel rows of wooden benches with backrests, all oriented toward the statue and the street. The benches are the most-used area on the plaza. Their backrest construction and uniform orientation, however, discourage group social interaction. Additional seating is provided on a ledge at the base of the statue. The statue gives the plaza a dominant focal point but blocks the sight line from the benches to the sidewalk intersection. A row of trees softens the visual transition between the plaza and the Imperial Bank building and creates a circulation path for pedestrians passing behind the benches. Night lighting is provided.

On the sidewalk next to the plaza is a bus stop and a row of street trees that help mitigate the somewhat stark appearance of this open space. Pigeons are abundant in this plaza, as indicated by the droppings that stain the paving, benches, and sculpture.

Major Uses and Users

The users of Mechanics Plaza come from a wide variety of economic and cultural backgrounds. As with all downtown plazas, its use is highest during lunchtime when the brown baggers arrive. Office and construction workers arriving in small groups or alone are the dominant users. Men slightly outnumber women.

"Undesirables" are occasionally seen sleeping on the benches and rummaging through the trash cans but do not seem to bother anyone. A fourth user group consists of "resters" who use portions of the plaza for waiting or resting for brief periods before moving on. Other than the "undesirables," the users stayed for an average of twenty minutes. Because of its proximity to downtown pedestrian circulation, Mechanics Plaza functions nicely as a street-side, drop-in, short-duration use area.

Eating, reading, talking, and people watching are the dominant plaza activities. Most users sit on the wooden benches, except for the construction workers who tend to sit on the statue ledge facing the street.

Successful Features

- Ease of circulation
- Proximity to street and sidewalk activity
- Solar access
- Statue as focal point
- Separation of plaza space from sidewalk
- Water fountain on sidewalk
- Accessible to disabled people

Unsuccessful Features

- Accumulation of pigeon droppings
- Lack of adequate seating variety and orientation
- Bollards not usable for seating

3. Zellerbach Plaza: Corporate Foyer—the Impressive Forecourt[3]

Location and Context

Located on Sansome Street, between Market and Bush streets in the San Francisco financial district, Zellerbach Plaza consists of four main subareas, including a peripheral ledge, a sunken plaza (comprising the bulk of the overall plaza), an inner terrace, and a stepped entryway seating area. The Zellerbach Building forms the north edge of the plaza, and a one-story round retail building is located in the eastern plaza area. Three main access walkways lead into the main sunken plaza, although none creates an obvious sense of entry. The street-level buildings in the adjacent blocks are primarily financial.

[3] Compiled from reports written by students Sandra Wendel (1980) and Trudy Wischemann (1980).

Description

Zellerbach Plaza comprises four distinct but visually connected spaces. The peripheral ledge seat wall along Sansome Street is heavily used owing to its height, width, sunny location, and access to the Sansome Street sidewalk–street activity. A small street-level node extends the peripheral wall into and overlooking the main sunken plaza area and provides a gathering area for people out of the pedestrian flow along the sidewalk. Another peripheral wall along Market Street is in an ideal location to attract sitters, but it is too high to be used. A flower shop and newspaper stand occupy the Sansome–Market sidewalk corner.

The plaza's sunken area is recessed approximately eight feet below street level. This space is not used to

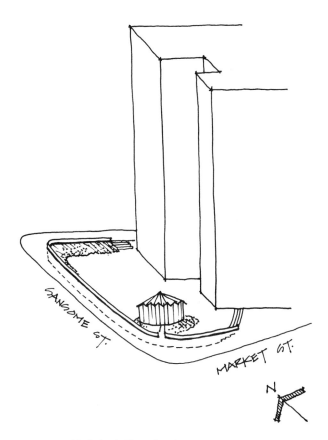

Location of Zellerbach Plaza, San Francisco.

its full potential owing to its poor sense of entry, its location below street level, its uncomfortable cobblestone paving, its lack of primary and secondary seating, and its absence of view to major street activity.

Zellerbach Plaza's partial success may be explained by its sunny position, its restricted yet interesting view to the sitters along the peripheral wall, its attractiveness as a protected and somewhat quiet gathering place, and its pleasant character created by a small fountain sculpture and ample vegetation.

Circulation flow patterns in the lower plaza area are channeled somewhat by the textural change between smooth concrete paths and cobblestones. Women in heeled shoes are more inclined to stay on the smooth concrete rather than the rough cobblestones.

A small stepped entryway to the lower plaza forms the third subarea in Zellerbach Plaza. It functions primarily as a walkway from the Market Street sidewalk and includes low steps that are used for seating. The greater use of this subarea rather than the sunken plaza attests to the need for seating in the lower plaza but supports Whyte's assertion that people like to be in the flow of traffic.

The fourth segment of Zellerbach Plaza is an entry court to the Zellerbach Building from Bush Street, and is composed of smooth marble flooring and an overhead roof plane created by the building itself. It is located at street level and offers an open view of the lower plaza and peripheral wall. There is no seating in the inner terrace, which receives minimal sun, and there is no direct access between this area and the sunken main plaza area below.

Major Uses and Users

The uses and users of the various plaza areas are somewhat stratified. The peripheral seatwall on Sansome Street is used mainly for lunchtime activities of sitting, eating, talking, and watching. The users tend to be

groups of male construction workers and bicycle messengers. Some male–female couples, male students, and groups of women are interspersed. This wall receives the heaviest use of any of the plaza's areas.

The sunken area is a more introverted space used more by office workers, couples, and women. Eating, reading, talking, sunning, and napping are the main activities. People tend to sit on the cobblestones in front of the fountain, often on some padding, or along the sunlit walls of the plaza's edges. Some users seek out shade and privacy on sunny days, which are afforded by small trees. The intended design of the lower plaza area seems to have been to create a semiprivate plaza for Zellerbach employees, rather than a high-use plaza for a variety of downtown users.

The stepped entry from Market Street is partially used for lunchtime seating by both men and women office workers. The entry court is used strictly by business people entering and exiting the Zellerbach Building. There is some waiting and standing conversation. No formal seating is provided, and building security guards prevent people from sitting on a railing that rings the terrace.

Successful Features

· "Hands-on" water feature
· Wind protection in recessed lower plaza
· Steps encouraging informal seating

Unsuccessful Features

· Lack of formal seating
· Inappropriate use of cobblestone walking surface, poor texture
· Poor sense of entry to lower plaza
· Wall along Market Street too high for seating
· Use of entry court discouraged by management
· Sunken plaza isolated from street
· Lack of color in vegetation
· Poor location in relation to major intersection
· Lack of food services
· No access between entry court and lower plaza
· No direct access between Sansome Street sidewalk and lower plaza

4. Giannini Plaza: Corporate Foyer—the Stage Set[4]

Location and Context

Giannini Plaza is part of the Bank of America complex in San Francisco's financial district. The Bank of America Tower rises from the plaza, which encircles the building. The main plaza area is located at the cor-

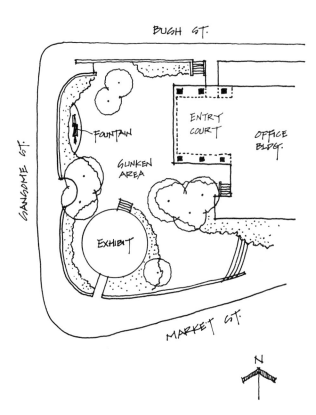

Site plan of Zellerbach Plaza, San Francisco.

[4] Compiled from reports by students Elizabeth Alden (1981), Daniel Machado (1988), Hitesh Mehta (1988), Katherine Wright (1981), and Jeanna Wyker (1981).

ner of Kearney and California streets, and smaller secondary plaza corridors extend along Kearney and Pine streets. Another secondary plaza is located on the east side of the bank tower and cannot be seen from the street. A mix of shops, cafés, and financial institutions occupy the ground-level buildings on adjacent streets.

Description

The plaza complex consists of four subareas of varying size and character (see site plan on p. 54). Area A, the largest but least-used portion of the plaza is a vast undifferentiated expanse accessible from the sidewalk along Kearney Street and via an impressive stairway starting well below plaza level, along California Street. This space contains several round planter beds, some of which are ringed by seat walls, a flower stand, flags, and a large sculpture of black stone of minimal user interest, except to the occasional children who try to climb it. The seating material throughout most of the plaza is hard granite, which is slow to warm, even in the sun. A rectangular fountain area once existed in Area A but has been converted to a planter–seat wall because of undesirable wind-borne fountain spray.

Area A is intended to be the main entry to the Bank of America Tower but was unfortunately situated on

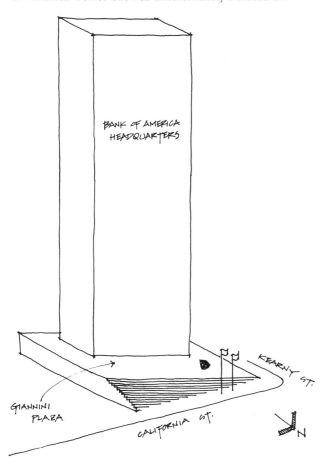

Location of Giannini Plaza, San Francisco.

the north rather than south side of the building, thus creating a continually shaded, uninviting, sparsely used plaza entrance to this dominating building.

Immediately adjacent to this expansive area is Subarea B, the smallest and most intimate space in the plaza. A hedgelike planter wall encloses the area and eliminates visual access to and from the main plaza and street. The hedgerow surrounds a number of wooden benches and planter seat walls, creating a sun-bathed and wind-protected microclimate during the peak hours of use. A variety of orientations allows individuals or groups a choice of seating arrangements. A branch office of the Bank of America can be reached through this space, but plants screen the entryway and there are no information signs.

A stairway leading to an enclosed minimall separates this secluded space from Subarea C which serves as a seating area and walkway connecting the north and south plazas. This linear space receives a good deal of lunch-hour sun but is completely hidden from the street between the walls of the newer Bank of America Tower and its older adjacent predecessor.

Three large rectangular planters, surrounded by fixed benches, contain trees whose canopies provide dappled shade and a mild sense of vertical enclosure, seemingly fitting for this area. An entry to the older Bank of America building is located here.

The last and sunniest Subarea D of Giannini Plaza is located along the south and west side of the bank tower. Street-level access is provided along Kearney Street and a portion of Pine Street. A planter area along Pine Street serves as a "lunch counter," as it is too high for most users to sit on. A seat wall along Kearney receives less sun and more wind, but its appropriate seating height and street orientation attract many users. People who sit along the Pine Street wall may inconspicuously watch the street activity below. Columns of the bank tower provide a popular backrest for users who sit on the ground. It is interesting that this heavily used area has no formal seating. A well-used entry to the Bank of America Tower is reached via this corridor subarea.

Major Uses and Users

Although Subareas B, C, and D all are popular spaces for lunch-hour use, Giannini Plaza is not, overall, a highly successful urban space. Area A is a vast space that is essentially lifeless except for pedestrian movement in and out of the bank tower. Had this expanse of space been built on the southern, rather than the northern, side of the building, the viability of the whole plaza as a healthy urban space would have increased tremendously. This example attests to the importance of sun as a crucial element in plaza design.

The users and uses of Subareas B, C, and D are those typically seen in other downtown plazas: lunch-

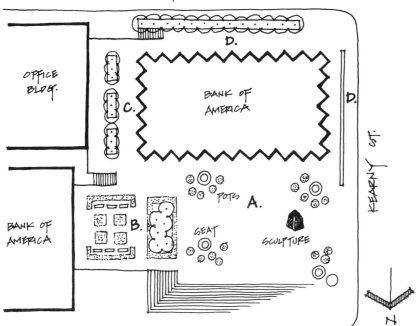

PINE ST.

OFFICE BLDG.

C.

D.

BANK OF AMERICA

D.

KEARNY ST.

BANK OF AMERICA

B.

POTS

A.

SEAT

SCULPTURE

N

CALIFORNIA ST.

Site plan of Giannini Plaza, San Francisco.

One of the few segments of Giannini Plaza that receives the sun at noon. (Photo: Robert Russell)

time activities of eating, reading, sunbathing, napping, conversing, and people watching. Men outnumber women by three to two. The visual isolation of Subarea B does not deter use by women in regard to safety issues. Typically, about two thirds of the users come alone, and one third come in groups of two or more. White-collar office workers are the most prevalent users. Construction workers tend to congregate along the street in Subarea D. The visual inaccessibility of Subareas B and C does not seem to inhibit their use, which contradicts Whyte's observation that to be successful, a space must have a view of the street. Both of these spaces, though somewhat hidden, have reasonable seating and receive good sun. They demonstrate that some urban users prefer to be isolated from the street action, and that visual isolation does not necessarily deter use by women.

Successful Features

• Hidden subareas that create private spaces for those users desiring privacy
• Good seating diversity and orientation in Subarea B

Unsuccessful Features

• The main plaza (Area A) is on the shaded north side of the bank tower rather than on the sunny south side
• Placement of fountain in a windy location, resulting in its removal
• Lack of programmed events to draw the users into Area A
• Inadequate seating in Subareas C and D
• Inadequate signing to inform users of bank entries and "hidden" plaza areas
• Poor choice of cold stone seating material rather than warmer seating materials
• Planter wall in Subarea D too high for sitting
• Blank wall views not screened by vegetation in Subarea C

5. TransAmerica Redwood Park: Urban Oasis —the Garden Oasis [5]

Location and Context

The TransAmerica Redwood Park is situated mid-block next to the TransAmerica Pyramid between Clay and Washington streets in downtown San Francisco. It is semienclosed by the dense peripheral planting of redwood trees that characterize the space and give the main visual clue to its presence. Although officially called a park, the TransAmerica Redwood Park func-

[5] Compiled from reports written by students Hitesh Mehta (1988), Imelda Reyes (1981), and Katherine Wright (1981).

tions as a plaza and so is included here. It has five entrances through unobtrusive steel gates which are locked on weekends when the plaza is closed. (The plaza is actually private property, owned by the TransAmerica Corporation.) Several small businesses line one entry corridor leading into the plaza from Sansome Street. The formal restaurant at the base of the TransAmerica Pyramid has a vast expanse of windows that allow diners a view of the redwoods. Several cafés are situated along Clay and Washington streets but provide limited take-out services for plaza users.

Description

The plaza has three subareas. Passing through either of the two Clay Street gateways, the user enters a fountain seating area. A modest fountain acts as a focal point for the diversely oriented bench and lawn seating nearby. The small lawn area has a backdrop of trees and is highly used. A dozen fixed wood and concrete benches are adjacent to the lawn and collectively form the plaza's dominant seating area. Flower planters and raised ashtrays can be found around the fountain and between the benches. Sunshine fills this area throughout the lunch period. Five jets of water enliven the fountain when it is turned on. Waste receptacles are located throughout the plaza and are emptied by maintenance people so that garbage does not overflow during peak-use periods.

The ministage, a second subarea, is visually and physically linked to the fountain seating area. This space is characterized by a slightly elevated, step-up platform centered below the setback windows of the formal restaurant. These tinted windows minimize potential conflict between restaurant patrons and plaza users. The ministage platform serves as the focal point performance area for entertainers in the plaza. Major seating areas within the plaza have visual access to the stage, although people generally congregate closer during performances. Several benches, seat walls, and steps in the stage area provide day-to-day seating diversity. The ministage area also receives lots of sunshine.

An entry corridor lined by small shops leads directly into the plaza from Sansome Street. Additional seating matching the wood and concrete style benches found in the plaza line this corridor, along with several trees and a mid-corridor planter bed.

The subarea near Washington Street receives the least sun, although fortuitously the sun is present during the latter half of the lunch hour. This area is the smallest, most-enclosed area of the plaza and includes benches and a large square seat platform. Throughout the entire plaza, many edge-line "ins and outs" are incorporated into the design, creating a diversity of seating and user choice.

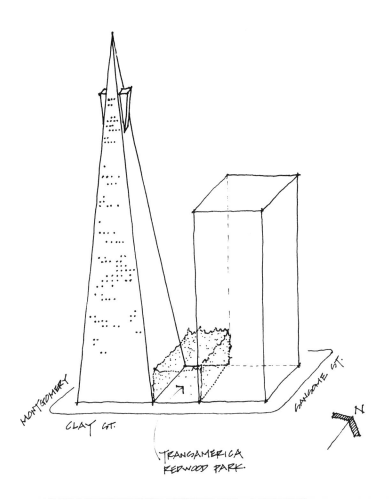

MONTGOMERY

CLAY ST.

SANSOME ST.

TRANSAMERICA
REDWOOD PARK

N

Location of TransAmerica
Redwood Park, San Francisco.

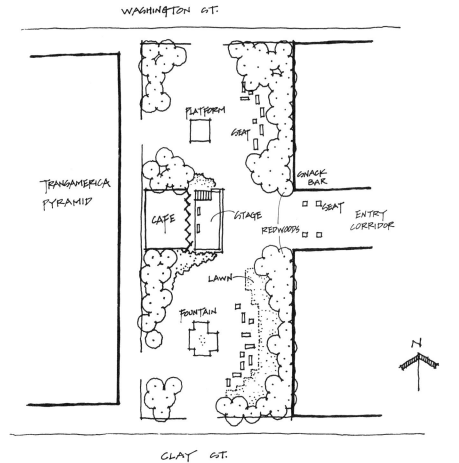

WASHINGTON ST.

TRANSAMERICA
PYRAMID

PLATFORM

SEAT

SNACK
BAR

CAFE

STAGE

SEAT

ENTRY
CORRIDOR

REDWOODS

LAWN

FOUNTAIN

N

CLAY ST.

Site plan of TransAmerica
Redwood Park, San Francisco.

56

Major Uses and Users

The plaza is, unfortunately, closed on weekends. It has a semiprivate, parklike character, owing to the redwoods and visual isolation from the urban street scene. The TransAmerica Redwood Park is a popular and successful space, although it does not have many of the typical features generally associated with a successful plaza. It is not located at a lively intersection; visual access into and out of the plaza is limited; and street vendors are not seen here. However, other crucial elements are present, including seating, sun, entertainment, and water. A plaza does not have to have every recommended feature to be a success.

Women outnumber men by three to two, a ratio indicative of how safe the space feels to users. During a sunny lunch period, all areas within the plaza are used, with migration from space to space as shadows replace sunlight. The lawn area is particularly popular for sunning and napping when the grass is not too damp and people can lie down. The principal activities are eating, reading, conversing, and people watching. The plaza is also used as a pass-through space for pedestrians. Unlike most plazas in San Francisco, no major buildings are accessible through the TransAmerica Redwood Park. The principal users are office workers, particularly during the lunch-hour period. A slightly younger, casual, more heterogeneous clientele seems to come here in the afternoon.

Successful Features

• Water feature
• Seating opportunities varied by form and orientation
• Diversity of spatial enclosures in three plaza subareas
• Adequate lighting
• Articulated edges
• Parklike atmosphere created by massing of redwoods and resulting sense of seclusion from urban surroundings

• Sense of security
• Well maintained
• Sunny during lunch hour

Unsuccessful Features

• Closed on weekends
• Steel gates and fencing
• No plaza-oriented food service

6. Berkeley BART Plaza: Transit Foyer— Subway Entrance Place[6]

Location and Context

Berkeley's Bay Area Rapid Transit (BART) Plaza is in downtown Berkeley and stretches along the west side of Shattuck Avenue between Allston Way and Center Street. It was created to accommodate the new downtown Berkeley BART station entrances. A twelve-story office building and bank borders the plaza at one end; a J.C. Penney store is at the other end, with various clothing stores and cafés in between. Nearby are the post office, the civic center, the Berkeley high school, the main library, the west end of the University of California campus, the YMCA, banks, hotels, shops, stores, and movie theaters. Residential areas close to the plaza are middle to low income. The residents are of various races and ages, as both students and the elderly constitute a significant portion of the area's population. The Shattuck Hotel, a block from the plaza, is both a residential and a tourist hotel.

Description

The plaza is essentially a widened sidewalk, one block long with a major entry and exit from the central Berkeley BART station at either end. One long side is bounded by stores and a bank building, the other by

[6] Compiled from reports written by students Julie Lower (1979), Eva Liebermann (1979), and Catherine Roha (1979).

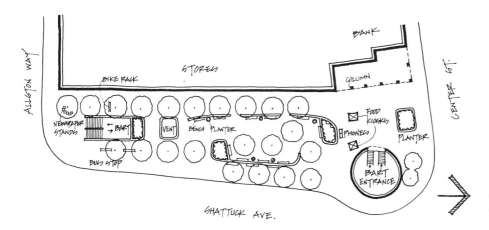

Site plan of the BART Plaza in Berkeley, California.

Shattuck Avenue, the main street of Berkeley. At the north end of the plaza, a round building of glass and steel marks the main escalator entrance to the BART station. A moderate-sized plaza space outside the station entry is punctuated by a planter and several mobile food kiosks serving commuters and shoppers. The arcade of the Great Western Savings Bank offers a sense of protection from the main pedestrian flows on the west side of this space. South of the main BART entrance is a rectangular sitting area, with low brick walls providing a sense of definition and protection from the pedestrian movement on either side. On the Shattuck Avenue side of this area, several outward-facing seats provide a waiting place for taxis. A major bus stop and interchange point marks the plaza's southernmost portion. Seating, planters, and pole lights are unified by means of the red brick paving on horizontal and vertical surfaces. Brick and concrete planters are placed throughout the site, but most are empty, with the replacement of damaged plant materials clearly a low priority.

Main Uses and Users

The main uses of this plaza fall into two categories: those that were consciously provided for, and those that have developed over time. The uses that were designed for comprise the following:

1. Pedestrian traffic entering and leaving the two BART entrances. Food kiosks, trash receptacles, telephone kiosks, and newspaper racks serve commuters and others using the rapid transit system.
2. People waiting for buses on Center Street and Shattuck Avenue. The stop on Shattuck Avenue is poorly designed, with bench seating available

for, at most, twelve people, whereas up to sixty people may be waiting at any one time during rush hours. There is no shelter for wet-weather waiting.
3. Pedestrians moving along the sidewalk beside the shops. This need is well designed for, as a low wall deflects this flow from passing through the sitting plaza.
4. Sitting, eating lunch, socializing, and the like. These are provided for in the sitting plaza where short wooden benches attached to the low brick wall defining the plaza can be "claimed" by individuals or couples. They usually are used by employees from local shops and offices eating bag lunches at noon; by elderly people who live in local hotels, who sit there in the afternoon; and by homeless people who in the late afternoon start appropriating the benches as sleeping places. The sitting area is not particularly attractive, with traces of gum and cigarettes on most of the paving, grease stains from food on the benches, dead plants in the tubs between the benches, and scars on the tree trunks from bicycles locked to them. Some potential users of the seating area seem intimidated by the presence of homeless people or by the shabbiness of the space.

Although use by the homeless is one function that spontaneously emerged in this downtown public space, another is use by teenagers and young adults as a hangout. For two decades, one particular planter outside the main BART exit at the north end of the plaza has been the leaning/sitting/sprawling stage for variously sized groups of adolescents. Some come to this place from nearby Berkeley high school, and others come by BART from other cities in the East Bay area. The

Berkeley BART Plaza.

groups are predominantly male and are particularly large on Friday and Saturday nights, when the plaza functions as a meeting place for party goers. The presence of these young people does not seem to be a problem for other users, who come and go from BART or pass by on adjacent sidewalks.

Successful Features

- Sunny location
- Located at busy intersection
- Open space in front of main BART entry
- Central sitting area focused inward

Unsuccessful Features

- Poorly appointed bus-waiting areas
- Seating not designed for groups
- Insufficient number of trash cans and bicycle racks
- Planters with more trash than greenery
- Poor maintenance
- Some conflicts between elderly and homeless users

7. *Justin Herman Plaza: Grand Public Place— the City Plaza*[7]

Location and Context

Justin Herman Plaza was built in the early 1970s as part of a massive program to revive San Francisco's deterio-

[7] Compiled from reports written by students Katherine Ashley (1976), Rene Bradshaw (1977), Thomas Franklin (1976), Katherine Gaunt (1980), Michael Marangio (1982), Jim McClane (1976), and David Peugh (1976).

rating Embarcadero district. Located at the terminus of Market Street and the edge of the financial district, it is bordered by high-rise office buildings, the Hyatt Regency Hotel, the Golden Gateway residential complex, and the historic Ferry Building. Restaurants, cafés, and retail shops are located at the plaza level of the bordering buildings. Terminals for the ferry, the rapid transit system, and trolley and bus lines, all located in the vicinity, ensure an even flow of passersby.

Description

Urban and large scale, the Justin Herman Plaza has as its focus the angular Vaillancourt Fountain located at one end of a large, slightly sunken, hard-surfaced open space. This area is depressed twelve to eighteen inches and is paved with bricks patterned to radiate toward the fountain sculpture. A seating podium and a covered stage in this open space make it a good location for large-scale staged events. An area for tables and chairs associated with the nearby restaurants and cafés forms the plaza's western edge. A tiled corridor between the Hyatt Regency and a high-rise office building, lined with small shops and take-out cafés, provides access to the financial district. Amidst the pedestrian circulation is a colorful bazaar of street vendors who have been displaced from the sidewalks of downtown San Francisco. Although currently fewer in number than in the 1970s, approximately ten to twelve vendors still find a market here for their wares.

The large brick-paved open space of the plaza has an unstructured pedestrian circulation that flows in all directions and provides a show for those seated on the steps and concrete seating walls that surround its periphery.

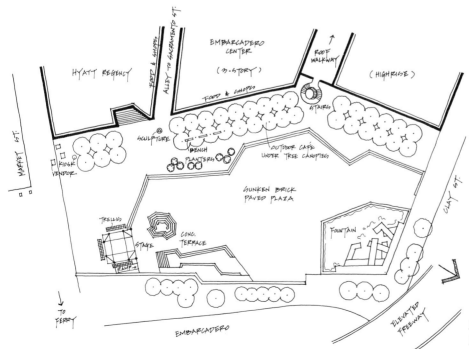

Site plan of Justin Herman Plaza, San Francisco.

Major Uses and Users

On weekdays, the plaza is used during the lunch period mainly by white-collar office workers from the surrounding office buildings. Approximately three hundred to four hundred people use the plaza during this time, and most are young white adults, with a slight majority being male. Brown baggers and take-out food customers line the outer edges of the plaza and the fountain. Restaurant patrons enjoy their lunch at outdoor tables. The large scale of the plaza is somewhat intimidating and encourages use principally on its outer edges, except when a concert or special event is held. The newly built high rises to the west now block out much of the afternoon sun. People can be observed following the sun patterns, a feature that in itself seems to dictate an upper limit on the number of users in a day.

Groups of children on a field trip can occasionally be seen at the plaza, and teenagers have found a stage here for their skateboarding. On a typical weekday, five to ten of these acrobats may be seen on top of and around the raised platforms, putting on a show for interested onlookers. On weekends their numbers are considerably larger; management is remarkably tolerant and has not—as in some plazas—attempted to evict them. Large concerts on summer weekends serve to introduce people from the larger Bay Area community to this plaza. On weekends throughout the year, the main users are tourists and street vendors.

Overall, Justin Herman Plaza is successful because its grand expanse and location invite attention and large groups of people. It is the preeminent site for large political rallies and the start of parades up Market Street. It is in effect San Francisco's town square, attracting a greater range of users (workers, tourists, performers, vendors, shoppers) and from a greater distance than any other downtown plaza. Such a space in any city should be considered as pivotal to the downtown's open-space system.

Successful Features

• Visible and accessible from many directions
• Accessible to a variety of users
• Take-out food and outdoor tables available
• Variety of formal and informal seating around plaza edge
• Eye-catching participatory fountain
• Large central open area that accommodates crowds at rallies or audiences at concerts
• Stage for noon-hour and weekend concerts
• Space for vendors and plenty of customers
• Informal use by weekend skateboarders tolerated by management

Unsuccessful Features

• When few people are present, space feels somewhat intimidating
• In drought years, fountain not running and perceived as "ugly" by many users
• Afternoon sun blocked by high-rise buildings to west

Warm spring day at Justin Herman Plaza: eating bag lunches and watching people from the ledge around the fountain. (Photo: Jennifer Webber)

8. Union Square: Grand Public Place—the City Square[8]

Location and Context

Union Square is located in the shopping district and on the fringe of the financial district of downtown San Francisco. Public transportation is available on all four streets that surround the square and link the area with the financial district, Chinatown, Japan Center, and residential areas near Golden Gate Park. Nearby are tourist interest spots centered on the cable cars, elegant hotels, and commercial stores. A wide spectrum of restaurants, bars, and low-income residential hotels are just a few blocks away.

Description

Union Square is sited on a south-facing slope. It is rectangular and occupies a full city block, with streets on each side. Entrances are at each corner at the street intersections. The design is formal and symmetrical,

[8] Compiled from reports written by students James Austen (1977), Sally Chafe (1975), Teri Flynn (1975), Laura Hartman (1975), Thomas Johnson (1975), Peter Koenig (1979), and Linda Yen (1977).

consisting of an outer belt of lawn surrounded by box hedges, an outer peripheral walkway, and an inner belt of grass that surrounds the central plaza. The central plaza is ringed with benches, and along its central axis are planters with a tall monument at the center. The formality of the plaza is reinforced by sixteen symmetrically placed trees and an equal number of lamp posts. At the west end of the plaza is a stage flanked by two flag poles.

Major Uses and Users

The square's diversity of use and users reflects the diversity of the surrounding area. The users are a mixture of occasional visitors and committed regulars. The occasional visitors include tourists and shoppers who stop by, usually briefly, for a photo or a snack, business people on their lunch hour during the week, spectators and participants in planned public events, and others on a weekend outing. The committed regulars are the nearby inhabitants—mostly elderly and male—from residential hotels for whom the square is the only public open space where they can enjoy the outdoors and socialize. Other frequent users are young people, usually single men hanging out and, increasingly, the homeless.

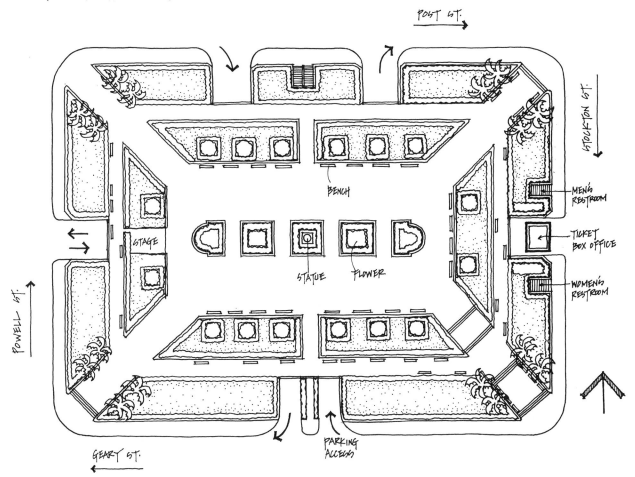

Site plan of Union Square, San Francisco.

Union Square is "home" to many lonely older people who live in small rooms in downtown hotels.

The varied activities occurring in the square reflect the differences in the users' ages and in the various subspaces. The elderly use the area as a place to sit and talk and be part of the busy city life. Through their regular and continued presence they claim various territories, one group preferring an entry where the benches are pulled closer together and other groups preferring to sit each day with those who speak their native language. Middle-aged users are largely shoppers and office employees who came here to eat, read, and to watch the action at midday. Many use the diagonals to shortcut through the square and use it only as a pleasant walking route. The lawn areas semienclosed by clipped hedges were originally designed just to look at, but now they have become places to lie down on hot afternoons, to take drugs, and to drink.

One of the most popular lawn areas—packed to capacity on warm days during the lunch hour—is a space that slopes at an angle up from Geary Street, giving the people sitting there an unobstructed view of the street activity while at the same time maintaining a degree of privacy. People also fill up all the available sitting spaces in the central plaza area and the quieter spots along the peripheral pathways.

Union Square was designed as a large public open space that can accommodate various activities, from a large public event to a nap on a park bench, as well as many different users. Although the design's formality restricts more varied seating and the lawns were not intended to be used, the various subspaces created by the level changes, the corner entries, the hedged areas, and the circulation pathways are successful in that they satisfy the requirements of this dense inner-city neighborhood's contextual diversity.

Although this category of downtown open space may seem obsolete, it is significant because it often marks the symbolic heart of a city and its historic focus and can accommodate a great range of users. This kind of space is as tolerant of diversity as the privatized corporate plaza is not, hence its importance in the downtown open-space system and the care that must be taken if such a space is redesigned, so that legitimate uses and users are not excluded.

Successful Features

• Visible and accessible to a wide variety of users
• Accommodates a wide range of users from the homeless to stylish downtown shoppers and tourists
• Sunlit for much of day
• Plenty of seating, both formal (benches) and informal (ledges, steps, lawns)
• Variety of green and hard-surfaced subspaces
• Symmetrical design with central monument and use for civic celebratory events
• Central rectangular plaza area to accommodate rallies and public gatherings
• Diagonal pathways for walking through square as shortcut
• Great range of seating areas for small groups of regulars on a semipermanent basis
• Small lawn areas functioning as semiprivate "outdoor rooms"
• Whole square functioning as "living room" for elderly men who live a short walk away in low-cost hotels

Unsuccessful Features

• Need to cross busy streets to reach square

• Some people inhibited from walking through square when having to pass between long rows of seated regulars
• No seating designed for groups to sit together
• Frequent predominance of male users inhibiting some women from using square

REFERENCES

Allor, David J., and Richard K. Murphy, Jr. 1980. Group behavior in a public space: A study of Fountain Square, Cincinnati, Ohio. *DAA Journal* (1):18–25.

American Society of Landscape Architects Foundation. 1976. *Barrier free design.* Washington, D.C.: U.S. Department of Housing and Urban Development.

Anderson, Stanford, ed. 1978. *On streets.* Cambridge, Mass.: MIT Press.

Architects' Journal. 1973. *Handbook of urban landscape.* New York: Whitney Library of Design.

Becker, Franklin D. 1973. A class-conscious evaluation: Going back to the Sacramento Mall. *Landscape Architecture* 64(1):448–457.

Bosselmann, Peter, Juan Flores, William Gray, Thomas Priestley, Robin Anderson, Edward Arens, Peter Dowty, Stanley So, Jong-Jin Kim. 1984. *Sun, wind and comfort: A study of open spaces and sidewalks in four downtown areas.* Berkeley. Institute of Urban and Regional Development, College of Environmental Design, University of California.

Chidister, Mark. 1986a. The effect of the context on the use of urban plazas. *Landscape Journal* 5(2):115–127.

——— 1986b. Response or prophecy? American plazas. Paper presented at the American Society of Landscape Architects annual meeting, San Francisco, November.

——— 1988. Reconsidering the piazza. *Landscape Architecture* 78(1):40–43.

City of New York. 1975. *New hope for plazas.* New York: New York City Planning Commission.

Cooper Marcus, Clare. 1975–1988. Unpublished student papers from Landscape Architecture 140, Social and psychological factors in open space design. Berkeley: University of California.

Cranz, Galen. 1984. Public attitudes. In *Tall buildings: Tight spaces.* A research project for Kaplan, McLaughlin, Diaz, Architects.

Crowhurst-Lennard, Suzanne H., and Henry L. Lennard. 1987. *Livable cities—People and places: Social and design principles for the future of the city.* Southampton, N.Y.: Gondolier Press.

——— 1984. *Public life in urban places: Social and architectural characteristics conducive to public life in European cities.* Southampton, N.Y.: Gondolier Press.

Cullen, Gordon. 1961. *Townscape.* London: Architectural Press.

Department of Landscape Architecture, University of Illinois at Champaign–Urbana. 1975. *First National Bank Plaza: A pilot study in post construction evaluation.* Champaign–Urbana: University of Illinois, Department of Landscape Architecture.

Dornbusch, David M., and Pat Gelb. 1977. High-rise impacts on the use of parks and plazas. In *Human response to tall buildings,* ed. Donald J. Conway, pp. 112–130. Stroudsberg, Pa.: Dowden, Hutchinson & Ross.

Eckbo, Garrett. 1964. *Urban landscape design.* New York: McGraw-Hill.

Francis, Mark. 1987. Urban open spaces. In *Advances in environment, behavior and design,* ed. E. Zube and G. Moore, pp. 71–106. New York: Plenum.

——— 1989. Control as a dimension of public space quality. In *Public places and spaces,* Vol. 10, *Human behavior and environment,* ed. I. Altman and E. Zube, pp. 147–172. New York: Plenum.

Fruin, John J. 1971. *Pedestrian planning and design.* New York: Metropolitan Association of Urban Designers and Environmental Planners.

Gehl, Jan. 1968. Mennisker til Fods. *Arkitekten* 70(2):429–446.

——— 1987. *Life between buildings: Using public space.* New York: Van Nostrand Reinhold.

Gibberd, Frederick. 1967. *Town design.* New York: Praeger.

Hasegawa, Sandra, and Steve Elliott. 1983. Public places by private enterprises. *Urban Land* 42(5):12–15.

Jackson, J. B. 1985. Vernacular space. *Texas Architect* 35(2): 58–61.

Jarvis, R. K. 1980. Urban environments as visual art or as social setting? A review. *Town Planning Review* 51(1): 50–66.

Jensen, Robert. 1979. Dreaming of urban plazas. In *Urban open spaces,* ed. L. Taylor, pp. 52–53. New York: Rizzoli.

Joardar, S. D., and J. W. Neill. 1978. The subtle differences in configuration of small public spaces. *Landscape Architecture* 68(11): 487–491.

Krier, Rob. 1979. *Urban space.* New York: Rizzoli.

Korosec-Serfaty, P. 1980. *The main square: Functions and Daily Uses of Størget, Malmo.* Malmo, Sweden: ARIS.

———— 1982. Public squares and sociability. Paper presented to the Lund (Sweden) Symposium on the Evaluation of Built Environments, March 25–27.

Korosec-Serfaty, P., and Psychology of Space Working Group. 1976. Protection of urban sites and appropriation of public squares. In *Appropriation of space* (Proceedings of June 1976 Conference of International Architectural Psychology in Strasbourg, France), ed. Perla Korosec-Serfaty, pp. 46–61. Louvain-la-Neuve, Belgium: CIACO.

Lieberman, Eva. 1984. People's needs and preferences as the basis of San Francisco's downtown open space plan. Paper presented at the eighth conference of the International Association for the Study of People and Their Physical Surroundings, Berlin, July.

Linday, Nancy. 1978. It all comes down to a comfortable place to sit and watch. *Landscape Architecture* 68(6):492–497.

Lynch, Kevin. 1971. *Site Planning* (second edition). Cambridge, Mass.: MIT Press.

Lynch, Kevin. 1981. *A theory of good city form.* Cambridge, Mass.: MIT Press.

Lynch, Kevin, and Gary Hack. 1984. *Site planning.* 3rd ed. Cambridge, Mass.: MIT Press.

Miles, Don, Robert Cook, and Cameron Roberts. 1978. *Plazas for people.* New York: Project for Public Spaces.

Montgomery, Roger. 1971. Center of action. In *Cities fit to live in and how we can make them happen,* ed. Walter McQuade, pp. 69–78. New York: Macmillan.

Mozingo, Louise. 1984. Women and downtown open space. MLA thesis, University of California at Berkeley, Department of Landscape Architecture.

Organization for Economic Cooperation and Development. 1974. *Streets for people.* Paris: OECD.

Plazas for people: Streetscape and residential plazas. 1976. New York: City Planning Commission.

Project for Public Spaces, Inc. 1975. Chase Manhattan Plaza study. Mimeo.

———— 1977a. Planning and zoning for public spaces in Seattle. Mimeo.

———— 1977b. Plazas for people: Seattle First National Bank Plaza. Mimeo.

———— 1978. Seattle Federal Building Plaza: A case study. Mimeo.

———— 1979a. The HUD Building, Washington, D.C. *A public space improvement plan.* New York: Project for Public Spaces.

———— 1979b. Seattle Federal Building Plaza: Events and improvements study. Mimeo.

———— 1984. *Managing downtown public spaces.* Chicago: Planners Press.

Purcell, Terry, and Ross Thorne. n.d. *Spaces for pedestrian use in the city of Sydney: A pilot study of city office and shop workers' attitudes and requirements for open space to be used in their lunch break.* Sydney, Australia: Architectural Psychology Research Unit, University of Sydney.

Pushkarev, Boris, and Jeffrey Zupan. 1975. *Urban space for pedestrians.* Cambridge, Mass.: MIT Press.

Rossi, Aldo. 1982. *The architecture of the city.* Cambridge, Mass.: MIT Press.

Rowe, Colin, and Fred Koetter. 1978. *Collage city.* Cambridge, Mass.: MIT Press.

Rudofsky, Bernard. 1969. *Streets for people: A primer for Americans.* Garden City, N.Y.: Anchor Press/Doubleday.

Sitte, Camillo. (1889) 1945. *The art of building cities: City building according to artistic fundamentals.* First published in German, 1889; trans. Charles Stewart. New York: Reinhold.

Storr, Robert. 1985. Tilted arc. *Art in America* 73(9):90–97; 73(11):5–7.

Whyte, William. 1974. The best street life in the world. *New York Magazine,* July 15, pp. 26–33.

———— 1980. *The social life of small urban spaces.* Washington, D.C.: Conservation Foundation.

DESIGN REVIEW CHECKLIST

PRELIMINARY QUESTIONS

1. Does the analysis of nearby public open space indicate that a proposed new space will be welcomed and used?

2. Have the client and designer determined for which functions the plaza should be designed? Such as a visual setback for a building, transition zone, lunchtime relaxation, bus waiting, sidewalk cafés, displays or exhibits, performances, or mid-block pedestrian thoroughfare?

3. Have the correlations between block location and type of space been considered, either in choosing a location for the plaza at the outset of the site planning for the entire development or in determining how best to configure and detail a particularly located plaza? For example, high-use potential of a corner location at grade, oasis potential of a mid-block cul-de-sac location?

4. Assuming a catchment area of nine hundred feet, will a currently unserved population be served by the proposed development?

5. Are there many workers in the catchment area, to ensure a lunchtime clientele?

6. Is the plaza located where a diversity of people can use it? Workers, tourists, and shoppers?

7. Does the location of the plaza tie into an existing, or proposed, pedestrian system for downtown?

8. Does the local climate warrant providing a plaza? If an outdoor space can be used for less than three months of the year, an additional public indoor space should be considered.

SIZE

9. Taking into account that every location and context is different, have the suggestions by Lynch and Gehl been considered in regard to limiting the plaza's dimensions? Lynch recommended twenty-five to one hundred meters, and Gehl, seventy to one hundred meters—the maximum distance for seeing events—as comfortable dimensions.

VISUAL COMPLEXITY

10. Does the design incorporate a wide variety of forms, colors, textures—fountains, sculptures, different places to sit, nooks and corners, plants and shrubs, changes in level?

11. If a complex view from the plaza is possible, has the design capitalized on it?

USES AND ACTIVITIES

12. Has the plaza been designed to accommodate either lingerers or passers-through, or if both functions are to be included, have they been provided in distinct subareas of the plaza, to avoid conflict?

13. If people are encouraged to take shortcuts through the plaza, have barriers between the sidewalk and plaza, including grade changes, been eliminated?

14. To encourage people to stop and linger in the plaza, have dense furnishings, attractive focal elements, and defined edges been used? If concerts, rallies, and so on are anticipated, have unimpeded open areas been provided?

15. Does the plaza design address the differences between men's predominant preference for a "front yard"—public, interactive—experience and many women's desire for a relaxed and secure "backyard" experience?

16. Has the plaza been designed to encourage heavy use, as a way to minimize vandalism and the presence of "undesirables" (or to render them inconspicuous in the crowd), rather than by "hardening" the design?

MICROCLIMATE

17. Is the plaza sited to receive maximum, year-round sunshine?

18. Where the summers are very hot, is shade provided by means of vegetation, canopies, trellises, and so on?

19. As a city policy, is building height and mass controlled to preserve and enhance sunlight reaching public open spaces?

20. Does the plaza site have lunchtime temperatures at or above 55°F for at least three months of the year? If not, an additional indoor public space should be considered.

21. For those months when lunchtime temperatures average 55°F or more, have sun–shade patterns been calculated to predict where seating areas should be located?

22. Does glare from adjacent buildings create unpleasant visual and/or temperature conditions in the plaza?

23. Can reflected light off adjacent buildings be used to brighten the plaza's shadowed areas?

24. Have wind patterns been evaluated for the plaza site? Will windiness lead to nonuse, particularly in cities with marginally hot summers?

BOUNDARIES

25. Do boundaries such as paving changes or planting define the plaza as a distinct space from the sidewalk without rendering the plaza visually or functionally inaccessible to passersby?

26. Does the plaza have at least two sides exposed to public rights-of-way, unless it is intended to function as an oasis?

27. Have plaza design features such as plantings been extended into the public right-of-way, to draw attention to the plaza?

28. Can any needed grade change between the plaza and sidewalk be kept below three feet?

29. Have the visual and functional transitions between the plaza and adjacent buildings been considered? Has the personal space of either the plaza users or the building users been violated by placing seating, tables, or desks too close on either side of windows or doors?

30. Do ground-level building uses enliven the plaza, incorporating retail stores and cafés rather than offices or blank walls?

31. Is outdoor café seating available, in attractive colors to draw people in?

32. Have the plaza's edges been designed with many nooks and corners, to provide a variety of seating and viewing opportunities?

SUBSPACES

33. If it is a large plaza, has it been divided into subspaces to provide a variety of experiential settings for users?

34. Have such features as grade changes, planting diversity, and seating arrangement been used to create subareas?

35. Are subspaces separated from one another without creating in any of them a sense of isolation for users?

36. Are subspaces large enough so that users entering an area will not feel as though they are intruding if someone is already in that space?

37. Are subspaces scaled so that a person will not feel intimidated or alienated sitting there alone or with few others present?

CIRCULATION

38. Has the plaza been designed to mesh with, or enhance, existing downtown circulation patterns?

39. Are plazas linked by a system of safe pedestrian walkways, malls, street closures, and the like, to encourage walking?

40. Has thought been given to predicting the direct routes between sidewalk and building entries that people will take at rush hours?

41. Does the plaza layout also allow easy access to a café, bank, or retail establishment peripheral to the plaza; access to seating or viewing areas; and opportunities for shortcuts or pleasant walk-throughs?

42. If there is a need or desire to guide pedestrian flows, have physical barriers such as walls, planters, bollards, or distinct changes in level or texture been used to do so, rather than color or pattern changes in paving, which have been shown to be ineffective?

43. Does the plaza design allow for the tendency of pedestrians to walk in the center of spaces and sitters to gravitate to the edges of spaces?

44. Does the plaza accommodate the needs of the disabled, the elderly, parents with strollers, and vendors with carts? Do ramps parallel stairs whenever possible, or at least allow access to every level?

SEATING

45. Does the design recognize that seating is the most important element in encouraging plaza use?

46. Does the seating meet the needs of the varying types of sitters commonly found in most plazas?

47. Has seating been placed in those locations that are sunny during lunch hours or, in very hot locations, where it will be shaded?

48. Does the plaza seating reflect that sitters are commonly drawn to locations where they can see other people passing by?

49. Has secondary seating (mounds of grass, steps with a view, seating walls, retaining walls that allow sitting) been incorporated into the plaza design, to increase overall seating capacity without creating a "sea of benches" that might intimidate potential users when sparsely populated?

50. Is there at least as much primary as secondary seating in the plaza?

51. Are elements intended as secondary seating (with the exception of lawns) within the optimal sixteen- to thirty-inch height range?

52. Have wooden benches been given high priority, and do they include those that are three by six feet and backless, for flexible use?

53. Is some seating linear (benches, steps or ledges) or circular and outward facing to allow people to sit close to strangers without the need for eye contact or interaction?

54. Are there wide, backless benches, right-angle arrangements, and movable chairs and tables to accommodate groups?

55. Has seating been located to allow a range of choices, from sunny to shady?

56. Has a sense of privacy been created for some of the seating, through the placement of planters or other designed elements?

57. Have a variety of seating orientations been included to allow water views, distant views, views of entertainers, foliage views, views of passersby?

58. Have seating materials been used that seem "warm," such as wood, and have those been avoided that seem "cold" (concrete, metal, stone) or that even look as though they might damage clothing if sat on?

59. In determining the appropriate amount of seating, has the Project for Public Space recommendation of one linear foot of seating per thirty square feet of plaza or the San Francisco Downtown Plan guideline of one linear foot of seating for each linear foot of plaza perimeter been followed?

PLANTING

60. Has a variety of planting been used to heighten and enliven the users' perception of change in color, light, ground slope, smells, sounds, and textures?

61. Have feathery leaved, quasi-open trees been selected where a see-through effect to other subareas is desirable?

62. If a plaza must be sunken, have trees been planted that will soon grow above sidewalk level?

63. Have open canopy trees been selected for windy plazas, to reduce potential damage associated with dense foliage and high winds?

64. Have a variety of annuals, perennials, shrubs, and trees been selected for their color and fragrance?

65. Has the eventual height and mass of mature plants been considered, in regard to views, shade, maintenance?

66. Have tree plantings been used that screen out adjacent building walls but that, if necessary, allow light to reach building windows?

67. Is there adequate seating so that people are not forced to sit in planted areas, thus damaging the vegetation? Are planter seat walls wide enough to prevent users from sitting in planted areas?

68. Do lawns vary the plaza's overall character and encourage picnicking, sleeping, reading, sunbathing, sprawling, and other casual activities?

69. Is the lawn area raised or sloped to improve seating and viewing opportunities, and has it avoided creating a vast "prairie" expanse in favor of smaller more intimate areas?

LEVEL CHANGES

70. Have some modest but observable changes in level been included in the plaza design, to create smaller subareas?

71. Have level changes been considered as a means to separate seating areas and circulation?

72. If level changes are used, has a visual connection between levels been maintained?

73. Where level changes are incorporated, have ramps been provided to allow access to disabled people, those with baby strollers, and so forth?

74. Is there an elevated vantage point, with a wall or railing to lean on while watching people?

75. Have dramatic grade changes between plaza and sidewalk (either up or down) been avoided, as such plazas will be underused?

76. If a plaza must be sunken more than slightly, has some eye-catching feature been included to encourage people to enter?

77. If a plaza must be raised more than slightly, has planting been used to ''announce'' its presence and draw people upward?

PUBLIC ART

78. If public art has been included in the plaza design, will it be able to create a sense of joy and delight, stimulate play and creativity, and promote communication among viewers?

79. Can people interact with any planned public art—touch it, climb on it, move it, play in it?

80. Is the art likely to ''speak'' to a large proportion of the public, rather than an elite few?

FOUNTAINS

81. Has a fountain or other water feature been included in the plaza design, for its visual and aural attraction?

82. Does the sound of the fountain screen out traffic noise?

83. Is the fountain in scale with the plaza space?

84. Will wind cause water spray to blow, thereby making sitting areas unusable? If so, could a full-time gardener or plaza manager be available to adjust the fountain?

85. Has the fountain been designed to be ''hands on,'' so that plaza visitors can interact with it?

86. Have the operational costs of running the fountain been calculated to ensure that the fountain can be operated?

SCULPTURE

87. If sculptural elements are to be used in the plaza, will they be scaled to the plaza itself?

88. Is some of the sculpture experiential; that is, can people sit around it, climb on it, alter its shape?

89. Is the sculpture located so as not to impede plaza circulation patterns and sight lines?

90. Has sculpture been located off center, to avoid creating the impression that the plaza is merely a background for it?

PAVING

91. Do major circulation routes follow the plaza users' principal ''desire lines''?

92. If a design's intention is to channel pedestrian movement have cobbles or large gravel been used where walking needs to be discouraged?

93. Has a change in paving been used to signify the transition from sidewalk to plaza, without discouraging entry?

FOOD

94. Are any food services available in and next to the plaza, such as food vendors, a food kiosk, or an indoor–outdoor café?

95. Are there comfortable places to sit and eat either a bag lunch or food bought from a vendor?

96. Have drinking fountains, restrooms, and telephones been provided to augment the facilities for eating, as one would find in a restaurant?

97. Have enough trash containers been distributed around the plaza to prevent littering of food wrappers and containers?

PROGRAMS

98. Do the plaza's management policies encourage special events in the plaza, such as temporary exhibits, concerts, and theatrical events?

99. Does the plaza design include a functional stage area that can be used for sitting, eating lunch, and so on during nonperformance periods?

100. Is the stage situated to avoid undue disruption to pedestrian circulation and to avoid making the audience face directly into the sun?

101. Will movable chairs be provided for the audience, and is there storage nearby for such chairs when not in use?

102. Are there places on the plaza to post event schedules and notices, so that they will be readily visible to plaza users?

103. Is there some method available to announce an event—decorations, banners?

104. Is there a place for temporary concessions to set up on event days?

VENDORS

105. Has the plaza been designed to accommodate vendors, whose presence will add to the vitality of the space, provide a measure of security, and often increase the popularity of surrounding retail outlets?

106. Have vendors been considered especially for plazas that are already popular for lunchtime use, poorly used and in need of something to draw users, and/or sidewalk or transit plazas with many pedestrians?

107. Does the plaza include an area that can be used for a farmers' market?

108. When providing for a market or vendors, could a colorful, fabric ''roof'' be provided for that area, to draw attention to the facility, provide shelter and shade, and contrast with the scale of the downtown buildings?

109. Has the area for vendors or a market been situated so as to be easily accessible and highly visible, yet not impede regular plaza circulation?

INFORMATION AND SIGNS

110. Is the name of the building clearly displayed and well lit after dark?

111. Is the main entrance to the building obvious?

112. After entering the building, is an information/reception desk immediately visible, or are there at least clear signs to one?

113. Are there signs directing visitors to elevators, restrooms, telephones, and cafeteria or coffee shop?

114. On leaving the building, are there clear signs indicating the way to transit stops, taxi ranks, and nearby streets?

115. Has a simple, clear map of the neighborhood been considered?

MAINTENANCE AND AMENITIES

116. Will there be adequate staff to maintain plantings, so that lawns are green and trimmed, dead flowers are removed, and so forth? If there is some question about the availability of maintenance, an effort should be made to use attractive yet low-maintenance planting.

117. Are there enough litter containers and a collection schedule that will prevent their overflowing?

118. Will lawns, as well as shrubs and flowers in planters that double as seats, be watered so as to be dry during lunchtime?

2

NEIGHBORHOOD PARKS

Clare Cooper Marcus, with
Clare Miller Watsky, Elliot Insley, and Carolyn Francis

The premise of this book is that local variation is essential if designed spaces are to meet the users' needs but that some qualitative design guidelines also need to be considered. The recommendations in this chapter are based on numerous park studies that observed activities, interviewed users, and analyzed what forms of design do and do not work for people. The guidelines are intentionally performance based, rather than specifically prescriptive, and they are presented as component parts that can be applied to a specific design job or used to assess or develop a program for a park design. The chapter is divided into six sections: History of American Parks; Future of Neighborhood Parks; Literature on Parks; Design Recommendations; Park Typology; and Case Studies.

HISTORY OF AMERICAN PARKS

Galen Cranz identified four major periods in the development of the American park since the mid-nineteenth century: the pleasure ground, the reform park, the recreation facility, and the open space system (Cranz 1982). The pleasure ground, which dates from the period between 1850 and 1900, was developed at least in part as a response to the overcrowded, unsanitary conditions of the newly industrialized cities. The model for this type of park was the aristocratic manor park of England and Europe in the Romantic period, which idealized wilderness and the pastoral landscape. Pleasure grounds, usually located on a city's outskirts, were intended for special Sunday outings and were characterized by large trees, spacious lawns, undulating terrain, meandering walks, and naturalistic water features. Here, it was hoped, workers would maintain

their health through relaxed outdoor recreation, and the norms of middle-class behavior would "rub off" on the poor, as all social groups shared this public facility.

The reform parks, appearing around 1900, were an outgrowth of the Progressive and social work movements and, like earlier parks, were intended to improve the living conditions of working people. Located in the inner city, these were the first true neighborhood parks. Their primary beneficiaries were to be the children and their families of the immediate neighborhood. Their most important feature was the children's playground. A reaction to what was seen as the elitist values of the Romantic landscape aesthetic produced a stark functionalism in the design of reform parks, which were defined by hard paving, buildings, and activity areas laid out in symmetrical arrangements using straight lines and right angles.

Eventually the concepts of the social work movement were incorporated into mainstream society. The recreation facility, established in American towns and cities starting around 1930, severed the ties between parks and the goals of social reform, instead emphasizing athletic fields and equipment (the word *recreation* became synonymous with developed athletic facilities) and organized programs. With the growth of the suburbs and increasing automobile use, new and larger parks were built that provided a myriad of courts, swimming pools, and fields. The parks' catchment or service area increased, and transportation to the park was often by car. Physical exercise—team sports in particular—was deemed as important to maintaining morale in hard times as it was to biological and public health purposes, which had motivated earlier reformers.

A typical neighborhood park of the 1980s contains a mix of elements of park-design philosophy. This park in suburban San Mateo, California, contains a children's play area, sports fields, a community building, and picnic areas.

The open space concept, which has developed since 1965, combines separate pieces of land, such as mini-parks, playgrounds, and urban plazas, into a system—in theory, at least. The open space idea grew concurrently with the urban renaissance that is part of the emerging appreciation of city vitality. The centrally located neighborhood park is only one of several potential dispersed locales (e.g., amusement parks, shopping centers, flea markets, street fairs, and state and regional parks) where people spend their leisure time.

Today, most neighborhood parks embody elements from all four periods of park history, and there are few, if any, pure types. Resistance to changes in parks may sometimes be traced to the belief that a park should conform to only one model. However, in Cranz's view, designers tend to throw together a hodgepodge of elements from each model because they do not know what is truly appropriate. To fulfill actual needs, Cranz believes, park policies must be based on sensitive analyses of current social problems and attitudes towards cities.

FUTURE OF NEIGHBORHOOD PARKS

In the past several decades there has been little outward sign of change in the design and management of local parks. Old, outdated facilities sit in disrepair as maintenance levels decrease, depressing reminders of the irrelevance of many parks to the current needs of potential park users. Seymour Gold wrote of the necessity of integrating local parks into the mainstream of modern life (Gold 1972), and Galen Cranz has referred to parks as the "fuddy-duddys" of urban recreation (Cranz 1982).

Several writers have presented their visions of the parks' future. In regard to their management and planning, Gold recommended citizen involvement in all as-

pects of park development and management, renewal or relocation of existing parks that fail to meet users' needs, and voluntary program leadership and self-maintenance whenever possible (Gold 1974). Gold believes that the future demands new activities, institutions, and concepts to guide the development of urban recreation, perhaps a combination of publicly and privately owned facilities, from rooftop gardens to urban campgrounds (Gold 1980).

Distinctions that we now make between downtown and residential areas may become obsolete as the mixed-use concept takes hold. New parks near commercial centers already seem to be cropping up spontaneously in the suburbs, and the tendency to view park and commercial uses as incompatible seems to be decreasing, at least among park users, who frequently request such amenities as food concessions and equipment rentals in parks. Public parks can and should continue to cater to the needs of the whole community's physical and mental well-being. Women continue to constitute a definite minority among park users, and, Galen Cranz argued, they should start to demand a fair share of park resources (Cranz 1981). Along with improving existing athletic facilities for women, health centers, community gardens, and day care centers might be park functions that would benefit both women and men.

As cultural patterns of space usage are better understood, park design may be jolted out of its mass-produced, institutional rut. A single, centralized park may be irrelevant to a community that depends on active street life to sustain its social networks (Laurie 1975). Acres of greenery may have little meaning in a culture with a "plaza" rather than a "park" tradition. Provision of space to wash and display cars, for instance, may be accepted as a legitimate function of a local park, instead of being "designed out," as it was in one California park (Hernandez n.d.).

Although there is little evidence of a widespread grassroots movement to change local parks (indifference is more often the case), it seems possible that in a future of increased housing densities, more expensive fuel, and shrinking budgets for centralized park maintenance, there will be a new appreciation for the possibilities of local open space. Asked what she would like to see in her local park, a twelve-year-old girl replied: "Tennis courts should have pink nets that shine like lightning." Maybe someday parks will reflect the life and spirit of their communities.

LITERATURE ON PARKS

A large part of the literature on social issues and urban parks deals with the history of large city parks and the individuals who guided their development (Chadwick 1966; Laurie 1975). Cranz described the changing forms of both large and small parks as a reflection of their social and political contexts (Cranz 1982). Finally, Rutledge looked at how the contributions of designers, planners, administrators, and the community affect the resulting park (Rutledge 1971).

In *The Death and Life of Great American Cities*, published in 1961, Jacobs criticized the application of unvarying rules and standards without regard to cultural, geographical, and other differences, which resulted in the social failure of many neighborhood parks. Several articles by various writers followed, which attempted to describe and explain the phenomenon that Gold named the *nonuse* of neighborhood parks (French 1970; Gold 1972; Johnson 1979). Several writers have commented on the use of park design as an instrument of social control (intentional or otherwise), often to the detriment of legitimate user groups (Cranz 1981, Gold 1974, Sommer and Becker 1969).

Starting in the early 1970s, investigators began using surveys and questionnaires to establish the actual use patterns of parks (Bangs and Mahler 1970, Deyak and Parliament 1975). Later researchers used systematic on-site observation techniques, sometimes combined with interviews and questionnaires, to draw a detailed picture of park activities (Cooper Marcus, 1975–1988, Gold 1980, Linday 1977, Rutledge 1981, Taylor 1978). By the late 1970s and early 1980s, specific problems in parks were being highlighted in research reports, such as on vandalism in the city parks of Boston (Welch, Ladd, and Zeisel 1978), San Jose (Parks and Recreation Department, San Jose 1981), and Seattle (Wise et. al. 1982).

More recently, researchers have looked at the public's response to vegetation in parks (Gold and Sutton 1980) and at the essential differences between the park and the garden aesthetic (Francis 1987). Finally, writers have advocated community participation in the planning and design process, through meetings, workdays, and so forth. The direct participation of local residents, together with systematically recorded behavioral data, is seen as the best way to obtain credible data for use in park design (Francis, Cashdan, and Paxson 1981; Hester 1975).

Although offering guidelines on park design may seem to contradict community participation, we believe that both are necessary. An analysis of how existing park facilities and layouts work is important if we are to avoid repeating past mistakes. The community's involvement in a specific park design (or redesign) is essential, but the designer or facilitator may find the following guidelines a useful means of presenting alternatives and a means of informing both himself or herself and the community about the needs of those who are usually not well represented at community meetings —children, teens, the elderly—but who often are the principal park users.

DESIGN RECOMMENDATIONS

Two frequently cited reasons for park use are: a desire to be in a natural setting and a need for human contact.

Need for a Natural Setting

A park is often considered as an oasis of greenery in a concrete desert. For passersby as well as those who come into a park, its natural elements provide visual relief, seasonal change, and a link with the natural world.

According to two major interview studies of park use, in San Francisco and London, the most frequently cited reason for park use was "contact with nature." In London, this motivation was cited more frequently by women than by men, by older rather than younger people, and by upper-income rather than lower-income users. Similarly, according to a study of heavily used midtown Manhattan parks, the most frequently cited reason for their use was simply to relax and rest. When asked to describe these parks in three words, more than half offered descriptions that could be classified under the general heading "park as retreat," using such words as *greenery, nature, relaxing, comfortable, tranquil, peaceful, calm, urban oasis,* and *sanctuary.*

The need for a park as a retreat or oasis is probably most pressing in high-density sectors of the inner city, but a study of suburban parks in relatively low-density Sacramento, California, found that even there the amount and type of vegetation strongly influenced the park users' degree of satisfaction (Gold and Sutton 1980).

Jurgen Milchert suggested that there is a basic human "need to experience or imagine 'wilderness' i.e. 'untamed nature' as a contrast to a technological and planned urban environment." He further cautioned that "the spiritual component of the relationship between man and nature, the desire for an unestranged, primeval and magical relationship with it, is an important reason behind the necessity for quantitatively sufficient and qualitatively attractive open space in towns and cities" (Milchert 1983, pp. 771, 774). To support such a relationship, Milchert recommended leaving certain areas of the park to grow naturally, or to be designed by the park users themselves. He also pointed out that "the everyday character of nature also includes being able to experience its changing aspects: unfortunately old and diseased trees are still felled in large parks . . . it [is] important to be able to observe their slow natural decay, which is just as important as their growth" (Milchert 1983, pp. 776).

The following guidelines are suggested to fulfill park users' needs:

- Create a rich and varied aesthetic environment to maximize the desired feeling of contact with nature. For example, provide plants of varied colors, textures, and shapes; plant fragrant and flowering trees and shrubs; plant species that attract birds or butterflies; provide water that is moving (e.g., a fountain or waterfall) or is still (e.g., an ornamental pool). The soothing sounds of falling water create a sense of well-being and calm. Similarly, an isolated spot away from activity and noise may satisfy the person in need of a calm and silent niche. A German study of park use found that the main reason why people visit open spaces is to experience silence (Garbrecht 1976).
- Allow space for trees that do not need drastic pruning. By defining and enclosing spaces with

their mass and bulk, large trees may do more to establish a natural ambience than can the expanses of turf that are often associated with the word *park*. In London's classic Georgian squares, it is more the immense plane trees that define these much-used spaces than the patches of grass and flower beds beneath them. Trees also can be used for shade and windbreaks.

- Provide meandering pathways through or alongside natural settings. People in need of privacy may wish to stroll along a circuitous path system with varied views, alternating settings of enclosure and openness, and opportunities to sit and rest. Perhaps one of the most pleasing types of park paths is around an expanse of water. The meandering path around the lake in St. James Park, London, for example, is used by hundreds of office workers every lunch hour, to stretch their legs, view the ducks and other waterfowl, and to create a pleasant hiatus in what is often a desk-bound working day.
- Create an area in the park that can be allowed to grow naturally. In an urban setting, such an area may provide an important spiritual link between humanity and nature.
- Isolated tables should be provided for those people wanting to eat, read, or study outdoors in a natural setting. Quiet areas should be usable, and their silent and tranquil mood should be expressed clearly and strongly enough to discourage other more intense or noisy activities, such as large picnic groups.
- Provide some areas for sitting close to the park perimeter yet partially screened from street noise and activity. People with only a few minutes to spend,

Levi's Park, San Francisco, designed by Lawrence Halprin. Although some designers have criticized this park for its lack of aesthetic connection to context— warehouses, office buildings, wharves, and shipping piers—its naturalistic milieu is immensely popular with nearby office and dock workers. Thick perimeter planting, sloping lawns, an artificial stream, rocks, and informal seating combine to create a green oasis in a very urban setting.

those with limited mobility, and those who are security conscious may wish to choose areas where one can observe green and natural spaces yet not be totally inside the park.

- Be aware of the microclimate(s) of the site when locating quiet seating areas. Degrees of sun, shade, and wind protection will have an important impact on the park's use. Consider the extremes of climatic conditions likely to be experienced (which might include summer heat and/or winter wind), and design for both these and normal conditions. Deciduous trees are often the best choice for areas with both hot summers and cold winters. A seating spot catching sunshine at midday in the winter may be equally appreciated for its shade in summer.

- Place benches in planted areas, facing pleasing views of open green areas. Those benches backed by structures such as walls, plants, or trees provide a greater sense of security than do benches situated in the open. The textures, odors, and microclimate around such benches can also enhance the sense of being in nature.

Need for Human Contact

Although most park users claim that "contact with nature" is their main motivation for going to a park, observation of what people actually do in parks suggests that social contact—both overt and covert—is equally important. It is easier for most people to say they use a park because they like the greenery than to say instead (or in addition) that a park offers opportunities to meet or watch other people.

All parks should offer the opportunity for both overt socializing, or getting together, and covert socializing, or watching the world go by. The location of the park will, in large measure, determine which will predominate. Parks in higher-density neighborhoods may be better for people watching, and parks in family-oriented, low-density residential neighborhoods may be best for getting together for picnics, games, sports, and so on. The park's design—seating patterns, circulation system, recreation facilities, and so on—also will be affected by which of these two forms of human contact is perceived to be more important. Thus, a downtown park where many people come alone to relax might need a more meandering circulation system to maximize a lunch-hour walk, with benches designed for either sitting alone or alongside strangers. Conversely, a park in an established residential neighborhood where most people come to use a specific facility probably needs a circulation system that enables more direct, easy access to its component parts.

Overt Socializing

At least two varieties of overt socializing can be observed in contemporary parks: (1) coming to the park with others, for the purpose of talking and/or eating together; and (2) coming to a park in the hope of meeting other "regulars" whom one expects to see there.

Coming to the Park with Others

Teenagers may plan to meet after school in the park to talk before they go home; parents may plan to take their children to a favorite play space and to chat while their children are playing.

Whatever the scenario (the location will determine which is most likely), all or some of the following guidelines will apply:

- Design a space for a meeting place that can easily be described to another person.

- Choose seating arrangements to support the type of social contact desired. The arrangement of benches can either support or preclude social contact. That is, two benches arranged at right angles encourage contact between people or groups, whereas two benches arranged one behind the other have the opposite effect. Two benches facing each other force people to confront each other (or to avoid even sitting down) if they are too close together, or they may prevent contact if they are too far apart or are separated by a path with heavy pedestrian traffic. In general, a concave arrangement encourages contact, and a convex arrangement discourages contact.

- Provide movable seats for self-structured social environments. The flexibility gained by being able to arrange one's bench, garden seat, or deck chair can greatly enhance social interaction, in addition to allowing the user to have more control over his or her own comfort. Deck chairs can be rented for a nominal sum per hour in London parks and are very popular, allowing people to choose where they sit, with whom, and so on. William Whyte's stop-frame movies of plaza use in New York City indicate that when movable seats are provided, people will often rearrange them slightly for no obvious reason, seemingly to assert some personal control over their temporary environment.

- Provide picnic tables. Picnic tables are desirable not only in places where families or groups come to barbecue but also when placed in semisecluded spots for eating lunch together in a downtown park or just as an "anchor" for a group to sit around.

- Provide a visually attractive walk-through. For those who may use the park only for a leisurely group stroll, a wide pathway passing through varied and attractive spaces can be a pleasing solution. The path should be wide enough so that passing pedestrians will not disturb bench sitters.

- Design the park to permit regular groups of users to lay claim to certain areas. A regular group of users, distinguishable by age, gender, or recreation interest, should have the opportunity to claim a subsetting within the park, for example, a particular seating area, group of tables, or portion of a beach. Claim to a particular territory, however informal, may be necessary for them to maintain a sense of group cohesion and identity and to be able to predict where and when to meet their friends. Gray's study of a park in Long Beach, California, identified two groups of regular users with distinguishable territories: lower-class indigents and winos in the park's older section and retired men and women in a redeveloped section of the park (Gray 1966). Observations of the use of Portsmouth Square in Chinatown, San Francisco, indicate another form of time and activity zoning that allows different user groups to use the same space. For example, local residents use the park intensively for conversation and games of chance; tourists use it just for passing through or occasional ceremonies. This same park, because of a design on several levels, permits different subgroups of regular users to claim different segments: elderly Chinese men on the upper level, elderly Chinese women and children on the lower level, and Caucasian lunchers on one or two benches nearest the financial district (Cooper Marcus 1975–1988).

Many people—especially men—use downtown parks, such as Rice Park in St. Paul, Minnesota, for what might be termed covert socializing.

Coming to the Park to Meet Others

A park's layout and details can enhance casual meetings in the park. School-aged children may come to the park to find a playmate; a teenager may cruise by or through a park looking for friends; and a young adult, with tennis racket, may come in hopes of finding a partner.

These kinds of park encounters can be facilitated by all or some of the following guidelines:

- Provide a relatively open layout to facilitate scanning the park for a friend or group.
- Attach benches to certain specific facilities (e.g., tennis court, tot lot, recreation building) so that one can safely assume that a fellow bench user is at the park for a similar purpose, an assumption that may offer a social opening.
- Create a circulation system that leads people past potential social contact areas without forcing them to stop. People prefer freedom of choice as to when and where they make contact with others. Thus it is unwise to have a path lead to, and terminate at, a setting where contact seems likely—for example, benches grouped around a focal point likely to stimulate conversation. Rather, pathways should allow people to pass close by to these settings, to see in and to pass on if that is their desire.

Covert Socializing

Many people of all ages come to parks merely to watch people, with no intention of conversing or meeting with them. Many elderly people engage in this activity, and more guidelines can be found in the section for the elderly. In general, it is important to situate benches so that the people moving through the park or along adjacent sidewalks can be observed unobtrusively.

SPECIAL USER GROUP NEEDS

Several user groups frequent parks, or would like to, whose needs are often not understood or incorporated into the parks' design. These groups are the elderly, the disabled, preschool children, school-aged children, and teenagers.

Retired and Elderly Park Users

Our inner cities and older suburban neighborhoods are increasingly inhabited by elderly people who may be lonely or bored. For them, leaving a lonely room or house and spending time in a nearby park is a welcome, inexpensive respite. Frequently, such people go to the park alone and return alone, and they may spend much of the day sitting alone, yet around many similar others. For some, this is not a time of life for active recreation or even active socializing; rather, it is a time for reflection and observation of the passing world.

Some older people, however, may go to the park to seek friends. A park, if properly designed and located for ease of access, can satisfy enough of the elderly's social needs to support a regular senior constituency. A study of a downtown Long Beach, California, park described it as "a great outdoor living room in which a daily open house takes place. There people are visited, games are played, issues are debated, and the time of day is passed" (Gray 1966, p. 10). Older people in this instance are interested in meeting new people and being entertained. Indeed, their regular friends are often acquaintances they have made in the park. A study of regular elderly users of MacArthur Park in Los Angeles reported that two thirds were using the park every day and came there on foot from hotels or rooming houses within a four-block radius. Most were men who lived alone, and although nearly all were observed coming to the park alone, more than two thirds gravitated to high concentrations of people in the park and spent most of their time conversing with one or more friends (Byerts 1970).

The following guidelines apply to any park—inner city or suburban—that elderly people are likely to visit:

- Situate some seating areas just inside the park's entrance. Seating located near a park entrance or busy thoroughfare is a good place to watch people and may enhance a feeling of security.
- Locate the main entrance to the park near bus stops with shelters and crosswalks. Just getting across a street can be difficult for some elderly people and so can discourage them from using a park. At a minimum, crosswalks to parks should be provided. Traffic lights should be timed to allow for the safe crossing of a slowly moving person. The traffic signal box should be equipped with a pedestrian button to stop traffic.
- Place drinking fountains, restrooms, and seating shelters in convenient areas. When a park becomes one's "outdoor living room," these facilities become essential. If the drinking fountains are used almost entirely by seniors, the fountains should be built high enough off the ground to permit their use without having to stoop down to a child's height. A step can be built into one side, or spigots provided at two heights, to allow access to children and those in wheelchairs. Elderly people are more greatly affected by heat, cold, and glare than are younger people and appreciate a shelter or gazebo close, if possible, to toilet and food facilities. A shelter need not be elaborate, just a place to get out of the weather for a while, perhaps to play cards or chat with friends. In San Francisco,

for example, elderly people complained that they cannot spend time looking at the ocean along Ocean Beach because it is usually too cold for them, and there are no sheltered seating places. Glass-sided shelters on the seafront are very popular with the elderly residents of many British seaside towns which have become attractive places for retirement.

- If the surrounding neighborhood includes many elderly people living alone, provide places for their meeting together; if more elderly live in group situations with facilities and programs encouraging social contact, emphasize natural surroundings and areas for quiet walking. Although many elderly people go to the park to meet and talk with friends or acquaintances, a considerable number also go just to be in an attractive, peaceful, natural setting, to walk, sit, and contemplate nature or to dream and doze in the open air. One study of the use of a downtown Los Angeles park indicated that elderly people living in apartments, hotels, and retirement homes with facilities or programs encouraging social contact, tend to use parks to enjoy the natural setting rather than to meet people. Those living alone in apartments or rooms tend to use the park for a variety of activities, but especially those promoting social interaction (Byerts 1970).
- Place benches in a variety of arrangements to facilitate conversation. If seating is not conducive to conversation or is uncomfortable for long periods of sitting, older people who, according to one writer "look to the park primarily for the satisfaction of their social needs," might have to look elsewhere (Gray 1966). The design and placement of benches can therefore greatly influence use of a park by the elderly. If a bench is relatively short and can be claimed by one person and his or her belongings, it is unlikely that anyone else will sit there; thus, unwanted contact can be avoided. If a bench is very long, people tend to take the two end positions, possibly too far apart for conversation; a third person may find it difficult to take the middle position and may prefer to keep walking or look for another place to sit. A bench should therefore be long enough for two to four to sit without infringing on one another's personal space and yet close enough for a conversation. Because many elderly people are hard of hearing, conversations between two or more people on a linear bench can be difficult.
- If it is a park in a neighborhood with many older residents, include some continuous looped walkways designed with only a gradual slope (or none). Paths that loop and connect to various routes allow use by those with differing physical abilities. Where appropriate, a variety of grades will provide challenges for those who want regular exercise.

Many elderly men who live in single rooms in Chinatown come to Portsmouth Square, San Francisco, every day to play mah-jongg, chat with friends, or sit alone. (Photo: Anthony Poon)

- Use stairs only when necessary, and then provide handrails. Steps should have a nonslip surface and should not have overhanging treads that can trip climbers.
- Place benches along pathways, especially at the top of inclines, so that older people can rest frequently. If benches are widely spaced or not present at all along pathways, less active people will be discouraged from strolling.
- Protect the backs of benches. Placing benches directly in front of walls or plant masses increases the sense of security.
- Provide benches with backs and with arms that project slightly beyond the seat. Benches without backs and armrests are uncomfortable for long stretches of sitting. Elderly people also may have problems with balance and with getting up from a seated position. (For more information, see chapter 5.)
- For walkways, use surfacing materials that are smooth, yet not slippery and are free of glare. Gravel, brick, or any other uneven surfacing may make walking difficult for older people, particularly those who have mobility problems or are using canes. At an attractive brick crosswalk on Solano Avenue in Berkeley, elderly people often cross the street just outside the crosswalk, on the smoother street pavement, for fear that the bricks may be uneven. Concrete walks, though smooth, are not popular with older persons, who are afraid that the hardness of the concrete might hurt them if they fell down. They also may be affected by glare from

light surfaces; most elderly people, therefore, seem to prefer dark-colored asphalt.
- When possible, provide programmed activities and games for the elderly. The natural environment of a park is not enough to attract some elderly users, but a park with many activity programs can stimulate social exchange and create a sense of belonging. In a study of a highly used park in downtown Long Beach, California, Gray found that on an average day, 150 to 200 men and women walked up to five blocks to the park to spend several hours playing bridge or pinochle together. Many were living on pensions; most lived alone; and, as one described the benefits of playing cards in the park: "It keeps us alive, keeps our minds alert (you have to think to play cards), maintains social contact, encourages interest in current events and politics, provides the exercise walking back and forth, and prevents us from giving in to our feelings and becoming neurotic" (Gray 1966, p. 8). Popular activities for elderly persons are shuffleboard, table games, bocce ball, horseshoes, and lawn bowling. Interest in these and other activities varies by cultural background and socio-economic class.
- Provide game tables in both sun and shade.
- Provide seating for spectators around game courts, with equipment lockers and coat pegs nearby.
- If plots for gardens are made available, be sure to provide storage lockers for gardening implements. Garden plots are best located in fenced and locked community gardens or in a segment of the park set aside for this use and protected from vandals.

Disabled Park Users

Virtually everyone is disabled at some point in their lives, whether by illness, accident, or old age. Physical disability should not preclude enjoyment of the outdoors; indeed, the healing powers of exercise and contact with nature have long been recognized. When designers create barrier-free environments, the result is often a place that is more comfortable also for people without obvious disabilities. For example, curb cuts intended for wheelchair-users are convenient also for bicyclists, skateboarders, and people wheeling shopping carts or baby strollers.

While it is impossible to anticipate the needs of every individual, the limitations of most common disabilities can be minimized by manipulating the physical environment.

Walks

- Follow contours (traverse slopes) as much as possible when laying out pathways and sequential activity centers.
- Make sure that no path crosses a ramped access way, as this can be a difficult maneuver for someone in a wheelchair.
- Use a change in paving material to show changes in level, path intersections, or changes in type of use.

Stairs and Ramps

- Provide double handrails, a lower one for children and people in wheelchairs and a higher one for ambulatory adults.
- Do not design stairs to be so steep as to be exhausting to climb. A landing should be provided after every four feet in rise.

Parking

- Passenger-unloading zones should be designated near major park entrances and activity areas.
- Provide parking spaces for drivers who transfer into wheelchairs.
- Avoid curbs unless absolutely necessary for drainage edging or safety. When curbs are necessary, they should be painted to increase visibility.

Vegetation

- Keep away from paths deciduous trees and plants with a large amount of fruit, which could pose a hazard to safe footing.
- Prune plants so as not to hang down or jut out into pathways.

Signs

- Make signs of dark lettering on a light background, the most legible combination. If possible, signs should be lighted, with the main focal point at a height of about four feet.
- Place Braille strips at the base of signs where they can easily be felt.

Furniture

- Make some tables directly accessible from hard-surfaced paths.
- Give drinking fountains two outlets, a lower one for children and people in wheelchairs and another, higher one.
- Put seating next to paths and hard-surfaced areas.

Preschool Users

Parks with facilities for children aged one through five are very popular. Day care supervisors, parents, and baby-sitters all bring young children to play with other children and to entertain themselves. The tot lot often becomes a social place for parents and/or baby-sitters, as well as for the children. Others may simply enjoy watching children play and gravitate to the play areas for this reason alone.

- Locate tot lots well away from streets. If they are too close, even if they are fenced, the fear of traffic danger will be enough to keep parents from relaxing.
- Ensure that restrooms are easily accessible and include diaper-changing facilities. Restrooms should be located close to children's play areas. Diaper-changing facilities are important to parents or baby-sitters with very small children because they permit them to stay at the park for longer periods of time. A fairly deep shelf fifteen to eighteen inches wide, three to four feet long, and braced to hold up to forty pounds will allow a child to lie down while being changed. The shelf should be thirty to thirty-six inches above the ground, finished in a nonporous material (such as formica) for easy cleaning, and, ideally, have an outer "lip" two to three inches high to prevent the child from rolling off. There should be space for a diaper bag or other supplies right at hand, adequate disposal facilities near or below the shelf, and a sink next to the shelf.
- Create smooth-surfaced walkways within and leading to the tot lot. The walk from the park perimeter or parking lot should be as direct and simple as possible, with a pathway wide and smooth enough for baby strollers and barely toddling children. In the tot lot, small children like to play in sand or on equipment and also to pull a wagon or ride a

A very poorly located tot lot provided by the developer of new suburban housing in St. Paul, Minnesota. It is situated beside a shopping center parking lot, has no sense of enclosure, offers no seating for adults, and provides limited play experiences for the children.

bicycle on a hard surface. Therefore, the path to the tot lot should also encircle it. Finally, because children playing in sandboxes or sand-surfaced tot lots often like to remove their shoes and resent putting them on again for the walk home, the surfaces between the tot lot and the sidewalk should be easy on bare feet.

- Enclose the tot lot with a three-foot fence or hedge to prevent animals from entering the area and to give children and adults a sense of enclosure and security. However, this fence or hedge should not be so high as to prevent seated adults from seeing out or passersby from looking in.
- Provide benches that overlook the play area. Preschool children and their parents feel more secure when they can see each other. A very small child, for example, a one-year-old just learning to walk, needs to be closer to his or her parents than an older pre-schooler. A bench-type edge to a sand box can fulfill the needs of the toddler, and benches slightly further away from the play area will suffice for the parents of older pre-schoolers.
- Arrange some benches to permit socializing among parents. Benches that are long enough to seat two adults comfortably, plus bags for extra clothes, bottles, diapers, and the like, are preferable.
- Make the play equipment strong enough to withstand occasional adult use. Sometimes parents sit on swings or other equipment. because their children want them to join in the fun or because they want to sit to talk with the other parents or to watch the children.
- Provide sand under play equipment. Sand is by far the most desirable surface under play equipment,

as it reduces injuries and provides a malleable play medium. Bark chips (tan bark) or rubber mats help prevent falling injuries but do not provide a creative play medium. Under no circumstances should equipment be placed over concrete or asphalt; grass also is unsatisfactory, as it is easily worn away and the exposed dust becomes muddy in wet weather.

- Provide a water source for both drinking and play. Children will become thirsty as they play, especially in hot weather. They are also likely to get dirty or sticky and to require a bit of clean-up, and adults will also appreciate a source of water within the tot lot. Equally important, the play potential of sand is increased exponentially with the addition of water with which to make it moldable, create rivers or moats, and so on. Many parks now provide a drinking fountain combined with a tap, and if the handle is spring-loaded to close when not held, the danger of flooding or overuse is eliminated. (See also chapter 6.)

Users Aged Six to Twelve

Children aged six to twelve are often the least-heard-from or least-designed-for group of park users, and consequently they often do not use parks for play. All of us remember the places where we most enjoyed playing as children, often overgrown, unmanicured areas that contained few overt messages about what we should do there. The mystery and excitement came from small things and sometimes from places that conveyed a slight element of danger. Empty lots have always been great favorites, for they offer freedom to make things or

A comfortable bench in a play area designed for school-aged children: a place for children and adults to rest, watch, or eat a snack. Although the equipment is not suitable for preschool children, they enjoy playing with the sand, and a concrete edge to the sand area permits adults to sit close to them.

play as one wants. Thus it is important to look back, analyze, and remember why certain places were special and why playing in them was so fulfilling.

- Leave some area of the park undesigned and natural. If vegetation occurs naturally, allow it to remain untouched, and if it does not occur naturally, plant indigenous species that require little maintenance. Allow the grass or weeds to grow unchecked in these areas, to allow children to dig in the dirt or explore the shrubbery, activities that give children more opportunities to fantasize than they would have in a designed environment.
- Vary the topography between undulating and flat areas. A varied topography can enhance the park greatly for children, by surprising them with places to roll on, run on, slide down, and hide behind. Flat grass areas are needed for sports, and flat paved areas can be enjoyed for hopscotch, marbles, jacks, four corners, and so on. Also, widened sections of a hard-surfaced pathway system often prove satisfactory for these purposes.
- Allow for water play. If any kind of watercourse exists on the site or can be constructed to double as a drainage channel, it should be left as natural as possible. A natural streambed is perhaps the most manipulable environment for children of all ages.
- Plant hardy, low branching trees away from fences, where the entire space around the tree can be used by children as well as the tree itself. Trees become entire environments for children. Too often, species are planted that will not withstand heavy use; either they die or elaborate measures must be em-

ployed to keep children off. Use strong, low-branching species that are easy and exciting for children to climb and are the types in which houses can easily be constructed.
- Take full advantage of natural elements as play possibilities. Children will gravitate toward natural elements such as sand areas, logs, boulders, and water areas if they are present in the park. (Or they will find them in nonpark settings.) They often prefer boulders to jungle gyms for climbing, if they are large enough to offer some challenge. The elements should be strategically placed, both near the designated play areas and in wild, undesigned spaces.
- Provide play equipment such as swings or rings that require physical exertion and challenge. Studies have shown that children often prefer old-fashioned metal swings, slides, and monkey bars to modern "sculptural" play equipment, for example, concrete turtles, dragons, and other catalog items. Swinging bridges, climbing nets, swinging balance beams, and other dynamic equipment can provide opportunities for increasing levels of challenge.
- Provide loose props for children to construct their own play environments. This manipulable aspect is one of the special qualities of play, which is rarely, if ever, provided for in parks. If the materials must be checked out and returned (e.g., Swedish-made chests of wooden building blocks), then a play leader and storage shed will be required. If this is not possible, the same kinds of activities can be assisted by periodically depositing loose boards, off-cuts of wood, bricks, and the like in the natural or deliberately overgrown sections of

An imaginatively designed park in a suburban housing project in Göteborg, Sweden. Material excavated for building construction was used to form natural-looking hills and swales. Grass on the valley floor is mowed for sports and running games, and vegetation on the hillsides is left to grow wild.

One of the most enjoyable activities for children on a hot summer's day is playing in the water of a shallow creek. In Ashland, Oregon, a much-loved linear park along Lithia Creek extends several miles from the center of town into the countryside.

the park. It is important to channel this activity into these areas since children like to build club houses and tree houses, in semi-private places, and adults and park-maintenance staff tend to be aesthetically offended by children's building efforts.

• If funds allow, hire a permanent recreation staff to (1) organize games and/or lend equipment with which children can organize their own games (e.g., volleyball nets, basketballs, tennis rackets), (2) be responsible for play props (large building blocks, stilts, and so on), and (3) serve as a community resource person. It is important that the supervisor enjoy children and working with them.

Teenaged Users

Teenagers have particular problems in regard to the use of public places, because our society does not fully acknowledge their special needs. Privacy is a strong need of this age group, and one problem that teens face is having few places to go that are not supervised by adults. One way that they circumvent adult control is by massing in large groups and taking possession of a particular spot. When dominance by teenagers precludes other people's use of the area, conflicts may result. Teenagers living in cities and without access to automobiles are restricted to meeting places that they

Children playing at Live Oak Park in Berkeley confirm what many observation studies have indicated—that swings are the most popular form of play equipment. A tire swing permits two or more children to engage in cooperative play.

Two boys building a house in a Swedish adventure playground. A trained play leader teaches the use of simple tools and ensures a ready supply of scrap lumber. Such building-play can happen without leaders or tools, where children have access to natural areas, or where prunings and the like are left in neighborhood parks.

can reach by public transport or on the way to and from school. For teens in this situation, the neighborhood park may be one important gathering place.

Neighborhood parks usually offer a basketball court and baseball backstops, but teenagers use parks for much more than organized sports. From late afternoon when school gets out and often into the evening, teenagers may use a park as their hangout, since alternative areas for gathering in groups are few. But many of the places that teenagers take over do not offer constructive activities; they become bored; and the stage is set for vandalism. Indeed, for many teenagers, vandalism may be nothing more than a way to relieve boredom.

- If there is a community building or recreation center in the park, include a special room and equipment for teens to use. A recreation staff may also be able to offer programs or activities that teens would enjoy.
- Provide an area for teen socializing near a major park entrance or at the busiest street intersection on·the park perimeter. The ideal location is where

both vehicular and pedestrian traffic passes by, providing the best chances for seeing and being seen by others. The area should be designed to optimize the chances for claiming territory but still allow other user groups to claim their own space. Entry seating at opposite sides of a park can be provided for both teens and elderly people.
- Locate a hangout area that maximizes views of and from passersby; clearly define the area; and provide seating for at least five to seven persons. A defining edge might be mounding, a retaining wall, steps (all of which could double as seating), or the backs of benches. A setting that allows sitting on various levels in various postures is best.
- Create a teen hangout area near a parking lot, where those with cars can easily pull in and join the group. If the park is large enough to justify building a parking lot, create a seating area facing the cars and close to the lot entrance so that teens cruising by can see whether their friends are there. Because teens tend to hang out where adult or official power of ownership over a particular setting is

A popular waiting and hangout spot near the main entry to a neighborhood park and close to a well-used recreation building at Live Oak Park in Berkeley, California.

weak and because most adults would not choose to sit facing a parking lot, teenagers may have few problems claiming this territory as their own. Even without seating provided, teenagers may use their cars to sit in or on or lean against.

• Consider creating private areas within the park, hidden from view, where small groups or couples can sit. This might offer a much-needed private space for a teenage gathering; however, it may also create a place for illegal or questionable activities.

Teenagers' Lunchtime Use of Parks

If a park is located very near a high or junior high school and is not considered off-limits to students, the park may be heavily used during the lunch hour. This may create problems for others, particularly other users and maintenance staff. At Martin Luther King Park in Berkeley, for example, high schoolers dominate the park during recess times and after school, preventing others from using it. Because it is a somewhat classic flat, green rectangle, other users cannot find subspaces to claim (Cooper Marcus 1975–1988).

If the park is near a fast-food outlet, litter may be a serious problem. For example, when the ninth grade of the Berkeley high school was transferred from the main campus to a location a mile away, a nearby Taco Bell franchise was a prime magnet for lunching teenagers. The four tables available soon overflowed, and then the young people discovered a newly created minipark a block away. They sat all over the play equipment and a few picnic tables and left the park badly littered each day. The designer had never expected such use.

Similarly, in a middle-class neighborhood of San Francisco, known as the Sunset, hordes of youths from a nearby high school buy Kentucky Fried Chicken and pour across the street into McCoppin Square every lunch hour. The square has very few trash receptacles; the park was originally designed more than fifty years ago for strolling through, playing tennis and softball, and for small children. One solution in such a park might be to create a clearly defined lunchtime, picnic-table area, convenient and attractive to high school students, well supplied with trash receptacles and well signed to encourage self-maintenance, in words and graphics that are attractive to teens.

TYPICAL ACTIVITIES

Typical activities in parks range across the entire spectrum of social acceptability. They may be conventional, such as tennis and picnicking, or unconventional, such as dog walking and bicycling, which may generate minor conflicts among users. Both of these kinds of activities differ from antisocial activities such as vagrancy and vandalism.

Conventional Activities

Court Games

• Provide benches, for spectators, adjacent to courts, and if possible, situate the courts so that they are overlooked by a gentle slope, permitting casual spectators.

• Locate game courts on the park's periphery, so that any associated noise and congestion will not bother quiet areas.

• Locate basketball courts away from children's play equipment. Basketball courts may become hang-

outs for teenagers and young adults which leads to age-related conflicts.
- Provide drinking fountains near the courts.
- Locate high trees away from courts, to reduce maintenance in removing leaves, pruning, and so forth.
- Locate windows and light fixtures where they are unlikely to be damaged accidentally by stray balls.
- Provide pegs for jackets and equipment storage near the court areas.
- Consider lighting the courts at night, to extend usable time and also make the park feel safer for other users.

Informal Recreation

Informal recreation spaces are those that carry an indirect rather than a direct message from the designer about what is expected to happen there. For instance, an open lawn area might be the setting for such diverse activities as a game of catch, informal picnics, sunbathing, or flying a kite. In general, it is important to create spaces for informal play and exercise that are compatible with a variety of uses yet are not so ambiguous as to discourage their use.

Sunbathing

- Provide areas for sunbathing that have a southeastern exposure, and protection from prevailing winds. These areas need not be large. Some quiet, semienclosed areas should be available to those who find passersby distracting. However, those who regard sunbathing as a more social activity may appreciate the exposure of a lawn or slope to passing pedestrians.

Lawn Games

- Provide at least one fairly large, relatively flat turf area. Questions have been raised, especially in the arid West, about the justification for large turf areas, but there is still no material as soft or durable as turf is for active use. The types of grass used in turf areas need to be tolerant of both drought and heavy use. Where turf areas are too steep or otherwise unsuitable for use, they may be planted instead with ground cover, without losing their landscape value.

Jogging

- Consider providing a running trail of packed earth. Locate the path far enough from plantings so that compaction of the soil will not damage plant roots. A par course for exercise is also popular with runners but should be situated so that its users do not damage planting en route or while using exercise stations.

Sledding

- Where the terrain and climate allow, provide areas for sledding and tobogganing. Slopes that in other seasons are used for picnicking or sunbathing can be used for sledding in winter.

Skating

- In regions with cold winters, consider using any sizable flat area as an outdoor skating rink. A baseball field surrounded by snowdrifts can be flooded for this purpose. Dugouts can then be used for spectators and as warming huts.

Picnicking

Picnic tables in neighborhood parks tend to be used by mothers and children on weekdays (morning through early afternoon) and by groups of children or teenagers (after school and into the evening). On weekends, families or groups of friends may come for a summer

Willard Park in Berkeley, California, is an open grass area with scattered trees. Its ambiguity of function serves this student-oriented neighborhood well: On any one day, people can be seen here meditating, socializing, walking dogs, doing exercises, playing music, studying, and playing frisbee or volleyball.

evening barbecue, when a trip by car to a regional park would be too long an excursion; or groups may meet for birthday celebrations, family reunions, or other gatherings.

- Locate parking areas close enough to eliminate long walks with picnic equipment yet far enough away to prevent intrusion on picnicking activity. In neighborhood parks, picnicking areas are used by people who come by both car and on foot, and so access to the area should be pleasant for both. Parking areas should be easily connected to picnic areas, for ease of moving children, bags, radios, and other equipment from cars. On the other hand, few enjoy the sounds or sights of passing traffic as they eat. A planting buffer may allow proximity without intrusion.
- Provide a comfortable and attractive setting for picnicking. This area should be defined and perhaps partially enclosed by planting; trellises or gazebos can create the sense of an outdoor room. The need for shelter from sun, wind, or thundershowers should be considered, depending on the local climate. Individual tables need not necessarily be screened from one another, as larger groups may want to share the space.
- Place picnic tables on a hard surface to prevent erosion, if heavy usage is anticipated. But remember that grass or hard-packed dirt is much more pleasing to the feet than is asphalt or gravel. Consider waiting until the picnic tables have been in use for a year before concluding that a hard surface is necessary.
- Provide a trash receptacle, source of water, and grill fairly near each table. The facilities needed in picnic areas should be convenient. For instance, trash cans should be near each table, for if people must walk any great distance, they often will not use them. A water source or faucet should be near the tables for the users' comfort and hygiene but is not necessary at each table, so long as it is easily accessible and does not seem to belong to just one group. Tables should be located upwind from grills.
- Provide oversized trash cans if maintenance is likely to be infrequent. They should be securely fastened or anchored so they cannot be overturned by children, dogs, or wildlife.
- Place some picnic tables near the play equipment. Before and after a picnic meal, children will want to play. Thus if picnic tables are within sight and sound of the play area, supervision is easier. Parents can also use the tables on weekdays to study or spread out work while watching their children.
- Provide shelters whenever possible, to permit use of the park in inclement weather. Simple shelters near bus stops, picnic tables, playing courts, and toddler play areas can screen sun, rain, snow, or wind. Shelters may be especially important in areas subject to summer thundershowers and may be needed for only half an hour before use can resume. In the damp Pacific Northwest, simple shelters can make play areas comfortable in the winter months for both parents and children.

Unconventional Activities

Activities that some people consider unsuitable in parks but that are not illegal are walking dogs; drinking and eating at cafés or kiosks; cycling, roller skating, and skateboarding; picking up people; and using radio-controlled vehicles. Let us consider how some of these uses can be accommodated.

A park in San Mateo, California, is a popular picnic area with a choice of tables in sun or shade and within easy viewing and calling distance of a children's play area.

Dog Walking

Dogs have become increasingly popular in cities, as companions and protectors and as an excuse to get out for regular walks. But dogs have to be exercised somewhere, and the pollution problem of their excrement has been addressed variously via fines for the fouling of sidewalks, "pooper-scooper" laws, and the prohibition of walking dogs in parks. The last may seem to those without dogs to be a reasonable response, but it can seem unduly discriminatory to those with dogs. A mounting conflict by two such groups in Berkeley resulted in a satisfactory solution: A section of the park was fenced off and designated as an "experimental dog park." The rules for its use include a limit of five dogs per owner, the owners' staying in the enclosure, and the owners' cleaning up after their dogs. This experimental park is a large, grassy field enclosed by a five-foot chain-link fence. It has a gate at either end, a water tap and receptacle, and a picnic table and benches. The experiment has proved so popular that people drive several miles to use the facility. Between 4 and 6 P.M. on a warm day, as many as twenty-five dogs and their owners can be found there. An active dog owners' association has been formed (Ohlone Dog Park Association) to maintain the park, welcome new users, and to fight a proposed ending of the experiment. Of course, not every neighborhood park has enough space to create a dog park. Some regional parks designate certain trails for dog walking (on or off the leash); for neighborhood parks, this is out of the question. But most cities have at least one park that could accommodate a "dogs only" section. This seems a more reasonable solution than banning dogs from all parks, a rule often impossible to enforce, anyway.

Cycling, Skateboarding, and Roller Skating

Wheeled (nonmotorized) sports are a major form of recreation in communities nationwide. Cycling is the major mode of personal transportation for millions of children and youth and so is often used for transportation to the park.

- Provide accommodations for cycling, skateboarding, and roller skating in the park. If these activities constitute a hazard to other park users, management policy could be changed to accommodate both groups of users. Closing off vehicular roads in parks for bike riding or establishing special areas or obstacle courses may be one solution.

- Locate bicycle racks in easily seen locations near high-activity centers and popular play equipment. The racks should be designed to allow bicycles to be secured by chain and padlock. The provision of racks will also prevent damage to trees, signs, and other facilities that otherwise will be used to secure bikes.

- Separate paths for wheeled sports from pedestrian paths, or construct walks that are wide enough to contain both pedestrians and riders at the same time and that indicate which side should be used by which group. Separation is especially important if elderly people are likely to use the park.

- Consider building special courses for bicyclists, skateboarders, and roller skaters, with mounds, banked curves, and challenging alignments. Because skateboarding is often prohibited on city streets, and bicycling may be hazardous, allow children some freedom to pursue these sports on special routes or in undeveloped areas of the park.

A unique solution to the "dog problem," in Ohlone Park, Berkeley, California, is a gated field for exercising dogs. This "dog park" emerged as a compromise between dog-owners and non-dog owners in the neighborhood during a participatory design process.

Antisocial Activities

Actual criminal offenses sometimes occur in parks, and clearly these are activities we want to discourage, by minimizing the environmental "supports" that assist the criminal (dense planting, blind corners, poor lighting), by maximizing park use so that no places are deserted or remote enough for such acts, or by encouraging police surveillance. Mounted patrols in some New York and London parks, for example, seem to be an acceptable form of police presence. In this section, we will discuss offenses that are not as serious, because they are crimes without victims: vagrancy, drug taking, gambling, and vandalism.

Vagrancy

In the nineteenth century, work left people physically tired, and so some of the first city parks were created to serve as the "lungs of the city," where workers could go to be refreshed, to relax, and to regain their strength for the coming week. Today, increasingly, work leaves people either stressed or bored, and so some go to parks looking for excitement.

Why do people choose parks to alleviate their boredom? First, parks are usually free. Parks are also, in a sense, the "last frontier" in the city. Just as some people moved west in the last century to settlements with little structured law enforcement and with an unspoken acceptance of certain behaviors frowned-upon back East (gambling, prostitution, drinking), so some people now retreat into parks to engage in certain activities deemed illegal or unsuitable by the rest of society. The irony is that people have to do these things in parks because they are poor; the middle and upper classes certainly have their share of gambling, heavy drinking,

drug taking, and prostitution, but they can do these things "out of sight" at home, a club, a bar, a massage parlor, or a resort.

If one lives in a tiny room in a hotel, or in an overcrowded housing project where there is no privacy, one may want to flee to the nearest free public space where one can be with like souls or at least find a kind of privacy through anonymity. The problems occur when people start to engage in activities that offend or intimidate passersby or other park users.

In the early 1970s, a neighborhood park in Richmond, California, was used primarily by white, middleclass youths (the local residents) for buying and using marijuana. Their parents petitioned the city to buy the land and close the park; that is, their reaction to the problem was to get rid of the place where it happened. At around the same time, commuters working in downtown Sacramento were offended by the presence of so many older men in City Hall Square, some of whom drank liquor while in the park. So they urged the city to address the problem, which it did by removing some of the huge trees that created deep shade in the park, and under which the men clustered on hot summer days. That is, the "solution" was the elimination of the attractive elements of the park that drew people there in the first place, and the result was that the men just clustered more closely under the trees that remained (Sommer and Becker 1969). In Berkeley, California, there is a park that spans either side of a street in a quiet, middle-class neighborhood. Local youths considered that segment of street to be a "no-man's land" and after school gathered there, on motorbikes and mopeds, in increasing numbers. The neighbors were alarmed (although some of the youth were their own children) and asked the police to "move them on."

A semiwild area in a Swedish park where children have made their own bicycle obstacle course through the landscape. City streets are dangerous for child-cyclists, and parks often prohibit this activity.

Here we are dealing with issues that are, for the most part, not illegal. But the presence of a *cluster* of youth on bikes, or ill-dressed men in a city park, is enough to arouse apprehension or fear in the hearts of onlookers or neighbors. Perhaps they are legitimately fearful for themselves or their children, but perhaps too it is just the human tendency to be suspicious of those unlike ourselves. The examples have no doubt been repeated in every city across the country. It is important therefore to look more closely at this anti-social park activity, and to suggest some ways of dealing with it.

It is ironic that among the functions of early parks was providing a place for city-dwellers to rest and reflect in natural surroundings. Today if you are a well-dressed individual in the financial district, or a mother with child at a tot lot, that is still ok. But if your appearance is dishevelled, or you are a young black male, or Hispanic, or you take an occasional drink from a bottle, or take a nap, or, worse still, you are in a group, that same rest and reflection may be labelled "vagrancy" or "loitering with intent."

Although the occasional group of loiterers in a park may be selling drugs, harassing passersby, or panhandling for money, the majority are law-abiding citizens who have nowhere else to go because they are poor and unemployed, live in tiny rooms in residential hotels, or want to spend time with peers after school. The problem is that we, as a society, seem unable to distinguish between legitimate and illegitimate users of public parks and so label them all as undesirable.

A solution suggested by William Whyte in *The Social Life of Small Urban Spaces* is to make a space so attractive to legitimate users that undesirables move on. Indeed, this was the approach used to reclaim Bryant Park in New York City from legions of drug dealers who had virtually taken over the park, which was

screened from the nearby sidewalks by planting and railings. Portable facilities for flower vendors, booksellers, and a café were moved into the park and after a period of anger and confusion, the drug dealers eventually moved on (Strickland and Sanders 1983). Although this approach effectively reclaims a particular space for legitimate users, it may just move the problem to the next space down the block.

What if one is designing a new park in a part of town where one expects vagrancy and a population of undesirables. Two examples from San Francisco may be helpful.

In the case of TransAmerica Redwood Park, the client was the corporation that owned the land and the adjacent building (the TransAmerica Pyramid). A very small piece of open space that functions as both a pass through (from one block to another) and a destination was designed as a beautiful green oasis, frequently used by local office workers. If "undesirables" come, they disappear in the crowd; if they are still there after the crowd disperses, there are two ways in which the owner handles the problem. Because this is a privately owned public space, the gardener or grounds keeper on duty can help maintain order, and the gates can be closed at dusk and on weekends, when "undesirables" might not be masked by legitimate users.

In the case of Boeddeker Park in the Tenderloin district of San Francisco, the client was the city parks department. There was a desperate need for park space in a district of rundown residential hotels, where recent Vietnamese immigrants had swelled the population, particularly the number of children. The locality was known to have a serious drug problem, a high degree of unemployment, and people with drinking problems. Information from a series of community meetings, questionnaires distributed to residents, and

Many homeless people use parks to drink, sleep, eat, and spend the night. (Photo: Anthony Poon)

pictures drawn by local children were used to develop a one-eighth acre park on the site of a former bowling alley.

The ways in which this park coped with the problem of "undesirables" included the following:

- Creating an active, well-used space in which any undesirable activity would either be dissipated or moved on.
- Incorporating a wide walkway that bisects the space, ensuring many shortcutting passers through and enabling a police car to pass through if necessary.
- Fencing the park with railings and gates, so that it can be shut after-hours. (Even so, people who want to sleep in the park have found a way in; the police turn a blind eye.)

Two day care center groups come daily to use the tot lot, and many elderly people sit nearby to watch. The park has proved to be immensely popular. Many people sit on the main diagonal pathway to watch the passing parade; a group of unemployed black men have taken over a table and benches just off the main path; and the basketball area has developed an unplanned use pattern, with Asian youths playing in the morning, blacks in the afternoon. So far, no group of users has identified another as undesirable. An amazing range of ages and ethnic groups use this park in parallel fashion.

Vandalism

Vandalism is an umbrella term used to describe several different types of damage to property. Psychologist Phillip Zimbardo called it "rebellion with a cause," the cause being a general societal breakdown, and recrea-

tionist George Kenline observed that indifferent parents may be the main cause (Kenline 1976). Some feel that the designer of the built environment may be at fault by the selection of inappropriate materials or lack of understanding of maintenance policies.

Although some recreation professionals are distressed by vandalism and constantly seek ways to stop it, others take a more philosophical approach, seeing it as merely a housekeeping problem, a part of managing public facilities. There are, however, obvious negative consequences of park vandalism. Apart from the cost to the taxpayer for replacing or repairing damaged property, there is an increased public perception of lack of personal safety in a park that has been vandalized, leading in turn to less use of the site by law-abiding citizens.

Though it seems unfair to hold designers entirely responsible for a problem as deep and pervasive as vandalism, there can be little doubt that the designers' insensitivity has sometimes exacerbated the problem. Yet until recently, little information about the behavioral aspects of vandalism was available to designers to enable them to decide where design interventions would help decrease damage.

A study by the Parks and Recreation Department of the City of San Jose, California, found that males between ten and twenty-five years of age were the most frequent perpetrators, that graffiti is the type of damage most often occurring, and that the time between sunset and sunrise on weekends is the time when the most damage occurs (Parks and Recreation 1981). Other associated factors are: boredom, drug abuse, fragmented family units, gang membership, lack of parental supervision, peer pressure, unemployment, an unresponsive school system, lack of adequate recreational programs,

Boedekker Park in the Tenderloin district of San Francisco provides a much-used meeting and recreation space for the residents of this multiracial, low-income neighborhood. Note the wide diagonal pathway for patrolling police cars and gates, which are locked at night.

and sometimes a recreational program itself (e.g., a fight after a dance).

Both knowledge of the precise type of damage and an attempt to discover the motivation for the behavior causing the damage are helpful in solving the problem. "A Survey of Vandalism in Outdoor Recreation" (Wise et al. 1982), from the Department of Architecture at the University of Washington, classified damage into four categories, the first three listed by increasing severity of impact:

1. User modification (e.g., a path cutting across a lawn, or a garbage can used as a ladder).
2. Destruction (use of wooden roofing shingles for firewood, broken windows and light fixtures).
3. Removal (theft of signs or light bulbs).
4. Defacement ("application of a semipermanent message or disfigurement of an approved message in a public setting," for example, graffiti).

The Seattle park facilities most likely to suffer damage and defacement (in order of frequency of incidents) were tables and benches, walls, restrooms, recreational equipment, trees, lights, signs, trash cans, doors, and lawns. The time of year in which most incidents occurred was the summer, May through August (Wise et al. 1982).

In the past, park designers and managers have tried to prevent vandalism by means of "target hardening" or overdesigning facilities to withstand maximum abuse. Similar design solutions include the actual removal of amenities (a picnic table that is not there cannot be damaged) or a design program whose first priority is ease of police patrol, often specifying flat topography, no shrubbery, chain-link fences, intensive lighting,

and elaborate security devices. These "solutions" may be effective, but we will not discuss them here, as they often conflict with the valued environmental amenities that we have recommended in other parts of this chapter (an attractive setting, an oasis effect). Rather, by using behavior analysis, more effective approaches have been discovered to alleviate a problem that no one is naive enough to claim can be completely solved.

Wise and his colleagues described a means of damage analysis whereby they examined the chain of circumstances, or "circuit," that "made the damage highly probable if not inevitable." The designer/planner might attempt to intervene in the process and break the circuit by means of "de-opportunizing design." This sometimes means attempting to manipulate the unconscious behavioral processes of park users, for example, with a roof design that reduces the perceived scale of the building mass, that is , when a building appears less obtrusive, it attracts less gratuitous damage. In many cases, it simply means becoming aware of the frustrations caused by poor design that are at the root of the damage and relieving those frustrations by modifying the design. The San Jose study, which was conducted with the help of community contacts, proposed extensive management and programming changes in an attempt to confront the deep societal problems and dissatisfactions that help cause many instances of vandalism.

Some general guidelines regarding vandalism are the following:

• Plan and locate park facilities to avoid potentially conflicting uses. Much damage to amenities results from poor planning.
• Provide adequate access to the park; inadequate

Some behavior labeled as vandalism might better be termed user modification. This shortcut through the landscaping into a Seattle park was made because the original design did not foresee the demand.

access may be the cause of cut fences, paths of convenience, and the like.

- Create a variety of settings that can be claimed by different groups, as opposed to one flat open space, to minimize user conflicts (which may lead to abuse).
- Locate permanent fixtures such as trash cans, benches, and barbecues in such a way that they cannot be used to reach rooftops.
- Construct gates or bollards that block direct auto access (but that can be removed for maintenance purposes), so as to make theft and destruction of property more difficult.
- Place windows and skylights out of direct sight lines from major access points, thereby reducing their potential as targets. In addition, particularly vulnerable windows should be made of plexiglas or covered with mesh.

Walls and Fences

- Fence public areas that are closed at certain times.
- Avoid high solid walls or gates that reduce visibility.
- Use materials that can be easily cleaned and painted.
- Use dark-colored exposed-aggregate concrete to discourage graffiti.
- Avoid large expanses of light-colored smooth material.
- Eliminate unnecessary fencing, to reduce frustration and irritation.

Tables and Benches

- Place benches along paths in such a way as to discourage cutting across planting beds.
- For picnic tables, use light-colored wood coated with varathane or a similar material. This type of surface is less attractive for carving purposes.

Trash Cans

- Provide heavy-duty trash cans that can withstand abuse. If conventional garbage cans are used, they should be kept in another receptacle, such as a wooden box, that blends in with the park's surroundings.
- Provide more cans in areas that have had a serious litter problem.

Signs

- Avoid large white background areas, to minimize space for graffiti.
- Use signposts made from wide, heavy timbers that are difficult to remove. Signs can be attached flush to the post, and if no part of the sign projects, the temptation to snap it off may be minimized.

Planting

- Protect young trees with guards.
- Reinforce lawns at path intersections and along shortcuts, with edging of concrete block or cobblestone.

Lights

- Use lighting fixtures that have a faceted design rather than one continuous surface. Globe fixtures provide a tempting target for rock throwers.

Management and Activity Programming

- Organize mural painting, or allow some spontaneous artworks to remain, to discourage less-acceptable graffiti.
- Provide quick and efficient maintenance to stop the vicious cycle of abuse, neglect, and misuse from becoming established.
- Offer financial incentives to youth groups that assist in curtailing damage and help with maintenance.
- Attract more users to the park with special programming (e.g., dances, family days, cultural arts celebration, theatre), to increase both pride in the park and natural surveillance.
- Establish a reporting procedure by which damage can be assessed. If damage is not intentional but is due to poor design, the design should be modified.
- Arrange regular police patrols by officers familiar with the park and the neighborhood to help increase the perception of safety (hence, use of the park).
- Plan operating hours of facilities, such as recreation centers and pools, to coincide as much as possible with the demand for their use. Closed buildings and unavailable facilities cause frustration, leading to vindictive damage or unauthorized, unsupervised use.

PARK TYPOLOGY AND CASE STUDIES

A useful way to look at neighborhood parks is to consider them in terms of a park typology that categorizes different parks according to the characteristics of their surrounding neighborhoods. Two factors seem to affect a park's use and therefore should inform its design: the overall housing density of the neighborhood and the income level of its inhabitants. Using these factors we have devised the six-celled matrix shown in Table 2.1. The parks named in each cell appear as case studies.

Low Density, Low to Medium Income

Parks for low-density, low- to medium-income neighborhoods tend to be in older suburban areas and were

TABLE 2.1 HOUSING DENSITY AND INCOME LEVELS

| Housing Density | Income Level | |
	Low to Medium	Medium to High
Low	Larkey Park, Walnut Creek	Orinda Community Park, Orinda
	San Pablo Park, Berkeley	Live Oak Park, Berkeley
Medium	Mission Dolores Park, San Francisco	Golden Gate Heights Park, San Francisco
High	Portsmouth Square, San Francisco	Sidney Walton Square, San Francisco
	Boeddeker Park, San Francisco	

established before and just after World War II. These parks often closely fit the recreational facility model: They have from two to ten acres, with at least two or three specialized sports facilities such as tennis and basketball courts, ball fields, and playground equipment for children. Other furnishings commonly include picnic tables, barbecue grills, and open, grassy "free play" areas. In addition, they often contain natural features such as water and mature trees and shrubs.

Many of the users of these parks arrive on foot from the immediate neighborhood; the regular (i.e., everyday) users are toddlers and their parents, elementary school children after school, and adults using the hard-surfaced game courts. Quite often the neighborhood and park are dominated by a single ethnic group.

Notably absent are teenagers and the elderly. Although older and new suburbs are considered ideal for raising young children, teenagers are often bored there, and their accommodation in neighborhood parks is often limited to negative design messages and restrictions on their activities. There is an increasing number of elderly in the older suburbs who have grown old with the area. Whether or not the elderly would be inclined to use neighborhood parks if they had a private backyard is unclear, but with the exception of a few athletic tennis players, they are excluded from these parks by the design emphasis on active, boisterous play.

Because of the lower housing density, greater availability of open space, and contact with vegetation in the suburbs (most residents have backyards, for instance), there may not be the same need for a natural retreat as there is in the city; rather, the park may offer a place for gathering, programs, and special equipment that the family home does not provide.

General Design Guidelines

- Determine the needs of the principal groups of users to be served. Most parks do not serve everybody, and it may be unrealistic to expect them to.

Participatory design can help set priorities and ensure that real local needs are addressed.

- Place a recreation building in a central, well-marked location, with a regularly attended bulletin board and signage. Provide some seating and gathering space next to the building so that the center will retain some social function even when the building is closed. In addition, closed buildings may be a more likely target of vandalism when such amenities are absent.

- Designate a dog-running area in a park that is big enough to accommodate one and if there appear to be many dog owners in the neighborhood. If the dogs are not fenced in, then they should be fenced out of the children's sand play areas.

- Design the majority of park spaces to be open and visible, to increase safety and the perception of safety. Using large trees rather than extensive shrubbery can be one way to retain a natural feeling while not creating a "creepy" sensation.

Larkey Park, Walnut Creek, California [1]

Location and Context

Larkey Park is at First and Buena Vista avenues in Walnut Creek, an outer suburb of the San Francisco Bay Area. A grocery store, church, and elementary school are nearby. The neighborhood is made up of single-family, detached houses, which are moderately well maintained. The residents have middle to lower-middle incomes and include young families, middle-aged and retired people; most are white. There are few sidewalks in the area, as automobiles are almost the only mode of transportation. The park opened in 1965 and has developed gradually since then.

[1] Compiled from reports by students Heather Clendenin and Victoria Davis, both written in 1977.

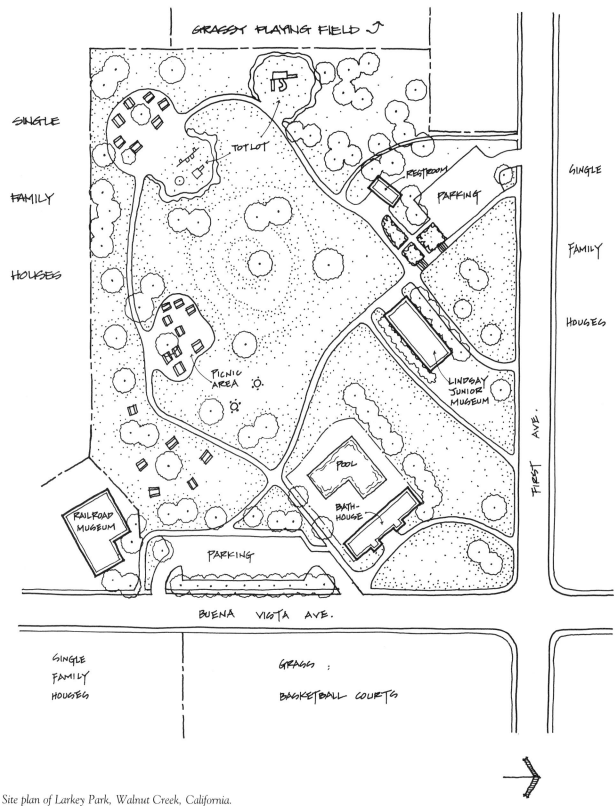

Site plan of Larkey Park, Walnut Creek, California.

Description

The park covers 16.4 acres of gently rolling terrain, with grassy mounds and a few Monterey pines. Its facilities are tennis courts, a multi-purpose playing field, basketball courts, recreation office, bathrooms, two playgrounds, a picnic area, tetherball, volleyball, horseshoes, swimming pool and bathhouse, and two parking lots. The park also contains a nature study area and a natural history museum where animals can be "borrowed" by children to take home for a short period.

Major Uses and Users

Parents and small children use the play areas heavily on weekdays until noon and all day on warm weekends. Typically, adults sprawl on the grass or on the molded edge of the play area while toddlers dig in the sand or older children climb, swing, and slide on a large play structure. Tennis players come after work and on weekends; business people eat their lunch here; teenagers hang out in both parking lots in their cars and smoke and drink; and older children come after school to visit the museum, ride their bikes on the mounds, and use the playground. People tend to come in family groups.

Successful Features

• Maintenance level very high, with users having much pride in the park
• Wheelchair access to park from parking lot
• Group picnic area in which tables can be moved
• Nature museum a strong draw for children and added source of pride to community
• Mounds and hilly pathways good for bike riding, which does not seem to be so intensive that it is seen as a problem
• Well-maintained toilets

Unsuccessful Features

• Not enough trash cans at picnic sites
• Heavy littering of parking lots by teens
• Dogs off leash a concern to some parents
• Shortcut paths across fields to residential areas

• Separate play areas for older and younger children a disadvantage to some, an advantage to others
• No indoor recreation space, only an administration office

San Pablo Park, Berkeley, California [2]

Location and Context

This park is bounded by Ward, Mabel, Russell, and Park streets in west Berkeley. The neighborhood is composed of small bungalows, one to two stories high and built in the 1920s and 1930s, and a few two- to three-story apartment buildings. The neighborhood residents are mainly employed and retired lower-middle-income blacks, with some white, Chinese, and Filipinos.

Description

This is a flat, rectangular park covering two city blocks. Its facilities are tennis and basketball courts, baseball diamonds, concrete picnic tables, a children's play area, a recreation center with bathrooms, and benches at the tennis and basketball courts. The vegetation consists of grass and a few sparse trees. The park is poorly maintained. It has dirt paths around the periphery, but no sidewalks. The park is completely open to the streets on all sides, except where fences enclose ball game areas.

[2] Compiled from reports by students Gilles Guignat (1977), Lorna Tansey (1977), Kim McDonald (1982), and Peter Bluhon (1988).

Larkey Park, Walnut Creek, California, on a Saturday afternoon in early spring. Note mounded concrete forms that function as play objects and keep the sand from spilling onto the pathways.

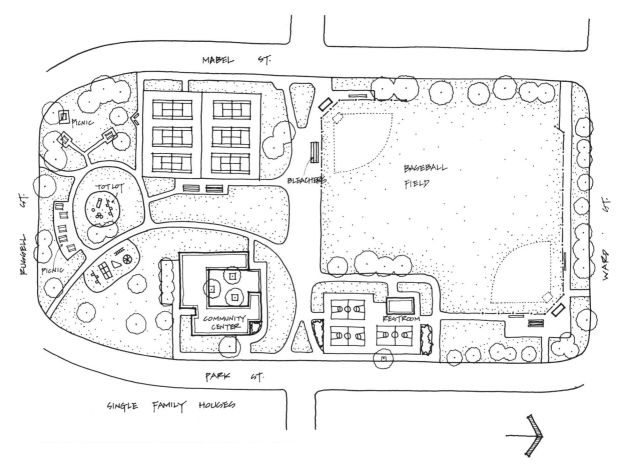

Site plan of San Pablo Park, Berkeley, California.

Although the picnic area at San Pablo Park, Berkeley, California, is located conveniently close to a play area, neither is often used, as the picnic tables are made of cold concrete and close to a peripheral street, and the catalog play equipment is boring and not scaled to children's needs.

94

Major Uses and Users

Athletic uses—tennis, basketball, and games organized by young adults for junior high students—predominate. The park is used at night as a hangout by young males who drink and smoke. Young children are very rarely brought to the park by their parents. Older children cut through the park after school and use the play equipment, yet feel that the play area is "not special." The recreation center typically offers a wide variety of activities: dance, weight-lifting, karate, drama, congo drumming, arts and crafts, photography, bridge lessons, and so on, but the building is badly maintained, and sometimes no schedule of its hours is posted. The San Pablo Tennis Club meets at this park, drawing young adults from all over the East Bay. Blacks are the principal users of this park.

Successful Features

• Basketball and tennis courts for both smaller and larger children; the lights, benches, and water encourage park use
• Picnic tables near tot lot well located for overseeing playing children; however, play equipment is unimaginative and does not hold children's interest

Unsuccessful Features

• A lot of leftover, unused, "ambiguous" spaces; boarded-up restroom building in basketball area contributes to demoralizing atmosphere
• No benches for informal socializing or quiet sitting
• Placement of trees limits size and versatility of playing fields
• "Putting green" is barely recognizable as such, from lack of use and maintenance; no indication that users desired such a facility
• Picnic tables and benches made of indestructible concrete; hard and cold
• Picnic tables located close to street; no sense of privacy or enclosure

Low Density, Medium to High Income

Parks in the low-density, medium- to high-income category can be found in both older and newer suburbs. In the older suburbs, these parks fit the recreational facility model, whereas new suburban parks fall into two categories: parks connected to civic buildings and the main shopping street, and larger community parks (twenty or more acres). In both cases, transportation to the parks is usually by automobile, and off-street parking is provided.

Most of the new suburban parks offer play equipment for both toddlers and older children. In addition, game courts, especially tennis courts, are usually provided; teenagers are often excluded by the lack of facilities

that interest them. Ironically, these parks sometimes work very well for their limited clientele, because they have managed to exclude groups or activities (e.g., teens hanging out) that are considered to degrade the park's image. A narrow spectrum of users provides a homogeneity that tends to lessen conflict. These suburban parks can have many uses, such as educational programs and day camps, requiring group cooperation and participation. There is often a high degree of community pride in and commitment to the park and fewer long-standing traditions concerning the park's use that can impede change.

General Guidelines

• If possible, locate the park near commercial or civic facilities, to create a larger pool of potential users. Ensure that the park lies on one or more bus routes, to encourage use of the park by elderly, teenagers, and others without cars.
• Provide some excitement for older children, such as a bike-riding course, game room, or a creek.
• Provide settings for group and cooperative activities, such as picnicking, team sports, or meeting places.

Orinda Community Park, Orinda, California [3]

Location and Context

This community park is located on Orinda Way, in Orinda, a suburb in the hills east of Oakland and Berkeley. It is a valley oak woodland setting intermingled with residential and commercial development. Most of the area's residents are white, with medium to high incomes, living in large single-family homes on spacious lots. The park is situated in the northernmost of two shopping areas separated by a rapid transit–freeway commuter corridor. The park opened in 1974 and has gradually been improved as finances become available through community donations.

Description

The park covers approximately three acres and is integrated with a popular community center. The park–community center site, formerly an elementary school, is the focal point for Orinda's recreation activities. Adjacent to the site is a library, church, private preschool, fire station, shopping area, and open hillside. The Orinda Senior Village HUD project is next to the park. The park's facilities are a tot lot, play structure for older children, tennis courts, picnic area, meandering path and par course, group-oriented amphitheater, gazebo, lawn open space, and natural area. The path is

---

[3] Compiled from a report by Rob Russell (1982).

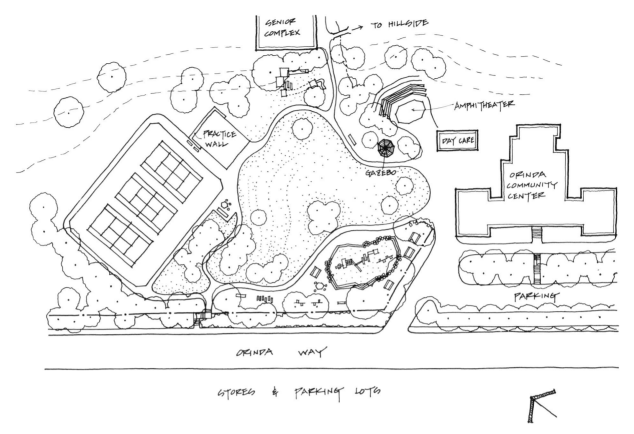

Site plan of Orinda Community Park, Orinda, California.

Mothers and children using the tot lot are among the most frequent users of this popular park in an upper middle–class suburban community.

used for walking, its par course, and bike riding. The park is not highly visible, as it is above the street, screened by vegetation, and lacking obvious entry and signage. Mature trees and shrubs ring the mounded central lawn and meadow area. Community concerts, a tennis tournament, and an art fair are held in the summer, attracting many non-Orinda residents.

Major Uses and Users

The tot lot and tennis courts attract 85 percent of the park's users. Mothers with children aged three to five dominate the tot lot. From morning to midday the tennis courts are predominantly used by female adults, before the postwork influx of males and more females.

The lighted courts receive the heaviest midweek use in afternoon and evening hours. The eleven-to-fifteen age group is almost absent. Older teens and young adults (sixteen to twenty-one) tend to concentrate in the small area overlooking the street and parking lot. These users comprise 12 percent of the total. Ten percent of users are in their twenties; another 30 percent are in their thirties. A relatively low proportion of users are over forty.

Successful Features

- High degree of community pride and support
- Overall community complex serving as the center for local recreation and culture
- Variety of park areas attempting to meet needs of diverse user groups
- Park clean and apparently safe for majority of users
- Large tot lot with variety of equipment; picnic tables nearby for supervising adults
- Separate play area for older children but too far from tot lot
- Path around central lawn frequently used by small children on bicycles

Unsuccessful Features

- Poor sense of entry to park and poor transition between park and community center
- Inadequate seating adjacent to tot lot and tennis courts
- No suitable park gathering area for teens
- Some conflict between parents in tot lot and teens at picnic tables
- Poor meadow drainage, thereby reducing use

Live Oak Park, Berkeley, California [4]

Location and Context

The park lies between Shattuck Avenue and Walnut Street, in north Berkeley. This neighborhood contains a mixture of older single-family houses dating from the early decades of the century, and apartment buildings built in the 1960s and 1970s. Many houses are occupied by their owners, and there is a mix of families, retired people, professionals, students, and artists. Most are white, with medium to upper-medium incomes. The street atmosphere is quiet, but just a few blocks away is a shopping area with a regional draw.

[4] Compiled from reports by students William Bull (1973), Erica Hames (1974), Marty Lynch (1986), Robert Paine (1981), Steven Perkins (1979), Moura Quayle (1981), Cynthia Rice (1974), Eric von Berg (1974), Alexandra Vondeling (1988), Steven Wong (1973), Katherine Wright (1981), and Flora Yeh (1988).

Description

The park, on four and a half acres, slopes downward from east to west and is divided by Codornices Creek. A wooded, wild section contains seating, picnic areas, and lawns. The formal recreation area provides basketball, volleyball, and tennis courts, with night lighting; a toddler play area; and multipurpose playing fields. Between the two halves is a large recreation center with a theater, craft workshop, gymnasium, kitchen, and a full schedule of after-school and evening classes.

Major Uses and Users

The park's main users are black and white males twenty to forty years old, who use the basketball and tennis courts. Basketball has long been an attraction here, with many professional-level players. White males, fifty years and older, use the tennis courts, and toddlers and parents use the play area. Secondary uses include dog walking, bike riding, frisbee, hopscotch, and football. A periodic popular use is for craft fairs, cultural festivals, and the like. After dark, some people drink and linger around the creek. In the late 1980s, some homeless people became semipermanent park residents. Noticeable nonusers are non-sports-playing adults, especially older women.

Successful Features

- Facilities for a wide variety of activities
- Central location of recreation center a good unifying force for the park and an important focal point for the community
- Lighting, enabling the courts to be used at night
- Little vandalism—evidence of community appreciation
- Open lawn areas frequently used on warm weekends for sunbathing, reading, and socializing
- Creek is attractive place for older children
- Play equipment for toddlers and for older children is adjacent but separate (the former is fenced)

Unsuccessful Features

- Parts of the park along the creek perceived by some as unsafe
- Not enough bike racks at recreation center
- Access to the creek limited in places by fencing
- Wasted grass area between tennis and basketball courts

Medium Density, Low to Medium Income

Medium density refers to attached housing such as duplexes and townhouses, often found in urban areas but now increasingly found in new suburban developments as well. Low- to medium-income inhabitants can cross the spectrum of users, from single parents to young

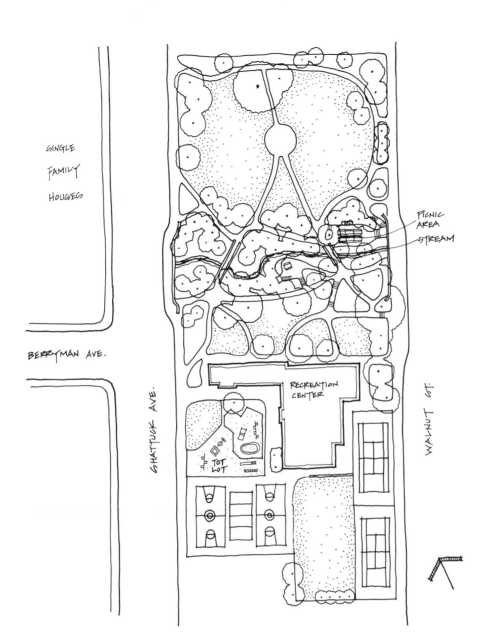

SINGLE FAMILY HOUSES

BERRYMAN AVE.

SHATTUCK AVE.

WALNUT ST.

PICNIC AREA

STREAM

RECREATION CENTER

TOT LOT

Site plan of Live Oak Park,
Berkeley, California.

Parents at Live Oak Park,
Berkeley, California, converse in
the shade on a hot day while
their children play nearby.

98

professionals to the elderly, and there is often a mix of ethnic groups.

Parks in such neighborhoods can reflect the probable conflicts in such a complex constituency. Sheer size or a sensitive design may allow parks to accommodate several groups separated by race, age, or activity. The most successful of these parks have ambiguous designs, which allow them to remain flexible over time and shifts of population and, at the same time, provide sufficient structure that some areas can be claimed. These parks are usually the principal public open space in the area and are used mainly by apartment dwellers and others with little or no access to private open space. Their value, however, may be more for social interaction than for their natural amenities.

A significant proportion of these parks' users come on foot or by public transportation, and they come to the park as part of an established routine. The park may be a central gathering place for particular groups who often have no other place to socialize. Territorial conflicts among user groups may be more likely to surface in these parks than in those serving a more homogenous population.

Most of these parks have the customary accoutrements such as children's play equipment and ball courts and fields, but in addition they may have a citywide reputation, say, for chess playing or sunbathing.

General Guidelines

- Determine major user groups and their needs, and provide separate areas for congregation and activity. Spaces should be highly articulated so as to reduce the possibility of conflict arising from ambiguity.
- Provide numerous access points to encourage use of the park. Areas claimed by some groups can thus be circumvented by others.
- Provide some large ambiguous space (e.g., a flat turf area) to accommodate the needs of rapidly changing city neighborhoods.
- Use signs, particularly at entrances, giving the park's name, information about hours, and the like. Such signs are especially important in city neighborhoods with a large transient population. The park should also be highly visible, with a strong image, to promote casual use by passersby.

Mission Dolores Park, San Francisco [5]

Location and Context

Bounded by 18th, 20th, Dolores, and Church streets and the municipal railway streetcar tracks, this large

[5] Compiled from reports by students Tom Quinn (1977), Jean Roggenkamp (1981), and Beth Stone (1981).

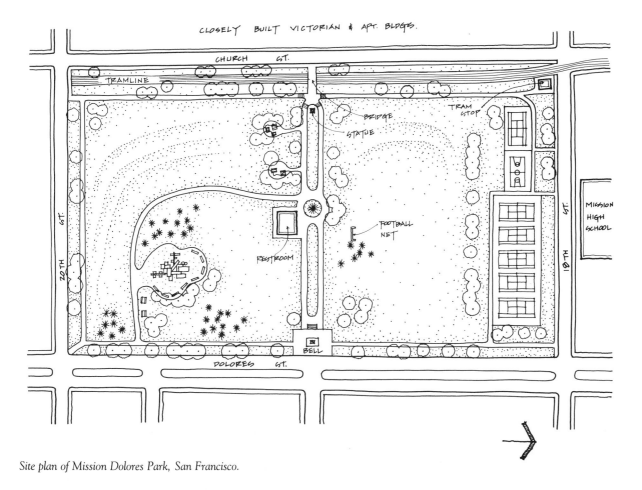

Site plan of Mission Dolores Park, San Francisco.

park lies between the Mission District and Noe Valley in San Francisco. Single-family, attached houses and apartments and three- to four-story apartment buildings are on three sides; Mission High School is on the northern border (18th Street). The neighborhood is a historic San Francisco district, and the park is one block from the Mission Dolores, built in 1782. This area was later the center of San Francisco's Jewish community, and the park itself was the site of the Jewish cemetery until it was moved to San Mateo in 1894. Later, the neighborhood was composed of blue-collar Irish and Germans and is now a gentrifying area composed of young families and professionals to the west of the park (most are white and many gay), and working- to middle-class Latinos in the Mission District to the east. The park is the principal open space in the area. At times it has been the scene of verbal and physical clashes among neighborhood residents, particularly gays and Latinos.

Description

The park comprises approximately 14.5 acres in a square shape, sloping from south to north. Grassy slopes are divided by pathways, and scattered palm and magnolia trees complete the vegetation. The park's facilities are six tennis courts, a basketball court, a children's playground, a small recreation building (game room upstairs, bathrooms downstairs), a designated dog exercise area, a plaza, benches, a multipurpose playing field, grassy open areas, picnic tables, horseshoe pits, and small paved areas. The park is accessible from most points on the periphery, as there are no fences, hedges, or other barriers.

Major Uses and Users

Male users outnumber females by two to one. The ethnic makeup of the users is approximately 50 percent Latino (primarily Mexican-American), 33 percent white, 10 percent Asian, and 7 percent black. The uses of the park are many and varied. Latino teenagers and young adults form a regular and significant group that hangs out at several of the major entrances where walls and steps provide sitting space. Aside from talking and socializing, activities for some include drinking, smoking, and drug dealing. In the early morning and evening hours (after work), young and middle-aged adults use the park for jogging, tennis, and dog walking (mostly on the park's perimeter). Toddlers and their parents in the playground are another regular user group. On sunny weekends gay men can frequently be found sunbathing on the upper grassy slopes, while others picnic, read, talk, or watch the people. Major public events such as theater, music, and political rallies are held in the park almost every weekend. The elderly and children aged six to fifteen rarely use the park.

Successful Features

• Ball field with backstop that can be (and is) used for several different activities such as soccer, volleyball, tai chi, or just sitting
• Backed benches lined up along path good for admiring the view or watching park action
• Accessibility of the park from all around its perimeter, enabling comfortable use by competing groups
• Lack of extensive tree cover appreciated by some users
• Park large enough to attract and accommodate a large number of diverse uses and users
• Diverse play equipment for small children

Unsuccessful Features

• Few sitting areas designed for socializing
• Paved entrances with ledges for sitting dominated by teens

A large, popular children's play area in Mission Dolores Park and view of downtown San Francisco on a foggy day.

• Only one drinking fountain in park
• Activities building often closed, vandalized, and unclear as to use
• Only one picnic area, which is dominated by teenagers and never used for picnicking
• Official signs are mostly negative and prohibitive in content; ineffective in influencing behavior
• Low level of maintenance

Medium Density, Medium to High Income

Medium-density, medium- to high-income parks tend to be in neighborhoods with fairly wealthy young families, middle-aged and elderly couples, and elderly individuals. The activities and facilities desired by this group are oriented toward family gatherings, active sports, and, for the elderly in particular, places to sit and talk or stroll. The park becomes an extension of their backyards. Areas for dogs can become an important issue in this category.

Golden Gate Heights Park, San Francisco[6]

Location and Context

Bounded on the north and east by Rockridge Drive and 12th Avenue, this park directly abuts the private backyards of single-family homes on the west and south.

[6] Compiled from reports by students Laura Lafler (1977) and Mimi Malayan (1986).

The neighborhood is primarily made up of modest, attached, two-story homes on relatively small lots. The residents are professionals, young families, and elderly people; most are white with medium-high incomes.

Description

Golden Gate Heights Park sits at the peak of a hill that starts to rise close to Golden Gate Park, one mile north. A relatively small 4.85 acres, quite secluded and natural/overgrown, Golden Gate Heights commands impressive views of the ocean, bay, and city. Used many years ago by the army, with gun emplacements overlooking the Pacific in World War II, the park still has a twelve-foot-wide paved "pathway" surrounding a central knoll—once used as an army battery—that dates from the war and seems oversized for a pedestrian way.

There are two tennis courts in the northeast corner, surrounded by a chain-link fence and plantings. To the south, at street level, is a children's play area and, beyond that, an open lawn (upper meadow). To the west of this meadow, the knoll is the highest spot in the park, with a few large sit-able rocks in the center. West of the tennis courts, the lower meadow slopes away from the park and is bounded by trees. The rest of the site is woodsy, overgrown, and often steep. Informal paths traverse parts of this area. Two locations in this undeveloped area, one open and one enclosed, offer especially good views. Three benches are dispersed around the central path, and a picnic table with

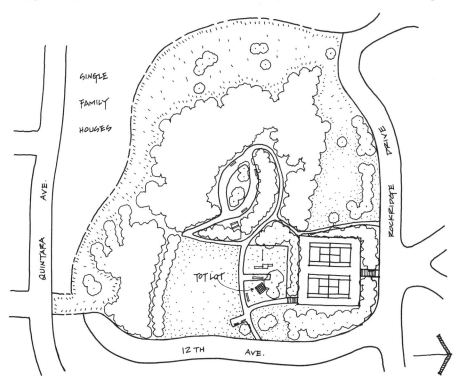

Site plan of Golden Gate Heights Park, San Francisco.

benches is nearby; two benches and a trash can are just inside the east entrance; and a double bench is in the middle of the sand play area, with benches also on its south and west sides. The main entry from 12th Avenue is unmarked and ambiguous, and owing to its topography, entry to the park is difficult from many directions.

Major Uses and Users

The park's principal users are dogs and their owners, mainly from the immediate neighborhood. Many of the dog owners are middle aged to elderly and are on familiar terms with one another and the regular canine users. These users are extremely happy with the park, tending to view its overgrown state as suitable for the dogs. Despite signs declaring "no dogs allowed" and "keep dogs on leash," the dogs are most often allowed free run of the park, including the tot lot, and the prevalence of dog feces deters other users.

A distinct subset of users is the tennis players, who come to the park only to use the courts and seldom any other area of the park. This separateness is underscored by the location of the tennis courts, which are visually and physically disconnected from other parts of the park.

Teenagers use the park especially at night, for drinking, smoking marijuana, and listening to loud music. They occasionally drive their cars into the park to go to the knoll, and they also walk to the viewpoints in the "wild" area.

Successful Features

• Park appreciated for its natural woodsy quality
• Tennis courts popular and well used, although in disrepair

• Upper meadow large and level enough to allow informal sports
• Benches provided at tot lot for supervising adults

Unsuccessful Features

• Conflict between dog owners and other actual or potential users
• Park difficult for many nearby residents to enter
• Tot lot boring, fairly isolated from rest of park, with nothing for school-aged children to do, and unsanitary because of dogs
• Walkways, based on army access roads, not related to any particular pedestrian use of site
• Picnic facilities too limited and poorly located
• Ambiguous entrance

High Density, Low to Medium Income

In high-density, low- to medium-income parks, the premium is on size and safety. Because of their location in densely populated urban areas, such parks tend to be small and heavily used. There is often no room for courts and playing fields, but there usually are play areas for children and benches and paths for talking, people watching, and walking. These parks are important to the very young and the very old, because these groups are the least mobile and cannot easily go to more distant parks. A natural setting with lots of greenery is especially welcome to people who live in the midst of so many hard surfaces and who have no backyards. In addition, the sound of falling water from a fountain can help mask the urban noise and create a sense of tranquillity.

Dogs and their owners are the chief users of this park; children use the play area as a meeting point before chasing and climbing games among the trees and wild areas.

Portsmouth Square, San Francisco [7]

Location and Context

The square is bounded by Clay, Washington, and Kearny streets and Brenham Place, one-half block from Chinatown's Grant Avenue, a major tourist and shopping street. The park is surrounded on three sides by four- to five-story tenement buildings that house restaurants and shops on the lower floors. To the east, across Kearny Street, is the Chinese Cultural Center, a Holiday Inn, and the central business district composed primarily of high-rise buildings. Most of the residents of the immediate neighborhood are low-income Chinese, often recent immigrants, who work in the sweatshops and restaurants of Chinatown. Many live in rooming houses in extremely crowded conditions. The

[7] Compiled from reports by students William Carney (1976), Doris Chew (1976), Joanna Fong (1977), Sherman Hom (1977), Richard Litwin (n.d.), Karen Pang (1977), Madis Pihlak (1977), and Jeff Yuen (1977).

square itself is historically important, being, with the Mission Dolores, the site of the first settlement in the city and was known as Yerba Buena Village in the early 1800s. San Francisco Bay was only one and one-half blocks away before landfill.

Description

Covering approximately 1.21 acres (three quarters of a city block), the park is built on two levels into a sunny, east-facing slope. The park was redesigned and built on top of a parking garage in the 1970s during a redevelopment project that included the building of the Holiday Inn and the Chinese Cultural Center. A pedestrian bridge from the Holiday Inn and the Chinese Cultural Center connects with the upper level of the park. Historical markers tell the story of the park's early days. The upper level has Chinese chessboards and benches, several seating areas, and pine trees, all with an Asian motif. On the lower level is a children's sand play area, with a dragon sculpture, swings, climbing structure, and slide. In addition,

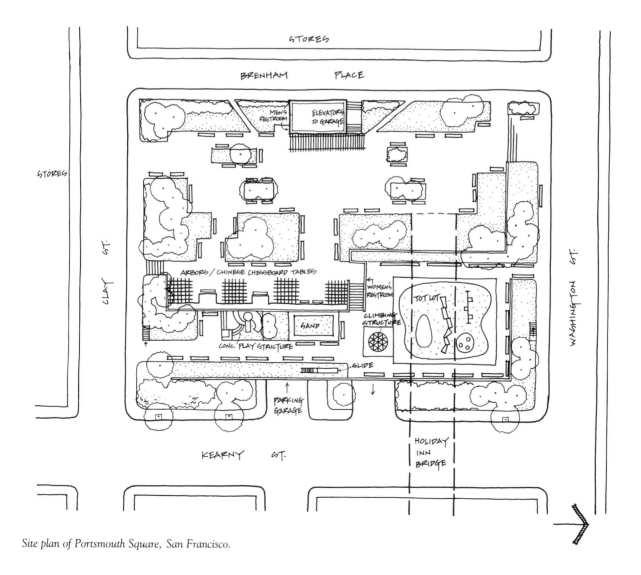

Site plan of Portsmouth Square, San Francisco.

there are small lawn areas, many benches, bathrooms, and several water fountains. There are four entrances to the park on the upper level and two on the lower level, including an elevator to the parking garage on the upper level. The park has a few poplar trees in addition to the pines, but overall the vegetation is sparse.

Major Uses and Users

The park's use is spatially quite distinct, with the upper level dominated by Chinese men, many elderly, who congregate to talk and play board games. A few transients gather in a separate area. The lower level is used mainly by Chinese women and children. Many elderly Chinese women come to the park without children but nevertheless congregate at the benches adjacent to the children's playground. A third space on the lower level is used by white office workers and tourists who eat lunch there.

The park has been described as an outdoor social club for elderly Chinese people. Aside from the martial arts, tai chi, and children's play, there is little physical activity in the park; it is primarily a sitting and gathering space. Teenagers and young adults are largely absent.

Successful Features

• Large entrance areas on Washington and Clay streets allowing view of park; farther in are protected areas
• Park not as marred by parking garage underneath as it might have been (with air vents, ramps, and the like)
• Lower-level sitting area good for elderly—shade from sun and protection from wind. Do not have to use stairs to reach it.
• Good management; park attendant looks out for people

Unsuccessful Features

• Lack of "sociable" seating for adults supervising children in the play area—benches lined up or parallel
• The redesign, which eliminated open, grassy character of park, missed by some users
• Pigeon droppings a maintenance problem
• Dangerous slide—children can easily fall off
• Pedestrian bridge little used and shades lower level
• Lack of adequate structure for displaying public information
• Bathrooms hard to find, signs confusing
• Grass areas too small and poorly maintained

Boeddeker Park, San Francisco [8]

Location and Context

The park is located in the Tenderloin district of San Francisco. Although the residential population is 27,000, the Tenderloin is not considered by most San Franciscans as a residential area. It is surrounded by a mixture of uses, ranging from commercial to civic to residential. Most of the structures in this area are four- to six-story masonry hotels and apartment buildings. The residential hotels were originally designed for tourists and are now housing low-income elderly, immigrants, and transients. The Tenderloin has the second-highest density, after Chinatown, in San Francisco. One third of the population is elderly people; one third is Southeast Asian refugees; and one third is transients, newcomers to the city, and the mentally disabled. Most of the Southeast Asian immigrants are apartment dwellers, whereas the seniors, whites, and blacks live in residential hotels. The Tenderloin has one of the highest crime rates in the city.

[8] Compiled from a report by student Amita Sinha (1985).

Elderly Chinese men on the upper terrace of Portsmouth Square, San Francisco. (Photo: Anthony Poon)

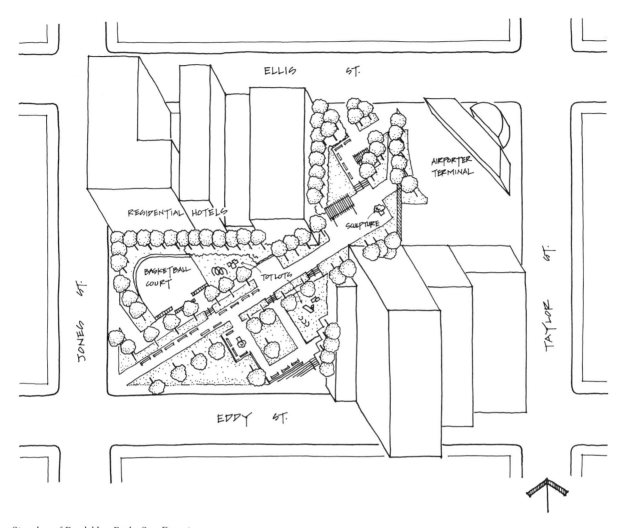

Site plan of Boedekker Park, San Francisco.

Description

The park covers 2.6 acres at the corner of Eddy and Jones streets. It is divided into two spatial zones which could be called active and passive areas. The active zone contains a half basketball court used by young adults; two grassy areas; a tot lot containing swings, a climbing structure with a slide and platforms; and a play area for slightly older children containing tire swings, parallel bars, a climbing structure and firemen's poles. In addition, there are a number of benches that alternate from side to side of the park's major axis. They are arranged so that supervising adults may sit next to either play area. The axis continues into the adult passive area, which contains two gazebos with game tables and benches. The two play areas contain sand, and brick is used throughout for paving. Trees are planted only along the edges of the park, and no shrub is higher than eighteen inches, following the design criterion of maintaining good visibility. The designer placed the one water fountain in the adult zone far from the children's play areas, in order to prevent

children from playing with sand and water and clogging the fountain.

Major Uses and Users

The park's use reflects the tremendous diversity of the neighborhood. At any given time, all ethnic and age groups are present. The designers (Royston, Hanamoto, Alley and Abbey, a landscape architecture firm in Marin County, California) attempted to segregate the users into well-demarcated zones through differences in level and texture, fences, and spatial distances. The main axial pathway is wide enough for a police squad car to go through the park and is also used for circulation, both within the park and between Ellis and Jones streets. The high usage of the park and the presence of people who are just passing through help deter crime. The designer's prime concerns were, within the limited space, security and satisfaction for all age groups. These criteria can be generalized to all inner-city parks where the crime rate is high and space is constricted. Because the park is one of only two in

Children and adults gather to listen to an informal music session at Boedekker Park, San Francisco, on a spring weekend.

the Tenderloin, it is heavily used by all age and ethnic groups. All settings appear to be overcapacity (more people using a setting than the norms and rules associated with a setting allow), giving rise to conflicts among age, ethnic, and interest groups. Mothers complain about older children's disrupting the toddlers' play; seniors feel that children and gays are taking over the park; and the Asian and black groups each want the basketball court exclusively for themselves.

Day care center children and preschoolers come in the morning, and many older children visit after school is over. The basketball court is occupied by young adults of all ethnic groups who, despite the complaints of one group or another about dominating the space, seem to have worked out a time schedule for using it. Elderly, gays, transvestites, and transients all use the park. Children use the whole park, including the adult area and the basketball court. Walking around the park is an activity for slightly older children who are bored with the fixed, single-activity kind of play equipment. They also use the equipment in unintended ways, such as making the top of the swings into a tightrope, running down the slide, and jumping from the top of the climbing structure and scaring the toddlers. The leaves of the growing trees have been plucked, and the lower branches are broken. The two raised green areas are no longer green because of their intensive usage. The Vietnamese children use them to play a game in which they flip coins into holes dug into the ground. The paved area next to the play areas is heavily used for tricycling, bicycling, jumping rope, playing marbles, and other activities associated with hardtop.

Successful Features

• Provides much needed open space in a high-density neighborhood
• High visibility acts as a deterrent to crime in this high-crime neighborhood
• Clear segregation of uses through separation of activity zones which prevents conflicts among the different user groups

Unsuccessful Features

• The play areas contain only fixed, single-activity equipment, unmalleable and unresponsive. The pieces of equipment are oriented to gross-motor activity, and there is little that a child can do with them except to slide, swing, climb, or jump. No fine-motor skills are involved, and no consideration has been given to children's cognitive, social, and emotional developmental needs. Manipulable materials such as water and loose parts such as balls and tires are not available. Sand and water have been consciously separated for maintenance reasons.
• The play equipment lends itself only to parallel kinds of play that do not involve the children in any cooperative, social activity.
• There is no spatial continuity between the two play areas, discouraging branching from one play activity to the next.
• The park is accessible to disabled people, but no attempt has been made to help them use it. None of the play equipment has been designed for use by disabled children.

High Density, Medium to High Income

Again, because of the land economics in high-density urban areas, parks in high-density, medium- to high-income neighborhoods tend to be small, often no more than one block square. People with high incomes often have many recreational options, such as health clubs, sailing, skiing, and backpacking and so do not depend on their neighborhood park as much for exercise and recreation as do people with fewer resources. Nevertheless, parks in such areas continue to serve the needed functions of providing a natural setting and social contact in an urban environment.

Sidney Walton Square, San Francisco[9]

Location and Context

Sidney Walton Square is a city-owned park, bounded on three sides by moderately busy streets and on the fourth side by upper-income housing. The heart of the financial district is less than a five-minute walk to the

[9] Compiled from reports by students Matthew Henning (1976), Olga Levene (1977), Mari Murayama (1977), Deborah Stein (1977), Ryoko Ueyama (1977), and Pam West (1976).

south. The "square" atmosphere is reinforced by brick townhouses that are connected to the park to the north and by the bordering two-story brick buildings housing offices and restaurants that contribute to the urban yet domestic scale of the park.

Description

Sidney Walton's area is less than one city block. It was clearly designed to be a contrast to the surrounding city, with meandering paths, grassy knolls, thick border planting, and a variety of views, vistas, and subspaces. Monterey pines grow around the square's edges and are pruned to allow visibility underneath to the shops and restaurants across the street. A small iron fence around the square helps separate the lawns from the sidewalk. Park entrances are delineated by lights, openings in the fence, and, at one entry, by a historic arch that was formerly part of the wholesale vegetable market that stood on this spot. A fountain and art pieces accentuate the subspaces and path meetings and offer some interest to the newcomer.

Tall bordering pines and a circle of Lombardy poplars help block the high rises to the south and allow the blue of the sky to dominate the high view. Gray, cement, and asphalt were designed to be at a minimum in the square.

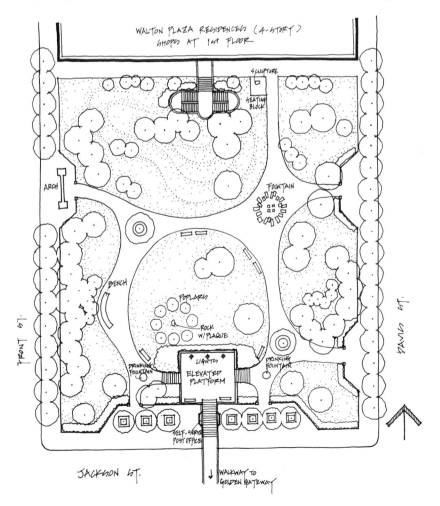

Site plan of Sidney Walton Square, San Francisco.

Major Uses and Users

Sidney Walton Square is very popular with office workers as a meeting place, lunch stop, or relaxing area. The rounded slopes at the north end are a favorite spot. Groups of office workers often come here to share a picnic, sending one of the party ahead to claim a space before the crowds arrive. Another popular area used principally by people sitting alone is the series of seating planters on the square's southern border. The higher condominiums to the south block the afternoon sun, which in turn reduces the attractiveness of the space after the noon hour. Weekend use is quite different: Families come to the square from Chinatown, and the children use the knolls and sculptures more actively than do the lunch-hour crowds. A few homeless people appear in the park at off-peak times.

Successful Features

• Located close to a high density of potential users
• Green-oasis character and bordering streets on three sides make it very visible and "imageable"
• Border fence and planting create a good sense of enclosure once in the park
• Tall trees partially block views of high-rise buildings and enhance the oasis effect
• Meandering pathways permit a variety of routes for strolling
• Grassy knolls create visual interest and permit temporary appropriation of subspaces by lunch-hour groups
• Accommodates both people coming to the park alone and those who arrive in groups
• Appeals equally to men and women users
• Art work displayed in park creates visual interest

• Park functions equally as a weekday office-worker lunch-hour oasis and a weekend neighborhood park for Chinatown families

Unsuccessful Features

• Nearby high-rise buildings block afternoon sun
• Poor drainage in central "hollow" precludes use after grass is irrigated
• Pines require heavy pruning to prevent some subspaces from becoming overgrown and shaded

A Particular Case: School Parks [10]

In the late 1960s and early 1970s, public money was made available in some communities for the redesign and rebuilding of public school playgrounds as "school parks," with not only play equipment for use during school recesses, but also benches, tables, grassy areas, planting, walkways, games areas, and so forth that would invite adults as well as children to use the park after school hours, especially on weekends.

The purpose was to create an efficient dual use of public land, especially in dense urban areas where there was little or no neighborhood park land available.

Two conflicting images are intrinsic to school park design. One grows out of the need to provide play space for large supervised groups of similarly aged children in a limited span of time, during school recesses. The other is the need for relaxed, unmanaged recreation places for adults and children of varying ages after school hours and on weekends. Another, newer con-

[10] Based on an earlier draft by Nanine Hilliard Greene.

Office workers enjoying Sidney Walton Square, San Francisco.

cern is to create an outdoor environment that supports both classroom curricula and children's social and physical development. Although such a park must meet the needs of the school population, a community-oriented school park is especially needed in urban areas with few public outdoor recreation facilities.

An innovative school playground remodeling project is the Washington Environmental Yard in Berkeley, California. A conventional flat school yard south of the Washington Elementary School in Berkeley was originally paved in asphalt, with an area for group games such as relay races, as well as the usual steel-pipe play equipment—swings, slides, and the like. In the early 1970s, under the leadership of landscape architect Robin Moore and his students at the University of California and with the support of the teachers and parents of the school, parts of the playground were transformed into an "environmental yard," including a nature study area with trees, shrubs, two small ponds and a creek; an adventure play area where children could build with real building materials and tools; and an area where children could grow vegetables in large raised planter boxes. The remaining hard-surfaced playground was also redesigned to improve circulation, offer a much wider range of opportunities and activities, and create a more pleasing appearance. After school and on weekends this school park is often used by the public, and for many years it was the home of a highly acclaimed summer program that brought together able-bodied and disabled children.

One of the earliest and most publicized school park renovations was that of the Watkins Buchanan School Park in Washington, D.C., located in a rundown, mostly black area within sight of the Capitol. Remodeled in 1968, this park set a fashion for crowding a play space with expensive cobblestone mounds, concrete forms, and steel cable and heavy timber play equipment. These design themes were imitated across the country in schools, neighborhoods, and miniparks. Although there were accolades from architectural magazines and newspapers, teachers, who were left out of the planning process, observed that there were not enough open spaces for group games for older children and that there were a number of playground accidents involving children colliding with sharp concrete. Recreation personnel, who supervised the area in the afternoon, felt that the design was strictly an architectural concept and did not offer flexible places for the programs of classroom teachers or afterschool recreation. In fact, the recreation workers preferred the open (and unimproved) grassy field across the street from the Watkins school.

Clearly, designing for the different users, or potential users, of a school park is difficult. Although the designers will know the number and ages of the school children, potential afterschool use will be less obvious. A neighborhood survey to determine the presence of family housing without yards, of day care programs, or of elderly residents may suggest the inclusion of particular elements or facilities. Likewise, community involvement in the design is likely to lead to a much higher incidence of neighborhood identification with, and care for, the school park. The importance of community involvement is crucial to a case like this, in which new users are encouraged to use a facility previously unavailable to them.

The Environmental Yard at Washington School, Berkeley, California. The original, all-asphalt school yard was transformed into diverse use zones, including an asphalt court for ball playing, play equipment over sand, and a wild area of dirt, ponds, and native vegetation.

Buchanan School, Washington, D.C.: a very expensive school-yard remodeling of the late 1960s that was copied across the country after accolades in the design press. It was, however, much disliked by recreation leaders and teachers at the school, who preferred an unimproved field across the street. (Photo: Nanine Hilliard Greene)

Design Guidelines

Many of the guidelines for miniparks and concepts discussed in Chapter 6 are relevant to the design of school parks. A few specific issues, however, are enumerated next:

1. Include some pleasant greenery in the view from the street. Trees, shrubs, and flowers indicate that more than a school playground is available. Interviews with adults suggest that the "greening" of a school yard is the factor most important to their increased use of a school park.

2. Design gates and gateposts that clearly indicate an entry and also are inviting. If they need to be shut during school hours, it should be obvious when they are open, to encourage neighborhood use.

3. Place attractive signs at entries, giving the name of the school park, the hours it is open to the public, any rules or regulations, and the name of the sponsoring agency.

4. Ensure that sidewalks approaching the main entry of a school park are wide enough for bike riders, wheelchairs, or two to three people walking abreast.

5. Provide a pedestrian-controlled stoplight if users will have to cross a busy street, for the safety of children coming after school hours without an adult.

6. Provide a safe drop-off place for children brought or picked up by car, where cars will not endanger pedestrians.

7. Place bicycle racks at the entry to the school park, allowing bikes to be parked and locked. If

the school park is too small for bike riding, then the racks should be located at the pickup/drop-off location, to indicate that bicycles are not wanted inside. But during unsupervised periods, some children will undoubtedly ride their bikes into the school park, and so the overall design should take this into account. Because school yards are one of the few places where children can ride bicycles away from traffic danger, we highly recommend allowing some area for this, whether it be a specially designed bike path or simply easy access to a paved sports area.

8. Provide benches at the entrance to the school park for children waiting for parents, parents waiting for children, or neighbors who want to spend a few minutes there. If convenient, this area might be combined with a transit stop.

9. Provide separate entries for delivery and maintenance vehicles coming to the school, which should be away from all pedestrian areas.

10. Use fences to protect those using the school park (e.g., for separation from traffic or hazardous areas) and to prevent the intrusion of people or equipment (such as balls) onto adjacent private property. If chain-link fencing must be used, disguise it with vines or with strips of colorful materials "woven" through it, or spray-paint it in an appealing color or pattern.

11. If the conversion of a school yard into a school park is to be confined to one particular part of the site, choose the area with the most favorable microclimate—most sun and/or summer shade, or least wind—and also consider the topography, current planting, views, and access.

12. Take advantage of existing topography and

planting to create subareas, lookouts, hillside slides, overgrown "adventurous" areas, or whatever.

13. Plan circulation on the site to accommodate peak school-hour use and to address the needs of fewer, more casual users after-hours.

14. Separate active and more quiet areas by means of berming, planting, log ends, or boulders.

15. Incorporate elements into the design that have an educational aspect—wind socks or banners, sundials, seasonal streams, or planting that attracts birds, bugs, or butterflies. Such elements will enhance the learning experience of the children while enriching the environment for all users.

16. Consult with teachers to determine some plants or planting areas that might support classroom programs, for example, vegetables, plants that produce natural dyes, or plants with seedpods or flowers that can be used for craft projects.

17. Avoid spiky, poisonous, staining, or abundant pollen–producing plants.

18. Provide a variety of benches around the site, some alone and some oriented to accommodate a group. Provide benches and tables for children to do class work or play games outside or to eat lunch; benches for spectators to watch an activity, or supervise children, or to sit and enjoy the sunshine. As in all public spaces, the best approach is to allow for many choices in seating.

19. Provide "secondary" seating in the form of grassy slopes, planter edges, boulders—for choice and for times of heavy use.

20. Consider providing some form of outside "stage" where children can put on either impromptu or planned events. Even if very rudimentary, such an area declares itself as a distinct place and will invite use. Audience seating should be provided, whether a grass slope, actual benches, or retaining wall-cum-seats.

21. If the space and neighborhood interest warrant it, consider adding a barbecue.

22. Make drinking fountains available; and if at all possible, provide access to a bathroom, perhaps even a portable toilet, if school facilities cannot be left open.

With this simple piece of play equipment, Swedish schoolchildren learn about pulleys, the weight of sand, gravity, trapdoors, and materials sliding down into wagons.

John Muir School Park, Berkeley, California [11]

Location and Context

The John Muir School Park is bounded by Claremont, Hazel, Domingo, and Ashby streets, approximately a mile south of the University of California campus. The park is at the dividing line between an elegant upper middle-income residential neighborhood and a small-scale commercial development and is within view of the Claremont Hotel, a resort complex. There is a heterogeneous mix of ages in the neighborhood.

Description

The park is a U-shaped, fairly flat open space surrounding an elementary school on three sides. Perimeter planting, chain-link fences, and the wall of an adjacent automotive garage limit most views out of the park. The park has metal and wood equipment in the play areas, an asphalt play area, a tot lot, a grass field, a natural creek area, and three entry areas.

Major Uses and Users

During the school year, the park is used mainly at recess times by children enrolled in the school and their teachers. After school hours, the park is frequented by parents with young children who use the play equip-

---

[11] Compiled from reports by students Andrew Blyholder (1981), Marian Cobb (1980), Annie Mosher (1980), and Liza Riddle (1981).

John Muir School, Berkeley, California: a formerly all-asphalt, grade school yard transformed into several sand-surfaced play equipment areas and a large multipurpose lawn.

ment. The park is also used by a smaller number of adults who come after school hours without children and who use the grass area for sitting, talking, reading, sleeping, and sunning. On weekends, the grass field is used for soccer practice, and for casual frisbee and baseball games, and for romping with dogs.

Successful Features

• Variety of activities in the park
• Natural area, running water
• Relatively high level of planting, greenery
• Level field large enough to support many sports activities

Unsuccessful Features

• Not enough seating in different locations
• Designed with few attractions for older children, teens, and the elderly
• Play spaces too "strung out," making it difficult to supervise simultaneously children in different areas

Leconte School Park, Berkeley, California [12]

Location and Context

The Leconte School Park and School are bordered by Oregon, Fulton, Russell, and Ellsworth streets in the flatlands of Berkeley. The surrounding neighborhood consists of one-story stucco and two-story wood shingle single-family houses occupied by middle-income families. Although only a block from busy streets, the

[12] Compiled from reports by students Nandita Amin (1980), Joseph P. Darrian (1981), Ken Mineau (1980), and Nora Watanabe (1981).

neighborhood is quiet owing to barriers that prevent through traffic. The neighborhood is predominantly white, although a couple of blocks south it is predominantly black. A few Asian families use the school park. Approximately 260 children from kindergarten through third grade are enrolled at the school, which also provides extended day care service after school hours.

Description

The school park is located to the west of the school building. The majority of the surface area is asphalt; this is tinted in tan, blue, and rust to designate basketball courts, a softball diamond, and locations for various games. Three distinct areas were added when the former hard-surfaced yard was made into a school park: a large lawn, a large tanbark area bounded by railroad ties and containing a variety of wood and metal play structures, and a small picnic table area.

Major Uses and Users

The hard-surface area is used mostly by boys for group games: kickball, handball, racing, basketball, softball; the play equipment area is used by both girls and boys; the lawn area is used for running games and some exercise classes; the picnic tables are used for eating bag lunches, socializing, and hanging out after school and on weekends. The park is used primarily by (1) the children during school recesses, some of whom return after school hours; (2) children in after-school care from 1 to 6 P.M.; (3) local parents with small children after 4 P.M. and on weekends; and (4) some teenagers who come in the late afternoon to use the basketball court. Older people seldom use the park.

Le Conte School, Berkeley, California: a formerly all-asphalt, grade school yard redesigned to include play equipment areas, picnic tables, a lawn, and asphalt areas for traditional games.

Successful Features

• Serves the school program well; teachers and children generally satisfied
• Serves as a neighborhood park for a few parents with young children
• Serves some schoolchildren after hours

Unsuccessful Features

• Not enough seating for adults
• Grassy area underused
• Too little shade
• Not enough equipment for very young children

REFERENCES

Baker, Mark L., Stephen G. Gang, and Gerald S. O'Morrow. 1979. *Prototypical park design access for the handicapped.* Athens, Ga.: Institute of Community and Area Development.

Bangs, Herbert, Jr., and Stuart Mahler. 1970. Users of local parks. *American Institute of Planners Journal* 36(5):330–334.

Byerts, Tom. 1970. Design of the urban park environment as an influence on the behavior and social interaction of the elderly. M. Arch. thesis, University of Southern California.

Chadwick, George F. 1966. *The park and the town.* London: Architectural Press.

Cooper-Marcus, Clare. 1975–1988. Student papers on park use in the San Francisco Bay Area. Typescript.

———. 1978. Remembrance of landscapes past. *Landscape* 22(3):34–43.

Cranz, Galen. 1981. Women in urban parks. In *Women and the American city,* ed. Catherine Stimson et al., pp. 76–92. Chicago: University of Chicago Press.

———. 1982. *The politics of park design.* Cambridge, Mass.: MIT Press.

Deyak, Timothy A., and Thomas Parliament. 1975. An analysis of youth participation at urban recreation facilities. *Land Economics* 51(2):172–176.

Francis, Mark. 1987. Some meanings attached to a city park and community gardens. *Landscape Journal* 6(2):101–112.

Francis, Mark, Lisa Cashdan, and Lynn Paxson. 1981. *The making of neighborhood open spaces: Community design, development and management of open spaces.* New York: City University of New York, Center for Human Environments.

French, Jere Stuart. 1970. The decline and deterioration of the American city park. *Parks and Recreation* 5(8):25–28, 40–43.

Garbrecht, Dietrich. 1976. The utilization of inner-city green open space. In *Proceedings of the 3rd International Architectural Psychology Conference, Strasbourg, France,* ed. P. Korosec-Serfaty, pp. 409–425.

Gold, Seymour. 1972. Nonuse of neighborhood parks. *American Institute of Planners Journal* 38(6):369–378.

———. 1974. Deviant behavior in urban parks. *Journal of Health, Physical Education and Recreation* 45 (November): 18–26.

———. 1980. *Recreation planning and design.* New York: McGraw-Hill.

Gold, Seymour, and John R. Sutton. 1980. User satisfaction and landscape quality in neighborhood parks. Unpublished study.

Gray, David. 1966. Uses of a downtown park. Redondo Beach: California, Remark before District IX of the California Park and Recreation Society, June 19. Working paper.

Groening, Gert. 1974. *Elderly and parks.* Berkeley, Ca., Working paper.

Guide for planning recreational parks in California. 1956. Sacramento, Calif.: Recreation Commission.

Guidelines for developing public recreational facility standards. 1976. Ontario, Canada: Ministry of Culture and Recreation, Sports and Fitness Division.

Hernandez, Rogelio. n.d. Briebach Park: A message to Chicanos—"Keep out." In Chicano teen-agers and park use, by David Bautista and Rogelio Hernandez. University of California, Department of Landscape Architecture. Term paper.

Hester, Randolph T., Jr. 1975. *Neighborhood space.* Stroudsberg, Pa.: Dowden, Hutchinson & Ross.

Jacobs, Jane. 1961. *The death and life of great American cities.* New York: Vintage Books.

Johnson, Ronald C. A. 1979. The obsolescence of urban parks. *Urban Land* 38(3):3–4.

Kenline, George. 1976. Vandalism, an overview. In *Vandalism and outdoor recreation symposium proceedings.* U.S. Department of Agriculture Forest Service Technical Report PSW-17. Pacific Southwest Forest and Range Experiment Station, Berkeley, Calif.

Laurie, Michael M. 1975. *An introduction to landscape architecture.* New York: Elsevier.

Linday, Nancy. 1977. Drawing socio-economic lines in Central Park. *Landscape Architecture* 67(6):515–520.

Milchert, Jurgen. 1983. On the desire for "wilderness" in urban open spaces. *Garten + Landschaft,* October, pp. 771–776.

Parks and Recreation Department. 1981. *A study of property damage in the parks of San Jose, California. Final Report.* San Jose: Parks and Recreation Department.

Rutledge, Albert J. 1971. *Anatomy of a park.* New York: McGraw-Hill.

———— 1981. *A visual approach to park design.* New York: Garland STPM Press.

Schroeder, Herbert W., and L. M. Anderson. 1984. Perception of personal safety in urban recreation sites. *Journal of Leisure Research* 16(2):178–194.

Sommer, Robert, and Franklin D. Becker. 1969. The old men in Plaza Park. *Landscape Architecture* 59(2):111–114.

Strickland, Roy, and James Sanders. 1983. Bryant Park's new lease on life. *Place* 3(7):1–4.

Taylor, Bill. 1978. Cruising, porch-sitting, cycling . . . Torrence Park designs fit neighborhood patterns. *Landscape Architecture* 68(5):399–404.

Ulrich, Roger S., and David L. Addoms. 1981. Psychological and recreational benefits of a residential park. *Journal of Leisure Research* 13(1):43–65.

Welch, Polly, Florence Ladd, and John Zeisel. 1978. Social dynamics of property damage in Boston park and recreation facilities. Cambridge, Mass.: Zeisel Research. Mimeo.

Whyte, William. 1980. *The social life of small urban spaces.* Washington, D.C.: Conservation Foundation.

Wise, James, David Fey, Reese Kaufman, et al. 1982. A survey of vandalism in outdoor recreation. Seattle: University of Washington, Department of Architecture. Mimeo.

Zeisel, John. 1981. *Inquiry by design: Tools for environment–behavior research.* Belmont, Calif.: Wadsworth.

DESIGN REVIEW CHECKLIST

GENERAL USER NEEDS

1. Are there a number of fairly isolated benches to give a sitter pleasant views of greenery?

2. Do planting and detailing create a rich and varied aesthetic environment, with ranges of color, texture, shape, and smell?

3. Have some trees been planted in locations that will allow them to grow to their full size without drastic pruning?

4. Are there meandering pathways passing by or through a variety of natural settings?

5. Have most benches been placed so that a wall, planting, or tree provides a "back," adding to a sense of security?

6. Are there some isolated tables and benches or chairs, where a person could eat, read, or study in a natural setting?

7. Are there some areas for sitting that are close to the park's perimeter, for use by those with mobility problems, little time, or concerns about security?

8. Have quiet sitting areas been situated with concern for the microclimate? Has placement beneath deciduous trees been considered for the winter sun or summer shade that they provide?

9. Has the park been designed so that subareas are imageable, enabling people to describe easily a planned meeting location?

10. Does the seating allow a variety of arrangements, both to support socializing and to permit use without intrusion by strangers?

11. Have some movable seats been provided, perhaps rentable deck chairs?

12. Are there picnic tables, both in large barbecuing areas and in more secluded locations?

13. Is there a wide pathway through the park, providing a pleasant experience for those who will only be walking through?

14. Have subareas been designed so that a regular group of users can claim a particular spot—a certain sitting area, group of tables—as theirs?

15. Is the main section of the park fairly open, to allow people to look for a group or friends who may be present?

16. Are there benches next to various facilities—tennis courts, tot lot, recreation building—to enable conversation among bench users?

17. Does the circulation system allow walkers to pass by and check out areas of potential social contact, without forcing them to enter?

18. Do some benches allow a sitter to watch the people moving through the park or along the adjacent sidewalks?

SPECIAL USER GROUP NEEDS

Elderly Persons

19. Are there seating areas just inside the park for elderly people who cannot or do not wish to walk farther into the park?

20. Have entries been planned to coincide with bus stops and crosswalks?

21. Are there drinking fountains, restroom facilities, and a sheltered area nearby, for use by older people?

22. If the surrounding neighborhood contains many elderly people living alone, does the park's design emphasize enjoyable places for meeting? And conversely, if there are many elderly residents of group facilities with social programs, is the emphasis on elements that will allow access to, and enjoyment of, the natural setting?

23. Have benches been chosen with dimensions conducive to socializing, and have they been oriented to that end, keeping in mind issues of lessened flexibility and hearing loss?

24. If there are quite a few elderly residents in the neighborhood, have one or more walkways been designed to have limited or no grade changes?

25. Are ramps used instead of stairs where possible, and if stairs are necessary, are they nonslip, without overhanging treads, and accompanied by a handrail?

26. Are benches placed at relatively short intervals along pathways, to allow frequent resting?

27. Are benches placed where a wall or planting behind them will add to a sense of security?

28. Have benches intended for use by elderly park users been provided with backs and armrests?

29. Are the surfacing materials for walkways smooth yet not slippery and free of glare?

30. If possible, are there programmed activities and games for the elderly?

31. Are there game tables in both sunny and shady locations, to allow a choice?

32. If game courts are to be provided for horseshoes, shuffleboard, lawn bowling, or other games that local residents are likely to enjoy, is there seating for spectators? Are equipment lockers and coat pegs located nearby?

33. If the neighborhood includes many elderly persons with no access to a private yard, has creating a fenced community garden within the park been considered? With storage lockers, adequate access to water, and perhaps raised beds?

Disabled People

34. Are walkways designed to follow the contours of the land?

35. Are cues such as paving-material changes used to indicate changes in level, path intersections, or type of use?

36. Are double handrails provided at ramps—a higher one for ambulatory adults and a lower one for those in wheelchairs and for children?

37. When stairs are used, is a landing provided for every four feet of rise?

38. Are passenger-unloading zones located near park entrances and activity areas?

39. Have curbs been avoided in the parking area or, if necessary, been painted to increase visibility?

40. Are deciduous trees and fruiting plants located so that falling vegetation will not create problems on walkways?

41. Will there be sufficient maintenance to ensure that plants are pruned away from pathways? If not, the planting design should reflect the need to keep pathways unobstructed.

42. Do park signs use dark lettering on a light background?

43. Are major park signs lit for night visibility?

44. Are Braille signs placed where they can easily be touched?

45. Do signs have their main focal point about four feet high?

46. Are some tables directly accessible from hard-surfaced paths?

47. Do drinking fountains have two spigots, easily operated —a lower one for children and people in wheelchairs, as well as a higher one?

Preschool Children

48. Is any tot-lot area located well away from the street?

49. Are restrooms with diaper-changing facilities easily accessible from the tot lot?

50. Are the walkways to and within the tot lot smooth surfaced?

51. Is the tot lot enclosed by a three-foot-high fence or dense planting, to prevent dogs and other animals from entering?

52. Do some benches overlook the tot lot, for supervising adults?

53. Are some benches oriented to encourage adults' socializing?

54. Is the play equipment strong enough to withstand occasional adult use?

55. Has sand been provided under play equipment, for its safety characteristics and its suitability for play?

56. Is there a water source in the tot lot, for drinking and for sand and water play?

School-aged Children

57. Has some area of the park been left undesigned or carefully crafted to be natural, leftover space?

58. Has this area been planned to allow digging in the dirt, crawling through the shrubbery, and so on?

59. Is the topography of the park varied, to create both undulating and flat areas?

60. Is there some provision for water play, with a natural streambed the most desirable?

61. Have hardy, low-branching trees been planted where the tree itself and the space around it can create a rich play environment for children?

62. Have natural elements such as logs and boulders been incorporated into the park design for their play potential?

63. Has moving equipment, and equipment requiring physical exertion and providing challenge, been chosen over "sculptural" elements?

64. Is there some provision for a supply of "loose parts" in the park—either through a play leader who can check out materials or through a periodic replenishing of loose boards, bricks, or whatever in the "leftover" section of the park?

65. Has the possibility been explored of having a permanent recreation staff in the park?

Teenagers

66. If there is a considerable teen population in the neighborhood, has a potential hangout area been created, preferably at a park entrance with both pedestrian and vehicular traffic, that will allow teens to claim the location without creating conflict between them and other users?

67. Is there good visual connection between passersby and teenagers using the hangout area?

68. Are the boundaries of the hangout clearly defined?

69. Is there seating for at least five to seven people in the hangout area?

70. Has the placement of this area near the parking lot been considered, to allow teens in cars to join the group?

71. Can a few small, private areas be created in the park, where couples or small groups can sit out of sight of authority?

72. If a nearby high school or junior high school suggests lunchtime use of a park, has an area of picnic tables and plentiful trash receptacles been provided? Has such an area been sited with the same concerns as a hangout and finished to be attractive to teens?

TYPICAL ACTIVITIES
Conventional Activities

73. Is seating for spectators located next to any game courts? Has a gently sloped lawn been considered for casual spectators?

74. Are game courts situated on the park's periphery, so that noise and congestion will not bother quiet areas?

75. Owing to their potential for use as a teen or young adult hangout, are basketball courts located at a distance from children's play equipment?

76. Are drinking fountains near all game courts?

77. Are courts placed away from high or overhanging trees, to reduce the maintenance required for pruning, leaf removal, and so forth?

78. Are courts away from any park buildings, so as to avoid damage by stray balls to windows or lighting fixtures?

79. Are jacket pegs and equipment storage areas near the courts?

80. Has night lighting of courts been considered, to extend usable time and to make the park safer in the evenings by encouraging its use?

81. Are there some areas, not necessarily large, for sunbathing, with a southeastern exposure and protection from the prevailing wind?

82. Is there a choice between somewhat secluded sunbathing areas and more public ones?

83. Is there at least one sizable, relatively flat area?

84. Has a packed-earth jogging trail been considered? A par course?

85. In areas with snowy winters, are slopes designed to accommodate picnicking and sunbathing in summer and sledding or tobogganing in winter? Are slowing-down and stopping distances free of obstruction or conflicting use?

86. Where temperatures drop below freezing in winter, has the possibility been considered of flooding a sizable flat area and using it as an outdoor skating rink?

87. Are picnic areas relatively near parking, to allow easy transportation of food and equipment, yet adequately removed or screened from instrusive parking lot activity?

88. Is there easy and pleasant access to the picnic area for those coming to the park on foot?

89. Is the picnic area attractive and comfortable, using planting, trellises, or gazebos to define and partially enclose the area?

90. If much picnicking is anticipated, have picnic tables been placed on a hard surface to prevent erosion? If picnicking is likely to be moderate or light, has the ground surface been left as grass or dirt?

91. Have picnic tables been placed upwind from the barbecue grills, to avoid smoke problems?

92. Are trash receptacles, a source of water, and grills available close to the tables?

93. Have oversized trash cans been provided where pick-up is infrequent?

94. Are trash receptacles securely fastened or anchored to prevent being overturned by children, dogs, or wildlife?

95. Are there some picnic tables near the tot lot, to allow young children to play within sight of the picnicking adults and to provide a work surface for the supervising adults at other times?

96. Are there shelters at bus stops and near picnic tables, game courts, and tot lots, to permit use of the park in inclement weather? Depending on climate, are there shelters for many users to be sheltered briefly from thundershowers?

Unconventional Park Activities

97. Has the creation of a ''dogs only'' section in the park been considered?

98. Is there provision for cycling, skateboarding, and roller skating in the park?

99. Are there bicycle racks in easily observable locations near high-activity areas and play equipment?

100. Are there separate paths for pedestrians and wheeled sports, or, at the least, walkways wide enough to accommodate simultaneous use and marked to show which side is intended for which use?

101. Have special courses been considered for bicyclists, skateboarders, and roller skaters, incorporating mounds, banked curves, and so on?

Antisocial Activities

102. Has the park been made so attractive to legitimate users that its heavy use will discourage antisocial activities?

103. Will an official gardener or groundskeeper be present in the park, to lend an air of authority and safety?

104. Does the park operate as a shortcut between two streets, to increase the number of people walking through and providing casual surveillance?

105. If illegitimate use of the park after-hours is expected, does it have attractive fencing and gates that can be locked during those times?

106. Are park facilities planned and located to avoid proximity of potentially conflicting uses, often the cause of vandalism?

107. Is there adequate access to the park, to avoid damaged fences, trampled planting, and the like?

108. Rather than one flat open space, are there a variety of spaces that can be claimed as territory by different groups to avoid conflict that may lead to abuse?

109. Are permanent fixtures such as benches, barbecues, and trash receptacles located where they will not provide climbable access to park building roofs?

110. Are gates or removable bollards used to block direct vehicle access to internal park roads, making theft and destruction of property more difficult?

111. Are men's and women's restroom entries located on the same side of the building, to increase casual surveillance, and are restrooms situated where they are not immediately accessible from park entrances?

112. Has an effort been made to avoid direct sight lines from main park access points and building windows or skylights, to decrease their target potential? Have especially vulnerable windows been made from plexiglas or covered with wire mesh?

113. Have public areas that are closed at certain times been fenced?

114. Have high, solid walls that reduce visibility been avoided?

115. Are walls and fences made of materials that can be easily cleaned and/or painted?

116. Has dark-colored, exposed-aggregate concrete—which discourages graffiti—been considered for especially vulnerable walls?

117. Have large expanses of light-colored, smooth material been avoided?

118. Has any unnecessary fencing been eliminated, to reduce users' frustration or irritation?

119. Have benches been placed along paths so as to discourage cutting across plant beds?

120. Has light-colored wood, treated with a material such as varathane, been used for picnic tables, to discourage carving?

121. Have heavy-duty trash receptacles been provided?

122. If standard garbage cans are provided, have they been placed in another receptacle, such as a wooden box, which blends in with the park's surroundings?

123. In a redesign, have more trash receptacles been provided in areas that have serious litter problems?

124. Do park signs avoid large white background areas, which invite graffiti?

125. Have heavy timber signposts been used, which are difficult to remove?

126. Have signs been attached flush along the post and, where more than one sign is used, attached to each other, to prevent their removal?

127. Are young trees protected by substantial guards?

128. Has an edging material such as concrete block or cobblestone been used to reinforce lawns at path intersections and along shortcuts?

129. Have faceted rather than globe light fixtures been used, to minimize target potential?

130. Has a community-created mural, or other more spontaneous artwork, been incorporated into the park, to discourage less-acceptable graffiti?

131. Has quick and efficient maintenance been planned and budgeted, to stop the vicious cycle of abuse, neglect, and misuse or nonuse?

132. Has consideration been given to offering financial incentives to youth groups that help prevent damage—often cheaper than repair and replacements?

133. If vandalism has been an ongoing problem, has there been an attempt to identify the perpetrators and to address solutions to that particular group?

134. Has special programming—dances, cultural celebrations—been considered to increase park use (and natural surveillance) as well as community pride in the park?

135. Is there a reporting system that will identify damage caused by poor design, rather than intention, to allow ongoing redesign?

136. Are there arrangements for police patrol of the park—preferably on foot or horseback and by officers familiar with the neighborhood—to increase perceived safety and use?

137. Have the operating hours of any recreation facilities been planned to coincide as closely as possible with demand, to avoid vandalism caused by frustration or unauthorized use?

3

MINIPARKS AND VEST-POCKET PARKS

*Clare Cooper Marcus, with
Nanine Hilliard Greene*

The history of small neighborhood parks in the United States is coming full circle. In Philadelphia in the early 1960s, students and faculty of the landscape architecture department at the University of Pennsylvania undertook an inventory of trash-ridden vacant lots and backyards. From this began a program called Neighborhood Commons, an effort to work with the citizens of low-income neighborhoods to reclaim these lots for gardens, sitting, and play areas and as land that would be owned, used, and controlled by the neighborhood (Linn 1968). But without the strong neighborhood organizations that have grown up since, the first Neighborhood Commons was bulldozed away for a school site and municipal agencies in Philadelphia began building what came to be called *vest-pocket* or *miniparks,* with federal and foundation money. Other cities followed suit.

The early miniparks were photographed and imitated across the country, but without serious evaluation (Clay 1971, 1972). Although most agreed on their size —somewhere between one and four house lots—there was, and is, some confusion over their purpose. Are they scaled-down versions of neighborhood parks? Are they primarily playgrounds, seating plazas for the el-

Vacant lots in low-income neighborhoods are often informally appropriated for social purposes, as this one in Philadelphia was in the 1960s. (Photo: Nanine Hilliard Greene)

derly, aesthetic green spaces in dense neighborhoods, or a little bit of each? Few directives or discussions of their design appeared in the professional literature; no official attempts were made to make available to one city the experience of others. A notable exception was the 1969 Workshop on Urban Open Space sponsored by the American Society of Landscape Architects Foundation. From this conference came a booklet and several articles that communicated to the users, city department personnel, and the funders just how complex the work actually was (ASLA 1969). According to a 1972 *Architectural Forum* article:

Numerous playgrounds and miniparks have been built simply because a lot was vacant. Demolished buildings, riots, fires, even private owners who don't want to cut their weeds, have caused in some cities a building boom in miniparks, more to tidy up the neighborhood than fit a daily need of either children or adults. Small parks have been a way for "city hall" to give evidence it is doing something while delays were occurring in more difficult programs such as housing. . . . In St. Louis, a misplaced $15,000 vest pocket park was returned to a parking area—for a second $15,000. (Clay 1972, p. 36)

Another article described how styles revealed the origins of these parks:

Those funded by wealthy foundations tend to be monumental, gratifying to the donor certainly, but tying up enormous sums of money in whimsical equipment. . . . Others, done by designers and students, tend to be furnished with gimmicky playshapes. Some, examples of neighborhood self-help or youth work, lie half-finished—badly planned, over-ambitious, unnecessarily difficult or dull to build. . . . Those sponsored by ladies' block or garden clubs have planted tender shrubs and flowers so vulnerable they must be caged in chain link fences and often don't survive one summer. . . . What all have in common is that after a few weeks or months of newness they are deadly dull. (Clay 1971, p. 24)

The name *minipark* is relative: In the big cities of New York and Philadelphia, a minipark may be only twenty feet wide. In Texas, one minipark turned out to be three acres. But usually they are one to three lots in size. They have ranged in cost from millions of dollars for Paley Park in New York, built with private funds on high-rent commercial land, to a few hundred dollars if built with volunteer labor and donated materials on leased land. In general, miniparks in midwestern and western U.S. cities are larger than those on the East Coast simply because lots are larger in less dense cities, and patches of undeveloped land still exist.

The usual design has included all or most of the following:

1. Planting or trees
2. A place for adults to sit
3. A place for children to play
4. Identifying logos: a mural, a name, a color scheme, or whatever
5. A basketball net
6. Sometimes areas large enough to play group games

Trying to include all these facilities in a very small park has led to problems, which we will discuss later.

Whatever their size or design, the difficulty of getting funds for programs or maintenance after they have been built has resulted in many miniparks' falling into decay or disuse. It thus would be advisable for a designer to review the fate of miniparks and vest-pocket parks in his or her own city in order to learn from the experience of others. Successful ones may have some local appeal not documented in this book; unsuccessful ones may have disappeared entirely. The great value of the land for other uses has also shortened the life of some miniparks and community gardens. Now, the aim of neighborhood organizations to construct small neighborhood parks and gardens, especially those on leased land in low-income neighborhoods, is again taking root in many communities. As Lisa Cashdan observed in 1982, "New York City now owns some 3,000 acres of vacant land. Rather than seeking to generate income by selling property that has measurable economic value as open space, the city could sell or lease some of this land—as open space—to community groups" (Cashdan, Stein, and Wright 1982, p. 90). The Trust for Public Land is one of the organizations that provides advice and financial help to neighborhood organizations trying to secure such small open spaces.

More than in almost any other open space plan, the designers of a vest-pocket or minipark will have to understand the neighborhood's social and political complexities. Because they are providing for a wide range of ages and habits of the people who may use the park at different times of day or night, they may want to get help from "facilitators" in recruiting representatives from the neighborhood, who can help the group make decisions about control, use, and design. This book offers some design possibilities. As Mark Francis, Lisa Cashdan, and Lynn Paxson reported, "The projects where groups felt they received good design assistance were ones where the designer played a facilitator role, provided options for the group to choose from, communicated the implications of each design decision, and became advocate for the group. The designers that were less successful tended to try to dominate and control the design process" (1984, p. 197).

DESIGN RECOMMENDATIONS

The research for this book was done mainly in California in the San Francisco Bay Area between 1975 and 1982. Miniparks were a significant feature of Joseph

A heavily overdesigned minipark of the 1960s that attracted design magazine photographers but had little play value. (Photo: Nanine Hilliard Greene)

Alioto's mayoral campaign in San Francisco in 1967, and after his inauguration, approximately twenty miniparks sprang up in the city, administered by the mayor's office and frequently featured in Sunday newspaper supplements. Meanwhile, in Berkeley, with less political fanfare, the Parks and Recreation Department built ten miniparks between 1972 and 1982.

Readers are cautioned to use the following recommendations only as guides, as the specific needs of a neighborhood, the dictates of the physical site, and the available budget for construction and subsequent maintenance may often take precedence.

Site Selection

Normally a minipark should be sited so that users from a four-block radius can walk to it without crossing a major street. The location of a minipark is crucial because whatever goes on around the park determines its use, the types of users, and their times of use and activities. A park can serve a great variety of users only if it is located where its potential users are concentrated: near high-density housing, activity centers, stores, and transportation. For example, in an area of neighborhood stores, a minipark next to a coin laundry may become a play place for children; if near a post office, it may be a meeting place for neighbors; and if near offices, factories, take-out food stores, it may become a lunch place. Even the roofs of buildings (such as the Oakland Museum) have been turned into small parks. A park to serve a specific user group (e.g., preschoolers) should be located only where there is a demonstrated need for it. A park built just to fill a vacant lot is a waste of public or private funds.

Sites not within walking distance of potential users may be suitable for specialized use. A park providing facilities not found elsewhere attracts users from a larger area, as well as those in the neighborhood. Some examples are tennis and handball courts or rented garden plots. An example in San Francisco is the Seward Street minipark, where a double, extralong concrete slide winds down a very steep lot, attracting children and their parents from all over the city as well as from the local neighborhood (see *Landscape Architecture*, October 1974).

If possible, plan the location and programming of miniparks in conjunction with neighborhood traffic plans. For example, a very small minipark can be considerably enhanced if it is situated approximately mid-block and extends into and across the street, thereby closing the street to through traffic. This not only offers an attractive and functional traffic diverter but also makes a small minipark more visible from nearby blocks.

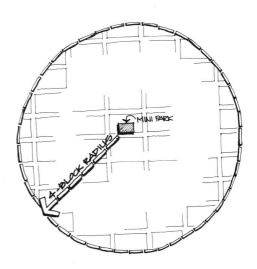

Few minipark users will walk more than four blocks, and most will come from a one- to two-block radius.

Deciduous trees let winter sunshine into this well-designed Berkeley, California, minipark. Note the sand play area, child-sized tables, drinking fountain, night lighting, and gated entry.

Consider how to capitalize on the existing topography while still meeting the neighborhood's demands. A site with existing mature trees and varied topography seems larger and can be developed more easily for walking, sunning, picnicking, and so on. A hilly site has possibilities for an amphitheater, snow, or earth slides. A flat, empty site is more easily used for paved walks for the elderly and disabled persons, children riding tricycles, and parents pushing baby carriages. If a site cannot be designed for its near neighborhood, it probably should not become a minipark at all. That is, if it attracts only people from outside the neighborhood, then questions of strangers, traffic, car parking will have to be addressed.

The designer should consider the microclimate in regard to a park's use in all types of weather. A park that is sunny and sheltered is used more frequently and attracts more parents with young children than does one that is windy or too cool or too hot. Parents prefer to sit and watch their young children in a comfortable place in both winter and summer. However, in a neighborhood with a great need for recreation space, a minipark will probably be used by six- to twelve-year-olds and teenagers, whatever the microclimate is.

Location and Size

There are essentially three basic locations for urban miniparks—corner lots, mid-block lots, or through-the-block lots. The site design of a corner lot should capitalize on its exposure to passersby on two of its four sides, by providing (1) a number of access points and, in particular, a pathway allowing the minipark to be used as a shortcut across the corner; (2) a fence or boundary design that allows controlled access and doubles as a bench, so that passersby can sit and rest facing the street, perhaps at a bus stop; and (3) where appropriate, planting to give a green experience to passing motorists.

A mid-block lot has both advantages and disadvantages. Among the disadvantages are an entrance onto the street that is perhaps only one house-lot wide and can easily be passed by without noticing that a park is there; and a lot that may be so long, narrow, and enclosed that the far end is rarely used. On a mid-block lot with only one entrance point (i.e., the park does not go through the block), a site that is about two and a half to four times as long as it is wide feels comfortable, whereas one that is about five or six times as long as it is wide can feel very uncomfortable, and the end one-third of the park may be rarely used (Cooper Marcus 1975). Among the advantages are that a mid-block lot may be quieter if it is designed for older people and more protected from traffic if it is designed for small children. It also may be more protected from the wind.

The advantages of a through-the-block lot are that it can connect two streets and may allow children and adults to walk more directly between home and school, shops, or friends. A through-the-block minipark may also connect two neighborhoods. Its disadvantages are that it may become a throughway for speeding bikes or a place of territorial conflict between rivals from different streets.

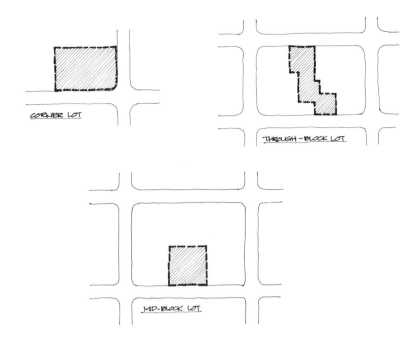

Three typical minipark locations.

A mid-block minipark, one house lot wide. From the street, this park is barely visible.

Design Program

In order to find out who the users of a minipark might be, the designer must analyze the area within a four-block radius of the park's site. Studies have shown that almost all the users of miniparks come on foot (Bangs and Mahler 1971; Gold 1972; Mason, Forrester, and Hermann 1975). Children will not walk a long way to reach a playground because they prefer to play near their homes and because they usually play in short intervals, after school and before dinner, after dinner and before bedtime, and so on, and so they do not have time for a long walk. Also, old people will not usually use a park unless it is very close by, as walking is often more diffi-

cult for them than for younger people. Interviews at Berkeley's miniparks revealed that by far the most frequently cited reason for going to a particular minipark was its convenience and closeness to home (Mason, Forrester, and Hermann 1975).

A design program should provide for those user groups who most need recreation space. In a detailed user study of six Berkeley miniparks, the chief user groups were (in order of importance) six- to twelve-year-olds, teenagers, and little children and their parents. The elderly rarely used miniparks. Observations in San Francisco indicated moderate use by the elderly, but only if (1) the park were very close to where they lived, (2) there were seats at or close to the entrance, and (3) the park had not been taken over by large groups of children or teenagers who made the elderly feel unwelcome (Cooper Marcus 1975).

After the area has been analyzed and after a cross section of people from the area have communicated their needs, the designers should assign priorities of use and try to reduce possible conflicts among user groups. For example, if the site is quite small and close to residences, it might be appropriate to exclude activities like basketball, which may create too much noise. A Berkeley minipark that had a half basketball court at its entrance and a lawn behind it attracted exclusively six- through eighteen-year-olds (almost all male). The noise of their play and the reverberations of a poorly designed metal basketball hoop and backboard caused

considerable resentment in the neighborhood. Even though there was seating and a sandbox at the back of the park, no preschoolers or elderly ever used the park because they felt uncomfortable sharing such a small site filled with ball players. In addition, the tot lot was out of view of the street and thus was often used for dealing drugs. This minipark was eventually redesigned: The original tot-lot portion was sold to a neighbor; the basketball area was removed (a neighborhood park with ample facilities was only three blocks away); and a new tot lot and sitting area were built close to the entrance. The minipark's use thereupon changed almost exclusively to small children, their parents, and the elderly.

If teenagers are known to be a group in need, it might be more appropriate to provide for their active games at a neighborhood park rather than a minipark, as they are more mobile than are younger children or the elderly. An active games area could be scaled down for younger children (i.e., shortened hoops, smaller areas) and would cause older children to seek full-scale equipment elsewhere. But if, for example, a small corner site is near moderately noisy traffic and/or non-residential buildings, it might well be developed exclusively for teenage basketball use. Indeed, if the only available lot in a dense urban area is being used for basketball by teenagers and adults, it may be answering more social needs than it would if redesigned for older people or younger children.

The elderly feel fairly comfortable near preschoolers and their parents, but not so comfortable close to older active children. If seating for the elderly is needed, place a clearly defined seating area at the entrance—with a choice of view into or out of the park—and place active areas as far away as possible.

In another Berkeley example in which the neighborhood sponsoring a new minipark wished to discourage its use at lunchtime by students at a high school one block away, it fenced the park on the sides closest to the high school. But the students came anyway, as an attractive play structure set in a large lawn was a good place for hanging out (Mason, Forrester, and Hermann 1975). A better solution might have been to negotiate with the school for more lunchtime facilities on the campus or on a vacant lot. Although designers may not agree with the demand for exclusive use, they should recognize that neighborhoods actively involved in the development of their own park may have strong territorial feelings about its use.

Community involvement in the design process is essential to a minipark's success. The minipark is a community facility, and the community generally knows best what it needs; designers should not impose their own values onto it. Residents will be able to identify with a park that the community has helped construct and so may be more inclined to use and take care of it (Mason, Forrester, and Hermann 1975).

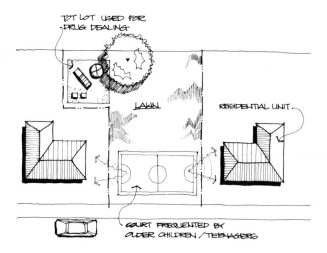

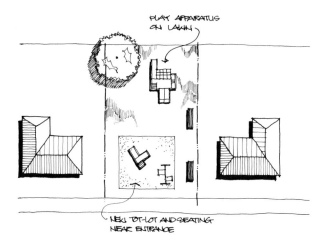

A Berkeley, California, minipark (top) originally designed with a basketball court at its entrance created noise problems and prevented parents and preschoolers from walking to a play area at the back of the lot. A successful redesign (bottom) moved the basketball court to a local neighborhood park, sold off the troublesome "out-of-sight" corner, and placed a tot lot with adult seating at the entrance.

Neighborhood involvement in actual construction is entirely feasible at the minipark scale, provided that the design can be carried out by nonskilled labor (Hewes and Beckwith 1974, Hogan 1974). However, a number of miniparks built in the late 1960s were never finished because the designer did not estimate correctly the amount of time that volunteer labor was willing to devote to the park. In order to complete the park with a sense of success, the construction effort should be concentrated into a relatively brief time-period. The park is much more likely to become a neighborhood focal point if neighbors worked together on its construction.

Prepare for both unplanned and planned consequences of the design. A design does not always function as envisioned; for example, an unplanned-for user group may start to use the facility. To accommodate such events, the budget should provide payments over a number of years, to make modifications and to allow the park to evolve with the needs of the neighborhood.

Allow for continuous feedback on the use of the park. The designers, for example, might be retained semipermanently for a small annual fee to modify the design in response to feedback from (1) neighborhood meetings called perhaps two or three times a year to discuss the park; (2) user studies of the park if the budget allows them; (3) casual observations of park use by client and designer; (4) regular reports on maintenance problems and use (and abuse) of the park by the gardeners, maintenance crew, or play leaders.

Leave unplanned areas for later modification as park use becomes established and predictable. A small portion of the park left in, perhaps, low-maintenance ground cover or as a dirt-digging area can be modified later to accommodate an unforeseen need. In one example, a portion of a Berkeley minipark next to a house that

was to be used as a community meeting place was left in low-maintenance ground cover until the needs associated with that structure become apparent.

Entrance

A small entrance plaza is essential to a minipark in a pedestrian-oriented, urban setting. Observations indicate that many adult passersby may wish to stop and rest for a while, watching the passing street activity, without actually entering the minipark. An example in San Francisco (at 24th and Bryant) has a brick-surfaced set back from the busy sidewalk, with wide backless benches facing onto the street and into the park, where people stop to sit or sometimes to sleep. Another alternative is to place some benches on the edge of the park facing out to the street and others on the curb side of the sidewalk facing into the park, thus giving passersby who wish to rest, a choice of two orientations.

A nameplate for the park and a community bulletin board are helpful. A nameplate identifies the park as a public space and tells the users about the organization responsible for its maintenance. A community bulletin board can aid communication among neighborhood residents and groups. The nameplate might be part of an entrance sculpture or totem, part of which could also be used for notices when necessary, but that does not look empty and un-neighborly when not used, as does an empty notice board.

Some miniparks are difficult to find because they are so small. The design should "announce" the location of the park to people approaching on foot or by car, by means of, for instance, noticeable paving extending out from the park to the street and/or striking street trees along the park's street frontage. If the park is only one house lot in width and space is at a premium, con-

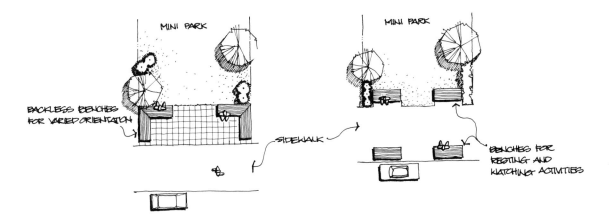

Entries to miniparks should be carefully designed to allow passing pedestrians to watch the activity while not fully entering the park. Elderly people especially appreciate these sidewalk benches.

sider extending it a short way into the street, by using the parking spaces adjacent to the entrance.

Mobile equipment should be taken into account. Depending on their size and location, some small parks are used for theater productions, concerts, and the like. Access and electrical outlets thus will be needed. For some occasions, portable toilets may be needed as well. Perhaps one parking space in front of the park could be reserved for a visiting bookmobile, a playmobile, or mobile food trucks.

Boundaries

Because of the inevitable proximity of public to private territory, the boundaries of a minipark should be clearly defined. The size of a neighborhood park often means that two or more of its boundaries are clearly defined by adjacent streets. But because a minipark is very small, two and often three sides are usually bounded by adjacent, frequently residential, properties. Consequently, if low fence boundaries mean that children can go from the park into nearby yards to play, recover lost balls, and so on, there will be complaints (Mason, Forrester, and Hermann 1975).

Because an inherent characteristic of a minipark is its very small size, every square foot should be used to advantage. "Keep-off" ground cover or shrub planting should be used only for places where people should not go. For example, there could be a border of such planting be-

tween active areas of the park and adjacent residential properties. But if the adjacent properties are industrial or commercial and children's play near or against the walls will not be a problem, "keep-off" planting should not be used, and active areas should extend right up to the property lines.

The vertical planes of surrounding buildings should be capitalized on where possible. A minipark at 24th and Bryant in San Francisco has stunning murals on three sides of its mid-block lot which add not only color to a very white/light/concrete setting but also add to its apparent size, by leading the eye out into jungle-like and riverside scenes. In contrast, the soaring white wall of an industrial building at the Howard and Langton minipark in San Francisco remains blank and useless.

If the property next to a minipark has lower floor windows that need light and maybe a filtered view, a good solution is to enclose the park with a chain-link (rather than a solid) fence and fast-growing vines. A chain-link fence with wood slats woven into it is not a good choice, as it invites children to pry the slats loose, and the fence will soon look messy. But passion flower vine, for example, in the right latitudes, can transform a chain-link fence in a short time.

Attention should be given to the park's street boundary. A low, attractive fence and perhaps a gate along the street frontage of the park might be considered in order to (1) channel pedestrian movement along pathways, (2) keep small children in, and (3) keep dogs out.

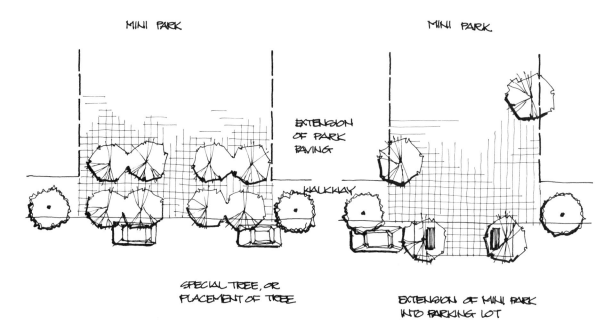

People can be attracted to a hard-to-find mid-block minipark by extending tree planting or paving from the park out to the curb or into the street itself, by appropriating one parking space.

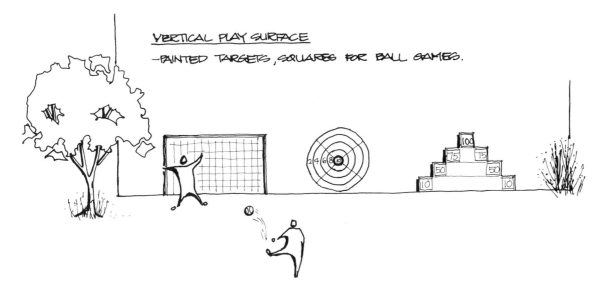

VERTICAL PLAY SURFACE
—PAINTED TARGETS, SQUARES FOR BALL GAMES.

In a small minipark, every square foot should have a use. If the adjacent buildings are not residential (factory, warehouse, storage) consideration should be given to painting murals or ball game "targets" on the buildings' walls.

An unobtrusive chain-link fence around this popular corner-location minipark in Berkeley, California, keeps small children inside and dogs outside.

Functional Areas

User spaces should take priority over visual spaces. Because a minipark is small and (one hopes) located only where it is needed, every square foot should be used carefully. The intended use of every portion should be considered —and reconsidered—and areas for aesthetic effect should always have a double purpose (e.g., trees that also cast shade where it is needed, lawns that also are comfortable for sunbathing).

Park forms should be varied and detailed, but from the entrance people should be able to see what activities and facilities are available and how to reach them.

Children's preferences for a varied, exciting environment should be respected in the design of the minipark, for they will be the predominant user group. Children prefer to play and move around in an environment that is varied and full of surprises. Children need choice and variety to retain their interest, as they rarely are engaged for long in one activity. While engaged in fantasy play they need some secluded places and places to hide. They also like to explore the natural world through plants, earth, rocks, water, and insects. The site plan should reflect this by being irregular, with as great a

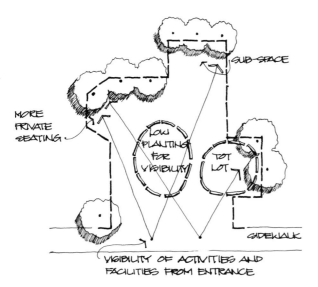

Prospective users should be able to see the facilities available in the park and how to reach them from the entrance.

Noisy and energetic ball games do not mix easily with preschool play areas on a small site. If basketball is provided for in a nearby school yard or neighborhood park, it should be excluded from a minipark. (Photo: Nanine Hilliard Greene)

variety of spaces, surfaces, levels, and plant materials as possible (Cooper Marcus and Sarkissian 1986).

Give special consideration to the positioning of noisy, ball-playing activities. In Berkeley minipark interviews, noise and broken windows were found to be the most frequent complaints of people living close to the parks (Mason, Forrester, and Hermann 1975). In this regard, therefore, consider (1) excluding noisy activities from the park design altogether, (2) situating noisy activities where they will give the least offense or be most likely to be screened out by nearby traffic or industrial noise, and (3) protecting nearby windows by means of fences or planting.

Provide some passive, "secret" places away from the street. Secluded areas offer space for intimate conversation or solitude. Children of all ages need to explore and fantasize by themselves, and teenagers, especially, need privacy. They need a place to talk, show off and flirt, but it should not be so secluded that the place is unsafe.

The overall site design should facilitate use of the park by people with disabilities. All miniparks should be designed to remove architectural barriers to people with disabilities. For example, there should be no steps without a parallel ramp for a wheelchair, and paths should be wide and level enough to accommodate people using wheelchairs and walkers.

Bicycles should be considered in the design. The designers should decide at the preliminary site-planning stage whether bicycles are to be included or excluded from the site. If they are to be included, paths should be wide and smooth and the corners gradual. If they are to be excluded, there needs to be some means of discouraging their entry into the park without, at the same time, precluding entry by a person using a wheelchair. In either case, raised planting edges can help prevent shortcutting, and bicycle racks should be provided at all entrances to the park.

Play Areas

Because children and teenagers are usually the chief users of a minipark in a residential area, it is crucial that the location and design of play areas be carefully considered. Traditionally in neighborhood parks, play areas for tots and older children have been separate. For a larger minipark (four to six house lots in size), this may still be desirable, but for a small minipark it may be best to have one combined play equipment area with parts of it (because of height, distance between steps on a ladder, distance of swing seat from ground) out of reach of younger children. The area thus could be vertically separated for older and younger children. Or, as often happens in play areas, there may be a temporal separation, with the younger children using the area more often in the morning, the older children after school and in the evenings.

Children usually do not try activities before they are physically ready for them. Designers frequently underestimate children's ability to engage in certain activities at certain ages: For example, observations of a play structure at a housing development in San Francisco revealed children as young as eighteen months or two years scaling a fifteen-foot play tower and safely descending to the ground by means of a long slide (Cooper Marcus 1975). If such equipment is designed for the smallest or most timid children, older children will view it as boring and try to use it in potentially dangerous ways. Rather, the key to designing a play structure to be used by both young and older children is the notion of graduated challenge; a range of climbing, swinging, sliding, and balancing activities can be undertaken successively by children as they grow older and become more skilled (Dattner 1969).

If the lot is so small that only one play area can be provided, it is probably better to locate it toward the back of the lot. Such a location will ensure (1) safety from traffic for young children, (2) privacy for older children and teenagers who may use it in the evenings, and (3) privacy for elderly users at the entrance area to the park.

However, a play area at the back of a deep or L-shaped lot may lead to problems such as use for antisocial or illegal activities.

If the park is large enough for two separate play areas and/or if the neighborhood indicates a strong need for this separation (i.e., large numbers of older children and younger children sent to park on their own), there may be some merit to locating the older children's area toward the back of the park. Older children tend to gravitate to the back of such spaces for privacy. Parents say that they feel happier about sending their small children to a park alone if (1) their play area is separate and they are therefore less likely to be roughed up by older children, (2) if the younger ones' area is at the front of the park and they do not have to go past the older children's area to get there, and (3) if its front location makes it visible from a number of nearby homes (Mason, Forrester, and Hermann 1975).

A play area exclusively for small children, or a portion of a larger play area intended for mixed ages, should have the following qualities: (1) Some scaled-down play equipment, especially slides, swings, climbing blocks, or platforms, is especially important to children aged

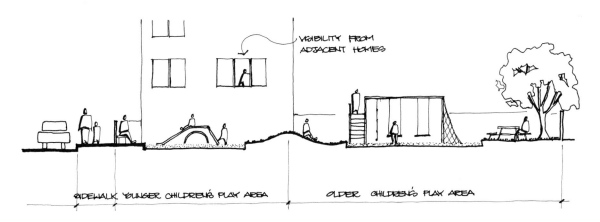

If a minipark is large enough for two play areas, the one for younger children should be located nearer the entrance.

A play area for small children should provide sand for manipulative play and for jumping into; bench or "lip" edges to enable adults to sit close by; hard surfaces for tricycles and wagons; and grass areas for running, rolling, or resting.

three years and up. (2) Sand under and around the play equipment serves as both a safety measure and a play resource for small children. A water spigot in the sand area or a water fountain nearby are most important, as sand as a play resource is much improved when it is wet. (3) The sand pit should be in the sun so that it can dry quickly after a rainstorm. It should also be sheltered from the wind to prevent the sand from blowing away. Moreover, a sand pit with nothing but sand in it will rarely, if ever, be used; therefore be sure to put climbing and swinging equipment in the sand area. A platform area that creates a shaded spot beneath which sand remains damp and malleable is an especially attractive spot for small children. A cautionary note: Do not put sand near a feature that invites breaking bottles, as the glass will have to be sifted out of the sand. (4) The sand area should be well drained and sunk six to eight inches below grade, with steps and a ramp going into it, to prevent too much sand from being blown or tracked out. A boundary that in places doubles as a wide bench seat is a great asset. Children or adults can chose to sit facing in or out of the tot area; children in the sand area can make sand pies on the bench, run model cars along it, and so on; it can also form a substantial barrier to prevent tots from easily getting out, dogs getting in, or older children riding their bikes through. This kind of boundary is preferable to, say, a four-foot chain link fence, which gives an area a cage-like appearance and is probably more of a barrier than is called for. (5) Benches for supervising adults should be placed in various locations around the toddlers' play area so that they can choose to be in the sun or shade, close to the children at play, or whatever. (6) One section of the tot-lot area should be hard

surfaced for small wheel toys, tricycles, and wagons. A circular path allows tricyclers to ride around and back to their parents. (7) Grass for rolling on should ideally be planted on a small incline.

Play equipment should be chosen with children's preferences in mind. Children enjoy play equipment on which they can use their motor skills, and on which they can have pleasurable kinesthetic experiences (Moore 1974b). Examples of such equipment are swings, slides, climbing structures, seesaws, monkey bars, and rings. The key is variety, as children move quickly from one activity to another and will quickly become bored in a park that provides only one or two forms of equipment. For example, one expensively designed minipark in San Francisco's Chinatown was rarely used by children when the total provision for play was two slides, some climbing logs, and sand. From observations of many miniparks in the Bay Area, it became clear that there is a close relationship between the variety of equipment in a minipark and the park's use. In one San Francisco example with just a square sandbox and nothing else for children, the park was used very little; another park, with a great variety of wooden forts, bridges, play towers, and the like, attracted many children. In fact, this relationship is so apparent that it seems safe to say that because miniparks are used predominantly by children and because children demand a great variety of play experiences, it is a waste of money to provide a minipark with no equipment or to locate one on such a small site that only equipment prompting a few activities can be provided.

Conventional or home-made equipment may be a better buy than expensive catalog pieces. All of our observations indicate that simple wooden climbing structures with

A concrete edge around a sand-filled play area prevents the sand from spilling out and provides a convenient place for an adult to sit close to playing preschoolers.

platforms at different levels and maybe a tire swing are much more often used than are expensive catalog pieces like "Walt Disney" horses on springs or Swiss Cheese cylinders. Also, construction costs can be reduced by using local labor. Telephone poles, railroad ties, old tires, and rope can also be made into marvelous play equipment (Hewes and Beckwith 1974, Hogan 1974). In one Berkeley minipark (Acton Street) a simply designed wooden play structure built by local residents cost only $600 (1975) in materials, whereas one for older children erected by a construction company at the same time cost $5,500 in materials and labor. For long-term use, it may sometimes be worth installing PVC-coated pipe-and-chain equipment combined with wooden structures, all of which should be inspected regularly for loose bolts, dry rot, or other signs of damage and deterioration.

Playgrounds should include elements that trigger children's imagination. Children need simple equipment that they can use to fill many roles. Therefore, a series of complex platforms, ladders, and rope swings is preferable to a catalog "rocket ship," as the former can become anything—a house, ship, fire engine, airplane —whereas the latter can be only a rocket ship.

Swings are almost always the most popular equipment in terms of frequency of use. Therefore if the budget is limited, provide these above all else. A tire swing that rotates is also popular, as it requires cooperative play.

Slides are used by all age groups. If the space or budget has room for only one slide, a high and longer one is best, as smaller children can be placed lower down the slide by their parents. Where possible, use topographical changes to make built-in slides.

Secret hiding places for children can easily be made on a minipark site. Children sometimes need a place of their own. A cement pipe can make a fine little house and can also be used as a place to learn about echoes. In Europe, small houses on a child's scale are provided at many park sites. Shrubs should also be considered for their "hideout" possibilities.

Children love water and are attracted to the smallest puddle. A small spray pool or pond might be provided on the site; it need not be elaborate or large. If this is not possible, a portable pool could be carried to various miniparks in hot weather, or the maintenance crew could be instructed to turn on the sprinklers in part of the park at peak times on hot days.

Children's greatest pleasures seem to come from manipulating very simple objects in the environment and creating their own "landscapes" from malleable materials. Because children will always find places to dig, a minipark should provide for this activity in (1) a sand area with a water source nearby and (2) a dirt area, perhaps under shrubs like rhododendrons that children can crawl under and that shade out ground cover. Because sticks, stones, twigs, leaves, small plastic containers, and the like can be the essential "bricks and mortar" of children's "landscaping" or "cake-making" enterprises, the maintenance crew should be discouraged from being too meticulous in picking up loose materials or "rubbish."

Children like to sit and talk, too. Child-sized tables and benches allow children to talk and play; there is no reason that a play place has to put all its emphasis on big-muscle play, as socializing may also be a reason for coming to the park.

Children are often just as intrigued by an old tree stump or a fallen tree as they are by expensive play equipment. (Photo: Nanine Hilliard Green)

Plant Materials

All plant materials should be potential resources for children. It is impossible to generalize about plant materials in a country with as many different climates as the United States has. It is also difficult to make suggestions about plants that apply to different cities and neighborhoods. For instance, in the deep humid South, greenery grows almost without assistance, and the problem is keeping it pruned. But in tiny lots in New York City it may be almost impossible to grow anything in the shadow of tall buildings or where use is so heavy that no plant can survive. In such a case, a minipark might be treated like a Mediterranean plaza, with interesting paving, sitting places, and gazebos.

The choice of trees on the site should be made with several criteria in mind. The trees should be climbable. If the site is barren and small trees must be planted, they should be well staked. In this case, it might be advisable to provide a large dead tree to be used for climbing until the young trees are strong enough for such use. Deciduous trees are preferable for two reasons: They provide needed shade during the summer and allow full exposure during the winter months, and they mark the seasons. Consider using fruit trees, as they provide color in spring time and fruit for adventurous climbers later in the year.

Trees must be located to provide some shaded sitting areas, on both benches and grass areas. In urban locations with considerable glare from surrounding sidewalks, buildings, and roadways, it is essential to provide shady spots to sit and rest. In one San Francisco minipark planted with only three spindly trees (and one had died), adults frequently clustered in and around the other two on hot days, leaving 95 percent of the park unused. In an example in Berkeley, the only trees planted in the park were situated so as to cast shade on a ground cover area that could not be used on a hot day. Trees planted around the boundary of a minipark can provide a nice frame and screen out adjacent buildings, if this is considered desirable.

Children too often need shaded areas to play in during hot seasons of the year, whereas some adults at the same time may like to sunbathe on open lawn areas. Because miniparks tend to be more heavily used in the afternoon than in the morning, plan the location of trees for shade at that time of day, especially during the summer.

Design tree wells with care. Tree wells should be set into hard-surface areas so that the dirt will not spill out and create a messy appearance, which can easily lead to littering, as users may feel that no one cares about the place. The tree wells in one park in San Francisco were flush with the surrounding concrete which was a continual mess of sand and dirt. A more successful arrangement is unmortared brick paving around the tree bases so that dirt is not washed or blown out and children on tricycles can ride across it, but this solution should not be used where loose bricks might be vandalized.

Vegetation is much appreciated by city dwellers even if they do not actually use the park. Kevin Lynch found that people feel a strong sentimental attachment to tiny patches of green in the city. Commuters described how they would take a longer route to work to drive past a favorite park or garden (Lynch 1960). People in cars are rarely counted as park users, but drivers, also, value green spaces highly. Thus lawns and leafy street trees should be placed near the street frontage of the park.

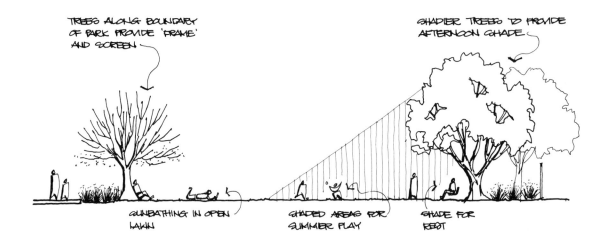

Trees should be carefully selected to "announce" the presence of a minipark at its entrance, to offer shade on hot summer afternoons, to provide trunks to lean against, and, where safe, to be climbed by small children.

Ground covers used specifically to keep people off should never be planted in as small a site as a minipark unless there is some compelling reason that people should be kept off a particular section of the site. Ground covers principally for show have no place in a minipark, unless it is a passive park intended only for sitting and looking.

All plant materials must be tough, impervious to trampling, fast growing, and not poisonous. Children need plants that they can use as swords, roofs for clubhouses, and so forth. Plants must be selected that are capable of bouncing back from such casual "pruning." Bamboo is a plant that is suitable as a play resource, as it is virtually indestructible.

Planted and grassed areas next to hard surfaces should have raised borders. Raised borders will prevent children from riding their bikes from hard surfaces into planted beds or over lawns. However, the border should not be so high as to prevent children from easily walking from pathways onto lawns. If the border is made of something with the width and height of, say, a railroad tie, it can double as a balancing walk for tiny children.

Surfaces

Different surfacing materials should be used for different purposes. Asphalt or another hard-surface material is preferable to dirt or sand for the main circulation route through a minipark. On such a surface, children can ride tricycles or pull wagons; adults can wheel baby carriages; and disabled people can have easy access to all areas of the minipark. During the rainy season this type of pathway will dry off quickly. Concrete may also be successful but should be used with caution in sunny urban settings where it just adds to the glare caused by sidewalks and buildings. The elderly are particularly susceptible to glare, and so if they are expected to be frequent users, pathways or sitting areas should be surfaced with brick or asphalt.

Soft surfaces (e.g., sand) should be placed under all play equipment to make falling off equipment less hazardous. Soft surfaces, such as grass, for rolling down on a slight incline, are often well used.

Carefully consider the use of lawn areas. Many designers place a sacred value on lawns, and too often they have been put in where they do not belong. Before adding a lawn to your design, therefore ask yourself the following questions:

1. Does the community really want a lawn?
2. Can a lawn be justified on a small site, bearing in mind that small lawn areas are much less heavily used than are sand, play equipment, or hard-surfaced areas?
3. Who will maintain the lawn, and will it be costly?
4. For what activities is the lawn designed?

5. Is it just leftover space that on the plan looks good filled in with green?

Some of the advantages of a lawn are the following:

1. An expanse of lawn tends to give a user or passerby more of a sense of greenery than do numbers of trees set in a hard surface, as the eye tends to take in ground-surface textures more readily.
2. Although studies indicate that children are less likely to play on grass in miniparks than on equipment or hard surfaces, a pleasantly located and sloped grass area can form an attractive place for sitting, lounging, and sunbathing.

If a lawn is included, and irrigation is necessary, the grass should be watered at night so that it will be dry and usable during the day. Recessed sprinkler heads should be used, as raised ones will curtail play, cause injuries, and invite vandalism.

Hard-surface areas should be included in miniparks designed for children's play. Observations of children in cluster housing indicate that they play more on hard surfaces than on any other kind (Cooper Marcus and Sarkissian 1986). Young children like hard-surfaced areas for riding trikes and wagons and for playing with wheeled toys. Older children use hard surfaces for ball games, running games, bike riding, hopscotch, jump rope, bouncing-ball games, roller skating, and so on. Hard-surface play areas thus should be part of the circulation system, perhaps as widened portions of the main pathway or a hard-surfaced section next to the play equipment area.

Site Furniture

Site furniture should be designed, bought, or constructed for specific users. For example, a bench suitable for an adult is not necessarily best for a child, and a bench suitable for an elderly person's rest and reflection is not necessarily the best design for a teenagers' hangout. In one San Francisco minipark (Anza and 7th) a nice addition is a low wooden footrest in front of each bench, which can also be used as a child's seat.

A drinking fountain may be desirable. A drinking fountain should have a step for younger children, or there should be another, lower fountain. A good design for a fountain is one with a water spigot on the side for filling buckets or cups or washing hands. Water needs to be accessible to children to use with sand. An ideal location for a fountain is at the edge of the sand area where overflow water will make the sand more malleable.

If the budget is limited, priorities must be determined. For example, in one San Francisco minipark, three checkers tables were installed but were rarely if ever used; on the other hand, a drinking fountain was

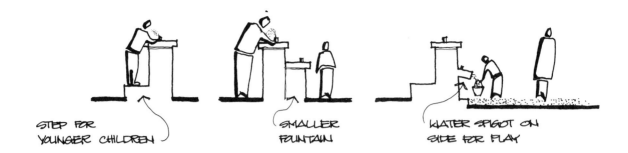

STEP FOR
YOUNGER CHILDREN

SMALLER
FOUNTAIN

WATER SPIGOT ON
SIDE FOR PLAY

Small children need to drink water more frequently than adults do. Child-sized drinking fountains are essential, and a water spigot for sand-and-water play is a welcome addition.

not provided, and a day care group that regularly uses the park finds this a great problem. Their visits, in fact, often have to be curtailed; small children need to drink much more often than adults.

Lighting may be an excellent addition to a minipark. Although few miniparks currently have lighting, it would help in the following ways: (1) The park could be used for longer periods of time, for example, by teenagers on summer evenings, and (2) it would become a safer place to walk in at night. However, if the budget is limited, play equipment, benches, and a water fountain should—except, of course, in high-crime areas— receive a higher priority than lighting does.

Litter cans are necessary. Children will not go far to throw away candy wrappers and so on, and thus litter cans should be placed throughout the site, but especially near activity areas and at the entrance or exit to the park. If there is to be a picnic area, it should have at least one can. Cans should not be able to be easily turned over by dogs or children but should be able to be easily emptied by garbage collectors or maintenance crews.

Provide multipurpose tables and benches. Minipark designers seem compelled to put in checkers tables. Observations in the San Francisco Bay Area suggest, however, that these are rarely used. Each designer should decide whether there really is a demand for checkers in the region where he or she is designing. If the demand is questionable, a much better investment is one or two regular picnic tables with a checkerboard set into one of them. There are two types of locations where picnic tables will be highly used: in a moderately high density residential area where some families in apartments have no private open space, and close to a high school or junior high school where students will gravitate to the park for lunch periods. In the latter situation, teenagers will use any play structure for socializing, eating lunch, and hanging out. Therefore, it should be sturdy enough to accommodate this behavior and have enough levels and semiprivate spaces for small peer groups to socialize together. There probably should be a hard, easily cleaned surface under the

picnic table so that food droppings can be hosed away.

If space allows, barbecues are a welcome attraction. A barbecue pit with logs around it for seating is an excellent addition to a minipark and can serve many different purposes, as a place for community fires and picnics, a stage, and a place for gathering.

In many neighborhoods a lockable bike rack should be provided near the entrance to the minipark. Children aged four and over ride bikes and trikes to miniparks. While they are playing in the park they may not want to use them, and so a safe place where they can keep them is essential. Adults and teenagers are using bikes more and more, and they also may need a bike rack.

If possible, toilets should be provided in a minipark. Children, especially, may need to use the toilet if they stay in the park for more than an hour or so. However, heavily constructed, fully plumbed toilets can be very expensive, and hence they are almost always eliminated from the program. Toilets are the most easily vandalized of all forms of park equipment and thus are impossible to provide in many neighborhoods. However, the light-weight, chemical toilets frequently used in state or regional parks are much less costly, and can be provided on special occasions. Siting, exterior painting, and planting can make toilets unobtrusive and yet accessible to park users.

A locked electrical outlet should be considered. An electrical outlet should be included only if there is a strong neighborhood demand for one, if the adjacent properties are not residential, or if nearby families are not bothered by noise.

Note: Guidelines on the design, orientation, and arrangement of benches can be found in the chapter on Neighborhood Parks.

Maintenance

An essential requirement of a minipark is that the space should be easy to care for and look neat in spite of heavy use. When planting is trampled on, path edges become worn, or shortcuts are made, the park begins to look shabby. The designer can help subsequent maintenance by restricting people to the spaces intended for them, by clearly communicating (using walls, barrier plantings) what activities are supposed to occur where and by accurately predicting circulation needs. It seems likely that people who live near a badly maintained park may feel that its poor condition reflects on the neighborhood as a whole and also on their own economic status.

It is essential that there be enough money for ongoing maintenance. The best design in the world can soon become a shambles without regular maintenance. If there is no money for continuing maintenance, the decision to provide a park in the first place should be reconsidered. A minipark that is sponsored and built by one city department, but maintained by another, is usually not a satisfactory arrangement.

If people in a neighborhood feel a sense of ownership of the park, they will take care of it and see that it is respected. People will feel that the park is their own if they are given a part in designing, building, and equipping it.

A park that is designed to be vandal-proof may defeat its own purpose and offend the users for whom it is intended. When faced with park facilities that are chained down or are constructed of monstrously heavy and immutable materials, users may feel that the park is there in spite of them, rather than for them, or that the park planners regard the users as opponents. Usually in such cases, the equipment is inflexible, uncomfortable, and unattractive. "Keep off" signs should be avoided, as they usually indicate a poor design solution and may promote the action rather than preventing it. Indeed, the signs themselves may also create a target for vandalism.

Personnel and Funding

Ideally, the budget for miniparks should be spent in increments to allow equipment and activities to be tested, to make additions or subtractions in the design, and to pay for ongoing programs and leaders. The design process should not be thought of as terminating on opening day or as concerning itself with only physical objects.

The possibilities for park activities can be increased enormously and the likelihood of vandalism correspondingly reduced if the minipark employs park play leaders. A successful program in Berkeley, California, in the 1970s had two play leaders and a playmobile ("The Great Pumpkin") shared among six of the most highly used miniparks in the city.

CASE STUDIES

Berkeley Way Minipark, Berkeley, California [1]

Location and Context

This minipark is located on Berkeley Way, just a block from University Avenue, a major thoroughfare con-

necting downtown Berkeley to the freeway. The park is located in a low- to moderate-income, racially mixed neighborhood of largely single-family houses. The traffic on Berkeley Way is relatively light, as the street terminates a block from the park.

Description

The park is a rectangular area, 0.43 acres (18,730 square feet) in size, or about four house lots. It is a flat site, open to the street along one long side and bounded by a high chain-link fence on the other three sides. The immediate neighbors to the park are two apartment buildings and a pedestrian way following a former railroad right-of-way. The park is 95 percent grass covered, with two play areas. One is a tot lot, partially enclosed by a low, vine-covered chain-link fence and containing bucket swings, and rocks set into redwood chips. The other play area—for older children—contains a large log and tubular steel play structure, set in redwood chips and bordered by seat-height wooden siding.

Major Uses and Users

The major users are neighborhood children aged approximately six to twelve, many of whom are allowed to come to the park on their own from within a three-block radius. The climbing structure is the facility most heavily used; the open grass area is large enough for ball games. A bench on the sidewalk allows older people to sit and watch the activity. According to a 1975 study, reactions to the park by users and neighbors were very positive. Over 90 percent of the park's neighbors liked living near the park, enjoyed looking over it, and considered it a "green oasis" in the neighborhood.

Successful Features

- Highly visible from street; secure
- Good balance of open grass area and play equipment
- Uninterrupted grass area permitting running and ball games
- Adjacent to a pedestrian way and bike path, facilitating safe access to park for children walking or biking alone
- Large play structures

Unsuccessful Features

- No large swings for older children
- Tot lot too small and lacking a variety of equipment
- Drainage problems in tot lot
- No seating in park; uncomfortable for parents accompanying children

[1] Compiled from reports by students Lee Bramhall, Charles Brandan, and Dennis Cadd, all written in 1975.

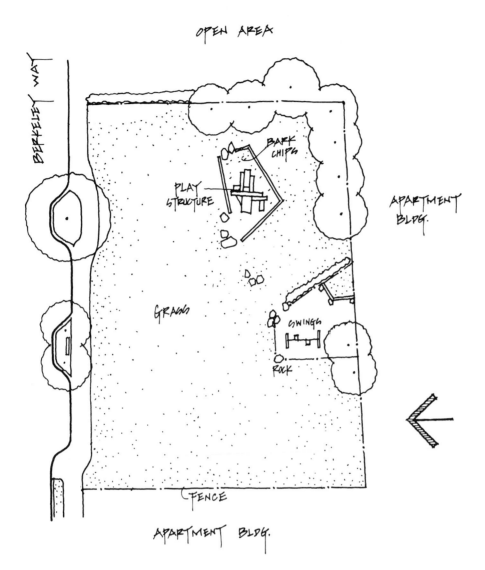

Berkeley Way Minipark,
Berkeley, California.

- No sand for playing
- No trees for shade in hot weather

Charlie Dorr Minipark, Berkeley, California [2]

Location and Context

This small park is in a largely black, low- to moderate-income residential neighborhood in the flatlands of west Berkeley. It is located on a narrow, quiet, tree-lined street of neat single-family houses. Two-story houses and their yards border the park on two sides; a Berkeley city maintenance yard is at the back of the park.

This minipark was created in 1973 after a heated protest by neighborhood residents about the lack of local open space and the renewal of a lease to the long-established Berkeley Lawn Bowling Club a block away. This club, with a clubhouse and two greens, was resented for its all-white, nonlocal membership. (Most members live in the affluent Berkeley Hills where there is no flat land.) A compromise was reached when the city of Berkeley acquired one house lot on Acton Street and created a minipark, which is named for a local resident, Charlie Dorr.

Description

The minipark is 0.22 of an acre (9,556 square feet) in size and forms a narrow slot of open space between two houses. Its narrow width fronts onto Acton Street. This narrow entrance, the adjacent houses, and lush street trees make this minipark virtually invisible. Only a small notice board and a name sign mark the entry from the sidewalk. A timber play structure with swings and a slide dominates the front of the park, and narrow asphalt paths bordered by a small patch of grass leads park users to a larger play area, a climbing structure set in sand forming the back "L" of the park.

[2] Compiled from reports by students Joe Friedlander, Terri Martin, Janet Pollock, and Sarah Sutton, all written in 1975.

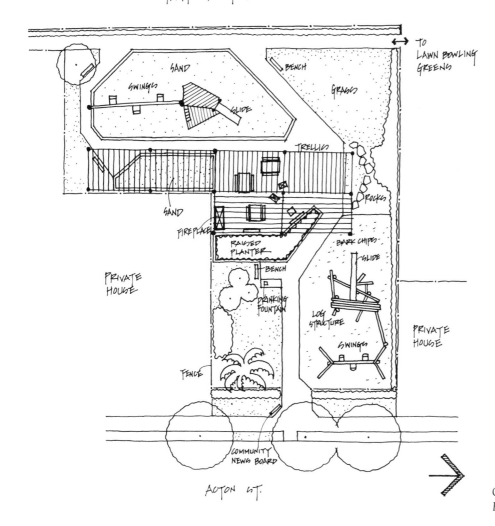

STREETS SANITATION
TRAFFIC MAINT. DIVISION

TO LAWN BOWLING GREENS

BENCH

SAND

SWINGS

GRASS

SLIDE

TRELLIS

SAND

ROCKS

FIREPLACE

RAISED PLANTER

BARK CHIPS

SLIDE

PRIVATE HOUSE

BENCH

DRINKING FOUNTAIN

LOG STRUCTURE

PRIVATE HOUSE

FENCE

SWINGS

COMMUNITY NEWS BOARD

ACTON ST.

*Charlie Dorr Minipark,
Berkeley, California.*

*A view from the back of Charlie
Dorr Minipark in Berkeley,
California, looking toward the
entrance on Acton Street. Few
use this rear play area, as it is at
a dead end. Men and teenaged
boys often use the tables under
the arbor as a hangout.*

137

An arbor that shades the seating and two picnic tables separates the front and back play areas. One bench and a drinking fountain are visible from the street. Shrubs and ground planting cover about 5 percent of the park; grass, another 5 percent; and hard surfaces (pathway and seating arbor), 12 percent. The remainder of the park is sand and redwood chip–surfaced play areas.

Major Uses and Users

Users walk or bike to this park from a three- to four-block radius. Six- to twelve-year-olds form the largest group. Teenagers and young adult males use the arbor area for hanging out. Relatively few parents come here with their children. According to a 1975 survey, Charlie Dorr was found to have the lowest use of the six Berkeley miniparks observed.

Successful Features

• Good use made of a very small site
• Variety of surfaces, textures, materials, and levels

• Vine-covered chain-link fences creating effective boundaries

Unsuccessful Features

• Park not very visible because of narrow entrance
• Play area very close to private residences
• Major seating area barely visible from street; does not encourage use

Berkeley Totland, Berkeley, California [3]

Location and Context

This long-established and popular minipark is located at the intersection of Virginia and McGee streets in Berkeley, in a medium-income neighborhood of largely owner-occupied single-family houses. Traffic barriers at the street intersection reduce the number of passing cars. The park is quiet and sunny.

[3] Compiled from reports by students Jon Rossen (1975) and Sofia Rosner (1989).

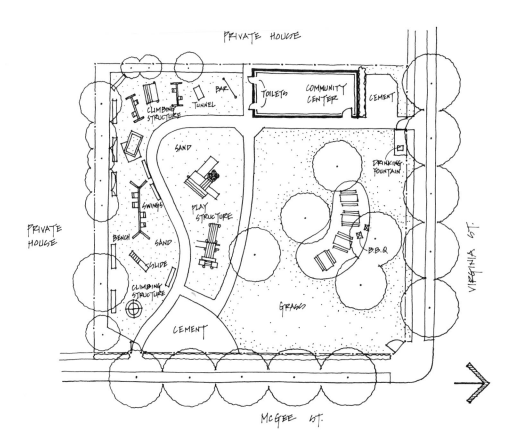

Berkeley Totland in Berkeley, California, is a popular minipark for parents and preschoolers.

Description

Totland is roughly square in shape and 0.37 of an acre (16,117 square feet) in size. The whole southern third of the park is a very large sand area with a variety of slides, swings, tunnels, climbing equipment, and spring toys. A concrete path borders and passes through the play area, with benches set in sand on either side. The northern two-thirds of the park is largely grass, with a few medium to small trees and four long picnic tables set on a concrete pad. A five-foot chain-link fence encloses the park on Virginia and McGee streets; a higher, vine-covered fence separates the other two sides from the adjacent houses. Three gated entries are kept closed to keep dogs out. A very pleasing ambience, variety of equipment, water fountains, picnic tables, public toilets, and a sometimes-open recreation building create a setting that is popular with both neighbors and users.

Major Uses and Users

This is almost exclusively a family park, mainly serving parents and preschool children. Very few older children, teens, or elderly persons use the park which, by its appearance and name, signals it as a place principally for small children. For its relatively small size, this park has an unusually wide draw; although many users walk from the immediate neighborhood, a remarkable number drive here from all over Berkeley. Many come almost daily, know one another, and socialize while their children play. A park-support group (with its notice board on the recreation building) helps maintain the park.

Most of the park's use focuses on the sand equipment area, although family groups and sometimes neighborhood organizations use the picnic area on fine days. The scattering of trees creates pools of shade in the grass area and makes the area unsuitable for older children's ball games. The whole park is easy to see from any one point; the gates are kept closed; and there are no hazards to prevent children from running freely. Not surprisingly, this has long been—and still is—one of the most highly used miniparks in Berkeley.

Successful Features

- Clear, simple layout
- Whole site highly visible and secure
- Park fenced for small children's safety
- Variety of equipment encouraging range of play behavior
- Picnic tables for adults to study, write, and eat on while watching children
- Trees creating pleasing ambience and summer shade
- Trees and picnic tables making site unsuitable for ball games, which could be hazardous for small children

Unsuccessful Features

- Most adult seating set in sand
- Picnic tables large and grouped together; not so comfortable for private use
- Little shade in sand area, so in summer sand is rarely damp and cool for manipulative play
- A few pieces of more challenging equipment needed for older siblings of small children

Berkeley Totland: A complex, integrated structure like this allows children to engage in a variety of activities—climbing, balancing, sliding, hiding, swinging—in a relatively small space.

REFERENCES

American Society of Landscape Architects' Foundation (ASLA). 1975. *Barrier free site design.* Washington, D.C.: U.S. Department of Housing and Urban Development, Office of Policy Development and Research.

Bangs, Herbert P., and Stuart Mahler. 1971. Users of local parks. *Journal of American Institute of Planners* 36 (5):330–334.

Cashdan, Lisa, Peter Stein, and David Wright. 1983. Roses from rubble: New uses for vacant urban land. *Urban Resources* 1 (3):89–96.

Clay, Nanine. 1971. Miniparks—Diminishing returns. *Parks and Recreation,* January.

———. 1972. Landscapes for urban play. *Architectural Forum* 137(3):34–39.

Cooper Marcus, Clare. 1970. Adventure playgrounds. *Landscape Architecture* 61 (1):18–29, 88–91.

———. 1974a. Children's play behavior at a low-rise, inner-city housing development. In *Proceedings of Fifth Annual Conference of Environmental Design Research Association,* ed. D. Carson, pp. 197–210. Milwaukee.

———. 1974b. Children in residential areas: Guidelines for designers. *Landscape Architecture* 65 (4):372–377, 415–416.

———. 1975. Informal observations at 13 San Francisco miniparks. Unpublished paper.

Cooper Marcus, Clare, and Wendy Sarkissian. 1986. *Housing as if people mattered: Site design guidelines for medium density family housing.* Berkeley and Los Angeles: University of California Press.

Dattner, Richard. 1969. *Design for play.* New York: Van Nostrand Reinhold.

Department of the Environment. 1973. *Children at play.* London: Her Majesty's Stationery Office.

Francis, Mark, Lisa Cashdan, and Lynn Paxson. 1984. *Community open spaces: Greening neighborhoods through community action and land conservation.* Covela, Calif.: Island Press.

———. 1984. *The making of neighborhood open spaces, community design, development and management of open spaces.* New York: Center for Human Environments, City University of New York, p. 25.

Gold, Seymour. 1972. Nonuse of neighborhood parks. *Journal of American Institute of Planners* 38(6):369–378.

Hart, Roger. 1974. The genesis of landscaping: Two years of discovery in a Vermont town. *Landscape Architecture* 65 (5): 356–363.

———. 1979. *Children's experience of place.* New York: Irvington.

Hewes, Jeremy Joan and Jay Beckwith. 1974. *Build your own playground.* Boston: Houghton Mifflin.

Hogan, Paul. 1974. *Playgrounds for free.* Cambridge, Mass.: MIT Press.

Lawson, Simpson, ed. 1971. *Workshop on urban open space.* Sponsored by American Society of Landscape Architects. Washington, D.C.: U.S. Department of Housing and Urban Development.

Lederman, A., and A. Trachsel. 1968. *Creative playgrounds and recreation centers.* New York: Praeger.

Linn, Karl. 1968. Neighborhood commons. *Architectural Design* 38 (8):379–382.

Lynch, Kevin. 1960. *The image of the city.* Cambridge, Mass.: MIT Press.

Mahoney, Anne. 1974. Public participation in neighborhood parks: The Berkeley miniparks program. Term paper, Department of Forestry, University of California.

Mason, Gary, Alex Forrester, and Robin Hermann. 1975. *Berkeley park use study.* Berkeley, Calif.: City of Berkeley Parks Department.

Moore, Robin C. 1974a. Anarchy zone: Encounters in a schoolyard. *Landscape Architecture* 65 (5): 364–371.

———. 1974b. Patterns of activity in time and space: The ecology of a neighborhood playground. In *Psychology and the built environment,* ed. D. Canter and T. Lee, pp. 118–131. London: Architectural Press.

DESIGN REVIEW CHECKLIST

SITE SELECTION

1. Is there a likely clientele of children and/or elderly people within a four-block radius of the potential site?

2. Will potential users within a four-block radius be able to walk to the park without crossing a major road?

3. If the potential site is mid-block on a quiet street, can the park be extended into the street to double as a traffic diverter?

4. If a mid-block site with only one entry point is being considered, is the lot less than four times as long as it is wide?

5. If a corner lot is being considered, would the park be enlivened by cross-corner pedestrian traffic?

6. If a through-block site is being considered, is a through-block shortcut needed for pedestrians who might enliven the space and create a sense of security?

7. If a number of sites are being considered, is there one with mature trees, changes of level in topography, and a sunny, sheltered location?

DESIGN PROGRAM

8. Is the community participating in the programming and design of the new park?

9. Has the construction and/or maintenance of the park by local residents been considered, and if so, has it been designed to be built or maintained by unskilled labor?

10. In programming the design, has priority been given to neighborhood residents most needing recreation space (such as preschool children? school-aged children? disabled persons)?

11. Has part of the budget been set aside for a postoccupancy study after one or two years of use?

12. Can part of the budget be saved, to be spent in increments on modifications and additions as the park's specific use becomes stabilized?

13. Has a small portion of the park been left undeveloped for later, unforeseen needs?

14. Do the planting, circulation, and facilities take account of the maintenance capabilities likely to be available when the park is in use?

ENTRANCE AND BOUNDARIES

15. Does the design of the park entrance provide casual seating for passersby who might not necessarily want to enter the park?

16. Does the streetside boundary of the park encourage entry yet provide a sense of enclosure and security for those inside?

17. If the minipark is small and/or in a mid-block location, does special planting, paving, or seating draw attention to its entrance?

18. Can a parking bay be created opposite the entrance for, say, a minivan dropping off a day care group or a playmobile?

19. Are there a nameplate and community notice board in a suitable entry location?

20. Have the boundaries of the minipark adjacent to private residents been adequately screened for privacy?

21. If the adjacent properties are not residential and are windowless walls (of, say, a factory or warehouse), can they be enlivened with murals to expand the apparent size of the park or with painted numbers and "targets" for ball games?

FUNCTIONAL AREAS AND CIRCULATION

22. Because a minipark is so small, has the use of every portion of the site been carefully considered?

23. Has the park been designed so that people entering can see what activities and facilities are available and how to reach them?

24. If the park is small and/or near residences, have noise-generating activities such as basketball been omitted?

25. If the design calls for a lawn area, can the community (or sponsoring agency) afford to maintain it?

26. Has asphalt or another dark-colored hard surface been used for the pathways?

27. Are there widened portions of pathways that children can use for games such as hopscotch and jacks?

28. Because children are likely to be the principal user group, have their needs for a varied environment been met—with places to explore and hide, places to have contact with natural elements?

PLAY AREAS

29. Are features and equipment that stimulate a great variety of play—swinging, sliding, climbing, balancing, jumping, hiding—included, as children are almost always the prime users?

30. Is there a play structure that offers graduated challenges?

31. Has the equipment been designed to allow children to use their imagination?

32. If one play equipment area is to serve several age groups, is it located toward the back of the park?

33. If the park size and service area warrant two play areas, has the one for older children been placed toward the back?

34. Has a play area intended partly or exclusively for preschool children been provided with suitably scaled swings, slide, and climbing blocks? Sand under and around the equipment? A hard-surfaced area for wheeled toys? And benches, for the supervising adults?

35. Are there rocks, blocks, or platforms in the sand so that children can jump from them?

36. Is the sand area well drained, and does it have a border such as a bench seat that will prevent sand from being blown or tracked out?

37. Is there a water spigot in the sand area or a water fountain nearby so that water can be carried to the sand?

38. In areas with hot, dry summers, does a tree or play tower create some shade so that some of the sand area will remain more damp and malleable?

39. Is the park and the play equipment accessible to children with disabilities?

40. If there are steep changes in slope, is there a slide set into the hill?

41. Does the park have a small water feature for play—wading pool, fountain, spigot?

42. Are there play leaders to create programs on the site, and has the park been designed with such activities in mind?

PLANT MATERIALS

43. Do the trees create shade when and where it is needed?

44. Does the planting design take into account the enjoyment of the park by passing motorists?

45. Can the trees (eventually) be climbed?

46. Are all the ground covers really necessary (i.e., to keep people away from a certain area)?

47. Are the specified plant materials fast growing, resilient, easily maintained, and not poisonous?

48. Are the planted beds and lawns bordered with raised edges to prevent soil from washing out and bicyclists from riding through them?

SITE FURNITURE

49. Do the benches satisfy the comfort needs of particular users? For example, do they have backrests and arms for elderly; have they been built in smaller scale for children?

50. Have multipurpose tables been provided?

51. If checkerboard tables are being considered, is there any evidence that local residents will use them?

52. Have a barbecue and picnic tables been provided?

53. Is the drinking fountain accessible by small children and people in wheelchairs?

54. Are there litter cans in critical locations (at the exit, near play area, near benches)?

55. Is there a rack for bikes near the park entrance?

56. Is there an inexpensive, suitably screened and painted, chemical toilet?

57. Has night lighting been considered?

58. Has the neighborhood requested an electrical outlet?

59. Have "keep off" signs and excessively vandal-proof equipment been avoided?

4

CAMPUS OUTDOOR SPACES

Clare Cooper Marcus, with
Trudy Wischemann

An important criterion for evaluating campus plans would be to ask whether the campus plan encourages the maximum number of impromptu encounters with other students, with other faculty members, with visitors, with works of art, with books, and with activities with which one is not himself a regular part . . . The efficiency of a campus plan is not merely to provide the physical setting in which the formal activities of the university are to take place. Much of the education of anybody occurs outside and separate from the formal courses in which he is registered, and only if the plan has the kinds of qualities which will stimulate curiosity, prompt casual encounters and conversation . . . will the atmosphere which it produces be truly educational in the broadest sense. (Keast 1967, p. 13)

Over many centuries, different campus plans have emerged in the Western world, from the urbane enclosed courtyards of Oxford and Cambridge, to the formal "academic village" of Jefferson's University of Virginia, to the mix of formal planning and ad hoc building on the Berkeley campus, to single megastructures at several Canadian locations, to the University of California at Santa Cruz plan where topography and ecology are the principal determinants of building locations.

Whatever the model selected and whatever the site, location, or region, a campus plan will almost always be some arrangement of buildings, with spaces created between them. Frequently ignored in texts on campus planning and design, these outdoor spaces—their use for circulation, study, relaxation, and aesthetic pleasure—deserve far greater attention than they have yet received. Observations on many campuses indicate that a great deal of the casual interchange, chance meetings, entertainment, and study between classes takes

place outdoors, when the weather permits. As in the modern city, campus life occurs to a great extent between scheduled events or specific buildings: Some would argue that this is the very stuff of life.

LITERATURE ON CAMPUS OPEN SPACES

A search for the published literature on how campus open spaces are used (or indeed how campus buildings are used!) proved to be a thankless task. A volume entitled *Campus Buildings That Work* (Association of University Architects 1972) and one named *Campus Planning and Design* (Schmertz 1972) proved to be architectural picture books with eye-catching photographs (usually devoid of people) and a minimal amount of text, dealing principally with technical innovations and issues of form. Though potentially useful for formal ideas to the architect of a new building, such books contain little that is helpful to the landscape architect or any professional concerned with the use and design of spaces between buildings. At the time these books were written (early 1970s), designers apparently felt that innovative buildings must be approached via monumental sets of stairs or across vast, empty plazas. There was little recognition of the need for pleasing, casual gathering places at building entries. The impression of a building from a distance was all-important, but the eye-level, day-to-day experience of passing through and using the spaces between buildings was seemingly of little consequence.

The literature on campus planning (as opposed to individual building design) is somewhat richer in number of volumes and intellectual content. Several books, case studies, and conference proceedings appeared in the 1960s, paralleling the increase in college enrollment and campus construction. But there is little in these texts to aid the designer of campus open space. Not unexpectedly, their focus is on fiscal issues, educational policy, and large-scale planning. One of the most useful is a collection of case studies of twelve campus plans and their subspaces, a project of a class of landscape architecture students at the University of Massachusetts, directed by Walt Cudnohufsky (Univ. of Mass. n.d.). But even this book presents the spaces in terms of how the designer expected them to function, not in terms of their real human use.

Some of the deficiencies in the literature on campus outdoor space use are beginning to be filled by studies written by students and faculty at schools where post-occupancy evaluation is part of the curriculum. These include, for example, the University of California at Irvine, School of Human Ecology (Campus Environment 1982); the University of Illinois at Champaign–Urbana, Department of Landscape Architecture (Kirk 1987); the University of New Mexico, Department of Architecture (Institute for Environmental Education 1982); and the University of California at Berkeley, Department of Landscape Architecture (Cooper Marcus and Wischemann 1983).

DESIGN RECOMMENDATIONS

A basic assumption is that the needs of the users of campus outdoor spaces should be critical to deciding how such spaces are designed. Although each North American campus is different, the use of outdoor spaces in such settings is relatively predictable. Thus, in reviewing the few existing studies of campus use, one can discern patterns repeated in similar settings and begin to establish guidelines for the design of such spaces. But like all guidelines or recommendations, they are true only in light of what we know at this time. When more sophisticated studies are available, no doubt such guidelines will be modified.

The following recommendations are based on a major study by a landscape architecture class of the Berkeley campus (Cooper Marcus and Wischemann 1983); less formal observations at other Bay Area campuses (Stanford University, Merritt College, Laney College, Foothill College); and monographs on outdoor space use at the University of New Mexico (Institute for Environmental Education 1982), the University of Illinois at Champaign–Urbana (Kirk 1987), and the University of California at Irvine (Campus Environment 1982). These guidelines deal principally with the design of outdoor spaces as areas to *be* in, rather than just to pass through. Thus, circulation patterns for a campus as a whole and the potential conflicts of pedestrians, autos, and bicycles are mentioned only tangentially. In addition, our guidelines do

Space between buildings: Lower Sproul Plaza, University of California at Berkeley.

not address student housing but, rather, the everyday use of space between classroom, research, and administration buildings.

Home Base: Spaces Adjacent to Specific Buildings

When thinking about campus outdoor space use, it is helpful to start with the notion that each student, employee, and faculty member probably has a work or home base around which his or her daily campus activities circulate. To find out whether or not students felt they had a home base on the Berkeley campus, in 1981 a random sample of four hundred were asked to indicate on a campus map which building or other space they would consider their home building or base. Surprisingly, 92 percent felt that they did have a home base; this is perhaps to be expected from graduate students, employees, and faculty who are all likely to have an office or desk, but it is equally true for undergraduates.

As might be expected, the home base was usually the students' major department. This was where they took most of their classes, where they saw their adviser, attended special departmental events, and so on. Apparently, the need to feel that one belongs to one spot is so compelling that most students, even those with no formal tie to any one building (i.e., those who had not yet chosen a major) still appropriated a place to which they returned daily. Given this psychological need to have a "home away from home," it may be useful, in planning the spaces around campus buildings, to look upon such buildings as "houses" and the adjacent outdoor places as having some of the elements of "front porches" and "front and back yards." In between these home-related spaces are the true common areas of the campus. Because these latter areas are not perceived as the territory of any particular building, their use is somewhat different.

Considerable confusion arises around campus buildings when the designer does not give enough thought to which is the "front door" or principal pedestrian entry, and which is the "back door," to be used for truck deliveries (or removals) of potentially toxic materials, as in departments such as chemistry and biology. Observations of many campus buildings suggest that whatever the designer may have planned, the entry that students use most frequently is the one that they consider the front or main entry. At this entrance, then, is where a front porch transition should be created for waiting, meeting, casual conversation, and so on. This may seem like common sense; yet many campus buildings fail to address this need.

The Front Porch

The front porch of a house offers an important physical and psychological transition from the public life of the community to the more private life of a smaller social group (usually a family). The front porch of a campus building can similarly offer this transition, from the campus as a whole to a department or college; it can also be a significant social/study/meeting/eating place. In a detailed study of behavior on the Long Beach State University campus, Deasy and Laswell noted that the main entries to buildings had the greatest concentration of outdoor campus use. In their interviews with students they discovered that what the students most needed were more places to study and eat comfortably outdoors, as well as opportunities to meet casually with faculty outside classes and office hours. Accordingly, Deasy and Laswell created a plan for redesigning campus entries that included study spaces, eating spaces, and casual seating. This, we feel, would be an excellent concept to emulate on campuses where the weather during much of the academic year is conducive to outdoor use.

In studying the Berkeley campus, we found approximately the same concentrations of use at main building entries. Those entries at Berkeley that already have some form of seating or steps to accommodate casual

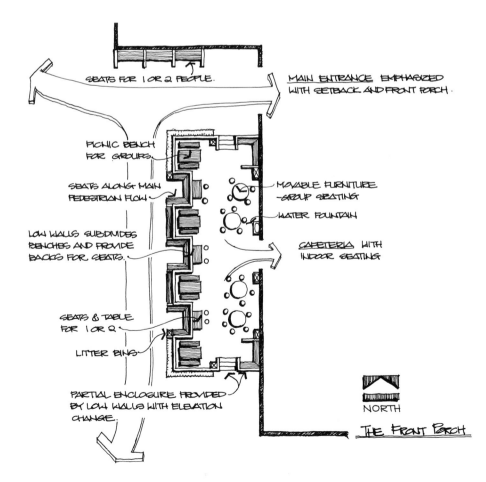

SEATS FOR 1 OR 2 PEOPLE.

MAIN ENTRANCE EMPHASIZED WITH SETBACK AND FRONT PORCH.

PICNIC BENCH FOR GROUPS.

SEATS ALONG MAIN PEDESTRIAN FLOW.

MOVABLE FURNITURE -GROUP SEATING

WATER FOUNTAIN

LOW WALLS SUBDIVIDES BENCHES AND PROVIDE BACKS FOR SEATS.

CAFETERIA WITH INDOOR SEATING

SEATS & TABLE FOR 1 OR 2.

LITTER BINS.

PARTIAL ENCLOSURE PROVIDED BY LOW WALLS WITH ELEVATION CHANGE.

NORTH

THE FRONT PORCH

The main entrance of every campus building needs to be made into a "front porch."

waiting and meeting are especially popular, but others are heavily used as well, even though they have no provision for sitting or studying. Indeed, the situation at one (Evans Hall), with vending machines just inside the building (encouraging quick snacks), enormous numbers of students entering and leaving the building, but no sense of front porch, has resulted in one of the worst entry problems on the campus.

Thus when designing a front porch, consider the following:

- When planning any new campus building, the designer should determine which the main entrance will be in terms of student pedestrian flows, ensure that this will be the main entrance architecturally, and accordingly design some kind of front porch.
- The front door/porch needs to be well lit at night, showing the name of the building and offering clear directions on entering inside.
- The front porch needs a partial enclosure, so that a person passing through senses a place of transition and a stationary user feels slightly apart from nearby campus foot or bicycle traffic.
- In regions with cool to warm weather throughout much of the year, it is comforting to users to create a sun trap, by arranging the building's walls, doorway, planting, seating, and so on so as to create as sheltered a spot as possible.
- Although the front porch might be used only rarely in the winter in northern latitudes, a propitious location—capturing the pale winter sun and the hot air from vents from the building—could help melt the snow and create a usable place dur-

ing warm spring and fall days.
- In very hot climates, overhangs, planting, and natural breezeways should be coordinated to create a cool and shaded place.
- Comfortable seating, with backs, should be located just to the side of the main pedestrian traffic entering the building.
- Some seating should be designed for one or two people to use comfortably and with some privacy; other arrangements should permit three or four to meet and talk as a group. On the University of New Mexico campus, the Mitchell Seating Hub is a popular building-entry feature. Shaped like a doughnut, the Hub provides semiprivate, sociopetal seating in the interior ring, and sociofugal, people-watching seating on the outer ring.
- Some picnic-type benches and tables might be provided for people eating bag lunches or groups studying together.
- A source of reasonably priced food and drink should be positioned at, or close to, the front porch/front door of major buildings.
- A water fountain and ample litter containers should be provided close to seating areas.
- Very long benches should be avoided, as they are intimidating to the single user and inhibit conversation among more than two people.
- In regions where outdoor use is unrealistic throughout much of the year, designers might consider the equivalent of a front porch just inside the main entrance, so that the same activities of casual meeting, eating, studying, and socializing can occur indoors, close to the main pedestrian flows.

Evans Hall, University of California at Berkeley, has an unsuccessful front porch: worn landscaping, people sitting on the ground, crowds jostling between classes, lines to use the vending machines just inside the building.

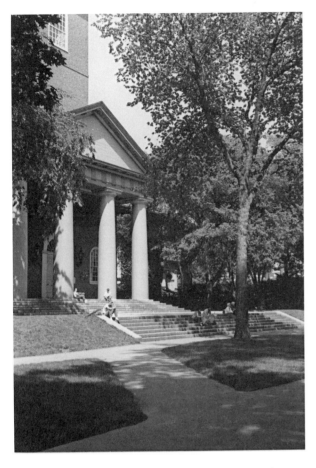

A classical step entry at Harvard University permits casual sitting, sunning, and socializing.

The Front Yard

While the front path and porch of a typical private house are hard surfaced, the front yard usually provides a soft, green transition or buffer between private and public space. Some campus buildings, too, appear to have "front yards"—significant green spaces where building residents can relax in a different way from on the front porch. Here one can go with a friend to talk in private, to sunbathe or sleep, to eat, to study, or to hold a class meeting close to home base. Clearly, a change of environment is important to people's mental health and stress level.

A casual experiment with a large class of Berkeley environmental design students several years ago revealed a marked difference between "inside" and "outside." The students were asked to spend five minutes somewhere inside Wurster Hall (College of Environmental Design), recording stream-of-consciousness impressions of what they were sensing and feeling; they then repeated the exercise outside. Words recorded inside included "enclosed—bored—frustrated—anxious —unrelaxed." When they moved outside, other sensations more readily surfaced: "Quiet—calm—relaxed— peaceful—green—comfortable—serene." This kind of experiential contrast probably holds for most of us: That is, buildings "expect" something of us (study, work, lecture, file, answer phone, go to meeting), whereas the outdoors expects nothing and therefore can be a calming antidote to the stresses of work and study, not to speak of some of the physiological stresses

A missed opportunity to create a pleasing and functional front porch: A single bench, parallel to the building, is not enough.

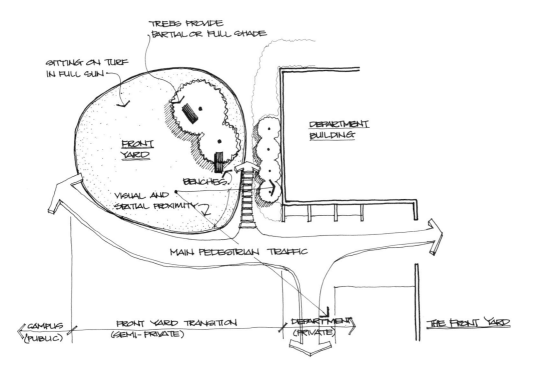

*A "front yard" close to the main entry can provide an area informally appropriated for sunning,
conversation, and outdoor study.*

of institutional buildings (air conditioning, fluorescent lighting, computer screens, building materials pollution, and so on).

For these reasons, the concept of the front yard is important. For some people, the idea of sunbathing or relaxing in a public space may be inhibiting. But resting, meditating, or daydreaming in a familiar place that feels like one's home base, around people one knows or recognizes, may be more acceptable.

To find out whether the concept of a yard or turf near home base had any validity, a sample of four hundred Berkeley students were asked to mark on a campus map the area they thought of as their home turf (Cooper Marcus and Wischemann 1983). The great majority (90 percent) of students interviewed *did* feel they had a home turf, or an area that was particularly comfortable and familiar. The size of the home turf ranged from just the immediate surroundings of their home base building (what we have designated as "the front yard") to a large adjacent segment of the campus. Undergraduates, moving between a number of buildings on campus for classes, tended to indicate the largest home turf areas. Graduates were more likely to indicate the immediate surroundings of their home-building. Faculty either responded that they had no home turf or just indicated a limited area around their home-base building. (There were no significant differences between male and female respondents.) Thus, the concept of a front yard may have most significance for graduate students and faculty, who spend most of their time on campus in and around a single building.

Clearly the pedestrian orientation of a campus has a lot to do with the perception of home turf. Where most campus-users walk between buildings, and where the climate is conducive to outdoor lunching/studying/relaxing much of the year, a gradual daily familiarity with place evolves into a sense of home territory. Like people in a residential neighborhood, students and faculty on the Berkeley campus felt comfortable in their home turf because they saw people there whom they knew. But we sensed that, even more importantly than in a residential area, people become attached to an area of campus because they use the outdoors as a resting place as well as a passing-through space, that is, they become familiar with its sights, sounds, sensations, and visual images while sitting, relaxing, eating, or conversing. It is possible that, in the large, institutional atmosphere of a major campus, people have a particular need for outdoor spaces where they feel at home and to which they can easily return each day to meet particular friends or just to relax.

When siting and designing a new campus building, consider the following regarding a front yard:

- Lawns, planting, and paths should be arranged to suggest (but not enforce) the notion of a front yard. There should be enough visual cues that users of a particular building can easily claim and feel comfortable in this space.
- It is preferable to provide areas of lawn in the full sun, plus other lawn areas fully or partially shaded. This not only provides pleasing visual contrasts for

Heavy use of a front-yard space at the University of California, Berkeley.

Students enjoying spring sunshine in the "front yard" of the main library, University of California, Berkeley.

passersby but also ensures contrasting microclimates for stationary users at different times of the year.

- Trees planted to create shade should not have any "unpleasant" characteristics likely to inhibit people from sitting or sleeping under them (e.g., the spiky fallen leaves of California live oaks or the sticky summer nectar of tulip trees).

- Regular bench-type seating might be provided around the edges of this space or around the base of particularly large and impressive trees.

- In seasons of the year when sitting on the grass is appropriate and irrigation is necessary, the grass should be watered in the evening or at night, so that it will have dried off by lunchtime.

The Backyard

Just as every home has a front yard that is generally open to the view of passersby and therefore semipublic, most homes also have a backyard that is fully or partially enclosed and used for both private relaxation and utilitarian functions. We believe that some campus buildings, too, should have backyards—spaces attached to or perhaps partially enclosed by buildings, where "residents" feel a greater sense of territory than in the front yard and where semiprivate departmental or college events can be held.

A good example of this is the U-shaped east courtyard of Wurster Hall (College of Environmental Design) on the Berkeley campus. Enclosed on three sides by the building it serves, this courtyard is used as one would use the backyard of a house. People come out in ones and twos to eat lunch on the peripheral benches. Although not the most attractive spot on campus, it is at least quiet, sheltered, and unhurried. Faculty and staff from the building often eat bag lunches here, avoiding the more lively, crowded west-facing "front porch" favored by students. Other uses of Wurster's semiprivate backyard are for design presentations, model building, photography, drawing classes, and volleyball games, as well as infrequent special events such as graduation, the Beaux Arts Ball, and memorial services for deceased faculty members. Clearly, this space is important to the sense of community in Wurster Hall. And in the hurried milieu of a large university, this sense of community is often sadly lacking. No doubt some departments such as environmental design, art, drama, and literature may have a greater need for some kind of backyard for informal class use, while in

other departments (engineering, biology, geology, and so on) the necessity of using laboratories or equipment precludes the use of outdoor space for teaching. Certainly, considerations of comfort (warm spots, shade) and function (seating, study, conversation) in such spaces need to be much more carefully addressed. Every campus observed seems to have ample examples of potential backyard spaces, usually courtyards that are desolate or empty because of inadequate concern for the details of aesthetics and functional needs.

Where a backyard seems appropriate, consider the following:

- This space should be away from major pedestrian flows and yet be easily accessible from the building it serves. Its presence should be obvious to the building's regular occupants but not so obvious to passersby.
- The majority of those passing through this space should have the building itself as a destination. The backyard space should not be a passageway for large numbers passing through. Rather, it should feel like an oasis, with occasional passersby.
- Although a hard-surfaced courtyard space may seem to be the most appropriate for a backyard, its materials should be warm and inviting. A study of an unused medical school quad at the University of California at Irvine revealed that the glaring concrete surfaces and the lack of shade precluded the students' using the few seats available. Changes proposed by a study team of environmental psychology students included the addition of a wooden deck, with a lattice for shade and movable seating (Campus Environment 1982).

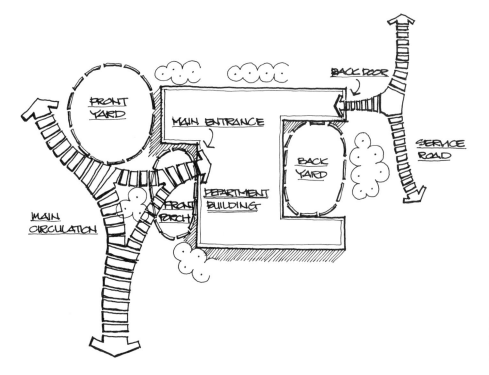

Each campus building should ideally have a front porch, front yard, back yard, and back door.

The Earth Sciences Building, University of California at Berkeley, has an unused rooftop "backyard." The circular "bulls-eye" space is a very uncomfortable place to sit: The area is visually removed from passersby and campus police, and only one of the surrounding buildings has a door opening onto it.

Latimer Plaza, University of California at Berkeley, is a backyard space next to a chemistry building that—with more attention to planting and seating—could have provided a pleasant setting for lunch and coffee breaks, but it is seldom used.

- Seating should be around the edges or attached to "islands" in this space, as people feel more comfortable with a wall or planting at their back.
- Where appropriate, movable seating and tables should be provided so that people can arrange their own clusters.
- A backyard space should be large enough for occasional "family" events—such as graduation—yet not so large and open that one or two users feel exposed or uncomfortable when in it alone.
- The space should be able to accommodate temporary seating for special events (e.g., graduation) and be wired for outdoor microphones.

The Backdoor

Most houses have a very different image at the front door compared with that at the backdoor. Similarly, a campus building should have an unmistakable backdoor or service entrance where (1) delivery trucks park and unload, (2) noxious materials are stored, and (3) garbage is picked up. Difficulties and annoyances occur when the front door and the backdoor are one and the same. It can be very irritating for people wishing to socialize, eat lunch, or study when at the same place and time trucks deliver products to the vending machines; library vans deliver and pick up books and so

The successful backyard of the College of Environmental Design at Berkeley is used for casual study, outdoor classes, model making, and special ceremonies.

Graduation ceremonies in the backyard of the College of Environmental Design at Berkeley. (Photo: Gilbert Haacke)

Confusion of front and back: A formal set of steps forms the "front door" to this building, while a "backdoor" for vehicular deliveries, garbage pickup, and so forth is located beneath, approached by a ramped roadway. A garbage dumpster at the top of the ramp conflicts with the formal pedestrian path.

152

on. The designated backdoor of a building thus should be (1) unmistakably a service entrance, (2) conveniently located for truck and van access without violating the front porch or front yard spaces of the same or neighboring buildings, and (3) located so that the noise of vehicles does not disturb nearby classrooms whose windows are open.

Common Turf: Campus Spaces Used by Everyone

If the spaces close to campus buildings can be thought of as adjuncts to a "house," then the common areas between them might be viewed as the streets and parks of the campus "town," those spaces that are not the territory of specific buildings or departments.

Campus Entrances

If the campus is in a rural or suburban context and students arrive by car or public transit, it may be counterproductive to plan one "grand entry," however appealing it may look on the plan. For example, the University of California at Irvine, which has many commuting students, was planned as a "wheel" of campus buildings and peripheral parking lots and so it has multiple entries. This makes sense functionally, although as a result the campus has a slightly disturbing lack of focus. At the University of California at Berkeley, by contrast, the formally designated main entry (at Bancroft and Telegraph avenues) is also the main gathering place (Sproul Plaza) and the principal entry point

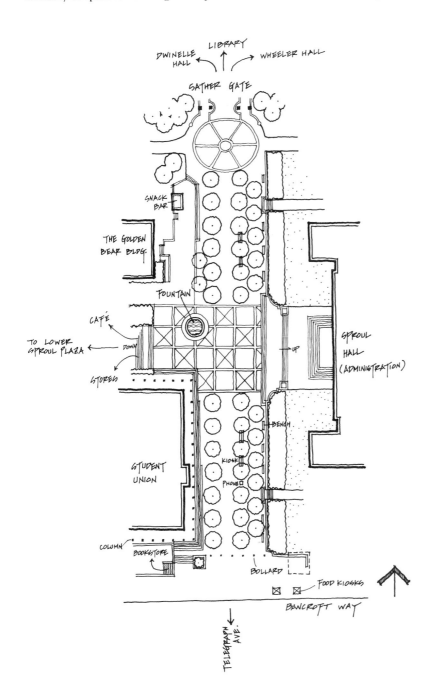

A successful main entry to the Berkeley campus is located where the main student street (Telegraph Avenue) empties into Sproul Plaza.

for students approaching on foot from Berkeley's south-side (where most of the cheaper student housing is located). All of these features, plus the lack of a vehicular entry here, combine to create a highly used and highly imageable "gateway" to the campus. Other entry points on the Berkeley campus are less successful: On the north side, pedestrians and cars shared a confused, unaesthetic entry until it was redesigned in 1990. On the west side, a formal entry conceived in Olmstead's original plan for the campus and redesigned by Thomas Church in the 1960s seems like a misplaced monument, as few enter the campus from this direction.

While campus entries should be placed where the majority of students will enter on foot, they should also provide pleasant sub-spaces for waiting, eating, casual studying, perusing notices, and picking up newspapers or flyers. Since many campuses do not conform to the surrounding contextual street pattern and buildings do not have street addresses, first-time visitors may have problems finding their way around. Major, and minor, entry points are important locations for legible, well-lit campus maps.

The success of Sproul Plaza at the University of California at Berkeley is due largely to its location at a main pedestrian entry point, a linear design that accommodates large pedestrian flows plus seating "eddies" off to the side, a central open space for rallies and speeches, and high-use buildings bordering the plaza.

Major Plaza Spaces

Almost every campus has some kind of central plaza or gathering place. Just as every traditional village or small town has its common green or town square, so each campus community seems to need a place where friends meet, bands play, displays are placed, rallies are staged, and people come to watch other people or just to relax between classes. The nature of these spaces varies greatly, from the grand central mall of grass and trees at the University of Illinois at Champaign–Urbana, to the large, buff-brick Smith Plaza at the University of New Mexico, to the distinctly urban Sproul Plaza at Berkeley.

Size. The size of the central plaza varies considerably, from that serving a major university to that serving a small junior or community college. Because the central plaza of a campus is likely to be where large rallies, speeches, or performances are scheduled, a space large enough to accommodate such gatherings may seem empty and ambiguous when not used for a scheduled event. A central green mall—such as that at the University of Illinois at Champaign–Urbana or at the University of Virginia—does not appear empty when unused, but a hard-surfaced space often does. At the University of New Mexico, for example, students regard Smith Plaza as the center of campus and recognize its value for rallies and fiestas. But when crowds are not present, campus users see the space as ambiguous, overwhelming, and uncomfortable to walk through. It is used, however, when relatively empty, by skateboarders and frisbee throwers, a sure sign on any campus that a plaza space is overscaled for study, conversation, and relaxation (Institute for Environmental Education 1982). The lower Sproul Plaza on the Berkeley campus is similarly perceived and used, whereas the upper Sproul Plaza splendidly enhances activities ranging from multithousand-person political rallies to quiet study and conversation. The subtle use of planting and paving creates a space for large gatherings that does not appear empty or ambiguous at other times.

Location. The central plaza must be located on "common turf," where the denizens of all buildings or precincts can feel equally comfortable. In a 1981 interview survey of almost four hundred Berkeley students, virtually all were able to name areas on campus they considered to be common turf; the largest number (almost two-thirds) mentioned the main entry/gathering place of Sproul Plaza.

- A central plaza should be bounded by places that generate a high degree of use throughout the day and into the evening. These might include a student center or student union, library, theatre,

"Red Square," University of Washington, Seattle, is intimidating for use by individuals or small groups, because of its immense size and lack of "eddy spaces," but it functions as a pedestrian circulation hub and is very frequently used by students and high school skateboarders.

gymnasium, cafeteria, administration building, bookstore, or post office.

- A central plaza must be located where major pedestrian flows pass by, so that many people become familiar with the place, see it in its different moods and seasons, and gradually "appropriate" the space cognitively. This parade of passersby is also important so that those who have come to watch people or wait for a friend have plenty to observe.

- A central plaza can be an important sociopsychological and perceptual orienting device. Hence pathways should naturally focus on it, bringing many people to the plaza. At the University of California at Santa Cruz, where the planners were specifically instructed not to include such a gathering place (for fear of repeating the Berkeley Free Speech, People's Park, and similar rallies), there is a noticeable sense of disorientation, even among campus regulars.

Spatial Attributes

- A main plaza on a large campus functions as a stage, where some come to "perform" (walk by, play music, give speeches, hand out literature) and others come to watch and perhaps to be watched. Thus, a successful plaza accommodates two basic activities—passing through and stationary behavior (sitting, studying, waiting, eating, watching). Its basic design must allow these two activities to proceed without impeding each other. A good analogy is a flowing river (pedestrian movement), with eddies off to the side (for sitting, watching). These eddies for seating should be provided in both prominent and less prominent positions. Observations on several major campuses indicate that a minority group often seeks out and claims a specific, highly visible seating area on the main plaza,

presumably for daily meetings with friends. At the Berkeley campus and at the University of Illinois at Champaign–Urbana, for example, black male students claim prominent seating walls close to the main entrance to the student union. Other individuals or groups may seek less prominent locations. For instance, on campuses in downtown city areas, elderly people (especially men) tend to use the main campus plaza as an outdoor living room but seek quiet, back-seat positions.

- As in any public place, people feel more comfortable sitting on the edge of a space with something at their back. Hence, a major campus plaza should allow as articulated an edge as possible and provide many "anchor" spots (e.g., trees, columns, planters). Observations at Sproul Plaza on the Berkeley campus indicate that women are much more likely than men to seek out edges, corners, and physical props in the environment. Men, on the other hand, are the predominant users of more exposed positions, such as lawns for sunbathing or a set of steps for obvious people watching. Thus a variety of seating locations should be provided.

- Informal and formal seating areas should be able to accommodate a great variety of needs, from quiet study to surreptitious people watching, to more blatant people watching, to waiting for a friend in a prominent place. More than any other single campus space, the main plaza needs to provide this great variety of seating locations.

- Because the users are so different, the actual form of seating in a central plaza should vary accordingly, from benches with and without backs, to steps, retaining walls, fountain edges, and so on.

- If bicycles are used on campus, there must be enough bicycle racks, or benches and trees will be used for this purpose, thus cluttering the environment, both visually and functionally.

- Boards for official notices may be glass-fronted cases, and those for unofficial notices may be kiosks or bulletin boards. Important details include locating open boards in places sheltered from the wind, providing a small overhang to protect paper from the rain, and placing seating near the notice boards in such a way that people neither feel inhibited from sitting there nor block the notices.
- A cafeteria or restaurant with outdoor seating (where climate permits) should be within view of the plaza, with food-vending kiosks or carts at which students can buy inexpensive snacks in or near the plaza. Observations in downtown office districts and campus plazas indicate that eating gives many people a needed excuse to be in a public space while at the same time reading, studying, or watching the world go by. Women seem to need such an excuse more than men do.
- Where the climate is appropriate, an eye-catching, participatory fountain can be a wonderful addition to a major plaza space. It can be an aesthetic focal point, an imageable symbol of the place, and if people can sit on its edge, trail their hands or feet in it, walk through it on stepping-stones, or otherwise interact with the water, it can be an attractive adult play space.

Favorite Outdoor Spaces

The campus environment remains one of the few North American urban areas where pedestrians predominate and usually have a right-of-way. Many campuses are a unique milieu in which urbanity and greenery are pleasantly juxtaposed. The 1981 Berkeley survey revealed that most students enjoyed having easy access to both types of environments, but the majority voted for "more open spaces and greenery" rather than more "malls and plazas." Judging the campus to be pleasantly balanced, they feared the encroachment of more buildings, parking lots and urbanity (Cooper Marcus and Wischemann 1983).

In the same survey, respondents were asked to indicate on a map their favorite spaces. The fact that virtually everyone was able, without hesitation, to indicate such a space, points to its importance. These favorite spaces tended to be green or "natural" environments, and/or were not seen as the territory or home base of any particular building or department. They seemed to be used much as a downtown office worker might use a park or other green public space, as a place to retreat to, to get away from the pressures of work and colleagues, to catch one's breath and relax. Respondents gave several reasons for choosing a favorite space:

Naturalness, trees, and greenery	60
Peace and quiet	36
Shade and sun	30
People and people watching	28
Proximity to water (a creek)	27
Grass and open space	26
Feeling free and comfortable	12

Though naturalness dominates the qualities of the most desirable spaces at Berkeley, what is meant by natural varies a great deal, from the neatly trimmed lawns and lines of pleached plane trees beneath the central Campanile, to the grassy, tree-bordered bowl of Faculty Glade, to a grove of towering eucalyptus trees by the

The Faculty Glade, University of California at Berkeley, was named in a student survey as the favorite space on campus.

meandering Strawberry Creek. What seems to be common to all these favorite spaces at Berkeley is that natural elements (trees, shrubs, grass, creeks) form their boundaries, largely or totally blocking out the presence of nearby buildings and roads. The activities engaged in are varied—from sunbathing and napping to occasional scheduled events (music, dance, receptions) to quiet study, conversation, eating, people watching, meditation, feeding birds and squirrels, and playing frisbee or catch.

What is clear is that such activities are essential to alleviate stress among students and university employees, rendering the intensity or boredom of classes, seminars, and office work more tolerable. Just as the city as a whole needs its "lungs" in the form of parks, beaches, and public outdoor spaces, so does the urban campus require its green spaces. The favorite space of students at the University of New Mexico campus is a duck pond with waterfalls and wooden footbridge, surrounded by sloping, lush lawns. On a campus bisected by a major traffic artery and experiencing hot summer weather, the duck pond provides a welcome oasis.

The Campanile Esplanade, University of California at Berkeley, is a favorite place for outdoor study and pausing between classes.

It is interesting to note that there may be a significant difference in the kinds of retreat places sought out by different campus age groups. In the 1981 study of the Berkeley campus, a large sample of mixed, undergraduate and graduate students named Sproul Plaza as one of their favorite places on campus. A later follow-up study (Higdon 1988) interviewed a much smaller sample of all graduate students about the favorite spaces cited in 1981. All of these students ranked Sproul Plaza as the least attractive of five such places on campus. "Most agreed that this is primarily a place for youth, specifically undergraduates, and many of the interviewees (graduate students) felt overwhelmed here. 'Busy—distracting—confusing—chaotic—and unpredictable' were some of the terms they used to describe this place" (Higdon 1988, p. 22). Graduate students clearly preferred quieter, more contemplative campus spaces.

In an informal, random sample asking people in general (i.e., not necessarily students) what publicly accessible place they might go to if feeling "low, depressed, or fed-up," most adolescents tended to cite a place of distraction (shopping mall, downtown, book-shop, active street), while most adults tended to cite a place of contemplation (beach, natural setting, quiet café) (Cooper Marcus 1989). This suggests that in a setting like a campus with a fairly wide age-range, from young freshman to professors and staff close to retirement, favorite places may need to span a range from active/urban to passive/natural. Since issues concerning the design of an active plaza space have already been discussed, the following recommendations will refer largely to natural spaces for relaxation and study.

- On a new campus, designate unique or particularly attractive natural features (e.g., a creek, pond, grove of trees, hillside) as "sacred," never to be built over or visually encroached on by neighboring buildings. On an existing campus, confirm by means of a survey or observations what the students' favorites are. Just as on a new site, such spaces should be documented and protected from urban encroachment.
- Plan for a variety of natural spaces, from large, open lawns or hillsides to secluded creekside spaces.
- Arrange seating, benches, and tables for studying, eating, and conversation. A user study of the University of New Mexico duck pond (referred to above) plus the adjacent Scholes Park, revealed lush, landscaped spaces quite inadequately provided with seating so that they could be fully enjoyed only by those willing to sprawl on the grass.
- Ensure that trees or other plant materials form a natural boundary for such spaces in the vertical and/or the horizontal plane. This may often entail careful, long-term planning regarding the location

The Bechtel Center roof garden, University of California at Berkeley, is a popular place to eat lunch, sit in the sun, and read.

of future buildings and the longevity and growth rate of trees.

- Plan the peripheral and internal planting of such spaces to satisfy the psychological need of many users to attach themselves to an edge or island at their backs.
- Ensure that such spaces are separate enough from campus buildings that they will not be claimed as the semiexclusive territory of any one department or group of students.
- Plan for major circulation routes to skirt these spaces so that they are easily accessible yet activities are not interrupted by crowds passing through.
- Provide adequate night lighting. The very nature of favorite spaces on a campus (separate from buildings, screened by vegetation) may also make them unsafe at night, particularly for women. Indeed, most of the "favorite spaces" cited by Berkeley students in 1981 were also perceived as being campus areas "most unsafe at night" (Cooper Marcus and Wischemann 1983).
- Water plants and trees at night or in the evening so that the grass will be dry during peak-use hours.

Outdoor Study Areas

Weather permitting, the "common turf" areas of a campus (as well as those related to buildings) can offer valuable locations for casual outdoor study between classes or for discussion with a friend that would be distracting in a library. In a survey during warm fall weather on the Berkeley campus, half the students questioned studied outdoors "often" or "sometimes." Factors inhibiting outdoor study were (in order of importance): too many people, nowhere to sit, lack of

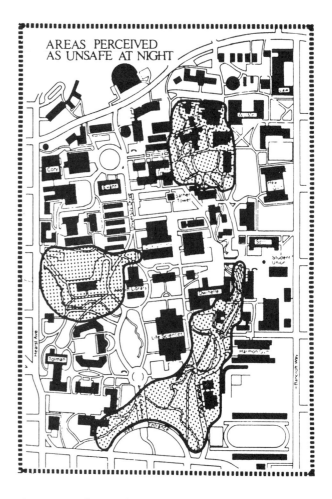

Areas perceived as unsafe at night in a survey of four hundred Berkeley students.

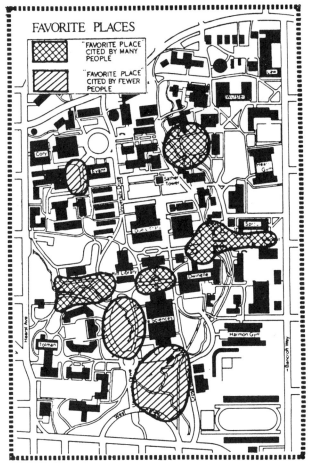

FAVORITE PLACES

"FAVORITE PLACE" CITED BY MANY PEOPLE

"FAVORITE PLACE" CITED BY FEWER PEOPLE

These spaces coincided with "favorite places" enjoyed in the day for their natural scenery and trees.

time, glare from sun and buildings on books and paper, noise from vehicles, outdoor distractions, dogs, and no place to write or lean on (Cooper Marcus and Wischemann 1983). If located, furnished, and detailed appropriately, places for outdoor reading and study will be actively used in the appropriate seasons, thus relieving pressure on overcrowded libraries and study halls.

The following locations appear to be the most favored for casual outdoor study:

- Major building entries, where between classes or at lunchtime, students can study close to their home base or in familiar territory.
- Areas close to sources of inexpensive food or snacks, as students often read and eat at the same time.
- Open lawn areas, for those who prefer to study close to their home bases or in a more public place, with lots of space around them.
- Secluded, small spaces for those who wish to do more contemplative or private work. One third of those questioned on the Berkeley campus wanted more places to sit and study along a creek that bisects the campus. (This has to be sensitively handled to avoid erosion problems.)
- Places away from vehicular traffic or parking areas, as the noise can be distracting.
- Semienclosed patios or terraces off libraries, to offer a change from indoor reading.
- "Eddy" spaces, just to the side of major pedestrian traffic flows.

Students—like most people— prefer to sit on the edge of an open space with seat back and planting protecting them from behind, as here, at the University of California at Berkeley.

- Spots under large mature trees that themselves create a subspace. A circular bench can create comfortable sociofugal seating where a number of people can sit and study who do not want to converse.
- Sites against the end or blank walls of buildings where the space is not perceived as the territory of a particular department.

When designing spaces that may be used for outdoor study, consider the following characteristics:

- Screen spaces from major pedestrian flows by means of distance, planting, level changes, and the like, so that the sights and sounds of large numbers of people passing by are not too distracting.
- Partly enclose some study spaces with defined boundaries, so that the user will feel sheltered from possible intrusion.
- Above all, provide comfortable seating. Sitting on a hard, cold, or backless bench is not conducive to outdoor study.
- Offer some kind of table. Although some people find comfortable seating sufficient for reading or conversation, others prefer to spread their books out on a hard surface and lean on a table while writing. Thus a variety of writing surfaces should be offered, from flip-up writing tablets to benches and tables. Because many people prefer to study alone or perhaps with one friend, small one- to two-person tables and seating arrangements may be preferable to large, picnic-sized tables. When asked what additions on the Berkeley campus

The Bechtel Center roof garden has small tables away from major pedestrian flows and under the dappled shade of an arbor. "More tables and benches" was the number one item requested by students to assist their use of the outdoors in a 1981 survey.

would enhance outdoor study, three quarters of those questioned cited "benches or tables." It is surprising that outdoor tables are rarely provided on campuses; it seems that they are specified by designers only as adjuncts to picnics and eating and only rarely as useful furniture for study use. One of the favorite places of many Berkeley students is the Bechtel Center's roof garden. Located on the roof of a partially sunken building, this space receives sun all day and contains a small café, seating, planting, and roofed outdoor study carrels surrounded on three sides by glass. The study tables are particularly popular.

Popular semioutdoor study carrels on the Bechtel Center roof garden have desks and electrical outlets.

Problems Inhibiting Campus Outdoor Use

Crime and Fear of Crime

When a large sample of Berkeley students were asked in 1981 to list problems affecting their general outdoor use of the campus, fear of crime emerged as the major issue. Those areas cited most frequently as unsafe included heavily planted areas, pockets of natural landscape, and streets or pathways infrequently used at night. However, this should not lead one to think that all the remaining areas are considered safe. A significant portion of the sample, all women, considered the entire campus to be unsafe at night. An equally significant portion of those interviewed felt safe anywhere on campus, but with the exception of one, all of them were men (Cooper Marcus and Wischemann 1983).

In a study of factors affecting perceptions of safety on the campus of the University of Illinois at Champaign–Urbana (Kirk 1987), highly vegetated and picturesque areas of the campus, such as the Cemetery and Illini Grove, were also perceived as the most dangerous areas on campus, especially by women. Factors that students rated as most important to the perception of danger were "poor lighting" and "places to hide." However, when asked to suggest improvements to increase campus safety, not one person (out of a random sample of sixty-seven men and women) suggested removing the vegetation. The most frequently cited improvements were better lighting, more police patrols, and more emergency phones.

A University of New Mexico study citing fear of crime as the main reason inhibiting general use of the campus at night, proposed designating an integrated series of well-lit and patrolled "night-safety paths" linking the main campus entries and nighttime activity areas (e.g., libraries, laboratories) (Institute for Environmental Education 1982). As on city streets, the combination of lighting plus people seems to be critical in inhibiting crime.

Traffic

When asked to cite problems (after crime) affecting their use of outdoor areas on the Berkeley campus, the biggest issues the students raised were moving traffic, vehicular noise, parking of cars, air pollution, and maintenance vehicles at building entries. Observations at Berkeley suggest that the use of mopeds—now insidiously infiltrating the campus and adding noise to otherwise pedestrian pathways—may become more of a problem in the future.

Traffic is important to the question of how outdoor spaces are used because it often affects stationary users, both directly and indirectly. Noise, congestion, smells, and heat associated with automobile traffic and pavement detract from the uses of an outdoor space, especially for rest and retreat. All of the most frequently cited favorite spaces on the Berkeley campus are removed from regular automobile traffic and service vehicle areas, both physically and visually.

Conflict among pedestrians, bicyclists, and automobiles seems to be a problem on many campuses. Many of those interviewed at Berkeley mentioned the lack of clear bicycle routes through campus, bicyclists riding on pedestrian routes, and the lack of adequate and secure bicycle parking, which is particularly needed, as bicycles are the most cost- and time-effective transportation for students.

Conflicts between pedestrians and automobiles on campuses tend to occur where (1) cars and pedestrians share an entry point to a campus, without designated sidewalks, (2) sidewalks are too narrow to accommodate peak pedestrian flows, (3) sidewalks empty into or cross roadways without a clearly marked crossing, (4) parking lots double as pedestrian routes, (5) service vehicles approach buildings via the "front porch" (i.e., no back door) and (6) the siting of new buildings and the planning of new roads and parking ignore existing pedestrian flows.

Although many campus plans encourage the use of bicycles by students, the mass parking of bicycles can clutter building entries, or—as here, at the University of California at Davis —virtually cut off a lawn area from use.

Because it is not the purpose of this chapter to deal with major campus-planning issues of vehicular circulation, parking, and so on, these are merely offered as pointers for traffic planners. Clearly, conflicts between cars (moving and parked) and pedestrians affect the use and enjoyment of outdoor space on every campus.

Campus Wear and Tear

Behavior traces in the landscape are the physical evidence of use, such as litter, worn landscaping, and people-made paths. The amount of campus litter is usually related to the availability of food, especially from vendors and vending machines, and to places where people like to eat lunch. Litter may result from carelessness, infrequency of trash-container pickups, and/or lack of adequate trash receptacles in obvious places. Litter may also relate to wind patterns and types of trash facilities: In places where turbulent eddies are caused by building placement or topography, litter may blow out of open trash bins. Their replacement with swing-top receptacles may be a solution.

Worn campus landscaping may result from overuse, careless use, neglect, improper placement or choice of plant materials, or shortcuts. Some shortcuts, especially those at corners, appear to be taken by careless or lazy pedestrians. Other shortcuts are the result of poor design, that is, the users' response to designated paths that are indirect and/or to landscaping meant to barricade what can be recognized as a natural path to an obvious destination. The last, and maybe the most important, reason that people leave designated sidewalks is just to walk on grass or dirt, among natural elements and/or away from crowds.

Not all shortcuts are necessarily unsightly or even problematic, except during rain and watering periods when the ground is soft and pedestrians trample ever-widening areas to avoid the mud. Softer, natural surfaces are a visual and physical amenity, distinguishing many campus areas from adjacent urban areas, and so finding ways to allow or even encourage their use without destroying them is a worthwhile challenge.

Some of the problems associated with shortcuts through the natural landscape of a campus are exemplified by the situation at the University of California at Santa Cruz, which was planned as a rural campus, with buildings situated in or close to a magnificent redwood forest. Major auto routes and parking were designated, but much less attention was paid to pedestrian routes. As a result, the campus is crisscrossed with student-made paths from residences to classrooms, to the library, and to sports facilities. Although the routes of these paths—through the forest or across areas of natural grassland—are attractive, they produce problems in the winter (when rainfall and fog make them muddy), at night (when they are dark), and where they go up steep slopes (and become dangerous to navigate). Al-

though some students enjoy the rural quality of this circulation system, it does make parts of the campus virtually inaccessible to those with disabilities or to those who wish to dress more formally.

Finding One's Way

Because they are on campus every day, habitual users tend to forget that it may cover a large area and accommodate as many people as does a sizable town. On some campuses—for example, the University of Southern California—some of the city streets cross the campus, thus making it more understandable to strangers. But on many other campuses, for example, University of California at Berkeley, where campus streets are generally not named and do not follow predictable patterns, newcomers are likely to become confused and disoriented. Just over half of those questioned at Berkeley in the 1981 survey felt that the maps and signs provided on campus were inadequate. Our recommendations for finding one's way are the following:

1. Place and maintain campus maps (well lit at night) at major entry points and along major routeways.
2. Place nameplates at the front entrances of all campus buildings, and make sure that these are lit at night.
3. Beneath the official name of the building, list the departments that it houses, for example, Earth Sciences Building: Departments of Paleontology, Geography, Geology, and Geophysics.
4. Place well-designed and well-lit directional signs at all major intersections.

Conclusion

Although our recommendations can probably be applied to any North American campus, when planning changes in or additions to an existing campus it is desirable to conduct some form of postoccupancy evaluation, so that the students' and employees' views can be gathered and analyzed and so that the details of outdoor use can be documented. When planning a new campus, these recommendations may help in the overall siting of buildings, the protection of special places, the location of campus entrances and main plazas, and the detailing of building entries and outdoor study spaces.

Campus outdoor spaces, too often it seems, have become what is left over after building decisions have been made. Perhaps this is another example of the landscape architect entering the design process too late, after major site-planning decisions have been made, and being expected to "shrub up" or detail a space, the use of which has scarcely been considered. In campus planning, as in any other form of site planning, professionals whose focus is the outdoors need to be involved from the start, pressing for front porches, aware of the need for common turf, sensitive to the protection of special places, and skilled in the use of planting and design and placement of site furniture so as to enhance the full use of the outdoors for study, relaxation, contemplation, socializing, and entertainment.

CASE STUDIES

Upper Sproul Plaza, University of California at Berkeley

Location and Context

Upper Sproul Plaza is located on the south side of the University of California campus at Berkeley. It is the major entry point to the campus and is a long, rectangular, tree-lined plaza bounded by the Student Union, Sproul Hall (university administration), and the Golden Bear (cafeteria and dining commons). It is connected by a set of wide steps to lower Sproul Plaza, a broader rectangular plaza bounded by Zellerbach Hall

Ludwig's Fountain, a favorite meeting point on Berkeley's Sproul Plaza, named after a dog who walked several miles each day in the 1960s to stand in the water and be fed and petted by the students.

(theater and auditorium), the Bear's Lair (café), the Golden Bear, and Eshelman Hall (offices of student organizations).

Description

Sproul Plaza is an axial design about 550 feet long and 75 to 100 feet wide. It connects the historic campus portal, Sather Gate, with the town and is the campus terminus of Telegraph Avenue. "The Avenue" houses coffee shops, bookshops, boutiques, and clothing stores in the few blocks close to campus and extends five miles south to downtown Oakland.

More of a street than a square, Sproul Plaza is bounded at Bancroft Way by a set of bollards, signaling that it is a totally pedestrian space. Its axial design is reinforced by rows of sycamore trees, creating a boulevardlike setting. Approximately halfway along its length, a major east–west axis crosses the plaza, linking Sproul Hall's impressive entrance to the activities on lower Sproul Plaza. At this crossing point of the two axes, the plaza opens up into a roughly square subspace, marked by a change in paving, a break in the rows of trees, and a fountain with a low seating edge. It is here that on October 1, 1964, Mario Savo climbed onto a police car and the Free Speech Movement was born. It was the location of the many rallies and meetings that made Berkeley famous in the 1960s and 1970s as the seat of student unrest. Important features of this central portion of the plaza enhance its use as a gathering place for political rallies and speeches: The steps of Sproul Hall act as a stage, the plaza itself as the auditorium, and terraces around the Golden Bear and steps and balconies around the Student Union provide gallery viewing for those at the back of the crowd.

Major Uses and Users

The designers of Sproul Plaza—architects Vernon DeMars, Donald Reay, and Donald Hardison and landscape architect Lawrence Halprin—set out in the late 1950s to design an arrangement of buildings and outdoor spaces that would become the social focus of the campus. As Roger Montgomery put it in a 1970 assessment of their efforts, "They succeeded and then some" (Montgomery 1971).

Sproul Plaza serves a multiplicity of users and activities and seems to serve them all well. The linear design creates a promenade for thousands of students who enter each day from the south side of campus (where most dormitories and other student housing is located) and head for the libraries and classroom buildings in the heart of campus. If this axial route way is envisaged as a river, then the trees, kiosks, bike racks, steps, and benches on either side create eddy spaces just out of the mainstream, where it is comfortable to stop and look at notices, chat with a friend, or watch the passing crowd. A wide sidewalk between the bollards at the plaza's southern terminus and the busy traffic of Ban-croft Way has become a favorite place for vendors to set up mobile food kiosks. As William Whyte so clearly demonstrated in his studies in Manhattan, the avail-ability of food much enhances the popularity of an urban plaza, and Sproul Plaza is no exception.

Looked at more closely, Sproul Plaza encourages use by people with subtly different needs. So-called street people (nonstudents who live around the campus) often stake out a territory where a set of steps parallel-ing the frontage of the Student Union turns the corner to face Telegraph Avenue; male students watching the passersby often sit on the steps of Sproul Hall and the union; female students tend to sit in slightly less ex-posed locations; black students—a minority group on campus—often cluster at lunchtime in a highly visible location near the Golden Bear building; and elderly men, who use Sproul Plaza on warm days as they might a city park, sit on the wooden benches with backs be-neath the trees on the eastern edge of the plaza.

Successful Features

• Buildings enclose space and funnel pedestrian traffic
• Distance between buildings allows for wide pedestrian flows plus seating on edges
• Tree placements enhance sense of boulevard and of eddy spaces for seating and kiosks
• Buildings edging plaza generate people activity
• Food is available from various sources

• Fountain forms an attractive focal point and meeting location
• Center of plaza creates wider space for rallies, speeches, and performances
• Steps to union and Sproul Hall provide informal edge seating facing pedestrians walking by
• Sycamore trees decrease scale of space for those sitting on edge of plaza

Unsuccessful Features

• Hard surfaces predominate
• Trees are deciduous and heavily pruned; hence greenery is present for only part of the year
• During active use times, there are no places to retreat far from activity
• Intensity of traffic, including bicycles, sometimes feels hazardous
• Intensity of use by one age group (aged eighteen to thirty) makes space relatively uncongenial for older graduate students, staff, and faculty

Faculty Glade, University of California at Berkeley

Location and Context

Faculty Glade is a grassy, bowl-shaped setting, sloping toward the northwest and bordered by mature trees and active pathways. This popular outdoor space on the

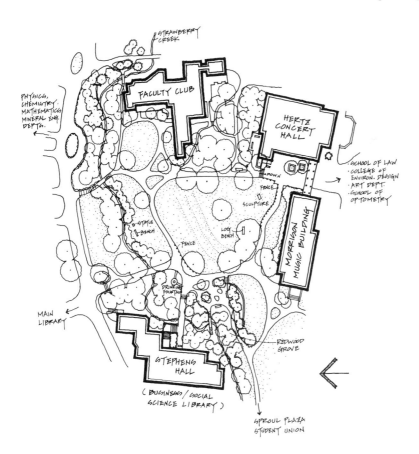

Site plan of Faculty Glade, University of California at Berkeley.

Berkeley campus is loosely framed by a number of low buildings, the faculty club, the music department, and the social sciences library, but the dense tree growth almost screens them from view. Faculty Glade is easily reached from the professional schools that cluster in the southeast quadrant of the campus, including law, environmental design, optometry, art, and music.

Description

This hillside bowl forms an informal grassy amphitheater as it slopes toward the vegetation along Strawberry Creek. Several of the trees in and bordering the glade are very old and gnarled, which adds a sense of history. There are views over the trees to the Campanile from the top of the slope, and at the foot of the slope is a flat area where musicians sometimes perform. There are several exits from and entrances to the site, making it convenient for many people to walk to or through the glade between classes. The entrances narrow as they pass through wooded areas, across bridges, and through arcades to enter the space, and so the sunny expansiveness of the glade creates an attractive contrast. The pathways skirt the main open space, leaving the hillside intact for sitting, sunbathing, and studying.

Faculty Glade: a favorite place to sit during the lunch hour, to eat, relax, study, and sometimes to listen to an informal country and western group.

Major Uses and Users

This natural, parklike setting surrounded by trees was cited by most of the students surveyed in a 1981 study as their favorite space on campus. Those who come, sit on the sunny hillside to study, socialize, eat lunch, or take a rest between classes. The pathways and one concrete bench are the only hard surfaces visible; the green setting is a pleasing contrast with the many high buildings just out of sight beyond the trees and with a major campus roadway screened from view and hearing by the vegetation along Strawberry Creek. During good weather, there is abundant sunshine here; the bowl of surrounding trees screens out the wind; and live oaks on the upper side of the hill provide shade. For those who seek a more secluded setting, there are subspaces around the edges of the glade to be quiet and alone, in a small grove of redwoods to the west and on the banks of Strawberry Creek.

Compared with the active, largely undergraduate focus of Sproul Plaza, Faculty Glade represents a sylvan retreat, enjoyed equally by faculty and students.

Successful Features

• Bowl-shaped setting
• Open grassy slope
• Surrounded by trees
• View of nearby buildings obscured by vegetation
• Pathways and pedestrian movement skirting edges of space
• Sun reaching space all day
• Location and form enhancing between-class recreation

Unsuccessful Features

• Desired pedestrian route from southeast to northwest entry points creating diagonal muddy shortcut across hillside until stopped by added fences
• Only three benches (one concrete, two wooden) for those who do not want to sit on grass
• No benches or tables on edges of glade, for studying on warm days
• Dense vegetative border and moderate lighting, creating a setting perceived as unsafe at night
• Speeding bike riders on down-slope pathways

Central Plaza, Laney College, Oakland, California

Location and Context

Laney College is a small, undergraduate state college, emphasizing vocational subjects and serving a local, largely black population. It is near downtown Oakland and forms part of a redeveloped section of the city, which includes the Oakland Museum, the Oakland Civic Center, and the Nimitz Freeway.

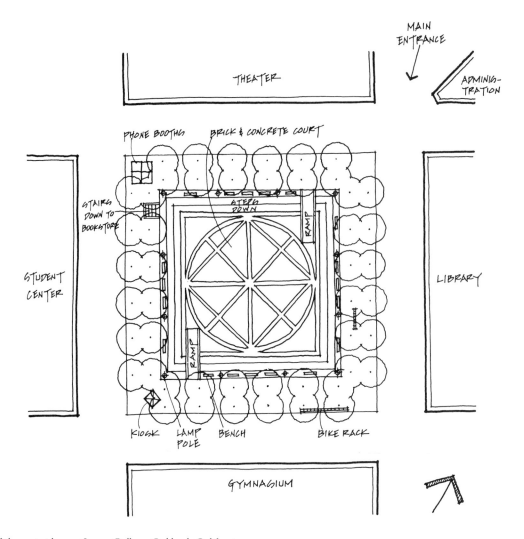

Site plan of the main plaza at Laney College, Oakland, California.

The college was designed by Skidmore, Owings and Merrill, in a compact, symmetrical plan. The buildings are mostly two story, except for an eight-story office tower that focuses attention on the main campus entry on Fallon Street. Unlike many campuses that intermix buildings, plazas, and green spaces, the planners of this campus decided to concentrate the buildings in a square mass like a medieval walled city, and to leave the remaining thirty acres for outdoor sports, recreation, and parking around the periphery.

Description

The plaza at Laney College sits exactly in the center of the square-shaped built-up part of the campus. Because the buildings are laid out on a grid, many straight pathways meet in this central area, bordered by four of the busiest buildings: the Student Center (including a cafeteria and bookstore), theater, library, and gymnasium.

The simple square plaza, approximately 120 by 120 feet in size, has four concentric zones. The outer perimeter contains a gray concrete walkway bordering the adjacent buildings. A second zone inside this comprises a hollow square of asphalt with double rows of trees and poster kiosks. On the inner edge of this zone are short backless benches. A third zone has a set of shallow steps leading down to the last zone, an open lower court paved in a pattern of bricks and concrete and intended for performances, speeches, and exhibits.

Major Uses and Users

Circulation tends to follow the plaza's perimeter with relatively few shortcuts across the central court. People who come, use the plaza for short periods between classes and for a little longer at lunchtime. Most sit around the edges of the inner court, leaning against trees or kiosks or sitting on the benches and steps. Users remark that the space is sometimes too hot and bright or too windy because of the funneling effects of the buildings. The wind often blows litter out of the few litter containers. Some students avoid the plaza because it is patrolled by the police and there are more pleasant and sunny areas overlooking the sports field where one can "hang out and not be harassed."

Although centrally located and bounded by potentially high-use buildings, Laney College Plaza is only partially successful, as two of the buildings (gymnasium and library) have blocked their exits into this plaza, and another building (theater) is only rarely used. Note the very poor choice of bench design, scaled more for a grade school than a college campus.

Successful Features

- Central location
- Adjacent to high-activity buildings
- Buildings that define but do not overwhelm outdoor space

Unsuccessful Features

- Site often windy and partially shaded; not comfortable for use
- Doors from two potential high-activity buildings onto space now blocked; main entries to those buildings relocated away from plaza
- Bench design more suited to a grade school use than a college campus (too narrow and fragile looking)

REFERENCES

Association of University Architects. 1972. *Campus buildings that work.* Philadelphia: North American Publishing.

Brawne, Michael, ed. 1967. *University planning and design.* London: Lund Humphries for the Architectural Association.

Campus Planning Study Group. 1978. *Campus historic resources survey.* Berkeley: University of California.

Campus Environment Assessment Team. 1982. Medical science quad area evaluation. Irvine: University of California. Mimeo.

Deasy, C. M. 1974. *Design for human affairs.* New York: Wiley.

DuVon, Jay. 1966. The campus landscape. In *American Education.* Washington, D.C.: U.S. Department of Health, Education and Welfare, Education Office, May.

Higdon, Cathy. 1988. Berkeley campus—Favorite places. Term paper. Department of Landscape Architecture, University of California.

Institute for Environmental Education. 1982. An evaluation of outdoor space use: The University of New Mexico campus. Albuquerque: University of New Mexico, Monograph No. 13.

Keast, William R. 1967. Introduction to Second Annual Conference, Society for College and University Planning, Ann Arbor, Mich., August 20–22. Ann Arbor, Mich.: Society for College and University Planning.

Kirk, Nana. 1987. Factors affecting perception of safety in the campus environment. Student report, University of Illinois, Department of Landscape Architecture.

Korobkin, Barry J. 1976. *Images for design: Communicating social science research to architects.* American Institute of Architects Research Report. Cambridge, Mass.: Architecture Research Office, Harvard University.

Cooper Marcus, Clare. 1989. Places people take their problems. Mimeo.

Cooper Marcus, Clare, and Trudy Wischemann. 1987. Outdoor spaces for living and learning. *Landscape Architecture,* March–April, pp. 54–61.

———. 1983. Campus open space: An underutilized potential. Mimeo. Department of Landscape Architecture, University of California.

Mayer, Frederick W., ed. 1967. *Contrasting concepts in campus planning.* Selected Papers from First Annual Conference, Society for College and University Planning, Portland State College, Portland, Oregon, August 13–14, 1966. Ann Arbor, Mich.: Society for College and University Planning.

Mayer, Frederick W., and Carl V. Schmult, Jr., eds. 1970. *The changing campus, people and process.* Selected

Papers from the Third Annual Conference, Society for College and University Planning, University of Kentucky, Lexington, August 19–21, 1968. New York: Society for College and University Planning.

———— 1968. *Campus planning 1967.* Selected Papers from the Second Annual Conference, Society for College and University Planning, University of Michigan, Ann Arbor, August 20–22, 1967. Ann Arbor: Society for College and University Planning.

Montgomery, Roger. 1971. Center of action. In *Cities fit to live in and how we can make them happen,* ed. Walter McQuade, pp. 69–78. New York: Macmillan.

Schmertz, Mildred F., ed. 1972. *Campus planning and design.* New York: McGraw-Hill.

Turner, Paul Venable. 1984. *Campus: An American planning tradition.* Cambridge, Mass.: MIT Press.

University of Massachusetts, Department of Landscape Architecture. n.d. *Case studies of campus plans.* Mimeo.

Use of the "front porch" at Wheeler Hall, University of California at Berkeley.

Use of a "front yard" space for an outdoor class on spring day at the University of California, Berkeley.

DESIGN REVIEW CHECKLIST

THE FRONT PORCH

1. Do the campus buildings have "front" and "back" doors?

2. Is there some indication of a "front porch" at the main entry, with provisions for casual study, eating, and socializing?

3. In regions where cool-to-warm weather predominates during the academic year, is the front porch designed to form a sun trap?

4. In latitudes with snowfall, can hot-air vents from the building be placed where they can help melt snow at the front porch?

5. In hot climates, can shading, planting, and natural breezeways be combined to create tolerable temperatures at the front porch?

6. Is the seating comfortable for one or two people to use singly and also for three or four to use as a group?

7. Are there some tables for eating or studying?

8. Is there a source of reasonably priced food and drink close by?

9. Are there adequate litter containers?

10. Is the main entry and name of every building well lit at night? Are the departments or functions of each building cited beneath the building's name?

11. Where the climate precludes sitting outside for most of the year, is there an indoor equivalent of a "front porch"?

THE FRONT YARD

12. Do visual cues indicate the presence of a "front yard" for all or most of the campus buildings?

13. Are there areas of sun and shade in each front yard area?

14. Will grassy areas—even under trees—be pleasant to sit on?

15. Is watering scheduled for night or early morning so that the grass will be dry enough to sit on during the day?

16. Is there seating along the perimeter of this space, and/or around any particularly impressive tree(s)?

THE BACKYARD

17. Do all or most campus buildings have "backyard" areas?

18. Is each backyard easily accessible to, and appropriated by, the users of the building it serves?

19. Does each backyard have the feeling of a "backwater" or "eddy space" away from major campus pedestrian flows?

20. Are the materials used in the backyard areas warm and inviting?

21. Depending on the local microclimate, are there a sufficient number of shaded areas and sunny areas for sitting, particularly during the lunch hour?

22. Is there seating in either "edge" or "island" locations?

23. Are movable benches and tables provided?

24. Can each backyard area be used for a special event (graduation, assembly) without seeming empty on a day-to-day basis?

THE BACKDOOR

25. Does each campus building have a backdoor that is unmistakably a service entrance for deliveries, garbage pickup, and so on?

26. Can trucks or other vehicles approach the backdoor without disturbing the front porch or front yard areas of the same or any other building and without disturbing nearby classrooms whose windows are open?

CAMPUS ENTRANCES

27. If the campus has one major entry, is it located where the majority of students will enter on foot, and is it designed for large pedestrian flows as well as waiting, eating, casual studying, perusing notices, and the like?

28. Where vehicles and pedestrians share an entrance, have the routes for each been carefully planned so as to avoid conflicts?

29. Do all campus entries have clearly designed, well-lit campus maps in prominent locations?

30. Does the campus have adequate directional signs to all major buildings?

31. If the campus roads have names, are they clearly marked?

MAJOR PLAZA SPACES

32. If the plaza area is intended as the principal gathering space on the campus, is it located on a major pedestrian route into or through the campus?

33. Is it bounded by buildings that will generate a high degree of use throughout the day and into the evening (e.g., student union, gym, theater, bookstore, administrative offices, post office)?

34. Is it designed to be large enough for rallies and performances, yet not seem empty when few people are present?

35. Is it designed so that two major daily activities—walking through and sitting—are comfortably accommodated?

36. Is the edge of the space reasonably articulated so as to provide seating and "anchor" spots where people might wait, study, eat, converse with friends, and so on?

37. Do the various forms of seating accommodate people watching, quiet study, sprawling, sitting alone, sitting in a group, and so on?

38. Are bicycle racks provided?

39. Are there notice boards or kiosks for advertising, and are they reasonably sheltered from the wind, with overhangs to protect them from the rain, and away from seating areas?

40. Are there sources of reasonably priced food available, either in or close to the main plaza?

41. Does the plaza contain some eye-catching features, such as a fountain or sculpture, to provide a visual focal point and an easily recognized meeting place?

FAVORITE SPACES

42. If the campus is new, does it have particularly attractive natural features—such as a pond, creek, grove of trees, or natural amphitheater—protected from buildings or the visual encroachment of neighboring buildings?

43. On an existing campus, has a survey of campus users been conducted to determine what the favorite spaces of different groups (undergraduates, graduate students, faculty, staff) are, and have these spaces been protected from change or encroachment?

44. Does the campus provide a variety of natural spaces, from large open lawns to more secluded creekside or woodland settings?

45. In such natural settings, do landscape plans provide for a partial or total boundary of trees, and are people able to "attach" themselves to an "edge" or an "island" when sitting?

46. Are actual or potential favorite spaces situated where they cannot be perceived as the semiexclusive territory or "front yard" of any particular building or department?

47. Have circulation routes been planned in actual or potential favorite spaces so as to permit passing through and sitting to take place without intruding on each other?

48. Are such spaces well lit at night?

OUTDOOR STUDY AREAS

49. Are there areas for outdoor study at major building entries? Close to sources of inexpensive food? In front yard areas? In favorite spaces? In small secluded spaces? In eddy spaces beside major pedestrian flows? Under large mature trees? Against the blank walls of buildings? In semienclosed patios or terraces?

50. Do each of these settings have comfortable seating and, where possible, picnic tables or small, one- to two-person tables for eating and/or studying?

51. Are some outdoor study areas separated from major pedestrian flows by means of distance, planting, level changes, and the like, so that people passing by are not too distracting?

FACTORS INHIBITING CAMPUS USE

52. Is the campus well lit for nighttime use, especially in heavily planted areas and along well-used pedestrian routes?

53. Are there an adequate number of emergency phones in prominent locations?

54. Is there sufficient safety patrol after dark, particularly along well-used routes?

55. Are bicycle routes on campus clearly marked?

56. Is there adequate and secure bicycle parking at each campus entry and at every major building entry?

57. Where cars are permitted on campus, are adjacent sidewalks wide enough for expected peak pedestrian flows? Are crossings clearly marked at major conflict points between pedestrians and cars?

58. In planning a new building or parking area, have existing pedestrian routes and potential desire lines been taken into account?

59. Have adequate litter containers been placed near takeout food sources and in areas favored for eating bag lunches?

60. Have litter containers been placed out of the way of prevailing winds and building-related wind turbulence?

61. Are there adequate pickups of litter from containers?

62. When building a new campus or constructing a new building on an existing campus, can the surfacing of some pedestrian routes be delayed until desire lines are established?

63. When possible, has the natural proclivity to walk in a straight line from one place to another been accommodated?

64. Are there some places on campus—along a creek, through a grove of trees—where people can walk on nondesignated footpaths?

65. Are all direct routes between the major destination points on campus hard surfaced, accessible to disabled persons, well lit, and provided with "eddy spots" or rest and study points?

66. Are well-lit campus maps provided along all major pedestrian routes?

PLANNING FOR THE FUTURE

67. In planning a new campus, have provisions been made to conduct a postoccupancy evaluation survey one or two years after completion of all or part of the campus, to discover what features or facilities need to be redesigned or modified?

68. Has part of the budget for a new campus been set aside for "fine tuning" or modifications as use patterns become established?

5

HOUSING AND OUTDOOR SPACES FOR THE ELDERLY

Diane Y. Carstens

DESIGN AND THE AGING PROCESS

Housing designed specifically for older people (usually defined as those over sixty-five years of age) is becoming a more common housing solution for many of today's elderly (Lawton 1980). More and more older people are now living independently away from their children and in dwellings shared with other people, than was true in previous years. If the current trends continue, the number of elderly (28 million, or approximately 12 percent of total U.S. population in 1984) will soar to 20 percent by the year 2030 (Riche 1986). The demand for such housing is likely to show similar increases. Of particular concern will be determining how to respond to the housing, health care, and service needs of the oldest old (those eighty and above), that segment of the population expected to grow the most rapidly in the next twenty-five years.

There seems no doubt that residents in elderly housing value the opportunity to view and/or use pleasant outdoor spaces. In a study documenting the preferences of 280 tenants of eight low- to moderate-income housing projects for the elderly in New Jersey, 46 percent said that they sat outside every day that weather permitted, and 82 percent said that they liked to sit outdoors in the summer (Cranz 1987). In a study of residents' responses to a high-rise elderly project in San Francisco, 75 percent reported using the outdoor area for sitting and exercise (Cooper Marcus 1990).

In a survey on services and facilities preferred in elderly housing, conducted in "an exclusive, high-income Southern California city," the desire for an outside landscaped area ranked eleventh out of seventy-seven items, the first ten being issues of kitchen design, building security, and emergency facilities (Regnier 1987). Interestingly, in this same survey, "lush landscaping" and a "small pool for exercise" also ranked high, whereas more traditional facilities such as shuffleboard, horseshoes, and a putting green were roundly rejected by a majority of those surveyed. Thus, although outdoor areas for viewing, exercise, and sitting in seem to be desired by the majority of elderly residents in age-segregated housing, the details of what particular facilities are considered important varies by region, previous life experiences, and income group. It is therefore important to use the following guidelines along with local knowledge and, ideally, preference-surveys with prospective residents.

A leading writer on design for the elderly wrote: "Although older people are, on the whole pretty much like the rest of us, there is an important message: where the capabilities of older people do differ from those of younger people, unique needs requiring unique satisfiers may result" (Lawton 1980, p. x). Growing older means a number of subtle and/or critical changes, in social/work role status, health, physical ability, and sensory acuity. These and other age-related changes may reduce the older person's sphere of activity, social networks, and self-confidence and make it more difficult for him or her to gain access to and enjoy the outdoors. Designing for older people thus requires finding design solutions for these needs.

For the elderly, comfort, safety and security, ease of access to the outdoors, and opportunities for meeting others and socializing become increasingly important aspects of outdoor use. Equally important are opportunities to enjoy nature and contribute to one's health and exercise, by taking a short walk or just feeling the

At 1760 Bush Street, a San Francisco Housing Authority Senior Residence, a secure sun pocket beside the entry offers a glimpse of street activity as well as an opportunity to watch residents coming and going. Note the clear street address, covered waiting area, and symbolic gate signifying the boundary between public and semiprivate.

sun on one's face. Yet outdoor spaces connected to housing for older people often consist primarily of functional elements, such as parking and service areas. And recreational enjoyment of the outdoors is often neglected, or treated in a stereotypical way, ignoring the real and varied needs of older people.

The influence of management on the residents' satisfaction with and use of the outdoor environment is also a concern. Programmed activities and events, such as barbecues, encourage use of the outdoors and should therefore be considered early in the planning and design process. Perhaps most importantly, those responsible need to allocate funds for the design and furnishing of outdoor space for use.

HOUSING FOR THE ELDERLY

Although most older people live in their own homes, (a proportion that will likely continue to be high), new kinds of housing designed expressly for older people are

available today, on a continuum from independent living to complete geriatric care. They range from individual homes or apartment units (offering the most independence); to congregate housing providing some level of group services and programs such as meals; to assisted living or residential care facilities providing nonmedical assistance such as bathing and grooming for frail individuals; to geriatric hospitals providing acute care. Each addresses particular needs and abilities, and each has important implications for the designer. These needs, however, may change over time as the resident population ages within a particular building, and they may also vary widely among housing types. Moreover, too many in-house services and support facilities may actually contribute to an "island effect," discouraging exploration of the facilities and services in the neighborhood. Yet, the more frail older person may indeed need more in-house assistance and support facilities. Thus the designer must be aware of this range of abilities and limitations and offer various levels of challenge and support.

It is often helpful to conceptualize three different but overlapping groups of older people (see Table 5.1). The first group is the "go go's," those active "young olds" who may choose a retirement community that offers a range of recreational and social opportunities, from golf and tennis to parties. On the other hand, the "slow go's," typically those in their mid-seventies and eighties, are more likely to choose an intermediate type of living arrangement, such as congregate or residential care communities where services and assistance with daily living are available. Usually, these individuals do not require medical supervision, but merely some assistance with the activities of daily life. They may enjoy more passive and social activity, such as walking, barbecues, card games, and lawn bowls. The third group, the "no go's" or the "old old," represent a small but rapidly growing segment of the aging population. Generally eighty years of age and older, these individuals often require greater levels of personal and medical care, such as is found in nursing homes. The types of activities they prefer tend to be more passive, such as sitting and socializing, watching birds, or taking a short stroll near the front door. There is no definitive list of outdoor amenities to provide in all housing schemes serving older people. The key is to understand the needs, preferences, and desires of the particular group to be served, and to respond with an appropriate program.

The common open spaces surrounding housing for the elderly may take many forms, from a landscaped area around a single high-rise building to a low-rise arrangement whose buildings enclose or define the outdoor spaces. Even in the high-rise alternative, the outdoor space may be relatively open to access or view from the surrounding streets, or it may be walled in for security and privacy.

TABLE 5.1 HOUSING ALTERNATIVES

	Young-Old	Old	Old-Old
Housing	Retirement communities, adult communities	Congregate care, continuing care centers, residential care	Nursing homes, residential care, personal care
Age	Approximately 55 to 70 and over	Approximately 70 to 80 and over	Approximately 80 and over
Ability	Independent, mobile	Semidependent, semimobile (in groups)	Dependent, limited mobility, greater need for health care
Types of Activity	Self-initiated, leisure, recreation, social, health/wellness related	Self- and group-initiated, more sedentary, social, health/wellness related	Limited (staff-initiated), group, sedentary, social, therapeutic

The guidelines and issues presented here do not address the design of open spaces for any particular housing type or layout for elderly persons, nor do they address regional preferences or the preferences and lifestyles of a particular socioeconomic cohort. Rather, we hope that these recommendations, based on the current research literature, can be adapted to any housing layout, location, or microclimate.

This chapter does not discuss site selection, although it obviously has important implications for older people's use of the outdoors. A carefully selected site, for instance, can help ensure residents' safety and security outdoors and provide reasons for outdoor use, be it strolling through the neighboring shopping district or enjoying a beautiful view. Sites close to shopping, services, and health care can also reduce the need for providing such amenities on the site, thus lowering development costs. (A few excellent sources are available on site selection, including Central Mortgage and Housing Corporation 1975, MSHDA 1974, and Zeisel, Epp, and Demos 1977.)

LITERATURE ON DESIGN AND AGING

As the proportion of older persons in the U.S. population began to increase, the literature on aging issues grew as well. Social scientists have addressed issues such as social interaction, privacy, personal space,

safety and security, and neighborhood mobility. The literature from other nondesign fields, such as leisure studies and recreation, can also aid in understanding factors that may affect the older person's participation in outdoor recreation, although most of the articles focus on indoor activities and facilities. New books in the gerontology field rarely address interactions between people and their environment, but there are some notable exceptions in the works of Lawton (1980), Pastalan (1970), and Regnier and Pynoos (1987).

Two major trends in the literature have become evident: (1) a call for a more comprehensive "systems" approach to the planning, design, and management of housing for older people and (2) the development of specific design manuals (most focus on indoor spaces).

The call for a more comprehensive systems approach to providing quality housing for the elderly came first in a short report, *Behavioral Requirements for Housing for the Elderly* (Byerts and Conway 1972), which examined housing as a "complex delivery system." The facility's design is but one supporting component of the total housing package, which also includes planning, leisure and service programming, and management. This is a particularly important approach, as older persons may spend more time at home and depend more on their immediate environment for friendship, activities, and support services. *Congregate Housing for Older*

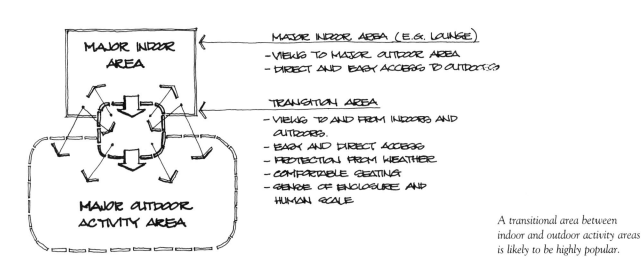

A transitional area between indoor and outdoor activity areas is likely to be highly popular.

People: A Solution for the 1980s (Chellis, Seagle, and Seagle 1982) takes a similar approach, discussing key issues surrounding the planning, development, and management of housing for the elderly, though it too focuses on interiors.

Housing for the Elderly: Privacy and Independence (Hoglund 1985) and *Housing for a Maturing Population* (Urban Land Institute 1983) examine the housing options currently available, the current thinking on the topic, and case examples complete with plans and photographs. The first book concentrates on options in northern Europe, and the second one looks at the United States, though both deal primarily with indoor spaces.

In regard to the literature on design guidelines, *Housing for the Elderly: The Development and Design Process* (Green et al. 1975) was a useful early guideline manual for the planning and design of indoor and outdoor spaces, as it covers all stages of the design process, from issues and guidelines for facility programming, site selection, and design, to technical standards. The performance criteria for the initial schematic stages of design, based on the needs and problems of older people, are covered in *Low Rise Housing for Older People: Behavioral Criteria for Design* (Zeisel, Epp, and Demos 1977). Its examples of designs of indoor and outdoor spaces, evaluations of numerous site plans from a low-rise housing design competition, and design review questions summarizing each chapter are extremely useful. Another publication by the same authors, *Midrise Housing for the Elderly* (Zeisel, Welch, Epp, and Demos 1981), covers similar issues for higher-density housing. An excellent discussion of the environmental needs of older people in high-rise housing, *Designing for Aging: Patterns of Use* (Howell 1980), deals mainly with private and shared indoor spaces but says little about the outdoors. Another interesting and useful approach is that of *Housing the Aged: Design Directives and Policy Considerations* (Regnier and Pynoos 1987). Each chapter is a well-illustrated report of a particular piece of research or programming strategy (each by a different author), and each chapter concludes with design directives and policy considerations.

Patterns of outdoor use in elderly housing are now beginning to be studied and reported. A University of California master's thesis (Wolfe 1975) was one of the first studies of the use of private and communal outdoor spaces in housing for the elderly. Inese and Lovering, in a 1983 analysis of thirteen congregate housing and nursing home settings in Canada identified four factors that they considered influential with regard to outdoor space use: motivation (attraction to active area of site), level of independence, microclimate, and seat comfort (Regnier 1985). And an observation study of an elderly housing project in Ohio by Brown (Regnier 1985) concluded that the three most significant design factors influencing outdoor use were a sense of orientation,

opportunities for sensory stimulation, and "control and mastery" over the environment.

A monograph by Victor Regnier (1985) presents case studies of outdoor space use at twelve housing developments for the elderly in the Los Angeles area. The monograph used various data-gathering methods, including focus groups and behavioral mapping, and concludes with a set of design directives "formulated . . . in order to communicate in the clearest way possible the implications of the research for design decision makers" (Regnier 1985, p. 131). Finally, Diane Carstens's *Site Planning and Design for the Elderly: Issues, Guidelines and Alternatives* (1985) was the first comprehensive guidebook to the needs of older people as they relate to the planning and design of outdoor spaces. (This chapter, by the same author, is both a summary and an expansion of that book.)

GUIDELINES FOR SITE PLANNING, DESIGN, AND DETAILING

The overall layout of outdoor spaces and the relationship among different on-site components can affect the use of outdoor spaces and amenities, as well as safety and security, orientation, efficiency of service delivery, and even the image of the community. Issues of building mass and height also pertain to the use and enjoyment of outdoor areas around elderly housing, in regard to sun and shade and wind patterns.

General Layout and Clustering

- Clustering together activities and services can increase the opportunities for drop-in use and thus the level of activity and use of amenities. Mail boxes, casual seating, and an outdoor patio, for example, may be clustered near the main entry, giving a sense of vitality to the project as a whole, and increasing the opportunities for chance meetings among the residents. If activities are too dispersed around the site, the community may appear "sleepy" and devoid of activity and vitality.
- Clustering residential units in groups of roughly twenty to thirty units gives a more residential character to the site and creates a sense of neighborhood, especially if small shared spaces are developed concurrently with the unit cluster.
- Circulation systems are a key component of clustering. A main walkway that connects all the major activity components also increases drop-in use and chance meetings, especially if the walkway connects such high-use areas as the parking lot, the dining room (if one is provided), and the main site/building entry.

Mixing Different Levels of Care on the Same Site

When different levels of care are offered on the same site, the job of the site planner becomes much more

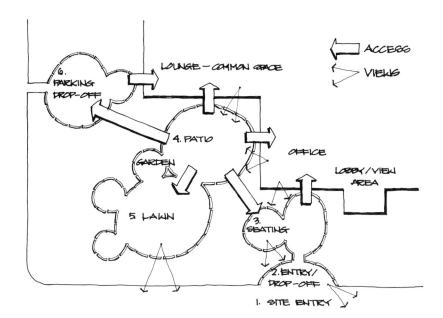

Clustering activity areas leads to greater casual use and a sense of liveliness and greater security.

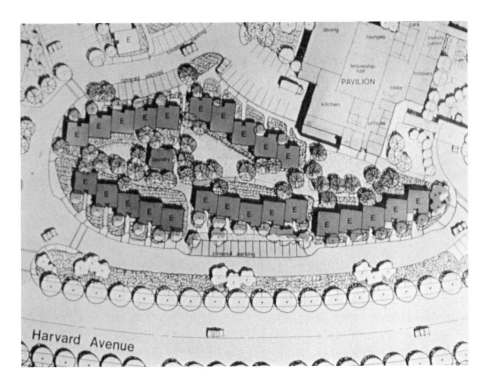

This unit cluster, in Regents' Point, Irvine, California, includes a shared walkway linking the units' backdoors to the shared utility/laundry facility and the main activity building. This arrangement can enhance chance encounters among residents of the cluster. (Photo: Diane Y. Carstens)

complicated. One question to be addressed is what and how to mix different levels of care and their associated services and amenities. Are residents willing to share facilities with those who are more frail? What is the most efficient and cost-effective method of management and service delivery? These questions cannot be addressed in depth in this chapter, but they are important enough to warrant consulting *Site Planning and Design for the Elderly* (Carstens 1985) and *Congregate Housing for the Elderly* (Chellis, Seagle, and Seagle 1982).

The way that different levels of care (such as independent living, assisted living, and nursing care) do or

do not relate to one another on the site has implications for social interaction, the image of the community, opportunities for mutual self-help, and even for the efficiency and cost of service delivery. Some considerations are as follows:

• As more levels of care are added to a site, it is important to avoid creating an institutional, or health care, image of the community. Planning and design variables that can help alleviate this problem are (1) a unit mix, the ratio of independent to care units; (2) location and relationship: Are different care levels located in the same building, adjacent, or separate? Do they share certain facilities and services, such as a multipurpose space or exercise course? and (3) design image, or the type and scale of the buildings and outdoor spaces and the level of detail and type of amenities, all of which create certain images of independence and health care.

- Certain amenities and facilities may be more suitable for sharing than others are, both in the minds of residents (the more able may not want to share with the frail and confused) and from a management perspective.

Microclimate

In a wind study of six high-rise projects for the elderly in Los Angeles, Regnier found four with serious uncontrolled down-draft problems on the first floor, where outdoor activities had been located. In one, wind currents were so severe that a courtyard had to be closed. On the other hand, an adequately controlled breeze can be an asset in hot locations and the lack of wind in enclosed courtyards can be a problem when temperatures are high (Regnier 1985, p. 138). Elderly people are particularly susceptible to changes in temperature, excessive heat, cold, windiness, and glare. The microclimate of twelve projects for the elderly in Los Angeles were studied by Regnier; nine had at least one major outdoor space that was severely limited during the afternoon because of excessive heat and glare. According to this study, elderly residents tended to do their shopping and household tasks in the morning and to use the outdoor spaces in the afternoon. Therefore, when planning outdoor areas at a new site, it is important to find out whether morning or afternoon use is

more popular and then to place buildings so that they either screen out the sunlight (in southern latitudes) or let it in (in northern latitudes).

Design Recommendations

- Use a wind tunnel analysis at the building-design stage so as to avoid wind problems after construction. Wind tunnel studies can pinpoint problems in time for their redesign or mitigation.
- Alleviate down-draft or crosswind problems by the appropriate location of overhangs, wind screens, buffer planting, walls, or berms.
- Situate courtyards and seating areas where they will catch summer breezes; this is especially important in regions where heat is a problem.
- Provide outdoor seating or strolling areas that allow a choice of sunny or shady locations, at different times of the day.
- Place trellises or awnings at building entries in order to mitigate problems with glare.
- Plant deciduous vine covers over trellises where appropriate, to screen out summer sun but to let in winter sun.
- Provide umbrella tables and awnings that residents or management can move around to get shade at different times of the day or year.
- Consider the shade and density of trees, as they can affect nearby seating.
- Use darker, nonreflective paving to reduce glare.

GUIDELINES BASED ON OLDER PEOPLE'S SOCIAL AND PSYCHOLOGICAL NEEDS

The concerns of older people about outdoor use, as well as their spatial requirements and preferences, sug-

At Kings Road, West Hollywood, California, movable seating, umbrella tables, and large trees allow for fine-tuning of temperature and level of sunlight. (Photo: Diane Y. Carstens)

gest several design issues for older people with declining health and smaller social networks.

Provide a "prosthetic environment" that offers appropriate levels of challenge and support when needed. A prosthetic environment is one that permits the older person to function, in spite of disabilities, by offering support when needed but allowing for independence, challenge, and learning. It requires recognizing the disabilities of the elderly and searching for environmental supports that facilitate a higher level of functioning (Lawton 1970b). Providing incremental "doses" of challenge and support is one approach, permitting the practice of skills and independence and reducing the likelihood of frustration, anxiety, or even withdrawal from too challenging an activity. Practice is essential to the maintenance of physical, cognitive, and social skills (Atchely 1972).

Design Recommendations

- Offer choices in length and difficulty of walking routes (e.g., routes with an incline and those on level ground).
- Include prosthetic elements or devices, such as handrails, to encourage participation by less-able residents.
- Allow for recreational options, ranging from the observation of activities to walking, gardening, and so forth.

Make available to residents a variety of outdoor areas and activities. Variety and choice should be available both outdoors and indoors, particularly in planned housing where many older persons must share the same "house" and where less-able residents will spend more time at "home" and depend more on their immediate environment to fulfill their needs. If given a choice, older people tend to select that activity best suited to their ability level (Lawton 1970a).

Design Recommendations

- Provide both informal and formal (i.e., programmed) outdoor areas.
- Create settings suitable for socializing with others, as well as for intimacy and privacy.
- Allow choices in the scale of spaces, from large open spaces to small "nooks."
- Provide settings for the pursuit of both individual and group activities and hobbies.

Encourage autonomy, independence, and a sense of usefulness by letting residents perform routine tasks for themselves. Some autonomy is sacrificed in housing that offers group services and facilities (Lawton 1980). In addition, retirement from the work force may create problems regarding a person's sense of usefulness and importance. Thus a design and management policy that allows residents of all ability levels to perform some or most tasks for themselves reinforces a sense of autonomy and self esteem.

Private patios and balconies off individual units help promote a sense of independence and usefulness. These spaces provide a setting for continuing many of the domestic tasks that are part of an active home life, such as gardening, airing bedding, drying clothes, storing things, tending visiting children, making repairs, and barbecuing. Front porches, backyards, patios, and gardens are good settings for domestic and personal activities that add to a sense of self. Each resident should have some private outdoor space for an independent domestic life (Wolfe 1975).

Design Recommendations

- Allow easy access to outdoor on-site facilities, designed for comfort and ease of use.
- Create options for the control of privacy, for example, drapes, blinds, patio screens.
- Provide opportunities for going outdoors.
- Encourage participation in outdoor maintenance and sharing responsibility for outdoor recreation planning, equipment, and the like.
- Include a private outdoor patio or balcony for each unit.
- Provide space that can be used for individual garden plots, and allow gardening also in the public areas of the grounds.

Use the design of outdoor spaces to reinforce both actual and perceived safety and security. The fear of falling or of being bothered by a stranger and not being helped is a concern of many people. The fear of crime also inhibits their going outdoors. Feeling safe and secure thus encourages outdoor use and is a strong determinant of older people's general life satisfaction (Lawton 1980). Thus, measures to enhance safety, security, and negotiability of outdoor spaces are critical.

Too often, unfortunately, management responds to perceived or real threats to security by locking doors. In five of twelve elderly projects that Regnier studied in Los Angeles, locked-door policies limited the use of outdoor spaces.

The locking of a door is such a simple procedure it often involves no direct cost whatsoever to management. . . . Because it is such a simple adjustment, it is not specified in any depth or detail on drawings for the building, nor are the policies regarding which doors are to be locked or unlocked clearly defined at the programming phase. (Regnier 1985, p. 139)

Design Recommendations

- Design outdoor spaces to be visible from indoor and outdoor areas frequented by staff and residents.

- Locate outdoor areas for physical and psychological protection, such as the enclosure offered by two sides of an L-shaped building.
- Clearly define the areas for residents' use and control, as opposed to public or neighborhood use.
- Include detailing and facilities such as lighting, ground cover, and high-branching plant materials that allow for surveillance and promote safety.
- Design walking paths that loop back to the building entrance, to improve safety in outdoor areas for use by residents who are confused and might otherwise get lost.
- Design outdoor spaces with "defensible space" principles in mind, and make them secure enough that doors to and from such spaces do not usually need to be locked.
- Plan at the programming stage which exterior doors will need to be locked, and ensure that these are not entrances to usable outdoor spaces.

Provide a transition or halfway zone between indoor and outdoor areas. Less-able elderly people may be unsure of their ability to participate in activities or to handle environments that demand more physical or psychological effort. A significant physiological change with age is the greater susceptibility to glare when moving from interior to outdoor spaces. A halfway zone for a moment's hesitation to adjust to changes in light, temperature, and sound, or for sitting and watching an activity, can provide needed time for sizing up the situation and preparing oneself before joining in, or at least a comfortable spot for watching.

Design Recommendations

- Create a transition area between major indoor and outdoor areas, such as a screened porch. This can offer protection from climate and glare, a sense of safety and security, and a place to sit and watch. According to one survey of nursing home residents, porches were more highly valued than was any other common space, including activity rooms (Hiatt 1980, p. 36).

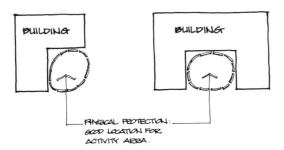

Outdoor space that is safe and secure, and perceived as such, will receive much greater use.

- Provide a handrail for a moment's hesitation and support.
- Include an overhang at all building exits, to allow gradual adjustment to changes in illumination and protection from weather.
- Locate private balconies and patios within sight of other private or public outdoor spaces, to make opportunities for social encounters without leaving the security of one's own territory.

Create subspaces for meeting others, for intimacy with a few friends, or for solitude. Meeting and talking with others seems to be the main reason for many older people's use of shared spaces. Separation from family, retirement, and declining health (and mobility) often make it more difficult to get out into the community and meet others. Thus opportunities for meeting others nearer home are particularly important.

Design can support a close, intimate relationship with a few friends by allowing the older person to appropriate smaller intimate spaces. In general, smaller spaces make it easier for an older person to meet and talk with others, because smaller spaces reduce the number of distractions that may contribute to the loss of a train of thought or confusion over who was speaking, even what was being said (*Time* 1981). In addition, smaller spaces are more easily approached and claimed as "our meeting place," particularly by the less able, who may be intimidated by larger spaces and larger groups of people—or by men, who may be intimidated by the preponderance of women in housing for older adults.

Design Recommendations

- Create a variety of small spaces for socializing and intimacy.
- Locate spaces for meeting others near centers of activity, for impromptu meetings and an interesting view.
- Make building entries and site entries prime locations for meeting others.
- Develop small subareas within larger spaces. Large multipurpose spaces are generally not suitable for informal socializing.
- Supply the appropriate furniture to allow spaces to be used as planned, for example, benches or light, movable chairs that allow for face-to-face interaction.
- Provide seating areas where a person can be alone. Many older people may tire of constantly being with others and prefer to sit outside alone. Indeed, the most popular sitting place at a Los Angeles high-rise project is a bench that can be appropriated by one person. It is located halfway along a popular promenade deck, which is backed up against the building and has a view of the sur-

At Rosa Parks Senior Apartments in San Francisco, Russian-speaking women in a multiethnic—multilingual housing project have laid claim to this pleasant bench, meeting daily to converse.

rounding downtown. "Residents claimed that the bench is so popular that others sitting nearby will wait for people to leave so that they can move there" (Regnier 1985, p. 34).

Arrange and design outdoor spaces to help older people orient themselves and find their way outdoors. One aspect of designing for outdoor use is deciding how the environment will be perceived and understood. Age-related changes in sensory processes may act as a "perceptual screen," filtering out particular kinds of information about the physical and social environment (De Long 1970). Thus many older people may depend on more limited sensory information when interacting with others, finding their way around the outdoors, or just enjoying being outside (De Long 1970, Pastalan 1971). Thus two major issues for design are orientation, and sensory stimulation and environmental comprehension.

Although many cognitive functions do not change with age, disease may result in failing memory and more difficulty for older people to orient themselves and find their way in a less familiar environment (Koncelik 1976). This is particularly true in monotonous undefined areas with few or unfamiliar clues for orienting oneself, too many directions to choose from, or too many distractions.

From a different perspective, Hiatt pointed out that outdoor settings have great potential for both individual memory development and group memory stimulation. Thus in an environment designed to balance comprehensibility with opportunities to enjoy seasonal and diurnal change, "these varied patterns of activity or growth may be natural stimuli to memory utilization and more valuable because of their combined familiarity and unpredictability" (Hiatt 1980, p. 35). It is important to identify where finding one's way between key destinations is an objective and to strike a balance between clarity, familiarity, and ambiguity.

Design Recommendations

- Use a basic organizational pattern that is easy to recognize and identify.
- Identify well-traveled routes by means of an unusual feature or focal point, which is supported by detailing to provide sensory clues and support the basic organizational scheme.
- Arrange spaces in hierarchies, with one space dominant, to provide spatial clues for orientation (De Long 1970, Pastalan 1971).
- Provide views from one area to another, views of landmarks, and signage to help people find their position in relation to the rest of the site.
- Construct an enclosed outdoor area or walkways that loop back to the door, which may be especially important in intensive-care facilities. Hiatt described (1980) one geriatric center where a protected area is situated between building walls, enclosed by a series of fences, hedgerows, and walls (the walls were sometimes concealed behind planting). This area consists of several subareas, including seating; there is no location from which closure is apparent; and hence there is no sense of confinement. Confused residents who might otherwise wander away are thus able to meander happily here, with minimal supervision.

Make available ample sensory information, to facilitate environmental comprehension and enjoyment. Sensorally loading the environment is one approach to compensating for age-related sensory losses. Tactile elements

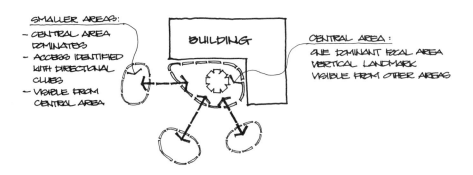

SMALLER AREAS:
- CENTRAL AREA DOMINATES
- ACCESS IDENTIFIED WITH DIRECTIONAL CLUES
- VISIBLE FROM CENTRAL AREA

BUILDING

CENTRAL AREA:
ONE DOMINANT FOCAL AREA
VERTICAL LANDMARK
VISIBLE FROM OTHER AREAS

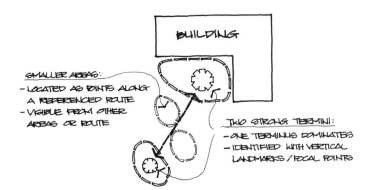

BUILDING

SMALLER AREAS:
- LOCATED AS POINTS ALONG A REFERENCED ROUTE
- VISIBLE FROM OTHER AREAS OR ROUTE

TWO STRONG TERMINI:
- ONE TERMINUS DOMINATES
- IDENTIFIED WITH VERTICAL LANDMARKS / FOCAL POINTS

Design components that make orientation easier include a readily understood circulation pattern, such as radial (top) or axial (bottom); hierarchy of spaces; and focal points and landmarks along the route.

This vertical landmark, visible from most parts of the site, helps residents orient themselves outdoors. (Photo: Diane Y. Carstens)

are particularly important, as vision and hearing are typically the first senses to decline with age.

Design Recommendations

- Offer visual, auditory, kinesthetic, and tactile stimulation. Tactile clues are particularly important, such as changes in paving texture at major traffic intersections or right before stairs.
- Use yellow, orange, and red where color differentiation is desired, as these are more easily "read." Blue, green, and violet are not as easily differentiated, owing to the yellowing of the eye lens, which acts as a filter.
- Provide planting with markedly different leaf textures, overall forms, and flower perfumes, to stimulate the visual and olfactory senses.
- Provide varieties of shade and enclosure and openings along walkways to allow a varied sensory experience, but avoid the juxtaposition of deep shadows and bright light on walking surfaces as this may be perceived as a change in grade.

Provide spaces to enhance social interaction. A popular misconception about older people is that they prefer a "peaceful and quiet environment" (Carstens 1982). But meeting and talking with others and feeling part of the activity is very important to many older people. Visiting with family or grandchildren outdoors may be an attractive alternative. Even sitting and watching the activities of others may be an active form of participation, particularly for the more frail (Carstens 1982).

Common spaces, which often are centers for social interaction, may become increasingly important to frail persons, who may not be able to get out into the community and meet others as often as they would like.

Several factors figure prominently in the success of a socializing area: in particular a location near activity, as well as safety, security, negotiability, comfort, and easy access.

Design Recommendations

- Locate outdoor socializing areas near indoor activities, such as building entries, lounges, dining rooms, or game areas. Provide enough space to accommodate the functional activities of the area and people passing by, as well as space for sitting, watching, and talking. "Coupled" seating, in which those sitting inside the lobby and those sitting just outside are visible to each other, seems especially popular (Regnier 1985).
- Choose a place for seating that feels safe and secure, such as near a building edge or an enclosed corner. Places visible from areas frequented by staff and residents generally feel secure. Avoid seating

Social areas located adjacent to indoor activity, such as this courtyard next to the dining room at the Duncaster Life Care Center in Bloomfield, Connecticut, can offer a place for drop-in socializing before and after meals. (Photo: Diane Y. Carstens)

arrangements in which residents would have their backs exposed to open space. As is true for most people, the elderly feel more secure when seating is backed by a building, wall, or planting.
- Put outdoor socializing areas close to indoor common spaces, for easy access. This is particularly important to the less agile, who may desire a quick retreat to the comforts of the building.
- Avoid seating arrangements that may create uncomfortable visual closeness for users. According to a detailed observation study of two Los Angeles projects with circular sociopetal bench designs, residents never used these facilities and complained about the uncomfortably close proxemic distances. "In some designs which take a circular or elliptical form of more than 180 degrees, a sense of enclosure is created which defines the space as an outdoor room. . . . One can either enter or leave the space but in so doing a commitment is made to interact with or ignore others" (Regnier 1985, p. 140).
- Create one right-angled or open U-shaped seating arrangement near the busiest entrance. This kind of design allows a few people to sit at conversational distance but does not create an "outdoor room" scenario. It seems that those who want to engage in group interaction often cluster near building entries.
- If the budget is limited, place seating along a highly used pathway rather than in quiet, landscaped areas, however attractive and comfortable they may be. "Seating located on, near, or within view of a [highly used] pedestrian circulation pathway is frequently the most popular sitting area. . . . These locations allow residents to enter into informal ad-hoc conversations" (Regnier 1985, p. 134).
- Position seating to allow residents to watch active local streets and thus to partake of neighborhood life. In one Los Angeles project, a covered seating arcade on the edge of the site permits residents to view the bustle of a nearby business district through dense planting, thus creating a virtual one-way mirror view. This proved to be an extremely popular place to sit (Regnier 1985, p. 135). And in an interview survey of 190 elderly residents of six age-segregated public housing schemes in San Francisco, about half indicated that they liked to sit outside, with the largest proportion choosing to sit "in front facing the street." Those who regularly spent time in this area had significantly higher housing satisfaction scores than did those who did not (Cranz 1987).
- In projects that provide meals, locate an outdoor seating area just outside the dining room, as it is often popular before and after mealtimes. Make sure that such a space receives sun at lunchtime or

This seating area, provided for an elderly housing project in Atlanta, fails on several accounts: The benches are oriented inwards, yet with nothing to look at, save someone sitting opposite; there is no provision for shade; there is no right-angle seating; and the area itself is separated by a street from the housing it serves.

Three-wheeler parking spaces designed as part of the main entry to the community building at Island Lake Village, a housing scheme for the elderly in Florida. (Photo: Diane Y. Carstens)

—in hot areas—has umbrellas or awnings that can be used to create shade.

- If the building has a family dining or party room that can be reserved, construct an outdoor patio next to it for a small-group barbecue, picnic, or cocktail party.
- Include "props," such as drinking fountains, bird feeders, game tables, and fountains, in the site's landscaped interiors, as they may create a reason for using a space, while at the same time offering comfort and interest.
- Cluster gardening beds so that residents can socialize while working and help one another. Also, provide a drinking fountain and place the beds in a visible area, with benches nearby for resting and for observing the action.

Provide specific areas for exercise. Health and exercise are concerns of many older people and are one reason for outdoor use (Carstens 1982). A series of studies on the preferences of over twenty-five thousand older adults across the United States conducted by Gerontological Services, Inc., indicate a growing interest in health and wellness-related facilities and that an outdoor walking/exercise course is often the most popular outdoor amenity. Some residents may be very active; whereas others may have health and mobility problems that limit their use of the outdoors, or they may feel that they "tire too easily." Thus there should be a variety of outdoor experiences and specific recreational facilities. In nursing homes an outdoor physical therapy area might help residents build strength while enjoying being outside and in turn lead to their greater use of the outdoor facilities. Hiatt described one facility where "a physical therapy area was developed outdoors where a small bridge and its handrails were used like indoor, parallel bars to encourage walking. Pulleys of carefully weighted plants were operated like the more mundane weights. Heated soil served to encourage exercising arthritic hands" (Hiatt 1980, p. 38).

Design Recommendations

- Offer activities that match the exertion level of prospective residents (e.g., very frail people will not use a shuffleboard court).
- Place areas for more passive exercise or just sitting in the sun close to the building, to encourage use by the less able.
- Make sure there are views of recreation areas from inside the building and patio areas, to provide a catalyst to participation and to allow surveillance by staff. Activity areas removed from major pathways or view may not often be used.
- Create walkway loops that offer choices in length and difficulty of routes, to accommodate people of all ability levels. Walking is a particularly popular activity among many older people.
- Consider building a ramped walkway with handrails as part of an exercise route. A study of a high-rise project in Los Angeles reported that non-handicapped residents frequently used a ramp connecting two plazas as an exercise course, where their progress in "laps" could easily be measured. This ramp was particularly supportive of exercise since it had a shallow incline; a rough texture that discouraged slipping; a landing at a half-way point; a handrail running the entire length of the ramp; and colorful plants on either side (Regnier 1985, p. 28).

- Consider building a covered arcade or veranda for an exercise area during poor weather. A fifteen-foot wide setback at ground level created an arcade all the way around a Los Angeles high-rise elderly scheme and was popular as an exercise track (Regnier 1985, p. 60).
- Check on the availability of suitable recreation facilities in nearby parks. Studies of San Francisco parks indicate a number where a semi-enclosed "card shack" is heavily used by elderly men who travel from their homes each day to play cards, dominos, checkers, and other games. It is unlikely that most of these men would abandon this social setting even if moving to a nearby elderly scheme with a card-playing area. Another issue is the number of residents in a project necessary to support a particular exercise or recreation facility. This critical mass may be impossible in schemes where the gender and/or native-language ratios of residents create many small subgroups.
- If an exercise facility is shared by two adjacent projects, make sure that the facility's location and detailing indicate that it is meant to be shared. For example, a shuffleboard court located between two Los Angeles projects, but physically closer to one of them, created territorial confusion and nonuse (Regnier 1985, p. 54).
- Construct specific recreational facilities based on the prospective residents' needs, abilities and desires. Those that also offer opportunities to socialize are often the most popular.
- Consider finishing outdoor activity spaces only after residents have moved in. Their involvement in deciding what to provide will ensure that the facilities are wanted and may increase the residents' use of them (Regnier 1985, p. 136).

A popular putting green in a housing scheme for the elderly, San Mateo, California.

- Use special detailing for facilities and equipment, in order to encourage participation by those with some infirmity. Finely graded playing surfaces for easy walking and brightly colored equipment for visibility are examples of such detailing.
- Provide resting spots in shade for those who tire more easily and those who are sensitive to heat or glare.
- Place drinking fountains near exercise areas.
- Be sure that restrooms are easily accessible from exercise areas.
- Provide storage for necessary equipment in a location that is easily accessible to residents.
- For nursing care facilities, consider creating an outdoor physical therapy area.

Provide outdoor spaces for enjoying nature. Residents frequently use private open space off individual units for sunning, breathing fresh air, checking the weather, watching the sky, growing plants, and feeding birds (Wolfe 1975). For more frail older persons, enjoying nature may encourage seasonal awareness and help maintain cognitive orientation to the passing of time, while offering variety and interest. Likewise, as Hiatt (1980) pointed out, grass, trees, and soil provide a welcome contrast with the smooth, fire-resistant, and easily cleaned surfaces characteristic of indoor institutional living. A slightly meandering walkway in the grounds of a mid-rise project for the elderly in Los Angeles is bordered by a variety of flowering plants, shrubs, and mature trees and is particularly appreciated by residents as a place to exercise. Large, mature trees were planted along with fast-growing species so that the landscape had a lush appearance from the first day of occupancy (Regnier 1985, p. 86).

Design Recommendations

- Situate some "green" areas for easy viewing from indoors and others more removed from the building, so as to encourage exercise and exploration.
- If the site permits, provide a variety of outdoor spaces, from formal gardens to more natural trails and wildlife areas.
- Use a variety of plant materials for seasonal color and form, to attract wildlife, and amenities such as bird feeders, to add interest and activity. Those too frail to go outdoors especially appreciate being able to see such color and wildlife from lounge windows.
- Create places for residents to participate in nature, such as garden plots and places for personal bird feeders. Gardening demand may vary from year to year, so avoid large bare areas for gardens.
- Build private or semiprivate patios and balconies off individual units to promote daily contact with the outdoors.
- Incorporate some garden plots with special facilities, such as raised work areas and planting beds accessible to the disabled.
- Provide a toolshed and water source near the garden area.
- Make sure to have a paved access way through the garden areas, for the less able.
- Consider building a greenhouse for gardening in the winter or for those who like to raise flowers. This could be located on an accessible rooftop, but heat and glare must be mitigated.

Provide for the enjoyment of the outdoors from within the building. Some older people may enjoy viewing the out-

A very popular feature at the Duncaster Life Care Center in Bloomfield, Connecticut, is this long, curving boardwalk leading through woods over wetlands to the community gardens. (Photo: Felice Frankel Photography)

A separate gardening area for serious gardeners is provided for the residents of Leisure World, Laguna Hills, California. The toolshed, housing shared tools purchased with the nominal annual gardening plot fee, also includes a shaded seating area and a drinking fountain for a comfortable respite from work. (Photo: Diane Y. Carstens)

doors most frequently from indoor areas. Views thus are a very important "window on the world." Two major aspects of views are what is viewed and from what position it is viewed. Views of activity and change (diurnal, seasonal) are generally the most popular, although a variety of views is best. Many people, particularly the less mobile, have a favorite chair where they like to sit and watch outdoor activity.

Design Recommendations

- Situate outdoor areas where they can be viewed from a seated position inside, especially from upper-story windows.
- In climates with frequent inclement weather, use architectural devices that allow for viewing from indoors. A solarium, for example, can be modified for exposure to the outdoors in good weather and for control of temperature and glare.
- Consider framing views with plant materials. The height of railings and window ledges should always allow for viewing from a seated position.
- Include night lighting to provide drama and interest as well as safety and security. But make sure that it does not interfere with the residents' sleep.
- Use architectural devices, window glazing, and planting to reduce glare.

In the previous section, we discussed some of the particular needs of older persons and the physical design recommendations to meet those needs. In this section, we reverse the procedure and discuss typical site components from the viewpoint of how they might best serve the needs of elderly residents.

What specific kinds of outdoor areas to include in a particular design is, of course, best determined by ana-

lyzing the existing site conditions and the needs, abilities, and preferences of the potential residents.

Site Entry

The site entry is important to both the residents' and the visitors' access, as well as to the community image. Safety, easy recognition, and access are the primary considerations.

Design Recommendations

- Consider site-specific qualities when determining the location of the site entry. Major traffic streets can offer high entrance visibility and easy access, whereas minor streets offer increased safety but may reduce entrance visibility (Green et al. 1975).
- Allow adequate sight distance in both directions down the street, for the street-crossing safety of older people, who may have poorer vision and slower reactions. A two-hundred-foot minimum view distance is often recommended (Green et al. 1975).
- Provide a covered transit stop near the site and building entry.
- Choose a type and size of entry that is easy to recognize but is not overpowering.
- Use high-branching trees or low plants that do not obscure vision around the entry.
- Use clear, bold signage and lighting to identify the entry and building.
- Put seating near the site entry clearly within the domain of the housing scheme, or it may be seen as public and be appropriated by outsiders.

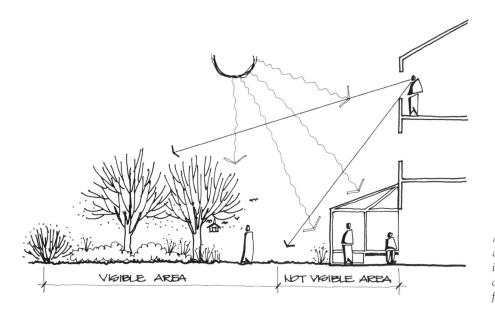

VISIBLE AREA   NOT VISIBLE AREA

A solarium at ground level allows an experience of outdoors in all types of weather yet can be designed not to block the views from upper-story windows.

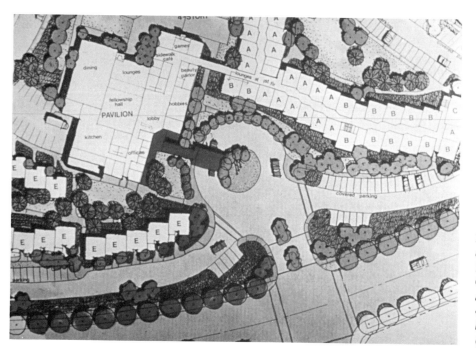

Located "up front," this entry drive and central drop-off area at Regents Point, Irvine, California, is easy to identify and welcoming to visitors. Those who want to park directly, bypass the covered drop-off area. (Photo: Diane Y. Carstens)

Entry Drive

An entry drive should provide safe and easy building access and passenger drop-off. A turnaround circular drive is the most convenient and accessible.

Design Recommendations

- Use an entry layout that is simple and easy to follow. The entry sequence should follow in a logical manner, such as building identification/recognition, followed by the option for parking or drop-off, and then the option for direct access to parking after drop-off, or exit from the site. For larger sites with much automobile traffic, an option for entering

the site and proceeding directly to the parking area (circumventing the drop-off) can reduce congestion. Separate delivery entries and access routes for ambulances may also be desirable.

- Build a curve in the road or speed bumps to help reduce traffic speed.
- When providing a close and convenient drop-off at the building entry, retain enough space for an outdoor arrival court, as many residents may want such an area for sitting.
- Arrange seating at or near the site entry for residents waiting for a taxi or a car to pick them up. It should be close enough to the building to offer a sense of security yet enable a clear view of ap-

proaching vehicles and only a short walk to a convenient pickup point.

- Create clear views of the drop-off area from the entry vestibule and/or lobby for those who prefer to wait inside.
- The radius and width of the entry drive must allow cars, vans, and buses to maneuver easily. A curb-to-curb minimum width of twenty-four feet for a single two-way road and twenty feet (each way) for a boulevard type of drive is often recommended.
- Ensure that the drop-off area includes ample space for wheelchairs, open car doors, and passing cars.

Main Entry/Arrival Court

The main entry is a favorite spot for sitting and watching the activity and for waiting for assistance on a short walk or to run errands. Thus this area must serve as both a building access and a seating/waiting/watching area.

Design Recommendations

- Create a space that has the quality of a "front porch" for a seating/waiting area at the main building entry, offering a small enclosed space, protection from weather, and views.
- Make sure that the seating/waiting area is protected from cold winds and other adverse climatic elements.
- Create easy views of the area from inside the building to assist those waiting for rides, add interest to indoor spaces, and increase safety.
- Consider placing a seating/waiting area slightly to the side of the entry walk, to provide ample room for safe and easy movement to and from the building and to reduce the possibility of "offensive" surveillance ("running the gauntlet").

- Provide a canopy or cover to offer protection from the weather. Some special considerations are (1) a canopy extending over the drop-off drive to protect those who take a longer time getting in and out of a car; (2) a canopy that is wide enough for several people to walk side by side, as well as for walkers and wheelchairs; (3) a canopy that is wide enough to protect from rain and snow when windy (e.g., by using siding); (4) a canopy that does not create a dark entry area (sky lights or a translucent cover are options); and (5) a canopy that does not have abrasive-surfaced supports, as residents may grab them for stability or brush against them.
- Make sure that the access from the car drop-off area to the building is direct and easy to identify. In addition, (1) the arrival court should be at grade with the entry drive; bollards can control automobile traffic; but avoid steps, curbs, and ramps. (2) If curbs and ramps are necessary, supply support rails that extend to the curb, to aid the less agile.
- Clearly mark and define areas of high pedestrian and vehicular movement, perhaps by means of changes in paving detail.
- Choose the lighting carefully. It should not create glare or deep shadows. Fixtures that direct the light downward and those that illuminate the paving edge are good choices.

Parking and Secondary Building Access

Many residents who drive may use a parking lot and/or secondary building entry more frequently than they do the main entry. These areas are important to residents' maintaining their independence, as well as to their safety and security.

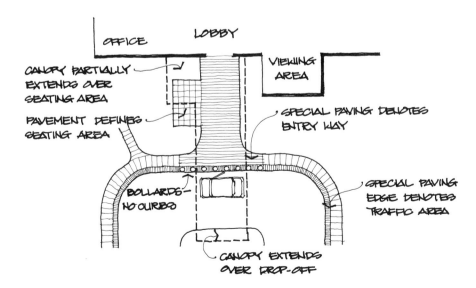

OFFICE   LOBBY

CANOPY PARTIALLY EXTENDS OVER SEATING AREA

VIEWING AREA

PAVEMENT DEFINES SEATING AREA

SPECIAL PAVING DENOTES ENTRY WAY

SPECIAL PAVING EDGE DENOTES TRAFFIC AREA

BOLLARDS — NO CURBS

CANOPY EXTENDS OVER DROP-OFF

Amenities and detailing that enhance the main entry and arrival court.

At the Duncaster Life Care Center in Bloomfield, Connecticut, changes in paving, but not in level, coupled with bollards to control the approach of cars, results in an effective entry sequence. The awning, glass doors to interior, and outside bench are also good design features. (Photo: Diane Y. Carstens)

Design Recommendations

- Place parking areas close to the building for convenience, even though this may not be the most aesthetically pleasing option.
- Provide a drop-off and seating/waiting area at the secondary entrance(s), with ample space for loading and unloading packages, groceries, and passengers.
- Include a cover over this drop-off, seating area, and building entry.
- Provide comfortable seating and a ledge for resting packages by the door while searching for keys.
- Use high-branching or low-growing plants to ensure visibility and reduce opportunities for concealment. A six-foot minimum viewing area under tree branches is often recommended (Green et al. 1975).
- Include security lighting for the secondary entrance and the entire parking area.
- Provide parking stalls for the disabled to use (twelve foot minimum width).

Shared Patios and Terraces

Patios and terraces may be centers for both small-group socializing and large-group activities, such as dances and barbecues. When appropriately designed, these areas may be frequented by less-able residents who require easy access, comfort, and security.

Design Recommendations

- Choose a location central to the building and site activity, with views and easy access to indoor areas. This promotes a sense of safety and security, allows for previewing from within the building,

and encourages informal patio use. Large-group activities and planned events may use both indoor and outdoor common spaces, if easy access is available.
- Locate patios near indoor facilities, such as kitchens and restrooms, and preferably adjacent to highly used interior social spaces, such as lounges or entry foyer.
- Choose a location where outdoor walkways leading to and from other on-site and off-site activities intersect, to support informal drop-in use and add interest. Walkways leading to parking lots are a good option. To reduce the possibility of offensive surveillance, however, create a subtle separation between the walkway and the seating area.
- Use a protected area—such as an enclosed corner where the right angles of a building meet—to create a warm pocket. This offers a sense of security and protection, as well as intimacy.
- Make sure that patios are large enough for planned group activities (e.g., barbecues, displays) but small enough for intimate groups. One design solution is to use smaller subareas within a larger space to accommodate both small and large groups.
- Use edge definition and other design detailing (e.g., arbors) to indicate subareas and create a sense of intimacy.
- Use more detail in patio areas. Sensory losses associated with growing older, and the greater amount of time that older people often spend in the same location, increase the importance of sensory stimulation through detailing.
- Use landscape elements and architectural devices to control exposure to weather. Too much wind, sun, shade, heat, or cold, or even bothersome insects, may reduce outdoor use.

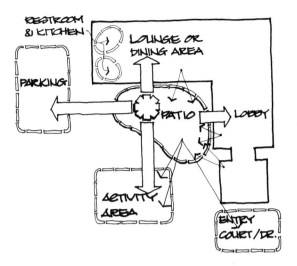

-VIEWS AND ACCESS TO ACTIVITY AREAS
-WALKWAYS LEADING FROM PARKING AND/OR ACTIVITY AREAS, INTERSECT AT THE PATIO.

THE PATIO SHOULD BE CENTRALLY LOCATED:
- VISUAL AND PHYSICAL ACCESS FROM INDOOR ACTIVITY AREAS.
- PHYSICAL PROTECTION FROM BUILDING EDGE OR CORNER.

A patio should be located to create physical and visual connections to other indoor and outdoor areas to enhance security; casual, spontaneous use; and convenience.

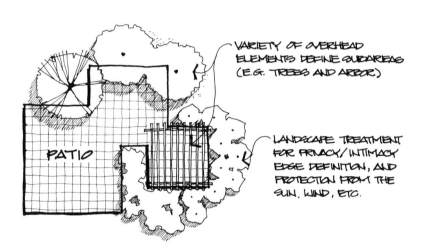

VARIETY OF OVERHEAD ELEMENTS DEFINE SUBAREAS (E.G. TREES AND ARBOR)

LANDSCAPE TREATMENT FOR PRIVACY/INTIMACY EDGE DEFINITION, AND PROTECTION FROM THE SUN, WIND, ETC.

A patio can be designed so that subareas for small, intimate groups connect to accommodate large groups.

- Provide ample comfortable seating and site furniture in both shade and sun. Easily moved furniture is preferable to fixed furniture, as it can be arranged for closer conversation distance. Fixed seating should both enable right-angle conversation and offer activity-oriented seating opportunities.
- Include amenities and detailing for interest and individual and group use, such as raised flower beds for close viewing without stooping, bird feeders and baths, and perhaps barbecues that are easy to use (e.g., gas or electric).
- Provide nearby electrical and water sources (including drinking fountains).
- Consider including night lighting, especially on patios, for balmy nights and to create dramatic views from indoors, as well as for security.
- Make sure that paving surfaces and grade changes have been designed to enhance safety and access by both disabled and able-bodied residents and visitors. A non-skid surface without excessive texture or jointing reduces the likelihood of tripping. Access should be at grade, or when changes in eleva-

tion are necessary, both steps and ramps should be supplied.
- Residents tend to use most frequently those outdoor seating areas that are within view of—or easily accessible from—popular indoor community rooms. A rectangular slab high-rise comprising 287 units in a busy commercial district of Los Angeles provided a single outdoor space in the form of a long, covered arcade running the length of the building, created by a fifteen-foot setback recess. Doors linked this space with a community room and television lounge; it was easily accessible by residents entering and leaving the main entrance to the building; a variety of seating options included movable chairs, chaise lounges, and benches; a dense but translucent buffer of planting between the arcade and a busy neighborhood allowed vicarious enjoyment of street activity; and cross breezes provided relief on hot summer days. This was one of the most highly used outdoor spaces in twelve buildings studied (Regnier 1985, pp. 43–46).

Lawn Areas

Lawn areas, although not absolutely necessary, are associated in the minds of many Americans with the idea of "home." Lawns are good for impromptu recreation, such as a croquet game, and special events. Less-able elderly people, however, may find it too difficult to walk on a soft, irregular lawn surface, and so there are several important design considerations that should be addressed if a lawn is to be included in the overall design.

Design Recommendations

- Place lawn areas near paved surfaces and seating areas for easy access and viewing.
- Make lawn areas for recreation visible from other major activity areas and from indoor sitting areas, for vicarious participation. They may also serve as additional "spill-over" spaces for large-group activities.
- If the lawn area is intended to be used—for example, for croquet—make sure that the microclimate is suitable. A croquet lawn in a Los Angeles project for the elderly was rarely used because heat from the late afternoon sun made it unbearable (Regnier 1985, p. 52).
- Provide adequate drainage, so that the lawn does not become a swamp in rainy weather.
- Clearly define the boundaries of a lawn area where it meets the street or property line. This is especially important to residents of intensive care facilities, who may unintentionally wander off the site if it does not have a clearly defined boundary.
- Where the paving meets the lawn, make sure that the edges meet at grade, so as to reduce the possibility of tripping (i.e., no edging).

- Grade the lawn area to be even or to incorporate a very gradual slope; that is, avoid any abrupt changes in grade.

Private Patios and Balconies [1]

All residents of multiunit housing—and especially the elderly—put great value on having an outdoor space that is their own (Cranz 1987; Wolfe 1975). A private patio or balcony attached to the individual unit makes the space seem more homelike and less institutional. It also gives the resident a personal connection to the outdoors and provides a setting for many personal and domestic activities that are part of an autonomous, independent home life.

The most common activities on patios and balconies are sitting in the sun and growing plants, and so a location that receives some direct sun each day is best. Ground-level patios should include a strip of earth with good topsoil around the edge of the patio, for planting directly in the ground. A majority of residents use such spaces when they are provided, and there is also benefit in knowing that one can garden, even when a patio is not actively used.

Private outdoor spaces give elderly people an opportunity for daily contact with nature—a place to watch the weather, get a breath of fresh air, see the night sky, feed the birds, and so forth. But elderly people are especially sensitive to exposure and therefore will not use outdoor spaces unless they are sheltered from sun, cold, and wind.

[1] The following two sections are based primarily on the M. A. thesis by Marian Faye Wolfe, "Outdoor Space in Special Housing for the Elderly," Department of City and Regional Planning, University of California at Berkeley, 1975.

At Bradley House in Tiburon, California, Mr. Lakenback has added several personal touches to his patio.

The interiors of residential units may lack stylistic variation and so the outdoor patio or balcony may be where the resident can establish a sense of individuality. Some residents turn their patios or balconies into small outdoor rooms that express their own personality and taste, by painting, carpeting the floor, putting up sunshades, and displaying personal possessions. These individual and homelike expressions may be particularly important, as the elderly resident will most likely be a tenant rather than an owner (Butterfield and Weidemann 1987).

Another important function of private outdoor spaces is as a place from which to view others' activities and to interact with other residents. For this reason, patios and balconies should face each other or look onto a well-used path or outdoor public area. The object is to create a space that is both private and part of a community. Fencing around patios should create privacy but should not obstruct the view from inside the unit. A gate that allows movement between the patio and the public open area makes the patio seem more like a backyard.

Elderly people also report that they value their private outdoor space as somewhere they can be alone, to enjoy solitude in the outdoors. Thus this space must provide a feeling of being both outside yet enclosed. Accordingly, patios and balconies with edges that are not well defined and that provide little or no screening are not often used. Better edges should create a feeling of security and privacy, while offering an opportunity to see out into a public area.

Design Recommendations

- Locate balconies and patios so that they face each other across a shared landscaped area or look onto a well-used public outdoor space.
- Locate balconies and patios so that they receive direct sun for a portion of the day.
- Offer protection from sun, cold, and wind.
- Use fencing materials that do not obstruct views from inside the unit.

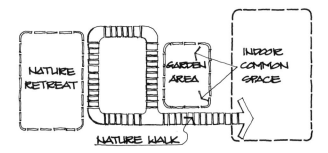

Nongardeners can enjoy the gardening beds if they are within easy view of an indoor social space or a well-used pathway.

- Use fencing or shrubbery to define the edge of the space and enclose it. Screening from adjacent neighbors is especially important, whereas defining the boundary between the patio and adjacent shared areas is optional.
- Put a gate in patio fences to allow movement directly into public areas.
- Include an exterior lock on patio units so that the door to the apartment can be locked from the outside.
- Leave a dirt border between the edge of the patio and the fence or planting that defines the space, for planting in the ground. Be sure this space has good topsoil.
- Provide a hose outlet on balconies and patios, for watering plants.

Gardening Areas

Gardening can be one of the most valuable activities provided for residents. Even if only a few residents choose to garden actively, to them, gardening offers great personal benefits. In addition, the gardening activities are shared in secondary and vicarious ways by many other residents.

Experience in the San Francisco Bay Area suggests that between 20 percent and 50 percent of residents can be expected to use personal gardening plots when they are provided. The gardeners are of all ages, including some of the very old. For some, gardening is primarily a recreational and social activity. But for others, having fresh vegetables to add to their diet and to extend a limited food budget is important. Gardening also provides a means to display personal skill and achievement. In some cases, the gardens become a symbol of pride for all the residents and, through shows and competitions, a vehicle for interaction with the larger community.

There are three types of locations for gardening on most elderly residential sites: on private balconies and patios, in specially laid out gardening plots, or in the public areas of the grounds. Gardening in the public area may be the sanctioned or unsanctioned participation of residents in the care and maintenance of the grounds, or it may be "unofficial" personal planting in areas not intended for that purpose.

Gardening can be encouraged by laying out official garden areas with small plots or raised beds for individual use. To be successful, these beds need good soil and several hours of bright sun daily. They should be clustered rather than placed next to individual units. Clustering creates a community of gardeners who can share their experience and help one another. It also provides an activity center where other residents can gather to observe and admire the gardeners' efforts. If fairly extensive raised planting areas are to be provided, an arrangement incorporating beds at several heights or

When a community garden was installed adjacent to an elderly housing project at 350 Ellis Street in San Francisco, enthusiasm and involvement were high from the outset.

Individual planting beds outside staggered unit entries allow for personal gardening touches that also enrich the public area. (Photo: Diane Y. Carstens)

gradually sloping (the planter itself or the ground surface) will allow each gardener to choose an appropriate working height. Other ways to improve access to raised beds are to provide toe space at the base, as with kitchen cabinets, and to minimize the width of the container's front lip, as it is wasted space (Rolls 1981).

Allowing residents to garden in the public areas of the grounds can have special benefits. Some residents would rather help to care for and maintain the grounds than to garden in an individual plot. Caring for the lawn, shrubbery, and flower beds may seem more like "real work" and, therefore, may give older people a greater sense of purpose and accomplishment. Also,

caring for the grounds may enable them to feel closer to the environment, to feel that the place "belongs to them." At a housing complex for the elderly in London, many residents take a hand in the general maintenance of the grounds.

They are not expected to, nor are the tenants interested in, mowing large unattractive areas of grass. But they enjoy mowing small lawns that are interspersed between other features, and the housing department has found that the residents now jealously guard the maintenance of their communal gardens with minimal help from the parks department. This produces obvious savings in costs to housing management and leads to much better maintained and more attractive gardens, and tenants who are rightly proud of "their" flowers and gardens. (Babbage 1981, p. 24)

Although not all elderly housing developments will have such energetic gardeners in residence, management policy should encourage this kind of participation.

Another form of gardening in public areas is the appropriation of unused spaces for private planting, but this is frequently viewed by management as undesirable. However, these ad hoc spaces are more like the residents' past gardening experience and therefore may be more satisfying than planting in an assigned plot. This activity is more likely to occur when maintenance is minimal and in areas that are close to the residents' units. This kind of gardening should not be prohibited but can be accommodated by putting inexpensive plants in some areas near the residents' units, which can be replaced with the residents' own planting if desired.

Design Recommendations

- Cluster individual garden plots to create a community garden.
- Locate garden plots where they will be seen from the residents' apartments and/or from well-used indoor common areas.
- Locate garden plots where they will receive several hours of direct sun each day.
- Place benches near garden plots.
- Provide some raised beds for the less mobile, preferably at a variety of heights and incorporating toe space at the bottom for increased access.
- Make sure that beds contain good topsoil.
- Provide gardening supplies and tools and an easily accessible storage space.
- Establish a management policy that permits gardening in public areas.
- Design the original landscaping to be flexible in areas near the residents' units.
- Work with the management and architectural teams to develop policies and interior amenities that support residents' gardening efforts (e.g., facilities for flower arranging with a sink and storage area, and a policy that allows for display of floral arrangements in common areas).

Walkways

Walking is a popular form of exercise among many older people and is a form of exercise recommended by doctors. However, concerns about slipping and falling are common among the elderly. Mobility problems, poor sense of balance, confusion or disorientation, declining vision (particularly depth perception, periph-

Raised work surfaces in the gardening area can eliminate much of the bending that prevents some less-able residents from working directly in the earth. (Photo: Diane Y. Carstens)

eral vision for the perception of movement, and discrimination of fine detail), slower reaction time, and decreased confidence all affect the ease and safety of walking.

Design Recommendations

- Locate most walkways within view of the building, particularly those areas frequented by staff and residents. Residents may not use walkways that are out of view, because of concern over not being seen if they fall or are bothered by strangers.
- Create walkways that pass by areas of on-site activity or are within view of off-site and neighborhood activity.
- Allow a few walkways to serve as a "retreat," such as one passing through a garden or natural area, offering privacy and solitude.
- Begin some walkways at frequently used building entries where residents may wait for someone to offer assistance.
- Consider creating a series of walkways that connect to form walking loops, that offer a choice of length and difficulty of routes as well as sensory

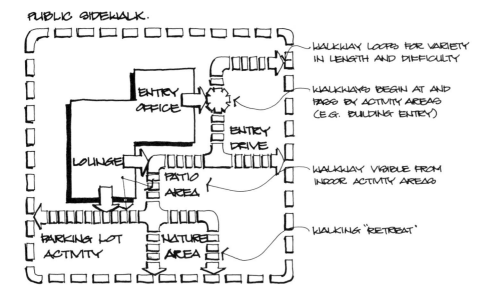

PUBLIC SIDEWALK.

WALKWAY LOOPS FOR VARIETY IN LENGTH AND DIFFICULTY

WALKWAYS BEGIN AT AND PASS BY ACTIVITY AREAS (E.G. BUILDING ENTRY)

WALKWAY VISIBLE FROM INDOOR ACTIVITY AREAS

WALKING "RETREAT"

ENTRY OFFICE

ENTRY DRIVE

LOUNGE

PATIO AREA

PARKING LOT ACTIVITY

NATURE AREA

"Walking loops" of various lengths, passing by activity areas, allows a range of experiences and levels of exertion.

interests, and that also return walkers to the building, to prevent their accidentally wandering off the site.
- Give residents with limited mobility opportunities to rest. Place benches or seating areas no more than fifty feet apart (Regnier 1985, p. 134).
- Provide rest stops and goals (e.g., mailboxes or an unusual tree) en route, to encourage walking. Walkway intersections or spots overlooking activities are good locations for seating areas.
- Consider providing an exercise par course and distance markers along a walkway. Commercially designed courses for older adults are available. Some facilities, even nursing homes, have made their exercise courses open to the public (with orange juice served to morning users), thus enhancing on-site activity and public relations.

Play Areas for Visiting Children

An outdoor play area for children may be welcomed by many residents with visiting grandchildren. Privacy, control, and noise, however, are concerns for many older people. Thus if an outdoor play area is to be provided on the site, consider the following:

Design Recommendations

- Place a play area away from quiet parts of the facility, such as the dwelling units and private spaces.
- Place a play area where it will be used only by visitors, and not taken over by neighborhood children, or place it on the perimeter of the property if such outside use is acceptable.
- Place benches at the play area for elderly and visiting adults to watch the children.

- Place a pathway and/or benches a slight distance away, to allow unrelated residents to observe the children's play.

Using the outdoors may not be very enjoyable for older people who cannot see the steps, read the signs, or get up from the bench. Certain site amenities and detailing are so important to older people's enjoyment and safety outdoors that they warrant special attention.

Seating

Chairs and benches should be designed specifically for older people who may spend much time seated. Muscle fatigue, general decline of muscle strength, compression of tissues, lessened flexibility, and other physiological changes associated with aging all create problems for older people in getting in and out of chairs and in sitting for long periods of time.

It is far better to supply a few comfortable seats than to provide many uncomfortable (usually less expensive) ones that will never be used.

Design Recommendations

- Use light, movable seating in preference to fixed furniture, as it can be moved to the desired location for sun, shade, or a close conversation distance.
- The most important criterion for bench and chair design is armrests and backrests. Such seating is often expensive but is critical to comfort. In addition, backrests should be solid, offering support to the lower back and shoulder regions. The leading edge of the armrest should extend to or beyond the seat's leading edge and provide a firm, rounded gripping surface. Many older people "pull" themselves out of a seat, owing to their decreased leg

*Movable seating can be arranged
for any kind of conversation
group or activity. (Photo:
Diane Y. Carstens)*

strength and difficulty in angling their legs under the seat. The seat should not tilt too far backward off the horizontal, nor be too high or too low, so as to enable easy movement in and out of the chair. A seat with a high or abrupt leading ledge should be avoided, as it may cut off circulation. Ninety percent of today's population from seventy-five to ninety-one years of age is between four foot seven inches and five foot four and one-half inches in height (Koncelik 1976). For these individuals (mostly women), the leading edge should be between 13.5 and 17 inches high. It would be most preferable to provide seats of varying heights within that range to allow residents to choose a comfortable height. A soft material, wood, or firm padding, is ideal for the seat. Hard materials that conduct heat or cold (e.g., concrete) are uncomfortable, particularly for older people who generally have less fatty and muscle tissue at the base of the hip bone to disperse the weight load (Koncelik 1976). Finally, chairs should be stable, with nonprotruding legs, to reduce the possibility of tripping or tipping over the chair.

- Provide some movable footrests and side tables for use with outdoor seating.

Tables

Outdoor tables increase the range of possibilities for outdoor activity.

Design Recommendations

- Offer a variety of shapes and sizes of tables for outdoor use.

- Make tables a separate unit from the chairs, for easy access and flexible seating arrangements.
- Use tables that allow easy seating in chairs with arms and wheelchairs. A height of approximately thirty inches (twenty-nine inches minimum) is best.
- Use only very stable tables, as older persons often use them for balance. Legs should not protrude beyond the tabletop.
- Use tables with a smooth or rolled (not cut square) edge, which offers an easy and safe gripping surface.

Walking Surfaces

Surface quality and ground plane elements may affect the ease and safety of walking. Older people are very aware of ground plane elements and textures; some may look directly down in front of their feet to see the ground plane, thereby drawing their attention away from the surrounding environment. This in turn decreases their opportunities to appreciate the outdoors.

Design Recommendations

- Make walking surfaces predictable, nonslip, and nonglare, such as stained light broom–finished concrete.
- Avoid changes in grade, irregular textures, jointing, and other protrusions on the ground plane that may create safety hazards. Changes in color and/or texture and other detailing may be used to signal upcoming traffic areas or stairs.
- Raise planters and planting beds along walkways for easy visibility (thirty-inch minimum is often

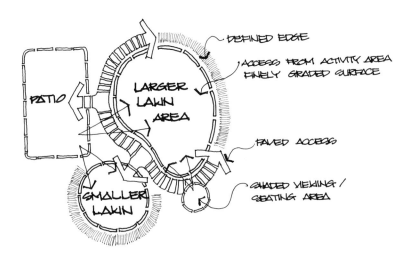

Views to and from various subareas of the site may encourage residents to use them and to watch others.

recommended), or place them directly at grade to avoid the possibility of tripping (Green et al. 1975). If the latter option is choosen, take care to prevent soil from washing out onto adjacent pathways.

- Ensure good surface drainage.
- Use small-leafed or evergreen trees along walkways, as wet leaves on walkways may be slippery.
- Make walkways wide enough to accommodate two people walking side by side or a walker and a friend in a wheelchair. A width of six feet (minimum) is often recommended for minor walkways (Green et al. 1975).
- Provide unobtrusive handrails along those routes likely to be used by less-able residents.

Ramps and Stairs

Ramps are not an ideal substitute for stairs because they are difficult for ambulatory people to negotiate: The rise of the ramp changes the walking gait, and in fact postural changes in many older people result in a forward shift of the center of balance, causing extreme difficulty in going either up or down a ramp (Hiatt 1980).

Design Recommendations

- Where changes in grade are necessary, supply both ramps and stairs. The standard accessibility specifications for ramps and other design features may serve as a general guide for designers. Older people may have multiple limitations, such as poor vision and reduced strength, agility, and stamina. A more gradual slope, more frequent resting spots, greater turning radii, and so on than indicated in most standards for accessibility can ensure access by all.
- Nonslip and nonglare surfaces are particularly important for ramps and stairs. A nonwhite, nonreflective surface can reduce glare.

- Clearly mark and light steps and ramps, particularly the leading edge of a step.
- Always provide handrails.

Handrails

Handrails offer older people both real and perceived safety. They should be available at changes in grade or where there might be some confusion or adjustment time needed, such as exiting from a dark room to the brighter outdoor light.

Design Recommendations

- For use by both ambulatory and nonambulatory residents, two handrails, one at thirty-two inches and the other at approximately twenty-six inches, are optimal (Koncelik 1976).
  twenty-six inches, are optimal (Koncelik 1976).
- For easy gripping, use handrails that are approximately two and three-quarters inches in diameter and are mounted approximately two inches from the wall (Koncelik 1976).
- Extend the length of the handrail up to one foot past the change in grade.
- Use indirect lighting along the handrail to increase visibility.

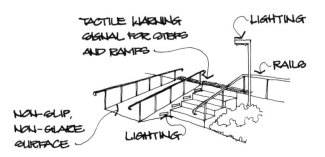

Ramps and stairs should be provided for any change in grade.

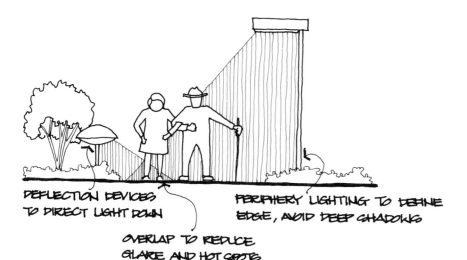

DEFLECTION DEVICES TO DIRECT LIGHT DOWN

OVERLAP TO REDUCE GLARE AND HOT SPOTS

PERIPHERY LIGHTING TO DEFINE EDGE, AVOID DEEP SHADOWS

Safety and security can be enhanced through thoughtful lighting and lead to the greater use of outdoor space.

- For handrails, use a material preferably impervious to weather, as metal becomes cold and slippery when wet, and hot in the sun. Consider plastic or vinyl coating.

Outdoor Lighting

Lighting may be used to accentuate an area or focal point, to define an area or edge, and to provide security. In general, higher levels of illumination are required for aging eyes (Koncelik 1976).

Design Recommendations

- Use higher-intensity lighting for the site and building entry and parking lot, for security. Light patios and other outdoor activity areas for special events and effects.
- Light highly used areas at their periphery, to help define the paving edge and prevent harsh shadows.
- Overlap lighting to avoid glare and hot spots (Green et al. 1975).
- Use lighting fixtures that direct light downward rather than up and out, to reduce glare.
- Wire one shared outdoor terrace or patio for electrical outlets and public address system jacks, for staging an outdoor event.

Outdoor Signs

Signs help residents and visitors find the site and its facilities and provide information about them. The need for many signs, however, may indicate poor site planning.

Design Recommendations

- Use signs in a consistent pattern and hierarchy (Green et al. 1975).
- Use oversized rather than undersized signs, but ensure a residential image.

- Use letter styles that are bold without serifs, for example, Helvetica or Futura letter styles. They should not be extended or condensed, as these are difficult to read (Green et al. 1975).
- Space the letters as on typewritten material, so that they are easy to read.
- Use white letters or images on a black or dark background, for the best legibility. If dark letters are used, they should be on a neutral gray background. If color is used, warmer colors are preferable to blues or greens (Koncelik 1976).
- Use symbols, textures, raised letters, and images to aid those with visual deficiencies.
- Use durable and nonreflective sign surfaces.
- Light signs for easy identification at night.
- Design signage to be compatible with local styles and preferences.

CASE STUDIES

Independent Apartments for Seniors, Lakewood, California [2]

Location and Context

This three-story elevator complex for low- to moderate-income seniors is located in a semiresidential neighborhood of Lakewood, California, approximately twenty miles from downtown Los Angeles. The community is designed for independent living, and being in Los Angeles County, residents rely heavily on their cars and a minivan service for getting about. Apartments are fully equipped, and no assistance with daily living is provided (with the exception of transportation). There are, however, several indoor facilities for social and recreational activities, including a community room, arts and crafts room, and a small TV room.

[2] Summarized from a study by Evelyn Cohen Associates, Santa Monica, California.

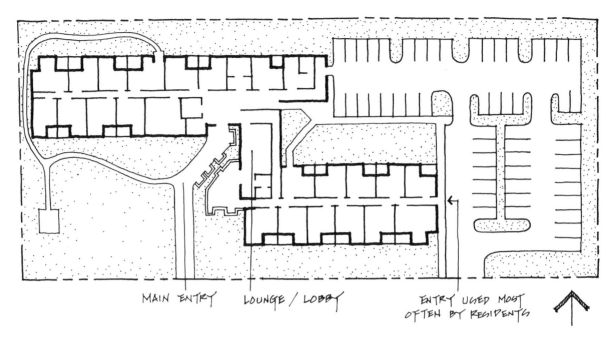

MAIN ENTRY   LOUNGE / LOBBY   ENTRY USED MOST
                                     OFTEN BY RESIDENTS

Site plan for Independent Apartments for Seniors, Lakewood, California.

Dramatically designed entries do not always ensure use. Instead of using this main entry, residents choose the side entry, which provides the most direct route to the parking lot. (Photo: Diane Y. Carstens)

Description

Two building entries are provided, one for pedestrian use only (the main entry) and the other linking the building to the parking area. The main entry is off Candlewood Avenue, a heavily traveled artery linking commercial districts. The main entry is elaborately designed with raised planters (with built-in seating), accent paving, and ornamental plantings. This entryway (approximately forty feet in length) runs from the street, past a semienclosed outdoor patio, to the front door and central core of indoor activity spaces. The large patio (approximately twenty by seventeen feet) is accessible only from the interior lounge. Perhaps this is to ensure building security, should the patio door be left ajar.

The secondary building entry is located at the end of the east residential wing, adjacent to the parking lot (indicated by an arrow on the plan). It consists of nothing more than a narrow sidewalk and door just a few feet away from the parking lot, and a view of the parking lot.

Major Uses and Users

Systematic observation indicated that the residents rarely used the main entry for entering or exiting the building or for sitting or informal socializing. They used the patio primarily when programmed activities were held in the adjacent lounge.

In contrast, the residents often used the secondary building entry. It was here that residents came and went from the building to their cars and waited to be picked up by the minivan or by friends. (Since the time of the original evaluation, covered seating has been added to the secondary entry area.)

Successful Features

• The main entry (ME) is located near the center of indoor activity and is visible from administrative spaces, for greater security.
• The ME has considerable visual interest, with a variety of detailed design features. It has a noninstitutional appearance.
• The secondary building entry is directly adjacent to the parking lot, for easy access and drop-off.

Unsuccessful Features

• The ME and patio area are not connected to the activity generated by the parking lot and drop-off.
• Located forty feet from the street, the ME does not provide for convenient drop-off, ride waiting, and so forth.
• Seating along the ME (built-in benches) is not especially comfortable.
• Seating at the ME does offer views of the street; however, street activity is limited to through traffic only, with little sidewalk activity. When sitting in this area, many residents felt vulnerable and on display to the passing traffic.
• Access to the parking lot requires passing through a residential corridor, thereby making this corridor more of a public area than a private residential one.
• The secondary entry door is not visible from interior common spaces, creating a potential security problem, especially if it should be left ajar.
• No seating/waiting area or covered drop-off is provided at the secondary entry.

Independent Apartments for Seniors, San Rafael Commons, California [3]

Location and Context

San Rafael Commons is an apartment complex for older adults, constructed under federal assistance (HUD, Section 121). It is located in a residential area,

and a neighborhood shopping district is just a few blocks away.

The three-story elevator building (47,000 square feet) houses eighty-three apartments, a manager's apartment, and a community room. The focus is on independent living.

The design concept for San Rafael Commons is similar to that of Martinelli House, a project previously completed by the same architects and also a housing complex for seniors. The design for San Rafael Commons integrates many design refinements based on a postoccupancy evaluation of Martinelli House. A follow-up evaluation of San Rafael Commons, however, indicated areas for even more improvement.

Description

The design concept is a central courtyard created by the three stories of units that encircle it in a U-shaped configuration. Open-air breezeways on each story offer views to the courtyard and the community room, which is located by the main entry.

In response to the evaluation of Martinelli House, the courtyard at San Rafael is larger and provides a greater variety of landscaped areas for sitting and conversing. The mail alcove, waiting area, and the community room are also clustered near the main entry. These public areas are oriented toward the street (for connection to neighborhood activity), while enclosing a secure, private courtyard.

Specific recommendations based on the Martinelli Housing evaluation included:

• Mail areas should be located along an "activity hub" to encourage conversation among residents.
• Furniture and amenities in the courtyard should enhance participation.
• Circulation should provide options for exercise and social exchange.
• Open spaces, including private areas, should be varied, and future designs should include more private or semiprivate areas.

Major Uses and Users

Most residents are enthusiastic about living in San Rafael Commons. They admire its architectural design, the courtyard and open-air breezeways, and its "Cape Cod" appearance. Two factors found to contribute to the project's success are its location (close to downtown, public transportation, and a grocery store across the street) and its price.

Although residents liked the appearance of the courtyard, observations indicated little use or socializing there. Rather, the residents preferred the open breezeways although only limited interaction was observed there; residents would often wave to one another, perhaps stop briefly, and then go on their way.

[3] Summarized from a study conducted by Kathryn H. Anthony, University of Illinois at Champaign-Urbana.

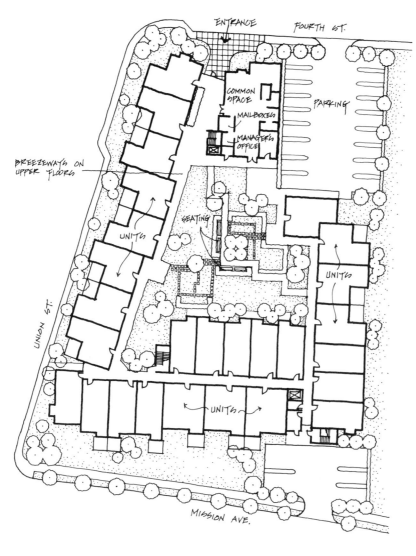

NORTH ARROW ↑

Site plan for San Rafael Commons, San Rafael, California.

Successful Features

• Clustering the community room, waiting area, and mail alcove near the main entry increases opportunities for drop-in use and chance meetings.
• The planting and paving detail in the courtyard offer visual interest and are appreciated by residents.
• Open-air breezeways surrounding the courtyard work well for management as a security monitoring device; they also are places for chance meetings among residents.

Unsuccessful Features

• The courtyard is too open and lacks a variety of smaller, more intimate spaces for socializing.

Residents enjoy overlooking the attractive courtyard but do not use the long, exposed benches, the only seating option.

• Although the planting of the courtyard provides visual interest, there are few amenities to support different types of activities.

• Two very long benches are provided in the courtyard, which are fixed at a ninety-degree angle and placed right in the middle of the courtyard. Because they are overexposed, they are rarely used.

• The design of the mail alcove area creates a wind tunnel, perhaps limiting interaction there.

• The breezeways do not have adequate space or furnishings to support socializing or extended viewing of the courtyard below.

• Management does not allow residents to personalize apartment entries or "furnish" the breezeways; this factor alone has severely curtailed their use as social spaces.

Nursing Home, Allendale, New Jersey

Location and Context

The Allendale Nursing Home is located in a middle- to upper-income area of New Jersey. Most of its roughly two hundred residents come from a ten-mile radius of the facility. The complex consists of two "sides," one for assisted living and the other for nursing care. Each has its own common spaces and dining room.

This case study examines the outdoor courtyard serving the nursing care residents. Enclosed and secure courtyards have often been recommended as an appropriate type of outdoor space for nursing home residents who may be confused and tend to wander. They ensure the residents' safety and make the staff's job of monitoring activities much easier.

The study is based on the perspective of one resident, Ethel, and on observations of the nursing care personnel.

Description

There is abundant land surrounding the nursing home, much of which will be used to expand the home's bed capacity. With the exception of the main entry, the central courtyard is the only well-developed outdoor space.

This rectangular courtyard, roughly sixty by one hundred feet, is surrounded on all four sides by the one-story nursing home building. Nursing care units front three sides of the courtyard. The other side is bounded by common spaces and the main entry area. Because of the low-rise building and the lack of large trees nearby, the courtyard receives sunlight most of the day.

The courtyard is accessible from two doors in the

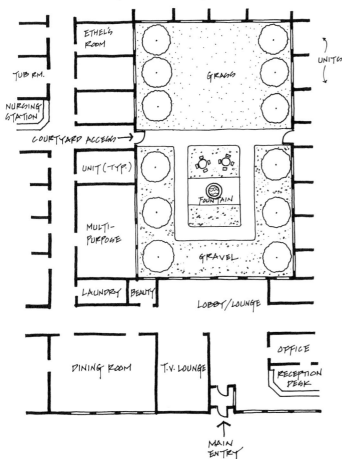

Site plan for Allendale Nursing Home, Allendale, New Jersey.

residential wings (near the nursing stations). Although the courtyard is visible from the multipurpose room and the main entry lounge, there is no access from these spaces.

The courtyard design is simple, sparsely landscaped, but well maintained. There is a concrete walkway and center seating area with a small fountain and some wrought iron chairs and umbrella tables. The planting consists of a grassed area, small trees surrounding the perimeter of the courtyard, and flowers potted in tubs scattered about on the graveled areas.

Major Uses and Users

Ethel is an eighty-six-year-old resident. Her mind is active and alert, but since her hip fracture nearly two years ago, her mobility has steadily declined. Now she rarely uses her walker and is confined most of the time to a wheelchair that she finds too heavy to wheel about very far. With another woman she shares a room, which is just three doors down the hall from the nursing station and the door that leads to the courtyard.

Ethel's trips from her room are becoming increasingly limited. She travels to the dining room for most of her meals, and to the multipurpose room for bingo but otherwise spends most of her time in her room.

Ethel, like most other residents, rarely uses the courtyard. When she does, it is often with a visiting friend or relative who helps wheel her outside, get her sun glasses on, and so on.

There are a few regular courtyard users. Most tend to sit near the edges and the trees where there is some shade and less glare. Visitors pull the wrought iron chairs and wheelchairs onto the grass near the trees, but the visits tend to be short.

Although Ethel lives near the courtyard (with a view), she finds that it takes too much effort to go there. The fire regulation door is too heavy to open without assistance. Once outside, she cannot move the wrought iron chairs by herself, and although they have arm and back rests, the surface is too hard and too cold to sit on for long. The sun reflects off the white concrete, gravel, and the light-colored building, creating a glare that is bothersome to even the younger visitors. Since her eye surgery Ethel wears prescription sunglasses which help somewhat. But even so, there is not much to do in the courtyard. The fountain is rarely turned on, and one cannot see the activity going on inside, nor those coming and going from the main entry (where most of the residents sit, inside).

It took some time for Ethel's grandchildren to realize that she did not like going into the courtyard, and they finally discovered an alternative outdoor destination— a grassy area (roughly thirty by sixty feet) that flanks the front door. It is cooler and greener, with large shade trees. Most importantly, it is somewhat private (removed to the side), but with a view of the front

door activity. Access to it also requires passing through the main lobby, affording an opportunity to see the others and to be seen (with the grandchildren). But traveling down the driveway and being lifted over the eight-inch curb scared Ethel. Nonetheless, she liked to tell the others that she had gone "outside," not just outside to the courtyard which was considered "safe" and somewhat pedestrian.

Two recent events, however, changed the value of the courtyard for Ethel and many other residents, at least for a while. First, her grandchildren brought a bird feeder and placed it just outside her window, so that she could see it even with her poor eyesight. Before long the birds came, and so did other bird feeders. The kitchen staff put out bread (residents watching), and the nurses filled the feeders.

The second and most exciting event was the arrival of a duck and eventually her dozen ducklings. The duck nested in a large flower pot, and the waiting began, along with a lottery to guess the date and time of the ducklings' arrival. Ethel won. The maintenance man put out a tub of water, complete with a ramp and "diving board." He changed the water daily (only warm water, or so the residents said). As the ducklings dove into the water and ventured across the grass, the lineup of residents around the windows grew. A few residents ventured outside to watch the ducklings, but the real excitement was inside. Photos of the ducklings appeared on walls, and there was even a local newspaper article about the residents and the ducklings. There was a lot to talk about and a lot to watch.

The ducklings have now flown away, and the courtyard is again quiet. They say that enclosed courtyards provide a safe place for the confused and frail nursing home resident. But there is obviously much more to creating a successful courtyard than ensuring the residents' safety. It appears that this safe enclosure was appreciated most by the mother duck, who brought some life into the quiet routine of this courtyard.

Successful Features

• The courtyard provides a safe outdoor area that residents can enjoy unattended.
• It is highly visible from inside and from the nursing station.
• Access is at grade.
• A variety of ground surface treatments add interest and choice.
• Staff and management allow personalization of outdoor space (e.g., feeders) and help bring outdoor activities to the indoors (with photos and the like).

Unsuccessful Features

• Choice of seating areas and sun/shade is limited.
• Materials (white concrete, gravel) magnify glare and heat.

• Recreational/walking options are limited.
• There is no connection from entry lounge or multipurpose room.
• Amenities are limited, and seating is uncomfortable and too heavy.
• Doors are too heavy for residents to open; thresholds are too high for many wheel chairs to pass unassisted.

Congregate Housing for Seniors, Aurora, Illinois [4]

Location and Context

Maple Terrace, a mid-rise housing facility for the elderly and disabled, in Aurora, Illinois, was the subject of an extensive postoccupancy evaluation by the Housing Research and Development Program at the University of Illinois, Champaign-Urbana. The study stemmed from high vacancy rates and reports of conflict among residents, resident dissatisfaction, and a poor image in the community.

The study examined those factors of the physical and social environment that contributed to the residents' satisfaction. Questionnaires, interviews, and scaled models were among the methods used to evaluate the physical design of interior and exterior spaces. Specific factors and general issues identified as important to resident satisfaction were then translated into a series of design options for improving the facility. A few of the key findings pertaining to outdoor spaces are presented here.

[4] Summarized from a study by Housing Research and Development Program, University of Illinois at Champaign-Urbana.

Description

Maple Terrace is a four-story congregate housing project (208 units), constructed in 1971 as a HUD Turnkey project. The building has the configuration of the letter H, formed by two residential wings that are linked by a one-story building containing primarily community spaces. These community spaces include a dining room, offices, lounge, and restrooms. Each residential wing was originally designed to function as an individual building and, in many instances, still does so. There are, for example, two separate mail box areas and separate street addresses.

The site slopes substantially from north to south. Thus the connecting link attaches to one residential building at the first-floor level and to the other at the second-floor level. There are a number of large older trees near the street, but only shrubs in the courtyard areas created by the H.

The west courtyard has been somewhat developed, with a circular paved area, seating, a fountain (which does not always work), and a walkway. The east courtyard is mainly for drainage, as it has a steep-sloped swale that prohibits its use by residents. The parking lot is east of the building. Access to the lot is not controlled, and there is no direct surveillance of the lot from the units or management offices.

Major Uses and Users

Although the interior lobbies at the two building entrances receive heavy use, the library, multipurpose room, and exterior spaces are underused. Other spaces are inappropriately used. For example, some residents

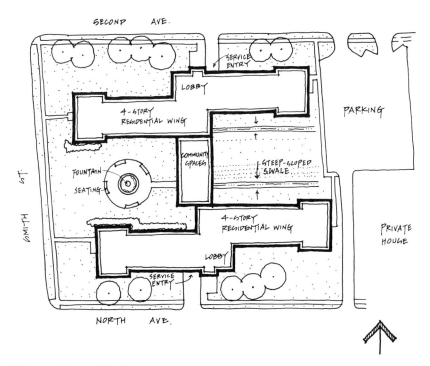

Site plan for Maple Terrace, Aurora, Illinois.

use the fire exit doors for ordinary entering and exiting, and leave them propped open.

When asked what residents liked most about living there, the responses fell into five categories of assets: living independently, the presence of friends, the location, the appearance, and the cost.

When asked what they disliked the most, the largest category pertained to the project's physical design. Interestingly, when individual factors related to satisfaction were grouped into broader issues, exterior issues came first, management issues second, and unit and resident issues third.

Of the exterior issues, security was the principal concern. Many residents did not feel safe outside. The parking lot, in particular, was a source of security concerns and a frequent location of crime and vandalism. Residents expressed interest in adding fencing, gates, and guards as ways to increase the security of the parking lot and other exterior spaces. The drainage swale in the east courtyard also presented some security concerns, primarily about peeping toms hiding there.

Other exterior issues pertained to the amenities and accessibility of outdoor spaces. Residents felt that outdoor seating areas were important (92 percent) but needed more variety in furnishings and location. Many also felt that it was important to have a balcony or patio and reported missing their own outdoor space (57 percent).

Successful Features

• The housing complex offers an opportunity to live independently but among friends.
• Its location, appearance, and cost were appreciated.

Unsuccessful Features

• The courtyards are not spatially defined as belonging to the residents. Underutilization and security problems are prevalent.
• The drainage swale in the east courtyard limits its use and is a security concern.
• There are few outdoor recreation and seating options available.
• The two building entrances limit social opportunities for the residents of the two buildings and actually allow suspicious and negative attitudes to form toward people in the adjacent building.
• Residents had no private outdoor spaces (patios, balconies).

Rosa Parks Towers, San Francisco [5]

Location and Context

Rosa Parks Towers is a high-rise, public housing project for low-income elderly, managed by the San Francisco Housing Authority. It is located in an area of San Francisco known as the Western Addition, which has been undergoing redevelopment since the early 1960s. The surrounding blocks consist mostly of low- to moderate-income medium density housing, a Safeway supermarket, a park, and several churches.

Description

The building was rehabilitated into elderly housing in 1985 from a heavily vandalized family project, originally built in 1962. Two hundred apartments for independent elderly people are housed in an eleven-story building. The building is shaped like the letter E, with sheltered courtyards enclosed by the wings. A covered walk leads to a locked front entry where a twenty-four-hour security guard monitors who comes and goes. Shared social spaces are clustered near the front entry and include an ample lobby, a large social room opening onto a patio, a smaller sun lounge, a library, and a laundry. Two landscaped courtyards contain walking paths, benches, card tables, a swing seat, ample planting, and raised gardening beds.

Major Uses and Users

The entry and elevator lobbies are the most often used social spaces, where residents collect their mail, talk with the manager or security guard, sit and watch people coming and going, and look out on the street activity. More than 70 percent of the residents participate in planned activities in the main lounge, including exercise and English classes, bingo, parties, and tenants' association meetings. The outdoor courtyards are used by 75 percent of the residents; going outside for a walk and to sit are the two most popular activities. The two favorite seating areas are just outside the sun lounge and just outside the main lounge, where trellises planted with wisteria create semishaded "transition areas," appreciated by the elderly who find it more difficult than do younger people to deal with the glare of bright sunlight.

Half the residents use the outdoor tables and the swing seat (provided because it was so popular at another elderly people's project in San Francisco). A total of 190 square feet of raised garden beds are used for growing vegetables; management has to keep a waiting list because the beds are in such high demand. Clearly, the number who wanted to garden was considerably underestimated. An area set aside for playing horseshoes would have been put to much better use as an area for gardening. No one ever uses the horseshoe

[5] Marquis Associates, Architects: Gita Dev, project architect; Richard Shadt, landscape architect; Deborah Sussman, color consultant; Clare Cooper Marcus, design program consultant. Summarized from a postoccupancy evaluation study by Cooper Marcus.

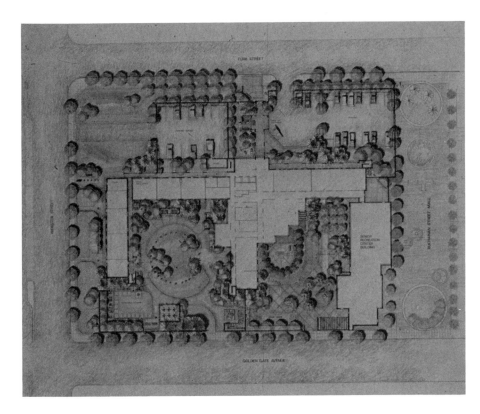

Site plan for Rosa Parks Towers, San Francisco.

Pathways provide shorter and longer walking loops in two landscaped courtyards. A sun lounge (ground level, left) is well used; enclosed corridors (above) with ample natural light encourage the cultivation of house plants at apartment entries.

area, partly because it is a men's game (and the men here, as in all elderly people's projects, are in the minority) and partly because the number of American-born men who would know how to play it is quite small. The building houses four major language groups, English, Spanish, Chinese, and Russian.

Successful Features

• Wings of buildings and walls enclose courtyards and protect them from the winds often present in this location.
• A variety of short and longer walking routes is offered.
• A variety of seating locations and orientations is available.
• Outdoor benches have comfortable backs and arms.
• A trellis-covered swing seat can be used by one to four people at a time.
• The planting offers seasonal variations.
• Star jasmine and other sweet-smelling plants are located near popular seating areas.
• Raised gardening beds for residents' use are available.
• Courtyards are pleasing to look out at—or down onto—for those residents who never venture outside because of ill health or disabilities.

Unsuccessful Features

• There are too many outdoor benches, sometimes creating an "empty" look.
• A semienclosed outdoor structure for card playing is never used.

• An area for playing horseshoes is never used.
• The number of residents who would like a raised garden bed was considerably underestimated.

Duncaster Life Care Center, Bloomfield, Connecticut[6]

Location and Context

Located on a seventy-two-acre site amid the rolling hills of Connecticut, Duncaster Life Care Center lies one mile from Bloomfield Center and twelve miles from downtown Hartford, allowing access to urban, suburban, and rural amenities while at the same time remaining sheltered and secluded. The 216 residential apartments, sixty-bed medical facility, and busy community center are clustered in the northwest portion of the site, leaving sixty acres for wetlands, woods, and meadows.

[6] Landscape Architects: Green Designs, Cape/Wilhelm Associates, Johnson and Richter Inc.; Michael Cegan, principal in charge. Architects: Stecker, La Bau, Arneill, McManus Inc.

Description

Modeled on several successful, Quaker-designed, life care communities in eastern Pennsylvania, Duncaster is laid out to replicate a small town with a village green. The commons area contains the green, a library, a post office, a bank, shops, a dining room, and many activity and meeting areas at ground level, with the medical center above. Three multistoried residential buildings extend out from the community center to create distinct residential neighborhoods, each with its own name, separate entrance, satellite parking lot, and distinctive lobbies, courtyards, interior, and landscape design details.

In response to the client's desire to draw people outward into the community and into nature, the designers provided a wide range of opportunities to both walk and garden, addressing the needs of all residents, from the most frail to the most robust. Residents can garden in small yards near their apartments, in common courtyards in their neighborhood, in a greenhouse in the commons or in raised beds outside the greenhouse, or in the substantial community garden that lies at the

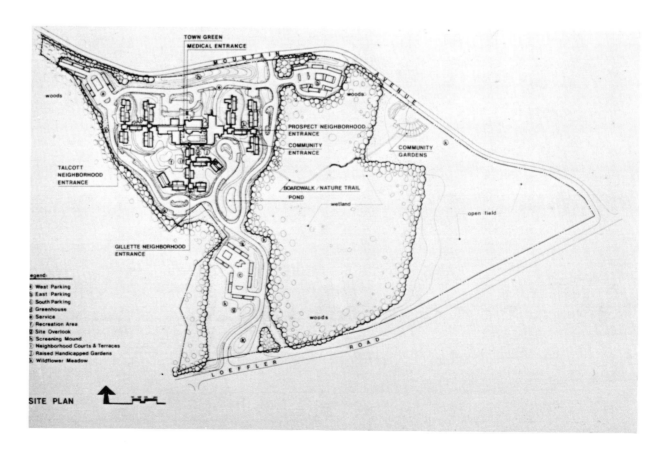

The Duncaster Life Care Center, Bloomfield, Connecticut.

The green at Duncaster is a central focus as well as a fine croquet ground (greenhouse to the left). (Photo: Felice Frankel Photography)

edge of the woods and the open field. A curving board-walk with wooden railings leads through the woods and across the wetlands from the east side of the complex to the community garden, following the contours of the land.

Major Uses and Users

Not surprisingly, the residents at Duncaster spend a lot of time outside. The more active and able ride bicy-cles, both on the path system provided and off the site, and many residents walk extensively on paths, nature trails, and the extremely popular boardwalk. Quite a few residents have dogs, which are permitted on most areas of the site, including the commons area (with the exception of the dining room). Croquet is popular with many residents, and most take advantage of the oppor-tunities to garden. Although a basketball court was provided for active residents, it is in fact used almost exclusively by staff during their lunch hour or breaks, although some residents enjoy watching these games. Five years after the facility was completed, some recre-ation areas are still unfinished, as they are intended for development based on the residents' desires and inter-ests. On-site management senses no unmet needs or wishes yet feels confident that other recreational facili-ties could be provided if there were enough interest.

Although provisions for the residents to enjoy being outdoors have been emphasized, year-round access to all facilities has been ensured by linking all buildings via closed and heated corridors. Visual access to out-doors is enabled by windows throughout the facility, at heights and angles determined to provide the best pos-sible views, without glare.

Successful and Unsuccessful Aspects of Design

All told, Duncaster is a very successful and highly pop-ular residential community. From the sensitive provi-sion of so many gardening options to its most popular feature—the boardwalk through the woods—there are numerous examples of successful design and manage-ment features. New residents are encouraged to bring not only favorite furnishings for use in common indoor areas (items too large for the apartments) but also fa-vorite plants from their gardens for the private or com-munal courtyards. One of the few shortcomings of outdoor spaces at Duncaster is that although many units have private outdoor space, not all do. While such outdoor space is ideally provided for all residents of an elderly housing scheme, the lack may be felt less when the common courtyard is so carefully planned to belong to those residents sharing it.

Another issue that may be problematic is the place-ment of the parking lots too far from the buildings. While this was done both purposefully and carefully to preserve the central area as a "pedestrian precinct," the outlying location may lead to some difficulty. Manage-ment has instituted a valet service for residents for whom the distance is too great, yet the potential com-plications and limitations of such a system many create problems.

The aging of Duncaster's residents will be a slowly evolving test of the success of its design. Currently, the majority of residents are relatively healthy and active and prefer that the medical facility be present yet un-obtrusive. Residents in the nursing facility indicated a preference to be part of the community yet to avoid having people wander through the medical quarters.

These two perspectives were addressed by placing the medical center on the second floor above the commons, overlooking the town green on one side and opening to a private, ground-level terrace (possible on the sloping site) on the other. This terrace is fully wheelchair accessible and incorporates raised planters for gardening and a low fence to prevent wandering by any disoriented residents. Although management believes that it would be possible, if bumpy, for an able person to push a wheelchair user along the boardwalk, this one example suggests the issues that may arise over time. Since the goal of a life-care community is to allow people to age in place, living independently as long as possible yet remaining on the site if or when they come to require long-term nursing care, the resident profile at Duncaster may be greatly changed in ten, fifteen, or twenty years. As a greater proportion use wheelchairs, walkers, or even gurneys, it may be desirable for an even greater portion of the site to be made even more accessible, not just in regard to gentle slopes and distances, but in terms of very particular surfaces and avoidance of even small barriers, and so on. Likewise, the larger part of the site may not adequately check wandering as more residents become confused. These challenges may be met by some combination of design and management response, with the worthy goal of maintaining the rich relationship between residents and environment which currently exists.

Successful Features

• Popular boardwalk through woods
• Residents encouraged to bring favorite furnishings and plants for apartments and common areas
• Placement of medical center overlooking commons, so as to be part of community yet slightly removed

Unsuccessful Features

• Private outdoor space not available for all units
• Potential problems with parking lots being too remote
• Boardwalk not amenable to wheelchairs
• Long walking distances between units and the commons

REFERENCES

Anderson, James, Robert Selby, Susan Edwards, and Lynne Allen. 1986. *A post occupancy evaluation of Maple Terrace: Housing for the elderly in Aurora, Illinois.* Champaign–Urbana: Housing Research and Development Program, University of Illinois.

Atchely, Robert C. 1972. *The social forces in later life.* Belmont, Calif.: Wadsworth.

Babbage, Tony. 1981. Meeting the client and user needs (illustrated by some sheltered housing schemes in Hammersmith). In *Gardens and grounds for disabled and elderly people,* ed. Penny Smith, pp. 19–24. London: Centre on Environment for the Elderly.

Byerts, Thomas Oakley. 1970. Design of the urban park environment as an influence on the behavior and social interaction of the elderly. M.A. thesis, University of Southern California, Department of Architecture.

Byerts, Thomas Oakley, and Don Conway, eds. 1972. *Behavioral requirements for housing for the elderly.* Report from a working conference, sponsored by the American Institute of Architects, Association for the Study of Man–Environment Relations, Gerontological Society, and National Tenants Association, Washington, D.C.

Butterfield, Dorothy, and Sue Weidemann. 1987. Housing satisfaction of the elderly. In *Housing the aged,* ed. Victor Regnier and John Pynoos, pp. 133–152. New York: Elsevier.

Carstens, Diane. 1982. Behavioral research applied to the redesign of exterior spaces: Housing for the elderly. In *EDRA 13: Knowledge for design,* ed. Polly Bart, Alex Chen, and Guido Francesco, pp. 354–369. Proceedings of the Thirteenth International Conference of the Environmental Design Research Association, College Park, Md.

———. 1985. *Site planning and design for the elderly: Issues, guidelines and alternatives.* New York: Van Nostrand Reinhold.

Central Mortgage and Housing Corporation, Minister of State of Affairs. 1975. *Housing the elderly.* Ottawa: Government of Canada.

Chellis, Robert, James Seagle, and Barbara Seagle. 1982. *Congregate housing for older people: A solution for the 1980's.* Lexington, Mass.: Lexington Books.

Cooper Marcus, Clare. 1990. High-rise rehabilitation for the elderly: The case of the Pink Palace. *Design intervention: The challenge of change,* ed. Wolfgang Preiser. New York: Van Nostrand Reinhold.

Cranz, Galen. 1987. Evaluating the physical environment: Conclusions from eight housing projects. In *Housing the aged: Design directives and policy considerations,* ed. Victor Regnier and Jon Pynoos, pp. 81–104. New York: Elsevier.

De Long, A. J. 1970. The micro-spatial structure of the older person: Some implications for planning the social and spatial environment. In *Spatial Behavior of Older People,* ed. L. Pastalan and D. Carson, pp. 68–87. Ann Arbor: University of Michigan Press.

Gerontological Services, Inc. 1983–1989. Market feasibility studies and computerized data bank. Santa Monica, Calif.

Green, Isaac, Bernard Fedewa, Charles Johnston, William Jackson and Howard Deardorff. 1975. *Housing for the elderly: The development and design process.* New York: Van Nostrand Reinhold.

Hiatt, Lorraine G. 1980. Care and design: Moving outside and making it a meaningful experience. *Nursing Homes* 29(3):34–39.

Hoglund, David J. 1985. *Housing for the elderly: Privacy and independence.* New York: Van Nostrand Reinhold.

Howell, Sandra. 1980. *Designing for aging: Patterns of use.* Cambridge, Mass.: MIT Press.

Koncelik, Joseph A. 1972. *Designing the open nursing home.* Stroudsburg, Pa.: Dowden, Hutchinson & Ross.

Koncelik, Joseph A. 1976. *Aging and the product environment.* Environmental Design Series, vol. 1. Stroudsburg, Pa.: Dowden, Hutchinson & Ross.

Lawton, M. Powell. 1970a. Ecology and aging. In *Spatial behavior of older people*, ed. L. Pastalan and D. Carson, pp. 40–67. Ann Arbor: University of Michigan Press.

———. 1970b. Planner's notebook: Planning environments for older people. *American Institute of Planners Journal* 36:127–129.

———. 1970c. Public behavior of older people in congregate housing. *Proceedings of the Second Annual Environmental Design Research Association (EDRA) Conference*, ed. John Archea and Charles Eastman, pp. 372–380. Pittsburgh: Carnegie-Mellon University.

———. 1975. *Planning and managing housing for the elderly.* New York: Wiley.

———. 1980. *Environment and aging.* Monterey, Calif.: Brooks/Cole.

Michigan State Housing Development Authority (MSHDA). 1974. *Housing for the elderly, development process.* Lansing: Michigan State Housing Development Authority.

Mirvis, Kenneth, and Cathryn M. Delude. 1988. Duncaster: A sense of belonging. *Landscape Architecture,* June, pp. 42–47.

Pastalan, Leon A. 1971. How the elderly negotiate their environment. Paper presented at the Environment for the Aged: A Working Conference on Behavioral Research, Utilization, and Environmental Policy, December, San Juan, Puerto Rico.

———. 1974. Privacy preferences among relocated institutionalized elderly. *Proceedings of the Fifth Annual Environmental Design Research Association (EDRA) Conference, (6) Privacy,* ed. D. Carson, pp. 73–82. Milwaukee: EDRA.

Pastalan, Leon A., and D. Carson, eds. 1970. *Spatial behavior of older people.* Ann Arbor: University of Michigan, Institute of Gerontology.

Place, Linna Funk, Linda Parker, and Forrest J. Berghorn. 1981. *Aging and the aged: An annotated bibliography and library research guide.* Boulder, Colo.: Westview Press.

Regnier, Victor. 1985. Behavioral and environmental aspects of outdoor space use in housing for the elderly. Los Angeles: Andrus Gerontology Center, University of Southern California.

———. 1987. Programming congregate housing: The preference of upper income elderly. In *Housing the aged,* ed. Victor Regnier and Jon Pynoos, pp. 207–226. New York: Elsevier.

Regnier, Victor, and Jon Pynoos. 1987. *Housing the aged: Design directives and policy considerations.* New York: Elsevier.

Riche, Martha. 1986. Retirement's life style pioneers. *American Demographics* 42–56.

Rolls, Eddie. 1981. Design of areas for horticultural therapy. In *Gardens and grounds for disabled and elderly people,* ed. Penny Smith, pp. 5–8. London: Centre on Environment for the Handicapped.

Time. July 1981, p. 81.

U.S. Department of Housing and Urban Development, Office of Policy Development and Research. 1979. *Housing for the elderly and handicapped. The experience of the Section 202 Program from 1959 to 1977* (HUD-PDR-301). Washington, D.C.: U.S. Government Printing Office.

Urban Land Institute. 1983. *Housing for a maturing population.* Washington, D.C.: Urban Land Institute.

Wolfe, Marian F. 1975. Outdoor space in special housing for the elderly. M.C.P. thesis, University of California at Berkeley.

Zeisel, J., G. Epp, and S. Demos. 1977. *Low rise housing for older people: Behavioral criteria for design* (HUD Publication 483). Washington, D.C.: U.S. Government Printing Office.

Zeisel, J., Polly Welch, Galye Epp, and Stephen Demos. 1983. *Midrise elevator housing for older people: Behavioral criteria for design.* Department of Housing and Urban Development, Office of Policy Development and Research. Washington, D.C.: U.S. Government Printing Office.

DESIGN REVIEW CHECKLIST

GOALS OF THE OUTDOOR SPACES

1. What are the goals of the developer or client for the outdoor spaces? Is it "marketing," or establishing a positive, noninstitutional image for the community? How can this goal and the needs and desires of future residents be addressed?

2. Does the design address the preferences of seniors in this region for outdoor space development, their expectations for a particular life-style?

3. Have homelike components of outdoor designs been incorporated into spaces, and have design features commonly associated with institutional design and group living been downplayed?

4. Have design concepts and features been included that encourage independence while providing support and assistance for outdoor use when needed?

5. Has a flexible design been created to accommodate changing needs and activity preferences over time? As the project matures and the residents "age in place," will the initial goals set for outdoor use be appropriate after seven to ten years with a more frail population?

USERS

6. What is the residents' anticipated ability level? If there are any special limitations, are design features included to ensure safety, accessibility, and comfort?

7. Have the residents' prior activity preferences been considered. Are there thoughtful details that would allow continuation of these activities, such as raised gardening planters or outdoor pursuits particular to a locality or ethnic group?

8. What are the adjacent indoor uses? Have complementary uses been developed to enhance the use of both indoor and outdoor spaces?

9. Will the project accept residents requiring different levels of care, from independent living arrangements to nursing care? Have opportunities been provided to encourage interaction among these different groups?

10. Is there management and activity programming to support outdoor use and broaden the residents' outdoor experiences?

BUILDING MASS AND MICROCLIMATE CONSIDERATIONS

11. Are activities and facilities on the site clustered to give a sense of vitality and use?

12. On a large site, are groups of units clustered to create a sense of neighborhood?

13. Have wind-tunnel studies been conducted to avoid what might be troublesome windy spots on the site?

14. Have potential wind or down-draft problems been alleviated by overhangs, wind screens, buffer plantings, walls, or berms?

15. Are seating, gardening, exercise areas, and so on located with concern for the site's microclimate?

16. In areas with hot summers, have courtyards and seating areas been situated to take advantage of summer breezes?

17. Do overhangs, trellises, or awnings at all building entries mitigate problems of glare?

18. Where winter sun would be appreciated, have trellises been planted with deciduous vines?

19. Does tree planting provide sunny and shady areas for outdoor seating?

20. Are umbrella tables and adjustable awnings provided to allow residents to control the amount of sun or shade available?

SITE ENTRY AND ARRIVAL COURT

21. Is the site entry on a relatively major street, for ease of visibility and access and, when possible, proximity to public transport?

22. Does the layout and location of the entry drive ensure safety and easy building identification and access?

23. Is the entry sequence clear and easy to follow, from site entry to building drop-off, parking, and site exit?

24. Is there adequate space for vehicular traffic, dropping off passengers, light deliveries, and development of a seating/waiting area at the main building entry?

25. Are separate access points for parking, deliveries, and ambulances required because of high traffic volume? Should this traffic be separated from drop-off traffic?

26. Is the entry inviting and noninstitutional in appearance?

27. Is the name of the building displayed at the site entry in clear, bold lettering, and is it well lit at night?

28. Is there some seating at the site entry for viewing street activity or waiting for a ride?

29. Does the traffic entry to the site permit easy drop-off or pickup at the building entry, followed by direct access to parking or exit from the site?

30. If pedestrians and cars share a site entry, will traffic be slowed by a curve or speed bumps?

31. Are there clear views to an auto pickup area for those waiting for rides in the main foyer or in a seating area just outside the principal entry?

32. Is there ample space at the drop-off and pickup area for wheelchairs, open car doors, passing cars, and nearby seating?

33. Does the entry drive have a curb-to-curb minimum width of twenty-four feet, or a twenty-foot minimum each way for a divided driveway?

34. Will the radius and width of the entry drive allow for pickups by ambulance, minibus, or van?

35. Does a canopy or cover extend from the front door to the pickup point, to offer protection from the weather? Is it wide enough to allow several people walking, or in wheelchairs, to move side by side?

36. Is the drop-off area at grade with the entry drive? Are bollards or other devices used to control automobile traffic?

37. Is there lighting at the building entry that illuminates the paving edges and does not create deep shadows or glare?

38. Is there a choice of seating/waiting areas—shaded, sunny, covered?

39. Is there a handrail between the building entry and the drop-off point, to increase safety and accessibility?

PARKING AND SECONDARY BUILDING ENTRANCES

40. Is there adequate lighting for the secondary entrance and entire parking area?

41. Is parking located for easy access to the building and for visibility from the building, to ensure security? Is parking clearly identified with the building or unit cluster?

42. Is it easy to load or unload passengers and packages at the building or unit entry?

43. Is the parking-lot layout clear and easy to follow, with good visibility and adequate turning radii?

44. Are secondary building entrances located for visibility (backdoors left ajar are potential security problems)?

45. Is there a comfortable waiting and seating "porch" at the building entry nearest to parking, so that residents who have been taken on an errand can wait for a friend or relative who is parking their vehicle?

CIRCULATION AND ORIENTATION

46. Has a simple organizational pattern been used in the design of outdoor circulation, such as a radial or linear plan?

47. Do reference points, such as subspaces, particular trees, or resting areas, make the circulation system easier to follow?

48. Has the outdoor area been designed with some kind of spatial hierarchy in mind to provide easily remembered visual cues to orientation?

49. Are subareas of the outdoors visible from one another to help residents locate their position?

50. Have walkways been designed to loop back to building entries, so that confused residents do not have to be monitored to ensure that they do not wander off the site?

51. Is there an outdoor area adjacent to the building that can be fully enclosed—although designed to seem unconfined through the development of subareas and use of a variety of fences, walls, and planting—to allow safe wandering by residents?

52. Are all walking surfaces nonslip and nonglare?

53. Has planting adjacent to walkways been selected so as to avoid leaves or blossoms falling on the path, which may be hazardous when wet?

54. When changes of grade are necessary, are both ramps and stairs provided?

55. Are ramps and stairs well lit at night?

56. Are handrails provided alongside all ramps and stairs?

57. Is seating provided for resting at the top and bottom of all ramps and stairs?

58. Is there a main walkway that passes by the activity areas, to maximize chance encounters?

59. Are there walking routes for pleasure that offer a choice in length and difficulty of route, changes in setting, and comfortable places to sit and rest along the way?

60. Are there thoughtful details to ensure safety and enjoyment outdoors, such as nonslip paving, raised planters for close-up viewing, and lighting accenting the pavement's edge?

61. Is the pavement wide enough for two people to pass with a wheelchair or walker?

62. Are walkways that connect frequently used areas (parking lots, game areas) direct and highly accessible?

63. Is the paving surface regular and predictable, without too much or too little texture? Does the material and color reduce glare?

TRANSITION ZONES

64. Does every building entry have a screened porch, awning, or trellis to offer protection from glare?

65. Is there a handrail or planter at a suitable height at each building entry, for a moment's hesitation or support?

66. Are private balconies and patios within sight of other private and shared spaces, to enhance opportunities for casual social encounters while on one's own "turf"?

LAWN AREAS

67. Are there lawns or grassed areas near paved pathways and seating areas, for easy access and viewing?

68. Are those lawn areas used for recreation visible from other major activity areas and from indoor sitting areas, for vicarious participation?

69. If the lawn area is intended for use—for example, for croquet or lawn bowling—is it located so that the temperature will be comfortable during the appropriate season(s)?

70. Is the grass area adequately drained?

71. Do grass areas meet adjacent pathways at grade?

72. Do grass areas avoid any abrupt changes in grade?

PRIVATE PATIOS AND BALCONIES

73. Have balconies and patios been situated so that they face each other across a shared landscaped area or look out onto a well-used public space?

74. Do they receive direct sun for a portion of the day?

75. Do they provide protection from the cold, wind, and hot sun?

76. Are patios and balconies enclosed in a way that will not obstruct views from inside the unit?

77. Has fencing or other material been used to provide some privacy between adjacent neighbors?

78. Have the boundaries between patios and adjacent shared areas been left low or optional, depending on the resident's need for privacy?

79. Is there direct paved access from patios to adjacent shared walkways?

80. Has an area of good topsoil been left between the edge of the paved patio and the fence or planting that defines the space?

81. Is there a hose outlet on each patio for watering?

GARDEN PLOTS

82. Are a variety of raised and not-raised garden plots clustered to form a community garden?

83. Is this garden area visible from residents' apartments and/or a well used indoor social space?

84. Is the garden area situated to receive several hours of direct sun each day, and to be protected from the prevailing winds?

85. Is there easily accessible tool storage and a water supply at the gardening area?

86. Are there benches for resting and socializing nearby?

PLAY AREAS

87. Has a play area for visiting children been considered for inclusion on site?

88. Is it located away from quiet areas of the facility—dwelling units, private spaces, nature retreats?

89. Has it been situated so that it is clearly only for the use of visiting children? Or, if use by neighborhood children is acceptable, is it located on the perimeter of the site?

90. Are there benches nearby for supervising adults?

91. Is there a walkway or bench a slight distance away to allow unrelated residents to watch the children playing?

SOCIAL AND PSYCHOLOGICAL NEEDS OF OLDER PEOPLE

Health and Exercise

92. Are there a variety of exercise opportunities for people of all ability levels?

93. Do on-site walking routes offer choices in length and difficulty?

94. Are there handrails, ramps, and resting points on some walking routes, to encourage more frail residents to exercise?

95. In a nursing care setting, is there an outdoor physical therapy area?

96. Are there outdoor areas for both informal exercise (walking, gardening) and programmed activities (croquet, horseshoes)?

97. Are raised garden plots provided in the shared outdoor space, at differing heights and incorporating recessed toe space and/or recessed front rims for improved access?

98. Have private patios, balconies, and window boxes been designed to support gardening or taking care of plants?

99. Has some of the shared landscaping been designed so that residents might help maintain or modify it, if they wish?

100. Are activity areas visible from major indoor gathering spaces (lounge, dining room, terrace) to allow for vicarious participation and staff surveillance?

101. Is there a covered arcade, veranda, or breezeway that might facilitate walking for exercise in poor weather?

102. Are there exercise or social facilities in nearby parks that might encourage residents to leave the building (e.g., to walk in a park, play cards or checkers, feed the ducks)? If an activity is available in a nearby park and it is questionable that the residential population will be able to support the same type of facility or setting on site, it may be preferable to provide other opportunities.

103. If an on-site exercise facility is to be shared with an adjacent project or senior center, is it clear that it is meant to be shared?

104. Are facilities for popular forms of exercise among the income and/or ethnic groups to be housed provided on the site where possible?

105. Can the facilities for these activities be adjusted so that people with different abilities can take part (e.g., ramped

entry to swimming pool for people in wheelchairs, emergency call buttons, brightly colored equipment)?

106. Do all exercise areas have places to rest nearby in the sun and shade, and access to a drinking fountain and nearby toilets?

107. Can the decision to furnish some exercise areas be made after the residents have moved in, so that their preferences can be taken into account?

108. If equipment is needed (e.g., for croquet, gardening), has storage been provided that is easily accessible to residents and very near to where they will need it?

Enjoying Nature

109. Are there a variety of opportunities for enjoying nature—areas easily viewed from indoors? Areas close to building entries? And more distant natural areas, to encourage exercise and exploration?

110. Have a variety of plant materials been used, to offer seasonal changes and splashes of color and to attract birds and butterflies?

111. Has a bird feeder been provided within view of a popular indoor space (lounge, foyer), so that those who cannot venture outdoors can enjoy watching the birds?

112. Is it possible to provide a greenhouse for residents who might like to raise plants, cacti, orchids?

113. When seated in their apartments, do residents have access to a view of near and/or distant natural features?

114. Has the height of all window ledges and balcony railings taken into account the need to see out from a seated position?

115. In areas of frequent inclement weather, is there a solarium or conservatory with indoor plants?

116. For those living on upper floors of a high-rise building and unable to go outside because of infirmity, does the ground plane provide visual interest with a variety of colors and shapes?

117. Does nighttime flood lighting of outdoor planting provide visual interest after dark?

Sensory Details

118. Has the outdoor environment been "sensorally loaded" (i.e., provided with greater-than-normal detailing) to provide stimulation and confidence for those residents experiencing age-related sensory losses?

119. Does design detailing give visual, auditory, kinesthetic, and tactile cues?

120. Does the planting have a marked variety of leaf textures, colors, plant forms, and perfumes?

121. Do pathways in sunny weather have a variety of deep shade, dappled shade, and sunny areas (without abrupt transitions) and a variety of open and enclosed areas?

122. Where colors are used, have those at the yellow/orange/red end of the spectrum been emphasized, rather than those in the blue/green/violet range?

Social Interaction

123. Are outdoor seating areas located close to—and visible from—indoor activity areas such as the entry foyer, dining room, lounge, and crafts area? Are these areas easily accessible from inside, and are the doors easily opened?

124. Is seating located in places that feel secure, such as near a building edge, in an enclosed corner, or backed by a wall, planter, or planting?

125. Have seating arrangements been avoided that force people into eye contact or create a strongly enclosed room-like space?

126. Have some seating areas—particularly near the main entrance—been designed to form a right-angle or an open U-shaped arrangement?

127. Is there seating near the most highly used pedestrian pathway?

128. When budgeting for seating areas, has priority been given to those that will enable residents to watch neighborhood or street activities from an on-site location?

129. If a choice has to be made, has seating in the "front porch" and "front yard" of the site been provided, rather than in "backyard" landscaped areas?

130. Are seating areas situated to be accessible by all and from all units? Do some locations for sitting outside minimize walking distances, exposure to inclement weather, steep slopes, and steps?

131. Are there logical reasons to pass near some seating areas, such as leaving the building, posting a letter, going for a walk?

132. Are there some seating areas where one or two people would feel comfortable sitting alone and some that support a group talking together?

133. Is there seating for viewing and socializing near activity areas such as places for outdoor games and gardening plots?

134. Is there a main terrace or patio for informal or programmed events, off the dining room or lounge?

135. Is this patio in a sheltered, sun-pocket location, to enhance a sense of security and protection?

136. Is the patio divided into subareas by means of an articulated edge or trellis roof, so that it feels equally comfortable for a few people there alone or a large social event (barbecue, birthday)?

137. Because some residents may use only the patio area or outdoor seating near the building entry, are these areas, in particular, richly detailed in regard to plant materials, seasonal changes, surface textures, building materials, outdoor artwork (sculpture, mosaic, fountain), or conversation pieces (aviary, bird feeder, fish pond)?

138. Has furniture that the residents can move been provided in the most popular locations—main patio, building entries—to allow for rearrangement and adjustments? Are these areas lit at night for use on balmy evenings?

Security

139. Are all outdoor spaces visible from indoor spaces that are frequented by residents and staff?

140. Are the boundaries of the site clearly marked by means of a fence, wall, or hedge, so that there is no ambiguity regarding the transition from completely public space to the shared area of the housing site?

141. Has a combination of high-branching trees and low ground cover been used at building entries or anywhere else where security may be a problem?

142. Have all outdoor areas been designed with "defensible space" principles in mind, and are they secure enough so that doors to and from such spaces do not need to be kept locked in the daytime?

143. Is there adequate night lighting on the site and at all building entries?

Encouragement of Independence

144. Are there spaces such as a porch at the front door, a private patio, garden, or balcony where residents can personalize their homes by means of plants, ornaments, wind chimes, and the like?

145. Is there a shelf next to the apartment entry, to hold parcels and bags while the resident opens the door?

146. Is a patio or balcony space available where a resident might hang out something to dry or air, do small repair or painting jobs, pursue hobbies, barbecue, and so forth?

147. Are patios and balconies designed so that residents may easily and inexpensively add a sense of privacy, by means of screening, trellis work, or planting, which is also a personal expression?

148. Does the design and management of the scheme encourage those who wish to participate in the maintenance of shared areas?

149. Are there raised gardening beds available to enable residents to grow vegetables or flowers?

150. Can a family room with adjacent patio be reserved by residents who wish to entertain family or friends in a space that is larger than their apartment?

151. Has consideration been given to providing a fenced area with seating, to allow visits from family and pets, preferably within view of a lounge or patio area, to allow vicarious participation by other residents?

152. Are the planted areas close to patios and apartment entries designed so that a resident can claim a small area for personal use and maintenance?

SITE FURNITURE AND DETAILING
Seating and Tables

153. Is there some light, movable seating?

154. Does all seating have backrests and armrests?

155. Do backrests support the lower back and shoulder region?

156. Does the leading edge of the armrest extend beyond the leading edge of the seat, and does it have a firm, rounded, gripping surface?

157. Are seats not tilted too far off the horizontal, and are leading edges of seats not more than seventeen inches high?

158. Are seats made of soft materials or wood and not of materials that readily conduct heat and cold?

159. Are there tables around thirty inches in height to allow for easy use with wheelchairs or chairs with arms?

160. Have a variety of table sizes been provided? Are table legs quite stable and not protruding beyond the tabletop?

161. Are table edges smooth or rolled?

162. Can some tables be used with movable seating?

Handrails

163. Where handrails are appropriate, have two rails been provided at approximately thirty-two and twenty-six inches, for ambulatory and nonambulatory residents?

164. For ease of use, are handrails approximately two and three-quarters inches in diameter and mounted approximately two inches from the wall?

165. Do the handrails extend approximately one foot beyond any change in grade?

166. Has a material been used for the handrails that is impervious to weather and temperature changes?

167. Does lighting enhance the visibility of handrails at night?

Lighting and Signage

168. Is there high-intensity lighting for security at building entries and in parking areas?

169. Are patio and landscaped areas lit for aesthetic effect?

170. Has lighting along pathways been installed so as to direct light downwards, to help define paving edges and to prevent deep shadows?

171. Do site and building signs have a consistent pattern and hierarchy?

172. Are letter styles bold and without serifs, for ease of reading?

173. Are letters spaced similarly to typewritten material, and are they oversized rather than undersized?

174. Have the surfaces of signs been selected so as to be durable and nonreflective?

175. Are symbols or images used for those who might have reading or language difficulties?

176. Is the lettering in white on a dark background? Have blues and greens been avoided when colors are used?

STAFFING AND MANAGEMENT

177. Will spaces or facilities that require staffing be included in the operational budget?

178. Will staff be willing and able to encourage participation in outdoor activities that some residents may find unfamiliar?

179. If outdoor areas are provided where movable chairs are intended for use, will there be a budget to pay for those chairs; has storage been provided for times when they are not in use; and will management allow or encourage seating in those particular places?

6

DAY CARE OUTDOOR SPACES

Carolyn Francis

The past twenty years have seen a steady increase in demand for the day care of children from six weeks through elementary school age and a concomitant rise in both the percentage and real numbers of working mothers. The U.S. Bureau of Labor Statistics reported in March 1984 a record number of full-time employed mothers of preschool or school-aged children, that is, six out of every ten, or 19.5 million women. Between 1960 and 1988, the percentage of employed mothers of preschoolers increased from 18.5 to 51.3 percent, and that figure is expected to reach 75 percent by 1995 (Triedman 1989). The proportion of children in a full-day day care program doubled during the 1970s, from 17 percent in 1970 to 34 percent in 1980, and continues to rise.

Such findings support the general consensus that parents seek preschool programs not only for child care during a parent's work day but for the social and developmental benefits possible in a peer group setting with trained professional care givers; and in an environment designed to enhance and facilitate that development. It has been pointed out that families often seek a day care center that might act as a surrogate neighborhood—a social community for both the children and adults which might replace the interactions that occurred "on the block" a generation ago. Considering the pressing and increasing need, and the magnitude and vulnerability of the affected population, it is clear that the question of care for these children is of national significance, demanding knowledgeable program development coupled with thoughtful and sensitive facilities design.

A child care program, such as at the New School, Berkeley, California, is a place to develop as a human being: to make friends, to try things out, and to learn and play. (Photo: Carolyn Francis)

215

IMPORTANCE OF THE ENVIRONMENT

Although there is certainly a problem of creating an adequate supply of day care to meet this growing need, issues of child development and educational philosophy have been addressed in the last two decades, resulting in a wide range of program philosophies. However, creating a supportive and stimulating environment for the various programs has been largely unrecognized or left to chance. This problem has been further exacerbated by the frequent use of secondhand or non-purpose built spaces for child care centers (church basements, storefronts, modified dwellings) which, though they sometimes can become wonderful and appropriate spaces, are almost never so before careful and informed refitting. Provence, Naylor, and Patterson spoke about the importance of the environment to the developing child:

The child's acting upon his environment is one of the processes through which physical, intellectual, and psycho-social development occur. The significance of activity in the development of motor competence, the importance of the active repetition of the passive experience as a psychic mechanism, the manipulation of objects as a condition for development of sensorimotor intelligence, the ability to mobilize physical and mental initiative—all these reflect the role of activity as an essential factor in development and learning. . . . The ability to be active in relation to his external world influences is closely related to the child's increasingly complex internal world of thought and feeling. Gradually, he comes to learn that he has choices to make, options to exercise, activities to initiate; he realizes that not only the powerful adult, but he too can choose and influence the environment of which he is a part. Some things he must be taught or told; many others he must be allowed to discover for himself. (1977, p. 83)

In the 1960s, as educators began to accept the premise that intelligence was both alterable and dependent on experiences, particularly during the first eight years of life, they also acknowledged the key role of the environment: "Since the goal of education for the very young was to provide opportunities for interaction with a stimulating environment, issues related to the design of early childhood settings assumed new significance" (*Journal of Man–Environment Relations* 1982, p. 3). Intellectual growth and cognitive learning thus were linked to wider experience in the environment, and it became generally accepted that experience- and action-based learning was more effective than a teacher-centered, lecture style of education:

A child's response to his environment is far more direct and energetic than an adult's. He is constantly making discoveries about highness and lowness, nearness and farness, hardness and softness, light and dark. The physical objects through which he explores these concepts can stimulate his imagination and reinforce his joy of learning. (Haase 1968, p. 9)

As designers and educators began to observe systematically the effects of carefully designed day care spaces, poorly designed spaces, and spaces that had been redesigned to support the program's goals, they found correlations between the quality of space and the children's behavior. Well-designed and organized spaces were found to support cooperation and productive as opposed to disruptive behavior and to reduce discipline problems and vandalism. Similarly, as play environments were enriched to include more varied opportunities and more comfortable conditions, the play behavior itself was observed to become more vital, sophisticated, and more effective as expression.

A barren and inhospitable setting discourages children's involvement, interest, and cooperation. Even if many more play items were brought out onto this patio area, its scale, hardness, abrupt transition from indoors, and monochromatic glare would not be conducive to children's play.

After an intensive three-year study of fifty day care centers, Kritchevsky and her colleagues concluded:

The higher the quality of space in a center, the more likely were teachers to be sensitive and friendly in their manner toward children, to encourage children in their self-chosen activities, and to teach consideration for the rights and feelings of self and others. Where spatial quality was low, children were less likely to be involved and interested, and teachers more likely to be neutral or insensitive in their manner, to use larger amounts of guidance and restriction, and to teach arbitrary rules of social living. (1969, p. 5)

Design should thus focus on young children's learning environments, with special attention to the outdoor space, or play yard, which has been miserably neglected. Gary Moore pointed out that "while outdoor activities are conceptually touted as an equal partner with indoor activities, the space programmed for them and the equipment provided for them is usually poor and an afterthought" (Cohen, McGinty, and Moore 1978, p. 392). The authors of *School Zone* concurred: "Playgrounds have a great deal of potential as learning tools, but they are the least utilized area for this purpose" (Taylor and Vlastos 1975 p. 18).

Actually, many guides and manuals for setting up a day care center suggest that although a good (or any) outdoor space is certainly an asset, it can be replaced by field trips, especially in a land-scarce urban setting. In fact, licensing requirements almost always stipulate a minimal outdoor space per child, but this does not address quality or the many unlicensed facilities. The idea that daily, casual outdoor play might be dispensable is highly questionable, especially for the urban child who may well live in an apartment with no yard or for the child in day care for most of his or her waking hours. Indeed, it is particularly troubling in light of research indicating that most adults recall from childhood an outdoor setting as the one most special or meaningful (Cooper Marcus 1978).

Because more and more children spend greater amounts of their time in a setting away from home, it is clear that we must design such spaces to encourage and enable the types of movement, social interaction, discovery, and development of self-esteem so important to a well-rounded child. Day care open space can be a setting for joy, contemplation, development of friendship, testing of skill, experience of biology and physics, multisensory stimulation, and so much more. Thoughtful design will allow it to be.

In this chapter we will be concerned primarily with day care centers for preschool (three- to five-year old) children. Some additional information intended specifically for babies and toddlers will be presented, although much of the preschool material is relevant to the younger children, keeping in mind differences in both physical and social maturity. Chapters 2 and 3, "Neighborhood Parks" and "Miniparks and Vestpocket Parks," include information on play areas which may also be useful, although the play situation is somewhat different from group care. Likewise, some of the information presented here can be applied to outdoor space for school-age children, taking into account their increased skills and sophistication. Indeed, many primary students attend after-school programs at preschools, frequently sharing some or all of the outdoor space.

One necessary clarification is that supervision is assumed within a day care center. The design may then include things that would not be considered adequately safe for young children alone or things that would be too vulnerable to misuse or vandalism in an uncontrolled setting like a playground. Many features such as garden areas will offer their maximum potential when some self-directed and some teacher-directed or -initi-

At the New School, Berkeley, California, the presence of a teacher allows a wider range of activities and materials than would be possible in a public playground. (Photo: Carolyn Francis)

ated activities are combined. The learning potential of such settings depends to some extent on their utilization by the teacher as a resource. The children can water or worm-hunt on their own initiative but will most likely learn from a teacher to distinguish weeds from crops.

On another level, this information is geared toward centers rather than family day care homes. Designers are much more likely to be involved with the former. Indications are that parents seeking a program, rather than babysitting, prefer day care centers, and it seems that centers will be constructed in greater numbers by government, employers, private enterprise, and others in the near future. Certainly home-care providers can use much of this material to advantage, and indeed so can parents in maximizing use of yards at home.

THE LITERATURE

There is little in the literature on day care outdoor space. Although there are a number of guides to setting up and running a day care center, when it comes to the outdoor environment, they are brief and not very specific. These books seem to accept and agree with the importance of outdoor space as a resource but are not able to provide much concrete guidance. In a different vein, there are a handful of imaginative and often do-it-yourself design manuals that are intended for playgrounds or schools and that include examples of thoughtful and responsive design in preschool settings. Although several of them are well illustrated and inspiring, they do not deal thoroughly or methodically with the various concepts and concerns that the design addresses. That is, one could copy their examples but might have trouble deciding whether or not this was the most appropriate response to one's own circumstances and constraints.

Notable exceptions to this tendency are the various publications by Kritchevsky and her colleagues at Pacific Oaks College in Pasadena, California, which are among the very few thorough and empirical studies of the relationship between day care environments and children's (and adults') behavior. After compiling and analyzing the observational data generated in their three-year, fifty-site study, they were able to formulate some important and pragmatic guidelines for establishing a supportive and enriching outdoor environment (their study encompassed both interior and outdoor spaces). Much of their information is supported by other researchers, who either formulated the concept in a slightly different format or arrived at similar conclusions by more intuitive means.

Another more thorough presentation, by educator and designer Fred Linn Osmon, appears in his *Patterns for Designing Children's Centers*, which is based on a literature review through about 1970, visits to many centers, and discussions with preschool educators. He

includes several patterns, or performance-based (as opposed to prescriptive) guidelines, that apply to the outdoor play environment and suggests possible design responses.

Also useful are the various documents produced by a study of both military and civilian children's centers and play areas, by Gary Moore and his colleagues at the University of Wisconsin at Milwaukee, under contract to the U.S. Army. The army, the country's largest employer-sponsor of child care centers, commissioned the study as a prelude to its plans to build new centers and renovate some older ones. The authors point out that in the army, "as a microcosm of the rest of the country, demand for developmentally-oriented quality care, both full-day and drop-in, including infant care, far exceeds current supply" (Cohen, McGinty, and Moore 1978, p. iv). The authors visited twenty-three child care facilities for environmental analysis, behavior observation, and focused interviews to determine successful aspects and conditions, shortcomings, and general patterns of need and use. In *Recommendations for Child Play Areas* this information, earlier research by the study group, and a review of related books and articles form the basis for fifteen planning recommendations and fifty-six design patterns. This book addresses the design of play spaces for housing areas, shopping centers, recreation centers, school grounds, neighborhood and regional parks, as well as child support facilities.

There is little available empirical research on day care environments. A 1979 literature review of fifteen hundred child–environment reports and articles revealed that less than 5 percent had an empirical base (Moore 1987), and although several authors indicated that such a study would be welcome, they also acknowledged the real problems of dealing with such a multivariate setting. The information in this chapter does draw on two such studies done as master's theses, (Simmons 1974, Sinha 1984), one in Berkeley, California, and the other in Blacksburg, Virginia; which are also used for two of the case studies at the end of the chapter. We also have used a professional report that discusses observations of twenty California day care center outdoor spaces, together with some conclusions regarding those elements necessary for a successful play area (Fields 1987, Chap. 1).

Finally, it is interesting but discouraging to note that the greatest range of literature on designing learning environments and play areas dates from the late 1960s to the mid 1970s. Essentially all of the child-centered, "learning through play in the environment at large" material is from that period; in fact, most of the reviews of children's facility design in the major architecture and landscape journals also date from that period.

It appears that the issue of child care has finally reached "critical mass" in this country, with both media and legislative attention being focused on the burgeoning need for programs, employer involvement, and reasonable pay and working conditions. However, this current attention has yet to address in any depth the question of day care environment. It is imperative that the issue of providing a setting to support both child development and the individual program be addressed; that in our haste to create more day care slots, we resist the tendency to create environments shaped only by building code or zoning requirements. Hopefully, we will begin to see reviews of new, sensitive, and exciting day care design; but it may be that in these more conservative times, the focus has shifted away from the need to provide environments that allow children to be children and that offer a supportive framework for the vital work of human development, namely, play.

PLAY AND DEVELOPMENT IN THE DAY CARE SETTING

The goal of both outdoor and indoor day care environments is to provide a setting conducive to the full range of normal child development and the various types of play that enable that development.

Physical development is most often associated with large-muscle or gross-motor activities, such as running, jumping, and climbing. Through these activities, children come to know their bodies, to be aware of their abilities and limitations, and to develop a sense of mastery or self-esteem by learning particular skills. Historically, outdoor play was also seen as an opportunity for letting off steam. While this is a valid concern, especially if indoor space is limited or the program is physically restrictive, outdoor space is capable of supporting the full range of child development.

Another type of development, which is both physical and intellectual, is frequently referred to as cognitive or perceptual. It is characterized by manipulative play of all types, by which children begin to formulate concepts of action and relationships, by actively manipulating the elements of the environment. It also is evident in play with small objects, requiring more fine-motor control. Many indoor toys are designed to promote fine-motor control, but it can be enhanced just as well by providing opportunities to collect pebbles in a cup, sort different shapes or sizes of leaves, or experiment with the properties of sand and water.

Social development, which is considered to encompass children's increasing expertise in interpersonal interaction and verbal ability, finds expression in dramatic or role-play behavior. Playing at games of house, fire fighters, space patrol, or whatever, children will increase their social skills.

Various studies indicate that provision of "loose parts" or props to embellish dramatic play leads to more invention and longer attention span of participants. Another finding with design implications is that while children seem always to be able to find a multitude of ways to use the natural environment (trees, rocks, bushes, etc.) there seems to be a level of ambiguity in designed play structures beyond which creative response declines. In other words, if a play structure is too ambiguous, it may remain so and receive little use. On the other hand, most experts believe detailed replicas of real objects are too limiting to the children's imaginations. A happy medium seems to be reached when a structure is open to a range of interpretations and includes a variety of challenges and ways to respond to the equipment without becoming vague or purely sculptural, a problem with quite a few professionally designed play environments. Essentially, if ambiguity is achieved through inclusion of many

Active play is most often supported by the outdoor play area design, which usually encourages gross-motor development. The challenge is to be equally supportive of cognitive and social development. (Photo: Carolyn Francis)

At the Pacific Oaks College Children's School, Pasadena, California, cognitive, or perceptual, development is enhanced by opportunities to manipulate elements in the environment, a role that pebbles, sand, leaves, and twigs fill as well as, if not better than, manufactured toys do. (Photo: Sharon Stine)

Adding props to a static piece of play equipment sets the scene for dramatic play at the Orange Coast College Children's Center, Costa Mesa, California. (Photo: Keila Fields)

possibilities and actions rather than exclusion of any-thing that would suggest a specific definition, the re-sults are likely to be satisfying.

Thus the best environment for children's physical, cognitive, and social development must offer opportu-nities for a wide range of play behavior. These different aspects of development are interrelated and interde-pendent. For example, "gross motor play, aids physical fitness as well as being critical in perceptual develop-ment and serving as a basis for later cognitive develop-ment" (Johnson, Shack, and Oster 1980, p. 65). Child development expert Burton White reminded us that the preschool years are a vital transitional period for social development, the principal experiences being "creating products" and "role play," both of which are believed to be important to developing competence (White 1975).

As a correlate to providing for all sorts of develop-mental play, Phyfe-Perkins stated:

Of special importance in an understanding of the influence of physical space on behavior is the need to analyze space in terms of whether it provides for a *full range of children's behav-ior.* Can a tired, unhappy child retreat to some private, cozy area and regroup his/her forces, or does the space provide only continued stimulation and frustration? Can shy children find small enclosed areas where they can interact with one or two other children, or are such children found on the perimeter of activities watching or playing by themselves? (Phyfe-Perkins 1982, p. 27, italics in original)

It may seem simply good sense that an environment expected to support a group of children, each with his or her own personality, for a good part of the day should incorporate spaces for a full range of moods, en-ergy levels, and kinds of social involvement. Unfortu-nately, in this case most outdoor spaces would be judged inadequate, as the general tendency is still to provide for active, gross-motor activities, and only barely adequately for those.

DESIGN RECOMMENDATIONS

Issues to Consider Before Design

Relationship of Program to Environment

At the very earliest stage of design, before any specific features have been decided, it is important to deter-mine the goals of the educational program. Several writers have concluded that one of the main reasons for a day care space to fail is the lack of agreement between environmental messages and opportunities, and the behavioral goals that the staff wish to achieve. Gary Moore found that the design and layout of a child care facility can affect the group activities, individual behavior, and psychological responses of the children and care givers. The environment

can either make it easier for staff to achieve their goals, or it can interfere. Spaces may not be large enough for planned activities, or they may be too large and thus encourage ran-dom, aimless behavior. . . . The planning and design of the facilities to house a child care program must be based on its philosophy, educational goals, and curriculum. The design of the facility, whether renovation of existing space or construc-tion of new facilities, must grow out of these program goals and support the curriculum. (Moore 1981, pp. 53–54)

He even suggested that in the case of a center not yet in operation, the future director be hired on a consult-ing basis to establish the educational program prior to design, as well as advocating the establishment of a user review committee and facility planning commit-tee.

Kritchevsky and her colleagues noted that "unless staff have a clear conception of the relationship be-tween goals and the play environment which they have created by their choice of contents, they may force be-havior which acts against the achievement of desired goals" (Kritchevsky and Prescott 1969, p. 17). Sutfin agreed, adding that a lack of agreement between physi-

Golden West College Child Care Center, Huntington Beach, California, has created a private little place for one or two children. (Photo: Keila Fields)

cal setting and expected behavior can lead to more disruptive behavior, shorter attention spans, and louder levels of conversation (Sutfin 1982). Examples of such situations, given by the authors, include:

- teacher goal to support autonomy via opportunities for children to make their own choices versus an environment so low in number of things to do per child that their choices are constantly thwarted.
- teacher goal to lengthen children's attention span by helping them retain interest in a self-chosen activity versus an environment offering only simple play opportunities (e.g., a slide, offering little chance for variation in play while remaining with the unit).
- teacher goal of children working independently from each other versus environment set up to accommodate groups with no one-child niches.

Kritchevsky also stated:

Goals in day care programs will often be concerned with providing the sort of warm, affectionate, individualized attention offered by home and mother. With a ratio of one teacher to up to 15 children, space which encourages children to go off and manage on their own will free the teacher to meet the needs of individual children as they occur. On the other hand, in a program emphasizing teacher direction of children's activities and closely restricting choices by children, the principal criterion of supportive space is that it not distract attention from the teacher. Teachers who arrange inviting activity centers and then require that children ignore them in order to pay attention to the teacher for extended periods are setting the stage for discipline problems. (Kritchevsky and Prescott 1969, p. 8)

That is, a design that invites the children's immediate self-directed involvement may well interfere with such a program's goals. Many studies have noted that the outdoor space of a day care facility is most often used for free play of varying degrees, so that even in a very highly structured program the outdoor space would largely be given over to self-directed activities. This in turn suggests that designers should be concerned more with free play when designing an outdoor space but nevertheless make sure that it is carefully designed. That is, if a play yard does indeed provide the main or only opportunity to "blow off steam" or go one's own way, then it is surely incumbent on the designer to create an environment requiring as little monitoring control and rule-enforcing by teachers as possible. Moreover, it is important for the designer to be aware of general policies for the use of space. For example, an understairs space might become a cozy and secret spot for one or two children. But if it is against the rules to use such a space in that way, there will need to be an adult-controlled barrier to remove the temptation. Also, a space may be unavailable for use as intended, such as a play house that has become a storage shed. When redesigning, then, the designer should take into account use patterns like this.

Numbers and Ages of Children Served

From a design viewpoint, two important aspects of the child population are the number of children to be served and their age range or age groupings. A basic issue in the design of child care outdoor space is whether to create several separate areas for use by different groups of children or instead to have one large space with differentiated areas that are accessible to all children outdoors at any given time. In larger centers, children are most frequently separated into smaller groups, or "classes," with a regular teacher or teachers and a designated interior space even if many areas are

Rather than placing it off limits, the staff at the New School, Berkeley, California, recognized the appeal of this unused animal hutch as a playhouse. Being open to unconventional uses is one way to avoid program–environment conflict. (Photo: Carolyn Francis)

shared. These smaller groups are often segregated by age, so that a preschool might include one or more groups of three-year-olds, four-year-olds, maybe even of toddlers or infants, and a group of school-aged before- and after-school children. Often this subgrouping extends to the outdoor space, where each group may have its own separate yard, or sometimes the groups share a yard, using it at different times of the day if the space is not big enough for all the children to play at once. In Keila Fields's study, this "time-sharing" of yards had several negative consequences:

Participants in Group A cannot conduct on-going building projects if they must come indoors and leave their projects exposed to Group B, who will then come out to play. When "outdoor time" is treated like recess (a time in which to run off steam in order to be able to return inside and be quiet) a child's approach to the use of the outdoor environment is one of simply running from one place to another. When several groups share a play yard, logistics create a set of problems that prioritize the schedule rather than the child's needs and the goals of the program. (Fields 1987, p. 20)

Fields found that the centers with high quality outdoor environments created sub-groups of 30–40 children (3yrs–up), and provided each group with its own yard.

Many factors should contribute to the decision on subdividing the outdoor area:

• Depending on the site itself and its relationship to the building, it may be natural, or even necessary, to develop a "front" and "back" yard, or north, south, east, and west yards based on site layout, building entrances, and so on. However, if such a division will create inequity (a much smaller yard for one group, lack of sunny areas, no access to trees . . .), then the interior layout of the building should be analyzed. Perhaps a reorganization of the internal areas will allow a more equitable relationship to the outdoor spaces. The development of the play yards should not be subservient to the building, but rather interactive with it. Clearly there is more latitude in the case of new construction, but it is far from impossible to move a door or window to create a better relationship between building and yard. If the design/remodel of the building and the design of the outdoor space are to be dealt with by different individuals or firms, the siting of the building and internal arrangement must be discussed in terms of the resulting play areas and their relation to the classrooms.

• Again, it is essential for the environment to respond to the educational program. Clearly, a center that sees outdoor play time as an opportunity for otherwise age-homogeneous groups to mingle with older and/or younger children will be ill served by an excessively compartmentalized yard. However, if the program's goal is to provide fine-tuned developmental challenges outdoors, then separate spaces may be necessary to avoid younger children's becoming frustrated or older ones' becoming bored. Or the goal of a program that serves children whose home lives are characterized by disruption may be to foster familiarity and dependence within a small group, also suggesting separate spaces.

• In regard to safety, the principal concern is preventing younger children from being either "run over" by the older ones or from attempting activities that are too advanced but that the older ones do. Actually, children on the whole show remarkable sense in determining their appropriate level of challenge, but if there is likely to be a problem providing adult supervision, younger children should probably not have uncontrolled access to play features that could prove harmful. The issue of being physically overwhelmed by older children's play is most relevant to infants and toddlers, who quite literally have trouble getting out of the way. These age groups should be given their own space, with visual access to the older group, if at all possible.

One appealing approach is that used by the Pacific Oaks College Children's School, which has six play yards, each of which acts as a "home turf" to a group of children housed adjacent but which the other children of the center can visit. There also used to be an infant group on the site, and at the teacher's discretion, the older children could assist or play with the babies, a practice that is continued with the toddlers in the "Boat Yard." A central "lane" provides for wheeled toys and connects the various yards. This approach allows the children to identify with a smaller area, while also offering opportunities to explore and enjoy the other yards.

Building on a Child's Scale

A chief failing of design is the creation of an environment that looks good in plan (bird's eye view) but that does not measure up as a person moves through it. When designing for children, special attention needs to be paid to the children's eye level as they walk, run, climb, or crawl through the play yard. For a piece of equipment or feature to be used, it must be easily visible to them. For example, a barrier that an adult can easily see over may entirely block the vision of a three- or five-year-old, who on average will be 37 to 43 inches tall. On the other hand, a four-inch concrete lip on a sandbox is probably not enough of a barrier to prevent a child intent on the attractions beyond, from running through the sandbox, scattering sand and demolishing castles. Barbara Scales, director of the Child

The child's view should be considered when designing for all types of activity—sitting, tricycling, running—so that design elements will enhance the experience. This modest planting along a wheeled toy path at the Good Shepherd Preschool, Irvine, California, designed by director Sue Ko, approximates the motorist's experience of a tree-lined avenue. (Photo: Keila Fields)

Study Center at the University of California at Berkeley, observed:

An attractive deck, built around a large shade tree in our play yard, failed to appeal to children. Later, when teachers stooped to take a child's eye view, they found that the deck and its access points virtually disappeared. This leafy retreat, designed for quiet pretend play, had meaning for an adult but was as visually "out of context" for children as the top of the refrigerator in my own home was for me. (Almy et al. 1987, p. 89)

Similarly, recognition of children's small stature explains the universal popularity of trees and towers to climb, both the novelty of "looking down from above" and the sense of powerfulness thereby engendered.

Another important issue of scale arises when designing settings for dramatic or fantasy play. Keila Fields discovered that even if the height of a mock kitchen counter is appropriate, the fantasy of being a grown-up preparing a meal will be destroyed if that counter is much longer than a real one. Likewise, in order to be successful, playhouses must take into account the child's experience of three-dimensional spatial volume and to avoid a common tendency to create overly tall spaces.

Variety and Opportunity

Many researchers have commented on the barrenness of outdoor play yards, which often fail to provide enrichment or even play opportunities. A yard for twenty-five or thirty children that has a simple sandbox, two swings, a slide, and three tricycles is clearly impoverished. On the other hand, a yard that is filled to capacity with equipment may offer only two types of activity, but in endless variation, for example, swinging and climbing. Neither of these situations can sup-

port developmentally complete play. To be effective, a preschool outdoor space must provide an abundance of what Kritchevsky and her colleagues call *play units*—something to play with and enough space in which to play with it (e.g., the "jump off and walk around" space around a slide that becomes part of that play unit). They found that in the yards judged to be successful, the ratio of play units (or opportunities) to children was somewhat greater than two to one. In other words, a yard for fifteen children would have thirty or more distinct play units. Thus, when a child felt ready to move from one activity to another, there would always be a variety of opportunities from which to choose. This allows a natural progression of play and makes it less necessary for the teacher to intervene in a change than when the ratio is one unit per child or less and the newly desired play unit is almost certainly already occupied.

Providing for a wide variety of activities may be a more elusive issue, as variety does not necessarily relate to amount of equipment. In fact, even in a yard with many things to do, if the majority are of one or two types, that is what will be seen. The possibility of variety within a play unit is what Kritchevsky and her colleagues named *complexity,* and it refers to the possibility of changing and refocusing ongoing play. For this to be possible, children must be able to use the unit in more than one way and to juxtapose and manipulate play materials. This type of built-in variety enables children to lengthen their attention span, as the play unit responds to their changing focus. The complexity of a play unit also refers to opportunity. The Pacific Oaks researchers found that a *simple* unit such as a swing or a trike is one play opportunity, whereas *complex* units, such as play dough and utensils or a toy farm with animals, offer four opportunities, and a *super* unit, such as a sand area with water and equipment, has eight. They strive to maintain a ratio of five play opportunities per child at the Pacific Oaks College Children's School. Simple units in the overall fabric of the play yard are valuable as places to pause or adjust and should be balanced (rather than replaced) with units capable of absorbing more children.

Variety, therefore, both in a given unit and in the play yard at large, is a measure of the environment's ability to keep the children interested and involved. An abundance of opportunities ensures that children will be able to respond naturally to that variety and to make a choice.

Sensory Stimulation

The outdoor environment naturally lends itself to sensory stimulation. The challenge is to highlight and enhance that stimulation, rather than applying a uniform layer of blacktop and some concrete "tree forms." As Suzanne de Moncheaux noted, "The young child senses the environment in a very immediate and detailed way. Many researchers have noted the 'fine grain' descriptions children give of their surroundings, and their frequent reference to animals, vegetation, natural phenomena, and human activities" (de Moncheaux 1981, p. 26). Likewise, when Kevin Lynch collected his students' recollections of their childhood environments, he found the descriptions to be full of detailed accounts of ground surfaces, climate, trees, and animals. Gary Moore believes that "the quality of the physical environment can have a direct, stimulating impact on children. Colors, textures, shapes of objects, and the layout of activity centers can encourage a child to interact with the environment and to learn from this interaction" (Moore 1981, p. 53).

Each phase and aspect of the design of a play yard can be thought of as a component in children's developing sensory awareness. They can see bright banners or flags and even hear them flapping or cracking in the wind. A garden provides dirt to touch and smell and a tomato or carrot to taste, touch, see, and smell. A wind chime can add music to the sound of wind in the trees; a prism can cast a rainbow. A bird feeder can bring birds to hear and see (and a stray feather to find, hold, and treasure). A stream over rocks makes a running sound, and slides through the fingers; a still pond reflects the clouds and might even hold fish. Different materials and surfaces focus attention on the world around us and are an important way to learn, one that is especially valuable to children with limited access to rich outdoor environments.

In 1966, Charles Dana Gibson (then chief of the California Department of Education's Bureau of Planning) presented his vision of the preschool environment:

The outdoor areas will be designed with the same care as the indoors. The transition from one area to the other will be fluid and simple. Instead of a sea of asphalt, outdoor space will have a variety of surfaces. Wherever possible, we will use the adjacent natural environment, hills, valleys, streams, to create dramatic changes in elevation and extend the young child's spatial experience . . . there can be many sorts of wall treatments, smooth and rough surfaces, soft and hard . . . there will be dry sand and wet sand, grass and brick areas; stone, concrete, and tan bark areas—in fact, all the various types of surfaces normally found in the vocabulary of a good landscape architect. We will also explore the world of color . . . as a child sees color, in a full spectrum of bright, vibrant hues. (Gibson 1968, p. 21)

Hopefully, the time has come to see his vision realized, even improved on.

The natural materials of an orchard, garden, and sandy "beach" at St. Elizabeth's Day Home, San Jose, California, offer a rich array of sensory stimuli. The outdoor areas were designed by Deanna Pini, based on Piagetian developmental theory. (Photo: Keila Fields)

Manipulation

Child development experts have attested to the importance of offering children opportunities to act on their environment, and both rigorous studies and casual observation have borne this out. Children have been found to play more creatively with materials whose play value is latent (e.g., sand, water, dirt, trees) than with already defined objects such as swings and slides. In fact, children most often look beyond the immediate designed purpose of objects in the environment, adapting and using them wherever possible for quite different ends. Children also learn mapping by manipulating their environment, developing both a concept of representation and of a bird's-eye view through the creation of dirt streets and sand, rock and twig buildings, bridges, and such.

In *Planning with Children in Mind* de Moncheaux identified children's need to touch the environment, to "physically and actively engage with it" expressed in "pressing buttons, picking up pebbles, rolling on grass, climbing trees, sliding down ramps, walking along walls, clambering on roofs, and so forth. Frequently however, this contact [is] prohibited or discouraged through design, custom, or instruction" (de Moncheaux 1981, pp. 90–91). Indeed, since it has been found that children in almost any setting adapt and manipulate their environment, if it is not designed to accommodate this need, they will most certainly find ways to do so anyway. Holes will be dug, bricks or rocks moved and stacked, and ornamental plantings trampled to create hidey-holes. This in turn leads to the definition of disruptive behavior, and the whole energy-draining cycle discussed under agreement of environment and program. The design must also address children's natural, inquisitive, and action-oriented behavior. A realistic and supportive program will recog-

nize and incorporate this need, but the importance of sensitive design may be even greater in a program less tolerant of disorder, where a clearly unintended use of the environment would create friction between children and teachers.

Another issue that is often considered undesirable by adults is children's need not just to build but also to destroy. Adventure Playgrounds, popular in Europe but not yet widely accepted in the United States, are dedicated to this process of making and unmaking. Equipping a manipulable environment can involve a full range of design responses, from providing for play with elements such as sand, water, and dirt (in conjunction with toys and tools appropriate to experimentation); to larger loose parts such as boards, barrels, boxes, rope, ladders, sawhorses, and other possible building materials; to using movable parts on the play equipment. A quick observation of play equipment indicates a considerably greater use of structures that contain steering wheels or revolving logs or tires, rather than only static pieces.

Outdoor Activities

Some educators maintain that the majority of, if not all, indoor preschool activities can be carried out as well or even better in a properly designed outdoor setting. In their study of child care facilities Gary Moore and his colleagues found that outdoor activity spaces— if they were well sited and landscaped and well related to one another—offered a "wealth of developmental opportunities hard to replicate in indoor spaces" (Cohen et al. 1979, p. 339). Children are often less inhibited doing artwork outdoors, and so in addition to providing an area for easels, the design of a play yard could incorporate paved areas especially suitable for chalk drawings or wall surfaces capable of either being

Painting is certainly not the only activity that can be brought outside successfully, but it may be one of the most enjoyable at the Child Educational Center, Caltech/JPL Community, La Cañada, California. (Photo: Keila Fields)

painted on or of having large rolls of paper attached on which to paint murals. Music is a traditional preschool activity that can easily move outdoors, and some musical elements might even be made part of the design, such as different types of chimes or bells or surfaces that can be tapped with a mallet or stick to elicit different tones. Storytelling and group singing can be enjoyable outdoors on a well-planned grassy slope or a circle of sitting rocks or stump ends. If an area is to be used for a more focused activity such as these, it needs to have a sense of enclosure and to be away from more active play. It also is a good idea to provide for this area a means of buffering sound, probably through vegetation. An area like this can also be used to advantage for show-and-tell activities or performing a play for an audience.

Other activities that are a normal part of the indoor program but do not come as readily to mind for the outdoors are sleeping and resting. One designer suggested providing hammocks, for a different type of experience, and it is easy to imagine a hot summer day when naps on blankets or mats under the trees might be far preferable to resting in a hot and airless indoor room. Likewise, a secure treehouse or platform with a cushioned area for resting could be a wonderful spot for a tired child to rest up before rejoining those playing and allow for either overlooking the play below or enjoying the patterns of tree branches against the sky.

Another routine set of activities deals with food, which when moved outdoors offers new and pleasant variations. An outdoor space could have one or more locations appropriate for picnicking, especially enjoyable if defined by a bright overhead canopy, or a framework to uphold a surplus parachute. And there is the question of preparing food outside or cooking over an outdoor fire. Proper supervision is, of course, essential, but it appears that children respond very well to the

necessary safety precautions when using a firepit or barbecue. Some writers have even suggested that for children who have no regular exposure to fire (an urban dweller with no fireplace at home), a controlled experience such as a preschool might offer can teach an understanding of the risks and dangers of fire without provoking fear.

As a correlate to bringing indoor activities outside is the issue of bringing outdoors the classroom, or structured learning experience. There are virtually endless opportunities for learning in the preschool outdoor space. For example, in a garden, plants can be labeled and their growth studied; insects, snails, and worms can be observed; and the harvest of vegetables or fruits can be picked, cut open to examine seeds and structure, and finally eaten. A sundial, thermometer, wind sock, weathervane, any type of solar-powered appliance, or rain gauge all can be used to teach concepts of time, season, and weather. The plants on the site can lead to an ongoing discussion of texture and color, smell, size, leaf types, and animal and insect habitats. In short, opportunities for teachers to demonstrate principles and concepts can be designed into virtually every part of the outdoor environment.

Another type of activity that should be part of the design is the opportunity for children to assist with or take responsibility for tasks that are part of the normal use and maintenance of the outdoor space. Children can develop skills and enhance self-esteem through such participation at child care.

For example, gardens can be set up to make it easy for children to water the plants or, with supervision, pick vegetables. It may be best to limit access to the garden by a gate, but if children will be allowed in to work, there should be paths wide enough to prevent accidental trampling of plants and some sort of edge around the beds to identify the appropriate areas to

When the weather is good, a picnic outdoors is enjoyable for children and adults at the Child Educational Center, Caltech/ JPL Community, La Cañada, California. (Photo: Keila Fields)

Although outside, this hard, hot, and featureless eating area brings none of the delight associated with an old blanket thrown down on the grass, perhaps under a tree for its dappled shade. Mere provision for an activity will not ensure a positive experience.

Children love to do "real work," which builds self-esteem and cooperation skills, as here at the Infant–Toddler Center, University of California at Irvine. (Photo: Keila Fields)

walk on. A faucet and sprinkling cans could be provided on the perimeter of the garden area, where, if left on too long, the faucet would not flood the beds. Or if it is a faucet that requires holding in the "on" position, with a flat surface below for the watering can, this problem can be eliminated. This might also encourage cooperation, with one child turning on the water while another maneuvers the can to fill it.

Animals can likewise allow for much child participation. Food and water can be replenished; straw or other bedding/nesting materials can be replaced; and in some cases, the animals can be groomed. There may also be opportunities for children to sweep up or wash off dirty surfaces. Indeed, whenever there is a routine task associated with the design, an attempt should be made to

use it to create opportunities for children to help, whether it means including a step or bench or providing something within a child's reach or at a child's eye level.

Site Characteristics

When studying the site, one of the most thoroughly documented and relevant facts is that children play everywhere. Hence, all areas that will be accessible to the children should be designed to incorporate as much play and learning value as possible and to be able to withstand use by the children. Not only will children play on the equipment and in designated play areas, but they will swing on the gate, hang from the tree

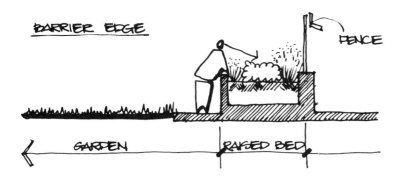

Raised garden beds will protect plants and can become attractive boundaries for an activity area.

Even the detailing of the edge can allow for "jumping practice."
(Photo: Carolyn Francis)

limbs, and attempt to scale the storage shed. A design that anticipates this will give far fewer headaches to the staff and less frustration to the children.

Amount of Space

The literature indicates that licensing requirements demand from 75 to 150 square feet of outdoor space per child (varying according to state and local ordinances). Virtually all educators and design researchers agree that this minimum should be expanded, if at all possible, to 200 square feet or more per child. To provide an adequate number of play opportunities supporting the range of developmental needs, as well as adequate circulation and buffering, this amount of space is more appropriate. In fact, the centers that were considered to have the highest quality outdoor environments in the Fields's study provided 300–400 square feet per child; and two highly regarded centers provide groups of forty children with one-half acre yards (530 + square feet per child). Clearly, such large amounts of space are not always, or even often, available. Yet if having such a resource is as important to child development as the evidence suggests, we must ask ourselves how it might be provided. Perhaps the current interest in having on-site child care in downtown corporate headquarters should be redirected. Certainly it would not be possible to provide any substantial outdoor space in a central business district, and what is provided will likely be shaded and windy due to tall buildings. The expense of providing prime commercial real estate for a center with negligible outdoor space might go much further in a more residential area.

Centers that are planned as part of suburban business parks may be able to occupy more space, although such use of potentially profitable area is still likely to be limited. These centers, unless very carefully planned, are subject to the problems of being cut off from any neighborhood setting (and possible walking trips), as well as the tendency to want them to reflect well on the developer/business park, and thus become sanitized "junior corporate" settings. An attractive adult vision of childhood may preclude much that is of value to the child.

Adjacent Uses

The designer should consider what surrounds the child care facility. Whereas adults usually prefer to be visually and aurally buffered from street traffic, children often find much to enjoy in the busy movement. Thus if it is possible to survey the street from the facility, the design could include either a section of nonsolid fencing, or a tower or tree platform near enough to the fence to see out. Children take great pleasure in

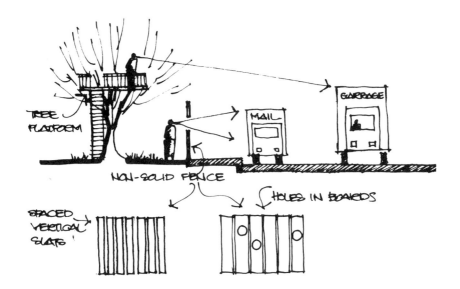

Children appreciate being able to see beyond the fence; street life is interesting, especially on garbage day!

If the view out is truly inappropriate, at least the wall should be treated to be interesting or attractive (vines growing on it, murals) rather than appearing as a stark barrier between the children and the outside world.

seeing, imitating, and discussing police cars, garbage trucks, fire engines, tree-trimming trucks, and the like. If, on the other hand, the facility is in a more suburban or rural setting, creating visual continuity between the play yard and the adjacent open, farm, or park space will add to the feeling of spaciousness. It may also provide subject matter for watching and discussing, whether it is views of animals, bigger children in a school yard, or arriving and departing parents. In any case, it is good to give the children a sense of being part of the neighborhood and the larger community, and thus some degree of outward orientation is appropriate. For reasons of safety, perimeter fencing must be at least four feet high and not climbable. Although it does provide visual continuity, the institutional quality

of chain-link fence makes it undesirable for all but short stretches. If it is already in place, climbing vines can be planted to soften its effect. Vertical slat fencing can be spaced to allow enough room between the boards to look out, or "knot holes" big enough to look out can be cut from boards at different eye levels. Horizontal slat fencing should obviously be avoided, as it might well be viewed as a ladder to be climbed.

Entry

The entry to any place is important, because it is the first thing one sees and because it conveys messages regarding whom this place is for, what it is like, and what is expected from those entering. In a child care center, the entry should—through scale, materials, sequence, and views—make clear that it is a place for children, a place to play and a place to try things and make discoveries. Frequently, the day care center is entered through a yard, courtyard, or patio area, and thus it is important that this entry area be more than a design statement: It should be inviting and contain elements with which a child can interact, such as a low wall to balance on, a child's height view of the play area beyond, or a gate made to swing on as it is opened. The entry should also be reassuring to the parents, letting them know that this is a good, nurturing place to leave their children. Features that parents appreciate at the entry are notice boards for general announcements and community interaction and enough room to stand and talk with a teacher or another parent for a few moments without blocking others. If the entry is residential in character, rather than institutional or commercial, both parent and child are likely to feel more comfortable. That is, abrupt openings in fences, blank or hard facades, and overdesigned "adult aesthetic" spaces should be avoided.

Topography

If the site includes any slopes, mounds, or hills, they should be incorporated into the design. In fact, when a site is flat, it is desirable to use any earth excavated for sand areas or water areas to create a mound, as changes in elevation provide many play opportunities. Many toys, and the children themselves, may be rolled down an incline. The vantage point at the top allows for a clearer understanding of the relationship among parts of the yard and easier location of a friend or teacher (and easier supervision by a teacher). A mound also provides a natural separation of play areas and moderates the effect of wind in the play yard. In addition, concrete pipe can be used for a tunnel through the base of the mound, and a slide can be set directly into the slope for an interesting and safe ride.

Natural Areas

The appeal of natural areas—overgrown, unmanaged spaces—to children is becoming widely recognized. Most adults can remember playing in an empty lot, along a drainage ditch, or in some other "wild" setting, frequently declared off-limits by their parents. In Europe, some housing developments are preserving natural areas for play or are even purposely planting in order to create such areas before construction, allowing several years for the natural ecology to become established. This same concern for a natural setting, incorporating several different ecological niches as well as a recirculating stream and pond, was used by designer Robin Moore at the Washington Environment Yard (or WEY, at the Washington Elementary School, Berkeley, California). A similar environment can be created in a preschool outdoor space, with unmowed grass and wildflowers, hardy bushes that can withstand exploring and hiding, and low-branching trees conducive to climbing. This space will be especially popular if the planting is dense enough to allow children to feel hidden, even though still visible through the foliage. Insects, birds, and even small animals should be encouraged through planting and the provision of rocks and cracked surfaces.

Building and Yard

The site's layout and the relationships among its elements are extremely important to the success of an outdoor play space. One basic relationship is that of the play space to the building. In a well-functioning outdoor space, the transition from indoors to outdoors is almost always clear, easy, and natural. Often the building's doors are glass or have glass panels, with child's-height windows next to the doors. This allows children to size up the situation before going out or to see whether there are specific people or objects outside to play with. The doors themselves should be easily oper-

This mound at St. Elizabeth's Day Home, San Jose, California, incorporates two tunnels that intersect at the center and a view from its top to the adjacent neighborhood. (Photo: Carolyn Francis)

A "wild" area with rocks, shrubs, and trees might even hold a lizard or two. (Photo: Carolyn Francis)

able by a child, with lever or bar openers and not too heavy. Once outside, many children will again stop to assess the activity or pause to watch it on the way in or out. Many studies have found that the best design solution to this pattern of behavior (and one that generates many other possibilities as well) is the creation of a "porch." The Moore study noted that "porches, arcades, and covered outdoor play areas are highly prized and highly used features of buildings. They provide a tremendous amount of flexibility and area at reasonable cost. Porches are multi-use spaces" (Cohen et al. 1978, p. 396). In fact, it was the authors' opinion that such space should be required for child support facilities. Apart from their value as a transitional space, porches also provide an easy and natural location for activities to extend out from indoors and, with adequate overhang, an area for outdoor play on rainy or overly hot days. Sharon Stine, a past director of Pacific Oaks, is equally convinced of the importance of porches. She believes that a porch also serves as an ideal location for quiet outdoor play during periods of heavy air pollution and a good spot for adults to chat and watch from.

Activity Areas and Paths

Most studies of children's outdoor play environments, or guidebooks for establishing such a space, emphasize the need to place equipment and elements in the correct places. As Gary Moore remarked, every indoor space should have an outdoor counterpart:

There should be individual activity pockets outdoors for cognitive, social, and individual activities as well as for motor activities, and they should be designed with the same consid-

erations as indoor spaces. They should be well-defined and yet partially connected to each other, so that circulation overlooks but does not interfere with the activity pockets. (Moore 1981, p. 63)

Playspaces for Preschoolers (Canada Mortgage and Housing Corporation 1976, revised 1980) suggests that areas for gross-motor physical play need some type of barrier to separate them from cognitive play areas but may be next to social and dramatic play settings. This report also includes a category of quiet or retreat play, which is more akin to cognitive play, and suggests placing such areas next to each other. Similarly, the authors of *Integrated Facilities* (Childhood Services Council of South Australia, ca. 1975) call for areas for vigorous, uninterrupted free movement situated where they will not conflict with children engaged in more quiet pursuits.

Of equal importance is the provision for a natural flow of play between areas, by not making the separation too extreme or the distances too great. Moore and his colleagues recommend medium to low foliage as an acoustic and partial visual barrier that still permits awareness of adjacent activities, a wall with seating that can also be used as a barrier, a few tires in sand, or a circulation path to create separation. Kritchevsky and Prescott (1969) believe that circulation paths with distinct goals, which allow sufficient room for each play unit (including necessary surrounding space), can channel children's energy into appropriate activities and prevent disruptions of ongoing activity. They warn against creating a "dead space," a large circle or square of empty space with no visible or tangible boundaries, which often leads to disorganized running and wres-

A swinging bench in the porch area provides a cozy spot to sit with a child, while watching others at play, at the Child Educational Center, Caltech/ JPL Community, La Cañada, California. (Photo: Keila Fields)

Wisteria growing over a trellis creates a beautiful, cool, green "room" for activities on hot days at the San Jose Day Nursery, San Jose, California. (Photo: Keila Fields)

tling. Furthermore, a path without a goal can lead children into such a space, but once in, they apparently find it difficult to leave. On the whole, Kritchevsky and Prescott found the best play yards to be one-third to one-half open space with no equipment, with the greater amount better for larger groups.

Microclimate

The climate and weather conditions in a preschool play yard will affect how and when the space is used. If there is excessive wind, even a moderately cold day will be uncomfortable for prolonged exposure. On the other hand, unfiltered sun on a hot day may make paved surfaces and play equipment too hot to play on

or with. Rain can make a poorly drained yard unusable even days later, and snow or ice may be seen as clear warnings to stay indoors. The design of the outdoor space thus should attempt to ameliorate unpleasant conditions and maximize the play potential of varying weather. For example, deciduous trees can be used to shade areas that otherwise would be too hot or bright in summer but that in winter benefit from receiving sunshine through the bare branches. Likewise, temporary canopies or trellis covers can provide shade only when needed. Wind can be lessened by earth mounding, or windbreak planting of trees, but if wind is strong enough to be problematic, consider including a windmill, which might even drive a paddle wheel or support a recirculating water system.

The importance of good drainage cannot be overstated. It might be useful to create zones in the play yard that dry out at different speeds. These areas should be organized so that the fastest-drying surfaces are closest to the building entry, so that the children will not have to walk through mud on their way to or from the dry area. If a wide porch area has been provided, the children can probably play there even while it is raining, and it might be fun to include an area of clear skylight so that the children can look straight up at the falling rain. If the day care center is in a region with a long rainy season, the yard might be designed so that a stream or waterfall forms after a certain amount of rainfall. Certainly, rain gauges or other catching and measuring devices should be provided.

In a climate that freezes and where snow falls, after providing for safe walkways and entrances (e.g., those that are easily shoveled, sanded, or salted), the designer should consider the transformations brought about by the season. For example, a mound might offer opportunities for sledding if it is not too hard to get to, and up, and if there is adequate open space at the base for stopping (or falling off). A warm-weather pond might become a skating rink or sliding surface, or a paved area could be flooded and frozen for a good sliding area. In such a climate, a porch area that could be fully enclosed, by means of a fairly simple system of panels, would be welcome. Finally, if children will be out in freezing weather, they should certainly be protected from the wind as much as possible, as resulting windchill factors may be physically harmful.

Elements and Equipment

It is clear that the specific features of and equipment in an outdoor play space should be provided in a way that enables children to use them easily, offers variety and challenge, and avoids disrupting natural play by requiring excessive intervention by the teacher.

Storage

Because so many outdoor activities require props, or "loose parts," in order to be enjoyed to the fullest, it is important that there be adequate storage for this assorted equipment at the location where it will be used. Many studies have shown that if items are stored in an inconvenient location, they are much less likely to be used. For example, if a teacher must collect and transport sand toys from indoors to the sand area every day, it is almost certain that the amount and variety of toys will be far smaller than if they were stored next to the sandbox. There is also frequently a problem having enough storage capacity. Therefore, when determining size requirements, remember that there will be new acquisitions and that over time, areas may be used in different ways and require storing items not currently on hand. Maintenance equipment—hoses, lawnmowers, shears, and the like—should have their own storage space, or else they will be stored in play storage areas. Also, make sure that outdoor storage spaces can be locked, so that there will not be a problem leaving things overnight or on weekends or vacations. If the staff feels that equipment may be stolen or vandalized,

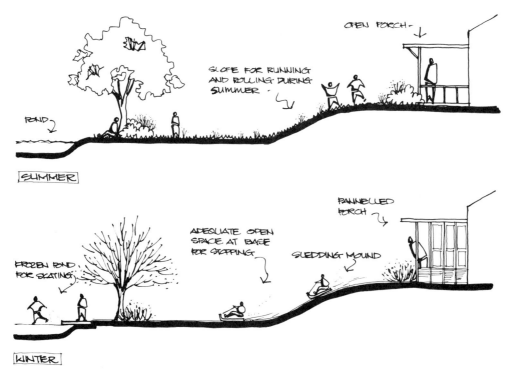

If the climate includes snow and ice, plan the outdoor space to take advantage of cold as well as warm seasons.

they will be reluctant to store it outdoors. Finally, when at all possible, allow equipment to be stored in such a way that the children may remove it and replace it with little or no assistance. A "garage" for wheeled toys, child's-height shelves, and easy-open drawers allow children to become responsible for the articles they play with, learn how to sort them, and participate in real work.

Planting

Planting is probably the most versatile and flexible of the designer's tools for creating a successful and stimulating preschool play yard. Suggestions for particular types or locations of plants are given throughout the text in regard to the specific design solution sought.

Sensory stimulation: A collection of plants and their related dirt, bark chips, rocks, and moss can demonstrate differences in texture, color, scent, and, in the case of vegetable gardens or fruit trees, taste. Sound can also be experienced as the effect of wind blowing through leaves and branches, tapping on trunks, or dropping a pebble or a seedpod into water.

Excitement and challenge: A densely planted area is good for exploration and discovery; a climbable tree offers a variety of challenges and levels of skill development.

Definition and separation: Planting can be used to mark a clear but permeable separation between areas. The height and density can determine degrees of acoustic or visual privacy, with even the smallest plants capable of defining an edge.

Climate control: As discussed earlier, plants can moderate the effects of sun and wind in the play yard.

Learning: As earlier discussed, plants can be labeled, seasons identified and studied via plants, insects dis-

covered and examined, pollination followed, and many other lessons taught by using the plants in the play yard.

Choosing Plants

The play value, hardiness, and absence of danger of any plant should be determined. Obviously, poisonous plants should be avoided; delicate plants should be used only in protected locations; and those with thorns, very sticky sap, or staining berries should be passed over in favor of less hazardous species.

The following guide to plant species is based on an appendix to Maureen Simmons's master's thesis (1974). We hope that it provides inspiration and a starting point.

Acacia decurrens: Children can play under canopy; has flowers, seeds, and seedpods.
Acer macrophyllum: Also other species; children can hide behind smaller species; winged seedpods are fun to drop.
Aesculus californica: Has enormous seedpods for collecting.
Alnus rhombifolius: Has small woody cones.
Arbutus unedo: Has small red fruits.
Crataegus phaenopyrum: Children can watch birds; has berries.
Eriobotrya japonica: Has fruit.
Eucalyptus ficifolia: Has especially large seedpods.
Eucalyptus species: What makes these trees bothersome to adults (litter) makes them very useful to playing children. Fallen leaves, bark, seeds or pods, fallen twigs all are useful for play.
Liquidambar species: Has thorny, brown burrlike seed balls.

A climbable tree creating built-in shade canopy, has many uses: play equipment, a setting for challenge and/or fantasy, a moderator of climate, a source of objects for nature study, and maybe even a home to insects or birds, as here, at the Golden West College Child Care Center, Huntington Beach, California. (Photo: Keila Fields)

Malus species: Has fruit.

Pinus radiata: Fallen needles and cones of this and other conifers are useful for many kinds of play.

Platanus species: Has large, dark-brown seedpods.

Prunus species: Fruiting kinds offer seasonal treats. Picking can be organized by staff or allowed to be done informally.

Quercus agrifolia: Children can collect larvae, pupae and oak moths. This tree is also good for climbing if low-branching specimens are selected.

Salix babylonica: May be too large for many yards, but the canopy is so appealing to hide under.

Bambusa species: Any of these can serve as a source of play sticks, and picking them will control spreading of the plant.

Blackberries: Requires some attention, but uses are obvious.

Callistemon species: Dense enough to hide behind, to watch hummingbirds, and to pick flowers.

Cotoneaster species: Has berries.

Heteromeles arbutifolia: Has berries; children can hide behind foliage.

Lantana species: Has flowers; children can watch bees.

Ligustrum japonicum: If children pick the leaves from this one, it just grows faster; also produces black berries.

Lonicera species: Children can pick the flowers and suck on them.

Mohania species: Has blue berries.

Nandian species: Has especially good flower and seed arrangements which look like miniature trees (for play with small cars and people).

Photinia fraseri: Very shiny red foliage invites picking; has flowers.

Pyracantha species: Has red berries.

Raphiolepis species: Has blue and black berries.

Carpobrotus edulis: Has flowers.

Hedra helix: Children can play with segments and look for insects in plants.

Oxalis corniculata: Children can pick flowers and chew stems (called *sour grass*).

Wisteria sinensis: Children can collect seeds and flowers (but watch very small children, for eating the seedpods can make them sick).

Water, Sand, and Dirt

Children need to interact physically with their environment, and a sandbox or water source (especially when combined) can occupy the greatest number of children for the longest period of time. Dirt carries much of the same allure, especially when it can be moistened to make mud. Its less prominent place in the literature is probably due to a combination of its less malleable quality (as opposed to that of wet sand) and its relatively rare provision as a play element. Also, mud is more difficult to clean up, and so if children are expected to remain tidy, sand and water are better. To provide the best sand–water–dirt experience, we recommend the following:

- Be sure child-controlled water is available to either sand or dirt play areas. A manual water pump has been used successfully in some yards. Although best if located nearby, if containers are available and the children can operate the water source, they will cooperate in getting the water to the sand. If there is no water source, the children will try to transport water from drinking fountains, which can easily be clogged by sand.
- If sand is used under play yard equipment to absorb impact, be sure to provide a distinct and enclosed

A dirt/mud pit with the addition of large "loose parts"—tires and planks—provides hours of satisfying involvement at the Assistance League of Newport Beach Child Day Care Center, Newport Beach, California. (Photo: Keila Fields)

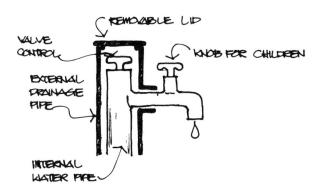

One way to provide a child-controlled water source at the teachers' discretion: On hot days the lid is removed (unlocked or by tool), and the main valve is opened. Then the lid is replaced, and the outside handle will control the tap.

sand play area. Otherwise, the children playing in the sand around the equipment and the children using the equipment will interfere with each other, and injuries might occur.

• Locate a sand or dirt play area out of the circulation path, to avoid shortcuts disrupting the children playing there. A low wall around a sand area will help prevent the sand's being scattered about the yard, define the area, and form a surface for toys and even sitting if it is wide enough or topped by a wide plank. When wheeled-toy paths follow the boundary of a sand play area, a border is important to keep the vehicles from skidding into the sand and to prevent the sand's moving onto the path where it can create a slippery surface.

• Apart from a water source such as a hose, faucet, or pump, provide larger quantities of water in a pond, pool, or elevated water table. One plastic washbasin per child might be nice in addition to a larger source, but cannot be considered an adequate substitute.

• Consider making available different kinds of sources of water. If a running stream can be incorporated or created, it will offer entirely new opportunities for discovery. At Pacific Oaks, the runoff from a specially designed water table can be directed (by an adult) either into a sewer or into a shallow, stone paved Japanese-garden style river which meanders across the grass. Likewise, a sprayer is much different from a still pool. A suggestion from Pacific Oaks is to hang sprinkle hoses in trees on hot days for a "rain forest" effect.

• Situate a dirt or mud play area away from the garden, so that overenthusiastic excavation does not damage the plants. It should be located where children can create a mud hole filled with water to jump across or into or to bridge with a piece of wood, but not where it can create a hazard for other children moving around the site.

• A sandbox should have at least eighteen inches of sand, be partially shaded to retain enough moisture to be molded, and be well drained. It should be covered when not in use, to prevent animals from soiling the sand. A simple yet effective cover consists of a wooden frame covered with the equivalent of chicken wire. The cover should not be solid, but allow the sun to sterilize the sand.

• Place the sandbox far enough from the building entrance so that children running inside will have shed most of the sand in their shoes and clothes before reaching the door.

This is not the best place to make a sand castle. A sand play area must be separate from the sand around equipment.

A child, a hose, and a streambed: a great combination on a hot day at the Pacific Oaks College Children's School, Pasadena, California. (Photo: Sharon Stine)

This tree shades the sandbox during the middle of the day at the Callison Day Home, Fremont, California, as well as making it a real "place" in the play yard. (Photo: Carolyn Francis)

Animals

Children both are fascinated by animals and can learn valuable lessons by interacting with them. Children can often empathize more easily with an animal than with another child and so can learn gentleness, sharing, and caring through their contact with animals. A preschool also offers an opportunity for children to be exposed to animals they probably do not see often at home. Chickens, ducks, rabbits, and even goats can be cared for in relatively little space. The children can learn about the life cycle, illustrated by the birth of babies to the death of old animals, and can learn re-

sponsibility by caring for the animals. Certainly, the staff of the facility must be interested and willing to be responsible for the animals, and if they are, a well-designed animal area can lead to a more natural and comfortable interaction between the children and the animals. The animals' cages should be large enough for free movement, provide some type of shelter or enclosure for bad weather or retreat, be easy to clean, allow the children to give them fresh food and water, and offer a place for the children to sit and quietly watch an animal for an extended period. There should be an enclosed or semienclosed space where a child can sit and stroke an animal or offer it a carrot, with minimal

Caring for and interacting with animals can be an important part of social development. (Photo: Carolyn Francis)

distraction to either. A larger fenced area might be modeled on petting zoos, where animals can spend much of their time out of cages and a few children are admitted to move among and pet them. La Loma Yard at Pacific Oaks has such an enclosure, open to all the center's children to visit with a teacher. The animals are caged overnight, for their protection.

Climbing, Sliding, and Swinging

Children especially enjoy the gross-motor, physical activities possible in an outdoor play area. To devise more pleasing ways for children to engage in those activities and also to provide play equipment on extremely limited budgets, some designers in the early 1970s began to experiment with telephone poles, cable spools, old tires, and such. Much of this ad hoc play equipment proved to be exciting and responsive, especially if some of the building materials were left loose or the structures could be altered in some way. Since the 1970s, several companies have marketed components purposely designed for creating large diversified structures, either according to designs they furnish or to client specifications.

In providing a preschool with opportunities to climb, swing, and slide it is important to keep in mind the pleasant texture of wood and group-swinging opportunities of horizontally hung tires, the popularity of steering wheels, and challenge of swinging bridges. On the other hand, it is good to note children's consistent use of traditional swings and the considerable popularity of child-powered merry-go-rounds, and to take Kritchevsky and Prescott's advice that traditional equipment may seem old-fashioned to adults, but is not so for children. Rather than apply any particular style or system, it is best to analyze the individual facility,

program, and site and then to plan the equipment accordingly. Some things to consider:

- Swings should be of the sling or tire variety, as serious injury can result from wooden or metal seats.
- An extra wide slide bed can accommodate more than one child sliding at a time. It also offers opportunities for going up and down, rolling objects, and so forth. In one preschool a knotted rope was hung down the slide to allow "mountain climbing" it.
- Children can climb on stumps, boulders, nets, ladders, and more, offering differing degrees of challenge.
- Structures can have a variety of detachable accessories, which can be changed periodically to sustain interest.

A word of warning from *Play for Preschoolers* about providing a single massive "all-in-one" piece of equipment:

Imagine for a minute if everyone were to really use it at once! The physical play children would swing monkey-like through the tea party, upset the social play on their scramble up to the top, dislodge the dreamer, and then leap down inadvertently onto the sand castle so creatively and painstakingly conceived. The children are acting their age. The designer is the one who has built-in these conflicts. (Canada Mortgage and Housing Corporation 1976, p. 19)

Loose Parts

Children react more creatively and remain engaged longer in complex play that allows for manipulation. Accordingly, they should have an adequate supply of

Traditional sling swings are always popular as these at the Golden West College Child Care Center, Huntington Beach, California, suggest. (Photo: Keila Fields)

All sorts of things are possible on a wide slide bed. (Photo: Carolyn Francis)

loose parts. The designer will probably have more influence on the provision of larger building materials than of props to support the various types of dramatic play, but as we already mentioned, sufficient storage may well encourage the staff to bring out the props more often. Building materials might encompass an area where, with supervision, children can actually hammer and saw, or it might be confined to a warehouse of boards, crates, drums, and the like for children to use in their play. Creative play areas in Europe and Canada have found that loose parts designed to fit together and form structures without the use of tools appeal highly to preschoolers (Cohen et al. 1979, pp. 607-1, 607-2).

Wheeled Toys

Older children enjoy riding tricycles or roller skating and thus need a path or paved area where they can do this without endangering or disrupting quieter play. Younger children also like nonpedal riding toys, and all ages enjoy giving one another rides in wagons. The paved vehicle area should also minimize the likelihood of traffic accidents; accordingly, a specific route may be more helpful than a large open area. Right-angle turns should be avoided, as they will often result in running off the road. Hard-surfaced paths designed for use with wheeled toys should accommodate two-way traffic or passing. This requires a width of five feet.

Real Vehicles

Another popular play element is a real car or boat that has been immobilized and stripped of dangerous features but not of play value. For example, a doorless, engineless car will provide countless imaginary trips to the zoo, country, store, and more. Likewise, a boat offers equally exciting possibilities for make-believe. This

The experience of playing with loose parts is as important as the result, here at the New School, Berkeley, California. (Photo: Carolyn Francis)

This tricycle path, designed by the director Sue Ko of the Good Shepherd Pre-school, Irvine, California, is curved, a bit bumpy for excitement, and has both interesting views and pausing points. (Photo: Keila Fields)

In contrast is the limited experience offered by a tricycle path consisting of a simple, curvilinear paved strip through a clipped lawn, with a few ornamental plantings and an outsized postmodern kiosk along the way.

241

is one instance in which a specific play element has no trouble generating creative responses. Nonetheless, if the play yard is very small, a vehicle may require too much room to justify the number of play opportunities it affords.

Spaces for Infants

The material in this chapter is intended to apply to preschool children, roughly three to five years of age. Although many of the concerns and suggestions are equally valid for outdoor spaces serving infants and toddlers, a few issues deserve special mention.

Development

Burton White stated in regard to babies up to twelve months (before they crawl) that their physical surroundings are probably more important (in comparison with their social environment) than at any later stage of development. During this period, after learning how to control their own body, babies become acquainted with the basic attributes of physical reality, for example, the permanence of objects and their properties and the laws of physics such as gravity and motion. Babies at this age need opportunities to practice pulling themselves to a sit, crawling, and cruising before they can learn to walk and run. They also need opportunities to explore cause-and-effect relationships, such as swinging doors open and closed, or operating light switches.

From one to three years of age, children spend much of their time exploring, investigating different objects, and mastering experiences that involve repetition of an action, for example, filling and emptying containers with water. These children also spend a lot of time in newly accomplished gross-motor activities, such as climbing stairs or other simple structures (White 1975, p. 27).

Protection and Enclosure

Nonmobile babies should be shielded from older, mobile children. The littlest children should have areas where they can lie, roll around, and creep without being constantly stood on or stumbled over by their newly walking counterparts. Similarly, the infant/toddler area, if it is part of a facility that also serves preschool or older children, should be physically separated but, if possible, visually connected to the older children's play yard. A gate could separate the areas but allows the older children to visit the babies at the teacher's discretion.

Very Tiny Babies

Sensory stimulation is important to babies, and mobiles, prisms, and wind chimes, as well as colorful and good-smelling plants (but out of reach, as babies and toddlers may try to eat almost everything), are appropriate. Both sun and shade should be provided, as sunlight works wonders for diaper rash but young skin burns quite easily. A soft swing made from an old tire can give even the youngest child a "moving" experience. Babies at this age, and older, like looking at themselves and so enjoy a mirrored (but shatterproof) surface placed low.

Crawling Babies

Crawling babies are ready to start enjoying water activities, either in dishpans or a sit-in pool filled only a few inches deep. They also enjoy traditional baby swings and may spend some time in walkers, which require a hard, level surface. Changes in surface, from paved to lawn, and minor changes in elevation also interest these babies. A series of wide low steps leading to a ramplike slide allow a variety of uses, including rolling toys. Babies can use handholds to pull themselves up to

Even very small babies can be placed in this type of cutaway tire swing at the San Jose Day Nursery, San Jose, California. (Photo: Keila Fields)

a stand and to cruise by means of benches, planters, or railings.

Toddlers

By the time children have become reasonably adept at walking and then running, they are capable of enjoying virtually all of the elements suggested for preschoolers, although sometimes on a smaller scale. Wheeled toys and push or pull toys are popular and require a hard surface. These children are now old enough to enjoy sand play without constant intervention to prevent their eating the sand. Between a year and a half and two years of age, most children begin to enjoy fantasy play and appreciate settings and props to support such activities. Toddlers are also ready to try their luck with slides, teeter-totters (although rocking boats may be more secure), and even a low-hung tire or sling swings. Kritchevsky and her colleagues (1969) noticed that yards for two-year-olds tended to be less interesting than those for preschoolers were, to include less variety and even fewer play opportunities per child. They suggested that these inadequacies may reflect general assumptions about two-year-olds, which in turn elicit and maintain those behaviors. It would be better to lean too far toward complexity and variety, to ensure the children's experiencing the satisfaction of self-directed choice and the chance to develop a longer attention span.

Developmental Grading

An interesting approach to providing a space supportive of the various achievement levels of an infant/toddler group is to organize the yard around developmental thresholds. In other words, to design barriers between areas so that by the time children can navigate the barriers, they will also be ready to handle the elements of the associated area. The Pacific Oaks Parent Infant Toddler Center is an example of such a design, providing, for instance, a series of wood stumps at the perimeter of the sand area. When children become capable of climbing the stumps, they have also passed the stage where they are most likely to eat the sand (Ferguson 1979). This is an appealing concept, as it frees the teacher from imposing limits on the children and allows a natural progression of skill acquisition.

Social Issues

Most sources touch on or specifically mention the need environmentally to support particular social behaviors. Maureen Simmons, in her master's thesis, discovered and documented social interactions that she had not anticipated but that were clearly at the heart of a yard's success or failure to support the children's development. Other authors have concurred with some of these findings or mentioned similar behavioral needs.

Watching

Many studies have found that between 25 percent and 50 percent of the children in a play yard are observing the other, active children. Because this can be a prelude to joining and is important in its own right, the design of a play yard should incorporate plenty of well-situated sitting and watching space.

Joining

The social dynamics of joining a group of playing children is complex and often unsuccessful. Simmons observed a pattern of repeated rebuffs lasting for days at a time, during which the unsuccessful joiner simply avoided other children but seemed to set in motion an insidious process whereby a child unskilled in joining would become identified as an undesirable playmate

A special place to take a nap, outside under a tree, at the Infant–Toddler Center, University of California at Irvine. (Photo: Keila Fields)

If you bring a shovel, you may be invited to join in, at the New School, Berkeley, California. (Photo: Carolyn Francis)

and then be turned away on that basis. The design of the outdoor space, however, can help the would-be joiner. As noted, many children watch before joining. Thus, if legitimate sitting or "hanging out" areas are located near frequently used play units, children will be able to spend time casually and (at least apparently) unconcernedly watching the action and then, at the appropriate moment, slipping into the group. Similarly, children appear to use "cover" items to allow them to approach a playing group without making apparent their interest in joining. One of the most frequently used cover items is the tricycle. A child can easily wheel up to a group, clearly be engaged in trike riding and thus not subject to the group's judgment, but then, at the appropriate moment, abandon the trike in favor of the group. To encourage this type of joining, the design can provide hard-surfaced, wheeled-toy paths that pass close to popular areas and, even better, with small "pull-off" nodes, so that a watching tricyclist will not disrupt ongoing play on the pathway. A final common method of joining involves "offerings": The child wishing to join determines what the playing group needs or might use, collects that object and brings it to them, and then is most likely invited to join (or at least tolerated) in return for the offering. This behavior depends mostly on the supply of loose parts and props, which are more under the control of the staff than the designer. However, the design still can encourage and facilitate the provision of such items, by offering adequate and conveniently located storage.

Backing Out

As children develop their skills in response to greater challenges, there will be times, when partway through

the process or even at the last moment, they decide not to carry through. For example, the slide down the pole may seem much scarier at the top than it looked from below, or the swinging bridge may seem suddenly too challenging. Because the goal of preschool programs is to enhance self-esteem and also to allow the children to develop faith in their own judgment, it is important that they not be teased by peers for deciding not to carry through or pressured into continuing despite their fears. The designer can facilitate "honorable" backing out by providing breakaway points and alternative uses on challenging equipment. For example, a child might be able to choose among a variety of ways to come down a structure. A fire-fighters pole, a slide, or a climbing net all could be accessible from the top and allow for graceful changes of mind.

Retreat

As mentioned earlier, children need cozy and private spaces that can accommodate one or two children. There is, in fact, a correlation between the lack of private or retreat space and aimless wandering and irritable and aggressive behavior (Phyfe-Perkins 1982). The appropriate type of space can be provided by tunnels, niches in walls or structures, areas at the center of clumps of bushes, small tree platforms, or such imaginative structures as the bean house or teepee described by Johnson, Shack, and Oster (1980). They suggested providing either a teepee shape, with a central pole and radiating strings, or a triangular tunnel shape, with string or wire sides, each of which would have vines climbing over and covering them. The resulting cozy, green retreat would undoubtedly appeal to children.

Whether a catalog-ordered play structure or a free-form climbing sculpture, offering easy and hard routes allows for changes of heart at the New School, Berkeley, California. (Photo: Carolyn Francis)

Just like adults, children sometimes want to be by themselves for a while.

TEEPEE WITH A CENTRAL POLE AND RADIATING STRINGS FOR VINES.

This cozy hideout might be planted with peas, to harvest and eat.

Alternatives to Ground-Level Playgrounds

Although a ground-level outdoor space opening directly off the child care facility is important, sometimes such a space is not feasible. Before considering alternatives, we recommend that all possible ways of creating or acquiring such a space be given serious consideration.

Rooftop Play Spaces

In high-density urban areas, it may be impossible to create a ground-level play yard, and in fact the child care facility itself may be above ground level. In these cases it may be worth exploring the possibility of a rooftop play area. There are certain advantages associated with such locations: their easy accessibility from the building but not by outside elements (important in relatively dangerous neighborhoods), potential for sun and fresh air, and separation from traffic. However, unless this is the only outdoor resource, the difficulties and limitations are formidable. Such an installation is likely to be extremely expensive, one reason being that most roofs are not designed to carry the added weight or to remain watertight under loading. Excessive wind is also likely to create problems. The Canada Mortgage and Housing Corporation [1] published a study outlining the possibilities and concerns related to developing such a space (Davis 1979). It examines both general and play potential and general and play constraints, followed by case studies and suggestions.

Several of the rooftop play spaces reviewed enthusiastically in the design journals in the mid-1970s were visited by the Moore study team, who judged them to be "awful." It seems clear that if designers are considering such a space, they should plan it well and determine whether it actually can support the types of play for which it is intended.

Indoor Street

One innovative concept that more closely resembles the "porch" space than an outdoor play yard is an indoor "street," like that at the United Community Day Care Center in Brooklyn, New York. In this facility, a double-loaded corridor with classrooms on each side was planned and developed to look like a street with skylights and trees. It is especially important to this facility, where the only classroom windows open onto the created street. This concept could also be used to advantage in other settings, perhaps in an outdoor room, also with a skylight and extensive planter boxes, a sand area, and climbing equipment. For an indoor space to be used in the same type of way as an outdoor

yard, it must be sound insulated and surfaced and furnished to accommodate the rough and boisterous play that is part of natural outdoor behavior.

A User's Handbook

A final consideration of the design of a preschool outdoor space might well be the creation of a "user's manual" that indicates the possibilities and considerations addressed by the design. Approached as a joint effort between the designer and the teachers, this manual could bridge the gap between vision and real use, as well as furnish a self-informing feedback loop; for example, changes and responses to the design could be entered into the handbook as the yard evolves. Often designers and users do not communicate clearly with each other which, with the likelihood of staff changes over time, means that many of the original concepts regarding the use of the space may be lost. On the other hand, a sensitive designer may have provided for future changes in use, but if these built-in options are not explained to future users, they probably will not be recognized or used. Thus a simple handbook describing the design of the play yard and giving examples of the ways in which the designer and teachers envisioned its being used may enable the play yard to be utilized to its greatest potential. A handbook could also contribute to the collaboration of the staff and designers in creating "an exciting outdoor environment giving [preschoolers] opportunities for creating, exploring, discovering and learning. In that environment, they need to invent and to improvise, to build and to destroy, to make things work and to learn how and why" (Evans, Shub, and Weinstein 1973, p. 207).

CASE STUDIES

Harold B. Jones Child Study Center, Berkeley, California [2]

Location and Context

The Jones Child Study Center is located at 2425 Atherton Street in Berkeley, California. It is a few blocks south of the University of California campus, on a one-block-long street that receives relatively little traffic. The immediate neighborhood is mostly apartment buildings and older, often Victorian homes that have been subdivided into units. Many university students live in the vicinity. The center's play yards are surrounded by a six-foot wooden fence that provides noise buffering and a visual screen for those inside and creates a low-key street presence. The facility itself is inward focused, with only a relatively narrow opening into Atherton Street. Both play yards open directly from their respective indoor areas, and both back onto Haste Street, a one-way fairly small but busy street.

---

[1] This report, *The Potential of Roof Deck Play Spaces*, can be obtained from the Canadian Housing Information Centre, CMHC National Office, Montreal Rd., Ottawa KIA 0P7. We highly recommend it for designers intending to provide a rooftop play area.

[2] Compiled from Gary Moore (1978) and Maureen Simmons (1974).

• Circulation that avoids conflict with main play areas
• Children able to take things from storage and return them by themselves

Unsuccessful Features

• Porch area gloomy, leaky
• Almost no vegetation, only two trees
• No regular child-controlled water source
• Riding toys not always available
• Transition area just outside classroom not buffered enough from rest of the yard
• No real "eddy" space just inside or outside door to stop and stir up activity without blocking traffic
• No "natural" area
• No garden or animal areas
• More paved "dead space" than appropriate

Blacksburg Christian Church Day Care Center, Blacksburg, Virginia [3]

Location and Context

The Blacksburg Christian Church Day Care Center is located in Blacksburg, Virginia. It occupies an undulating site bounded on one side by a parking lot, on another by the building, and on the other two by trees, with open land beyond.

[3] Compiled from Amita Sinha (1984).

Description

The center is run by a Chr[...]
and serves twenty-five chil[...]
age. The program philosop[...]
as "free play," and teachers[...]
the children in the play ya[...]

The play yard is rectang[...]
covered, and, with the exc[...]
and perimeter trees, contai[...]
areas: a set of three tire swi[...]
box at the east side of the y[...]
multipurpose timber climbi[...]
west corner; and a picnic ta[...]
rounded by sitting/balancin[...]

There is a clearly worn p[...]
climbing structure and from[...]
picnic table, and along the[...]
structure consists of multip[...]
climbing rings and a slide; [...]
kept around the structure.[...]

The yard can be entered[...]
though children are not all[...]
playtime or from the buildi[...]
higher than the main play [...]
of steep concrete steps or b[...]
children are discouraged fro[...]
not allowed to play on ther[...]
running down the hill, any[...]

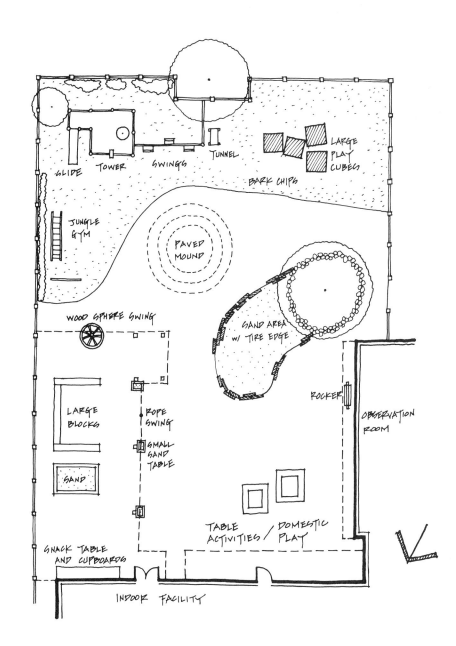

Site plan of Harold B. Jones Child Study Center, University of California at Berkeley.

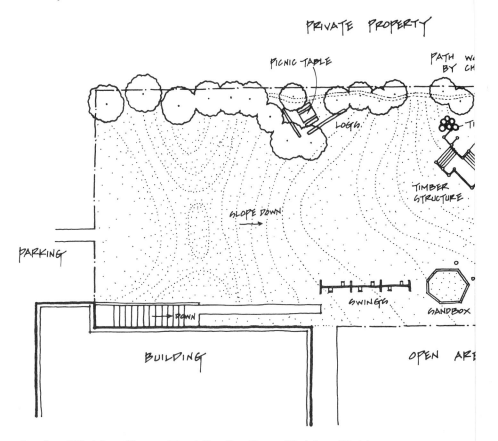

Site plan of Blacksburg Christian Church Day Care Center, Blacksburg, Virginia.

The Child Study Center in 1989, following extensive study and modification. Note, for example, the translucent roof panels covering the extended porch area.

247

Description

The center comprises two mirror-image preschool facilities with play yards, including an observation gallery running much of the length between them; offices and research and testing rooms are in a separate building across a covered walkway from the preschool facilities.

The yard studied was that of the University Child Study Center, a research and demonstration program of the Institute of Human Development. The other facility is run by the Berkeley Unified School District as a parent co-op nursery school. The Child Study Center has a paid staff of five, all holding advanced degrees related to child development, and four or five graduate student trainees each semester. Twenty-five children are present at a time—three-year-olds in the morning and four- and five-year-olds in the afternoon. Most of the children are from families affiliated with the university.

The program philosophy is to offer a variety of stimuli and planned settings that allow for child-initiated response and discovery. Help from staff is readily available, but overt direction is avoided.

The outdoor play area of the Child Study Center is a rectangular area of approximately five thousand square feet, three quarters of which is paved with asphalt. It has a north–south orientation, with access to the building at the north end of the yard, and is overall quite sunny. There is a covered transitional space of about one thousand square feet that acts as a buffer between indoors and outdoors, as well as extending along the east side of the yard to create a series of distinct activity areas. A large sand play area with tires around the perimeter and a tree at one end effectively divides the play yard. The section of the yard adjacent to the classroom is set up to support mostly cognitive and social play, and the outer section of the yard includes all the equipment for gross-motor activities—a jungle gym, large play cubes, a climbing tower with slide, a swing, a fifty-five-gallon drum tunnel, and a low asphalt mound. In the inner section of the yard, the covered "porch" area includes a small sandbox, cupboards holding sand play equipment, an area defined by more cupboards for large building block play, and a snack table. A wooden sphere swing capable of holding several children at once hangs at the end of the porch. The uncovered section of the inner yard includes a domestic play area with mock oven and sink, a table, cupboards holding sand and water play equipment, and a raised sand table. The inner yard is paved with asphalt, and the outer yard is surfaced with bark chips over compacted dirt.

This play yard was observed to contain a fairly extensive supply of "loose parts"—movable, multiuse play materials—which were stored at child's eye level and made available to children without adult assistance. A wide variety of props and clothes for fantasy

play, cars and tr
ing wheels affixe
were among the

Children's Use

Some children v
making directly
outer yard, all o
many children r
side to look thro
the activity tabl
circulation wher
they could play
area while sizing
and decide whet
were, or go back
found to be large
the table and th
damp and gloom
made it unsuitab

The large sand
used almost cons
both prevented t
vided a location
either that or ot
join a group). Si
most always in u
rate routes betwe
knotted rope, po
was also support
The jungle gym
vided by the staf
the children, and
The large play cu
about the site to
southwest corner
often kept was ur

Wagons were a
ing "joining" atte
occasionally. A s
days, and a hose
occasional offerir
Children made g
aged to take thin
assortment of tab
were quite often
which elicited ne
equipment.

Successful Fea

• Asphalt near b
• Lots of props ar
• Good provision
• Climbing struct
  opportunities, an
• Porch area for t

A combination of loose tires with a climbing structure allows many options. (Photo: Amita Sinha)

Children's Use of the Yard

The climbing structure was found to be the center's most popular play setting, followed by the paths. Play on the structure was both physical (gross-motor) and social, and a wide range of responses were enabled by the different routes available, the extrawide slide bed, and the inclusion of "loose parts" tires. Play on the paths and in the hidden areas around the trees was of a social nature and often involved fantasy play. The little niches among the trees provided retreat or hideout possibilities as well as natural explorable territory. There was a considerable amount of active play: ball and bat, racing on straight stretches of the path, running and rolling on the hill, and rolling the tires.

Teachers at the center generally chose a location from which they could view the children and then remained there, available to children requesting assistance but not involved in the play activities. They did not usually go down the path or to the picnic table but overlooked these activities from above, thus creating a certain privacy for the children engaged in social or fantasy play. Children were observed to play for relatively long times at the various play settings and to move easily and naturally between settings.

Successful Features

• Topographic variation
• Good relationship between play settings: visual connection, clear paths, adequate separation
• Good provision for motor play and good settings for social play (but lacks props)
• Provision of large-group spaces and smaller, one- or two-child spaces
• Some natural area for exploration

Unsuccessful Features

• Few "loose parts" and props
• No storage for props
• No child-controlled water source
• No quick-drying area for wet weather
• No covered porch or transition area
• No wheeled toys
• Sandbox only provision for cognitive play
• No garden or animal areas
• Relatively few different play niches for number of children

Hacienda Child Development Center, Pleasanton, California[4]

Location and Context

The Hacienda Child Development Center is located in the Hacienda Business Park, Pleasanton, California. The business park is quite new, and it has no mature vegetation. Hence the overall impression is of hard surfaces—fairly large corporate buildings, roads, and parking lots. The Child Development Center is essentially U shaped, with entry through an open courtyard in the center. A parking lot for staff and parents and a drop-off area are at the front. The play yards wrap around the building, and the three preschool play yards back onto a fairly substantial drainage ditch. Although liability issues precluded creating access from the yards to the ditch, a chain-link fence provides visual connection and a chance to see whatever wildlife may be present.

[4] Architect: Fee + Munson, Landscape Architect: POD.

• Circulation that avoids conflict with main play areas
• Children able to take things from storage and return them by themselves

Unsuccessful Features

• Porch area gloomy, leaky
• Almost no vegetation, only two trees
• No regular child-controlled water source
• Riding toys not always available
• Transition area just outside classroom not buffered enough from rest of the yard
• No real "eddy" space just inside or outside door to stop and stir up activity without blocking traffic
• No "natural" area
• No garden or animal areas
• More paved "dead space" than appropriate

Blacksburg Christian Church Day Care Center, Blacksburg, Virginia[3]

Location and Context

The Blacksburg Christian Church Day Care Center is located in Blacksburg, Virginia. It occupies an undulating site bounded on one side by a parking lot, on another by the building, and on the other two by trees, with open land beyond.

[3] Compiled from Amita Sinha (1984).

Description

The center is run by a Christian fundamentalist church and serves twenty-five children three to four years of age. The program philosophy identifies time outdoors as "free play," and teachers supervise rather than direct the children in the play yard.

The play yard is rectangular, almost entirely grass covered, and, with the exception of the natural slopes and perimeter trees, contains only four specific play areas: a set of three tire swings and a fairly large sandbox at the east side of the yard, by the building; a multipurpose timber climbing structure in the northwest corner; and a picnic table and benches, surrounded by sitting/balancing logs, on the east side.

There is a clearly worn path from the sandbox to the climbing structure and from there to (and around) the picnic table, and along the fence line. The climbing structure consists of multiple platforms with steel climbing rings and a slide; several rubber car tires are kept around the structure.

The yard can be entered from the parking lot, although children are not allowed to use this gate at playtime or from the building. The building entry is higher than the main play area, connected by a flight of steep concrete steps or by the natural slope. The children are discouraged from using the steps and are not allowed to play on them. They appear to prefer running down the hill, anyway.

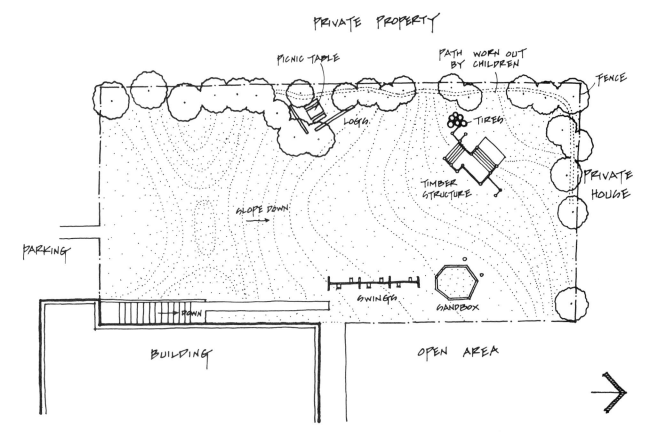

Site plan of Blacksburg Christian Church Day Care Center, Blacksburg, Virginia.

A combination of loose tires with a climbing structure allows many options. (Photo: Amita Sinha)

Children's Use of the Yard

The climbing structure was found to be the center's most popular play setting, followed by the paths. Play on the structure was both physical (gross-motor) and social, and a wide range of responses were enabled by the different routes available, the extrawide slide bed, and the inclusion of "loose parts" tires. Play on the paths and in the hidden areas around the trees was of a social nature and often involved fantasy play. The little niches among the trees provided retreat or hideout possibilities as well as natural explorable territory. There was a considerable amount of active play: ball and bat, racing on straight stretches of the path, running and rolling on the hill, and rolling the tires.

Teachers at the center generally chose a location from which they could view the children and then remained there, available to children requesting assistance but not involved in the play activities. They did not usually go down the path or to the picnic table but overlooked these activities from above, thus creating a certain privacy for the children engaged in social or fantasy play. Children were observed to play for relatively long times at the various play settings and to move easily and naturally between settings.

Successful Features

• Topographic variation
• Good relationship between play settings: visual connection, clear paths, adequate separation
• Good provision for motor play and good settings for social play (but lacks props)
• Provision of large-group spaces and smaller, one- or two-child spaces
• Some natural area for exploration

Unsuccessful Features

• Few "loose parts" and props
• No storage for props
• No child-controlled water source
• No quick-drying area for wet weather
• No covered porch or transition area
• No wheeled toys
• Sandbox only provision for cognitive play
• No garden or animal areas
• Relatively few different play niches for number of children

Hacienda Child Development Center, Pleasanton, California [4]

Location and Context

The Hacienda Child Development Center is located in the Hacienda Business Park, Pleasanton, California. The business park is quite new, and it has no mature vegetation. Hence the overall impression is of hard surfaces—fairly large corporate buildings, roads, and parking lots. The Child Development Center is essentially U shaped, with entry through an open courtyard in the center. A parking lot for staff and parents and a drop-off area are at the front. The play yards wrap around the building, and the three preschool play yards back onto a fairly substantial drainage ditch. Although liability issues precluded creating access from the yards to the ditch, a chain-link fence provides visual connection and a chance to see whatever wildlife may be present.

[4] Architect: Fee + Munson, Landscape Architect: POD.

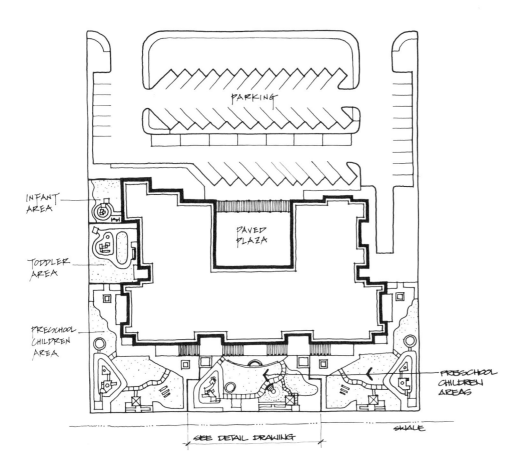

Site plan of Hacienda Child Development Center, Pleasanton, California.

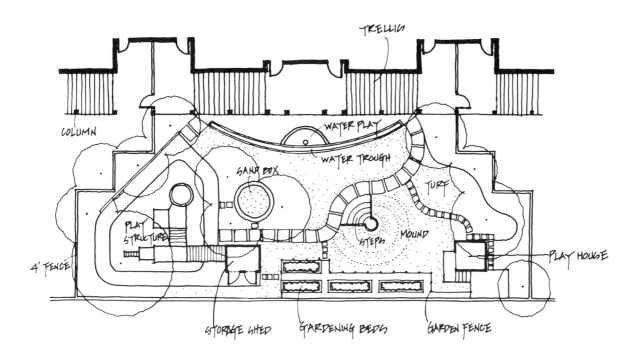

Site plan of preschool play yard, Hacienda Child Development Center.

Set in an office park, the center benefits by being close to many parents' workplaces, but it loses the benefits of being part of a neighborhood.

Description

The Hacienda Child Development Center was provided by the developer of the Hacienda Business Park. It was intended for use by the employees of companies locating in the park, with the expectation that some employers would provide benefits relating to its use. It is also open to use by residents in the area. With the clamor for employment-based child care, it seemed that a child care center in the park would be a valuable and socially conscientious amenity. Much research and expert guidance went into the project, and considerable care went into its design. The center was initially planned to serve two hundred children, in modules of about fifty children. These modules were further divided into two subgroups of approximately twenty-five children, each with its own main room, some shared indoor spaces, and a play yard serving each module.

The three preschool play yards, located along the rear of the site, have been developed to incorporate many elements and activities with a conceptual scheme of "urban–rural" transition. The urban end of the yard is more hard surfaced and includes the main climbing structure and sand area. The rural end contains a grassy mound and a garden area enclosed by a low fence. Each yard has a large paved porch area as transition from the interior, roofed by a wooden slat–trellis type of construction. The yards are similar; yet each has certain individual characteristics, for example, its own water feature. It is possible to see from one yard to the next, easily for adults and from certain places for children. Each of these three yards comprises, on the average, 3,750 square feet of usable space.

Children's Use of the Yard

This information is based on a site visit of two hours and on comments by teachers at the center. Therefore, this analysis is neither as complete nor as definite as is the information provided in the case studies based on master's theses. It is, however, indicative of the relationship between the physical elements and the children's behavior.

The first thing that became apparent when seeing the play yards in use was their relatively small size. Indeed, if all fifty children were to be in the yard at once, there would be only seventy-five square feet per child. When we visited, the two subgroups used the yard independently; yet the space still felt overly busy. Perhaps, as Fields suggested, this is the result of being "overdesigned," of not having allowed room for imagination. It was impossible to ignore the fact that nearly twice as much of the site was dedicated to parking, dropping off, and attendant automobile circulation as to the play yards. In this regard, the designers were no doubt constrained by regulations. One hopes that those of us designing or providing for children will actively question a system that elevates the storage of cars over the daily life of our children.

At any rate, the grassy mound was good for rolling, except that the children could roll onto the tricycle path. The tricycles had quite a lot of hard surface, but much of the path was too narrow, and the riders often conflicted with the children in and around the sand and equipment area or the porch area. There was no flat area for simply running. The children seemed to play in all areas of the yard but were constrained from using some spaces because of their ornamental planting. Considering the tightness of the space, it was disheartening to see perfect little one- and two-child nooks and niches placed off-limits to protect the planting. Likewise, we witnessed a group of children repeatedly attempting to crawl into a semienclosed space below the deck of a play house, only to be chased out by a teacher who explained that there was a drain and puddled water there, which the children were not to get into. This playhouse was not otherwise much used; it was not really built to proper scale, and its postmodern styling was likely more appealing to adults than to children.

The spacious patio area accommodated many activities and related well to the indoors. Yet its slat roof did not keep out the rain, and the teachers pointed out that there is a definite rainy season when such a space would be welcome, if it were dry. This roof was supported by many concrete columns, perhaps to give it a sense of enclosure, and yet such objects create a real hazard to preoccupied, moving children. The teachers confirmed that children ran into them and also felt that wood posts would have allowed them to tack up sheets for temporary partitions.

All in all, the play yards at Hacienda are less than satisfying. They contain some truly delightful elements, notably a system of water sprays and a water-play trough; yet the overall effect is not as wonderful as one would hope, considering the resources involved. Because this type of developer- or employer-provided child care center is being built with increasing frequency and because such centers will almost certainly have greater financial support than community-based centers do, we must learn how to create the most supportive setting possible. Certainly these yards provide a much richer range of opportunities than many other centers do. However, even with care, research, and resources, there are dangers. As Fields commented about Hacienda: "The designers really thought about the things children need. But it seems that they used a guidebook. As they provided a space or element that was suggested, they checked it off their list. They missed the spirit (the gestalt) of what is needed. . . . All the nifty pieces can be put together—it can even look good to the adult eye, and in reality it is not such a good place" (Fields 1987, draft notes).

Successful Features

- Provision for physical, cognitive, and social play
- Storage for toys and loose parts
- Paved porch areas
- Good transition from indoors
- Garden area (but because not generally open for children to use, takes away space from general use)

Unsuccessful Features

- Very small, seems too busy
- Too much of yard given to ornamental planting
- Tricycle path too narrow
- No "bad weather" outdoor play space
- Play house that appeals to adult aesthetic, wrong proportions
- Conflict between children playing in sand and those playing on climbing structure

Pacific Oaks College Children's School, Pasadena, California

Location and Context

Pacific Oaks is located in an old residential area of Pasadena, in a neighborhood of pleasant homes and trees. Its street presence is quite minimal and appears residential, except for the entrance to the narrow side of a rectangular parking lot. The center, comprising five buildings and six play yards, extends through the block to the next street. Children from the ages of about two to nine years are served by a variety of programs, each of which has its own indoor space and yard. The Children's School is part of the Pacific Oaks College, well known for its early childhood education program. The schools' philosophy is based on Piaget's and Erikson's theories, emphasizing support of the child's own explorations through both the environment and interactions with teachers.

Description and Use [5]

At the Pacific Oaks Children's School the term *yard* is used instead of classroom to designate the different programs for young children. This is a conscious decision to underscore the importance of the outside space in the children's learning and growing life.

During the six years that I was dean of children's programs, the environment of the Children's School (California campus) was continuously evaluated and upgraded, using teacher input, maintenance staff ideas, and hired architects. The changes reflect an overall plan to provide three kinds of outdoor spaces: (1) transition areas—low-level activity porches that could be used in both hot smoggy weather and rainy weather; (2) areas for various types of play—physical, creative, dramatic, social, constructive, imaginative, and cognitive; and (3) community areas where both adults and children could gather in small and larger groups.

The following are descriptions of the program's outside spaces now being used at the Pacific Oaks Children's School. The numerical order matches the numbers on the accompanying site plan, which indicates changes made through mid-1986.

1. *California Yard:* A program for children aged approximately two through three years (toddler/twos program). Note: All ages are as of the first of September (seventeen children). Although the children in this program do not have daily access to the other programs, they frequently walk to visit the animals. This is the only program in which children can watch street activity (buses, trash collection, parents coming and going) from their play structure, located near the northern fence on California Boulevard.

2. *Adventure Yard:* A program for children aged approximately six through nine years (grades 1, 2, and 3, thirty-three children). This is the only yard with a natural (dirt) mound to give children a sense of height. It is also the only program with a "wild" area of weeds, although it is hard to maintain because of the shortage of water in Southern California. Although the porch has not been built on the west side of the building, the plans have been drawn (in 1983), and it awaits only funding. Because this yard has a very large dirt area, children have frequently

<hr />

[5] Comments by Sharon Stine, dean of children's programs from 1980 to 1986.

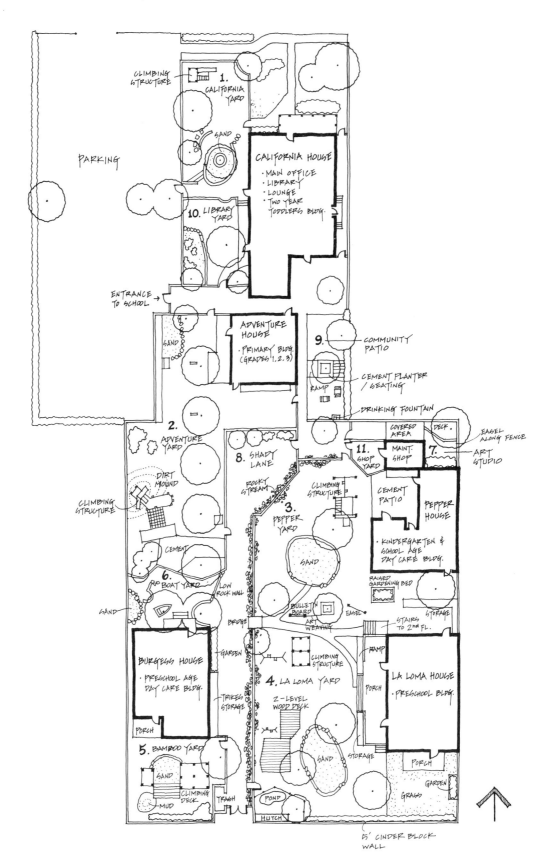

CLIMBING STRUCTURE

1. CALIFORNIA YARD

PARKING

SAND

CALIFORNIA HOUSE
• MAIN OFFICE
• LIBRARY
• LOUNGE
• TWO YEAR TODDLERS BLDG.

10. LIBRARY YARD

ENTRANCE TO SCHOOL →

SAND

ADVENTURE HOUSE
• PRIMARY BLDG. (GRADES 1, 2, 3)

9. COMMUNITY PATIO

CEMENT PLANTER / SEATING

RAMP

DRINKING FOUNTAIN

2. ADVENTURE YARD

8. SHADY LANE

COVERED AREA

DECK

EASEL ALONG FENCE

11. SHOP YARD

MAINT. SHOP

7. ART STUDIO

DIRT MOUND

CLIMBING STRUCTURE

ROCKY STREAM

CLIMBING STRUCTURE

CEMENT PATIO

PEPPER HOUSE
• KINDERGARTEN & SCHOOL AGE DAY CARE BLDG.

3. PEPPER YARD

CEMENT

SAND

6. BOAT YARD

LOW ROCK WALL

SAND

RAISED GARDENING BED

BULLETIN BOARD

ART WEAVING

EASEL

STAIRS TO 2ND FL.

STORAGE

BRIDGE

GARDEN

CLIMBING STRUCTURE

RAMP

BURGESS HOUSE
• PRESCHOOL AGE DAY CARE BLDG.

TRIKES STORAGE

4. LA LOMA YARD

2-LEVEL WOOD DECK

PORCH

LA LOMA HOUSE
• PRESCHOOL BLDG.

PORCH

5. BAMBOO YARD

SAND

CLIMBING DECK

TRASH

SAND

STORAGE

MUD

POND

HUTCH

GRASS

PORCH

GARDEN

5' CINDER BLOCK WALL

LA LOMA BLVD.

Site plan of Pacific Oaks College Children's School, Pasadena, California.

Shady Lane, with its arroyo stone creek, connects the individual yards at Pacific Oaks. (Photo: Sharon Stine)

studied fire in this program, by digging pits, circling them with rocks, and building fires in them (with teachers present).

3. *Pepper Yard:* A program for children aged approximately five through six (kindergarten, twenty-two children) in the mornings and children aged approximately five through nine in the early mornings and afternoons (school-aged care programs, thirty-five children). This yard includes the most successful garden, because it is a raised bed with good soil and sun, away from the toxic quality of the areas around the olive and oak trees. When the new building addition was built (to house the after-school care program), a cement patio was added. This is covered by an awning that provides shade or rain protection.

4. *La Loma Yard:* A program for children aged approximately three through five years (preschool, forty children). This yard has the only grass surface on the campus. It adds a much needed softness and, besides regular play activities, is used for large- and small-group gatherings on occasion. The animal area is located in this yard and includes rabbits and ducks with a pond. Children enter the area with a teacher. Animals are put in their hutches at night for safety. It is located here owing to easy access for draining the duck pond into the drainage on Shady Lane, into La Loma Street.

   A play structure was removed from this yard, and a large two-level wooden deck was built instead. This is used for hideouts, dramatic play

(adjacent to sand), and a gathering place, with spare parts (ladders, boards, ropes) that hook onto the low railing around the north and east sides of deck. The front porch on the west side of the building was also expanded and covered, making an observation deck from the second story. This porch is also used with the spare parts for physical play during rainy weather. The stairs were moved from the center of the building to the northwest corner, creating a more natural traffic flow from Shady Lane into both Pepper Yard and La Loma Yard and also to the upstairs. This yard is no longer separated in the middle by a pathway. The natural barrier between La Loma Yard and Pepper Yard is made up of a bulletin board, a tree with a sitting area around it, Plexiglas easels, a garden, and a place to hang artwork (there was a multicolored weaving made by children that added much needed color).

5/6. *Burgess House:* A day care program for pre-school-aged children.

5. *Bamboo Yard:* A program for children aged approximately three through five years (twenty-five children). This yard gets its name from the bamboo that completely covers the five-foot cinder-block fence that runs the entire length of La Loma Street (by neighborhood request). This greenery softens the yard. A play structure was added that is quite complex, with many ways to go up and down, a double slide, a tire swing, hanging ropes, and storage. There is also a sand area and a mud area in this yard that are separate from each other. The porch was upgraded and is used constantly for activities and meals during the long day.

6. *Boat Yard:* A program for children approximately two to three years (ten children). Although this is a part of the Burgess House day care program, the younger children have their own yard space. Shady Lane's activities are visible to these children over a low rock wall and through the fence that borders the lane. The boat is the only play structure. Spare parts are used exclusively to make structures in this yard and are stored in a large area along the building which when opened up is a hideaway place. A covered porch was added in 1985.

7. *Art Studio:* This is used by all children on a sign-up or designated day basis. It was built in 1982 under the inspiration of the faculty member who is the "artist in residence." The studio contains a covered area, a Plexiglas easel along the fence, a clay table, and a small deck. The large eucalyptus trees add a lovely fragrance, and the leaves are left in this area to provide texture and a special surface. It is isolated from the more

active yards because of the belief that sometimes children need quiet places to reflect and thus create. Art activities are also always available outside in the yards.

8. *Shady Lane:* This lane is used by all the children for wheeled-toy play, and it also functions well for observation and transit. This artery was upgraded in 1983 by resurfacing, construction of a streambed for drainage along the fence, rebuilding of all fencing, planting of shrubs and trees (at the north end by the Adventure Yard), widening of the north-end area for ease of trike turnaround, and addition of a new gate with stop sign mounted on it as a clear marker that bike traffic must go no farther (into the Community Patio area). The streambed is constructed with arroyo stones. Children frequently put hoses in the stream to play with the water as it flows down to La Loma Street. A small cement bridge was built over the streambed as an entrance/pathway marker into La Loma Yard and Pepper Yard. Wheeled toys are stored in cupboards along the east side of Burgess House. The fence is made of two-by-fours painted brown along the top and bottom, with vertical cedar (natural) grape stakes. It is about three feet high and a foot off the ground or streambed that meanders under and along its east side. The grape stakes are two inches apart, allowing a great deal of visibility.

9. *Community Patio:* The patio used by everyone as a gathering place to sit at tables and eat, to sell T-shirts or for other community functions, just to relax, or for visitors' gatherings and tour groups. This area was surfaced with pebbles in cement, with sufficient drainage added. It is on two levels, with steps and a ramp surrounding a planter that contains a flowering tree. Both this planter area and the redwood tables and benches are used for sitting. Planting is along the east fence. A large drinking fountain (child and adult height) drains into the plants and is a favorite spot for children to pause with parents when arriving at or leaving the campus.

10. *Library Yard:* This yard is to be used by everyone, and it should have been ready in the fall of 1986. It was planned for three years as a quiet space to listen to stories and read, next to the inside Children's Library.

11. *Shop Yard:* This yard was added in 1981 for maintenance-space purposes. It adjoins the shop area and is fenced by a six-foot cedar stake fence, for safety reasons. Located in the center of the campus, the maintenance staff are in and out and visible to the children, who like to watch or help with the many repairs (the campus is over eighty years old).

All yards have the following design qualities:

- Large sand areas (rebuilt 1981–1983) that are not in pathways, have water access, are not around play structures, have sand toy storage nearby, and are not around the large tree roots (causing water problems for the oak trees).
- Covered porches for transition from building to yard, with built-in seating along the edges. These areas are used daily for activities and for eating.
- Play structures with some traditional elements (swings, poles, slides).
- Dirt, logs, boulders, and large trees.
- Spare parts; ladders, wooden boxes, planks, saw horses, board holders, small portable steps.
- Portable water tables.
- Access to Shady Lane and wheel toys.
- Access to animal area.

Problems and things that are missing as design elements:

- There are not enough visual colors (I added some large banners I made a year ago to each yard, but it was not enough). With brown buildings, brown structures, and so much dirt there is a sense of missing color. Flowers have been nearly impossible to grow, owing to needed care and so many children tromping around.
- There is never enough storage, and it is expensive to build well so that it lasts. This is especially true because so many spare parts are used and a variety of activities are set up outside daily (art, dramatic play, construction, music).
- More natural sources of height (mounds), although all yards provide height through play structures.
- Hideaways are limited in natural setting. They are constantly built with spare parts, blankets, and the like but do not exist because of natural landscaping.
- Tracking of sand and dirt into the classrooms is a problem, even though there are porches. Children in the Adventure Yard program began taking off their shoes this last year, and it helped a great deal.
- There is no way to keep track of environmental elements (rain gauges, sun dials), which I think is a reflection of another attitude. I am not sure that the environment as a natural gift was treasured enough by everyone. When there are so many children exploring and engaging in various kinds of active play, being consistently caring of the natural setting is difficult.

Pacific Oaks has been fortunate never to have had a major vandalism problem. I question how this campus could have survived if that had been a serious issue.

Most people do not even know the area exists and are shocked to walk on campus, thinking it is just a collection of old homes.

REFERENCES

Ainslee, Ricardo C., ed. 1984. *The child and the day care setting.* New York: Praeger.

Allen, Lady of Hurtwood. 1968. *Planning for play.* Cambridge, Mass.: MIT Press.

Almy, M., P. Monighan, B. Scales, and J. Van Hoorn. 1987. *Research on play: The bridge between theory and practice.* New York: Columbia Teachers College Press.

Baker, Katherine. 1966. *Let's play outdoors.* Washington, D.C.: National Association for the Education of Young Children.

Bengtsson, A. 1970. *Environmental planning for children's play.* New York: Praeger.

Björklid, Pia. 1982. *Children's outdoor environment.* Stockholm: Stockholm Institute of Education, Department of Educational Research.

Canada Mortgage and Housing Corporation. 1976 (revised 1980). *Play spaces for preschoolers.* Ottawa: CMHC.

Childhood Services Council of South Australia. ca. 1975. *Integrated facilities for early childhood services.* South Australia: Government Printer.

Cohen, Uriel, Tim McGinty, and Gary T. Moore. 1978. *Case studies of child play areas and child support facilities.* Milwaukee: Center for Architecture and Urban Planning Research, University of Wisconsin.

Cohen, Uriel, Ann Hill, Carol Lane, Tim McGinty, and Gary Moore. 1979. *Recommendations for child play areas.* Milwaukee: Center for Architecture and Urban Planning Research, University of Wisconsin.

Cooper Marcus, Clare. 1978. Remembrance of landscapes past. *Landscape* 22(3): 34–43.

Davis, Kate (of Dan Matsushita Associates, Ltd.). 1979. *The potential of roof deck play spaces.* Vancouver: Canada Mortgage and Housing Corporation.

Early childhood facilities 3: Some sensible and outrageous ideas for the future—Community services and facilities for young children. 1972. Ann Arbor: University of Michigan Press.

The EIKOS Group. 1980. *Children's perceptions of play environments.* Vancouver: Canada Mortgage and Housing Corporation.

Ellison, Gail, 1974. *Play structures—Questions to discuss, designs to consider, directions for construction.* Pasadena, Calif.: Pacific Oaks College.

Essa, Eva L. 1981. An outdoor play area designed for learning. *Day Care and Early Education* 9(2): 37–42.

Evans, E. Belle, Beth Shub, and Marlene Weinstein. 1973. *Day care: How to plan, develop and operate a day care center.* Boston: Beacon Press.

Ferguson, Jerry. 1979. Creating growth-producing environments for infants and toddlers. In *Supporting the growth of infants, toddlers and parents,* ed. Elizabeth Jones, pp. 13–25. Pasadena, Calif.: Pacific Oaks College.

Fields, Keila. 1987. Outdoor environment for a child care center at the Presidio of San Francisco. Unpublished Professional Report, Department of Landscape Architecture, University of California at Berkeley.

Found spaces and equipment for children's centers. 1972. New York: Educational Facilities Laboratories.

Gibson, Charles Dana. 1968. Preschool educational housing. In *Housing for early childhood education.* Bulletin #22-A, pp. 17–22.

Haase, Ronald W. 1968. Space which allows. In *Housing for early childhood education.* Bulletin #22-A, pp. 7–10.

Hart, Roger. 1974. The genesis of landscaping. *Landscape Architecture,* 65(5): 356–363.

Hill, Ann B., and Carol Lane, with Uriel Cohen, Gary T. Moore, and Tim McGinty. 1978. *Abstracts of child play areas and child support facilities.* Milwaukee: Center for Architecture and Urban Planning Research, University of Wisconsin.

Hill, Dorothy. 1977. *Mud, sand, and water.* Washington, D.C.: National Association for the Education of Young Children.

Hirshen, Sanford, and Joe Ouye. 1971. *The infant care center.* San Francisco: Craftsman Press.

Hogan, Paul. 1974. *Playgrounds for free: The utilization of used and surplus materials in playground construction.* Cambridge, Mass.: MIT Press.

Johnson, Laura, Joel Shack, and Karen Oster. 1980. *Out of the cellar and into the parlour: Guidelines for the adaptation of residential space for young children.* Toronto: Canada Mortgage and Housing Corporation.

Kamerman, Sheila. 1983. Child-care services: A national picture. *Monthly Labor Review,* December, pp. 35–39.

Klein and Sears, Research/Planning/Architecture. 1980. *Lost and found: Recycling space for children.* Toronto: Canada Mortgage and Housing Corporation.

Kritchevsky, Sybil, and Elizabeth Prescott, with Lee Walling. 1969. *Planning environments for young children: Physical space.* Washington, D.C.: National Association for the Education of Young Children.

Mergen, Bernard. 1982. *Play and playthings.* Westport, Conn.: Greenwood Press.

de Moncheaux, Suzanne. 1981. *Planning with children in mind.* New South Wales, Australia: NSW Department of Environment and Planning.

Moore, Gary T. 1982. Child care facilities and equipment. In *Employers and child care: Establishing services through the workplace,* ed. K. S. Perry, pp. 54–64. Washington, D.C.: U.S. Government Printing Office and U.S. Department of Labor, Women's Bureau.

Moore, Gary T. 1987. The physical environment and cognitive development in child care centers. In *Spaces for children: The built environment and child development,* ed. Carol S. Weinstein and Thomas G. David, pp. 41–72. New York: Plenum.

Moore, Gary T., C. Lane, A. Hill, U. Cohen, and T. McGinty. 1979. *Recommendations for child care centers.* Milwaukee: University of Wisconsin, Center for Architecture and Urban Planning Research.

Nicholson, Simon. 1971. How not to cheat children: The theory of loose parts. *Landscape Architecture* 62:30–34.

Norén-Björn, Eva. 1982. *The impossible playground.* West Point, N.Y.: Leisure Press.

Osmon, Fred Linn. 1971. *Patterns for designing children's centers.* New York: Educational Facilities Laboratories.

Phyfe-Perkins, Elizabeth. 1982. The preschool setting and children's behavior: An environmental interven-

tion. *Journal of Man–Environment Relations* 1(3): 10–29.

Plath, Joyce. 1979. A center for infant day care. Master's thesis, University of California at Berkeley.

Provence, Sally, Audrey Naylor, and June Patterson. 1977. *The challenge of daycare.* New Haven, Conn.: Yale University Press.

Simmons, Maureen. 1974. Children's play areas: Designing for developmental play needs. Master's thesis, Department of Landscape Architecture, University of California at Berkeley.

Sinha, Amita. 1984. Continuity and branching in preschool playgrounds. Master's thesis, Architecture and Urban Studies, Virginia Polytechnic, Blacksburg, Va.

Stone, Jeanette G., and Nancy Rudolph. 1970. *Play and playgrounds.* Washington, D.C.: National Association for the Education of Young Children.

Sutfin, Harriet D. 1982. The effect on children's behavior of a change in the physical design of a kindergarten classroom. *Journal of Man–Environment Relations* 1(3): 30–41.

Taylor, Anne P., and George Vlastos. 1975. *School zone: Learning environments for children.* New York: Van Nostrand Reinhold.

Triedman, Kim. 1989. A mother's dilemma. Ms. 18(1 & 2): 59–63.

U.S. Department of Labor, Bureau of Labor Statistics. 1984. *News.* Thursday, July 26.

Utzinger, Robert C. 1970. *Early childhood facilities 2: Some European nursery schools and playgrounds.* Ann Arbor: University of Michigan Press.

White, Burton L. 1975. *The first three years of life.* Englewood Cliffs, N.J.: Prentice-Hall.

DESIGN REVIEW CHECKLIST

CHILD DEVELOPMENT

1. Is there provision for the children's physical development, that is, gross-motor activities such as running, jumping, and climbing?

2. Is cognitive/perceptual development addressed through opportunities to manipulate elements of the environment and develop fine-motor control?

3. Are settings provided that will encourage dramatic and role-play behavior and foster social development?

4. Are there settings to accommodate a full range of mood, energy level, and sociability? That is, are there quiet niches to be alone in, enclosed areas for two or three children, and larger open areas for big groups?

PROGRAM/PHILOSOPHY: ISSUES FOR DESIGN

5. Has the designer ascertained both the overall philosophy of the program and as much detail as possible regarding specific goals and curriculum plans to allow development of an environment with "good fit"?

6. If the program emphasizes the teacher's direction of activities and restriction of choices, does the design avoid creating too much distraction or inappropriate invitation?

7. If the program emphasizes child-initiated behavior, does the design permit autonomous action (are supplies visible and reachable); are there enough potential activities to allow successful choosing; and so on?

8. Does the center's philosophy/program require one large yard or several smaller ones?

9. Has the yard been designed to encourage active and exploratory use and yet require the least amount of monitoring, control, and rule enforcement possible?

10. Have any "attractive nuisances" been inadvertently created, such as a hiding space that the staff may want to put off limits?

11. Are the spaces the appropriate size for the activities planned?

CHILDREN SERVED

12. Can the yard accommodate the number of children who may be using it at any time?

13. Does the yard's organization support the school's philosophical goals, for example, age heterogeneity at play time, fine-tuned developmental opportunities, or small-group identification?

14. If there are infants or toddlers at the center, do they have their own space, but with visual connection?

CHILD SCALE

15. Are play opportunities visible at a child's level (thirty-six to forty-two inches)?

16. Are there opportunities to be "up high"? In trees, towers, and the like?

17. Have steps, door handles, fountains, and so forth been designed with a child's stature in mind?

VARIETY AND OPPORTUNITY

18. Is the ratio of play opportunities to children better than two to one?

19. Are there some "complex" play units, with built-in variety?

20. Are there many types of possible activities? Not just four ways to swing?

SENSORY STIMULATION

21. Have the colors, textures, and shapes of design elements been chosen to provide a range of sensory experience?

22. Are there bright flags, flowers, banners?

23. Is there a garden or fruit trees to provide edible, smellable, touchable objects?

24. Is there a wind chime, falling water, or rustling branches to hear?

25. Are there smooth stones, rough bark, wet water, fuzzy leaves or caterpillars, soft grass?

MANIPULATION

26. Can the children act on and manipulate the elements of the yard without causing damage?

27. Are there opportunities to un-make or destroy things?

28. Is there a supply of "loose parts" for the children to use and reuse?

29. Are manipulable elements such as sand, water, and dirt provided?

30. Does the equipment include movable parts such as steering wheels?

OUTDOOR ACTIVITIES

31. Are there outdoor settings that would support curricular activities such as art, music, storytelling, and drama?

32. Is there somewhere to nap outside?

33. Is there a place to eat outside?

34. Is it possible to cook outdoors? A fire pit or barbecue?

35. Have learning tools been incorporated in the yard design, for example, sundials, rain gauges, thermometers, wind socks, plant labels?

36. Can the children assist with "real work" such as garden care, weeding, and sweeping?

37. Are animal enclosures designed to allow the children to help maintain the animals—feed, change bedding material, clean?

SITE CHARACTERISTICS

38. Has the play/learning value of all parts of the yard been maximized?

39. Can all parts withstand use by children?

40. Is there at least 150 square feet of outdoor space per child (preferably 200 square feet or more)?

41. Has some sort of visual connection been made with spaces adjacent to the yard to allow connection with the neighborhood and use as a source of interest?

42. Is fencing designed to be visually permeable but not climbable?

43. Are any existing slopes, mounds, or hills incorporated into the design?

44. Was an elevation change provided by moving earth if there was not any to begin with?

45. Was a slide set into any available slope?

ENTRY

46. Is the entry inviting to children? Is there something with which they can interact?

47. Is the entry reassuring to parents, a safe, nurturing and interesting place?

48. Does the entry have a residential character?

49. Is the entry a place itself, not just an abrupt gate in a wall?

NATURAL AREA

50. Has a wild/natural area been preserved or created?

51. Have good climbing trees with low branches been included?

52. Are there bushes and tall grass to allow exploring and "secret hideouts"?

53. Have environments been created to support insect, bird, and/or small animal populations?

BUILDING/YARD TRANSITION

54. Is there easy access to the yard from indoors, with the possibility of "sizing up" before going out?

55. Is there a transitional or porch area between the building and the yard?

56. Is there a covered space sufficient to support considerable activity on a rainy day?

ACTIVITY AREAS AND PATHS

57. Have well-defined activity areas been created?

58. Do paths run adjacent to—but not intrude into—activity areas?

59. Are gross-motor physical play areas separated from quieter cognitive play areas?

60. Do barriers between areas allow for awareness of adjacent activities, while at the same time effectively separating potentially conflicting uses?

61. Do paths lead to distinct goals?

62. Is "dead space" avoided?

63. Is one third to one half of the space open, that is, containing no equipment?

MICROCLIMATE

64. Have trees, earth mounding, or buildings been situated to mitigate strong winds?

65. Have deciduous trees or trellises been used in areas needing summer shade and winter sun?

66. Is the yard well drained, so as to dry quickly after rain?

67. Is there a "porch" or other covered area that can be used even in bad weather?

68. In areas with strong winds or heavy rains, does the design attempt to benefit from these, as with a seasonal stream or windmill?

69. In a climate with freezing temperatures, have sliding or skating areas been provided?

70. Is there an opportunity for sledding?

71. In such a climate, can the porch area be completely enclosed in winter?

ELEMENTS AND EQUIPMENT

Storage

72. Is it possible to store loose parts, tools, or materials for an activity at the place where they will be used?

73. Does the storage capacity anticipate both new acquisitions and changes in use?

74. Is there enough storage space for maintenance equipment?

75. Can the outdoor storage space be locked?

76. Can the children remove most things from storage—and return them?

Planting

77. Has the planting been selected to maximize sensory stimulation?

78. Are excitement and challenge provided by planting—trees to climb, wild area to explore?

79. Has the planting been used effectively as a barrier or edge between areas?

80. Have plants been used to moderate the effects of wind and sun?

81. Have the learning possibilities of the plants been considered—unusual leaves, bird attraction?

82. Have plants been chosen on the basis of play value, hardiness, and absence of danger—have both poisonous and thorny/sticky/staining plants been avoided?

Water, Sand, and Dirt

83. Are sand, dirt, and water amply provided?

84. Is a distinct sand play area provided that is separate from the sand below equipment?

85. Are the sand and dirt areas off the circulation path?

86. Is the dirt/mud play area located away from the garden?

87. Is water available in conjunction with both sand and dirt and provided in such a way that sand cannot block up the water source?

88. If possible, is there both still and moving water?

89. Is there a pond, pool, or elevated water table as well as a hose, faucet, or pump?

90. Is the sandbox located some distance from the building entrance, to prevent the children's tracking in sand?

91. Does the sandbox have at least eighteen inches of sand, partial shading, and good drainage?

Animals

92. If staff will care for them, is there a variety of animals?

93. Are animal cages fairly large, with a shelter or enclosure?

94. Is there a place to be with an animal out of its cage?

95. Is it possible to have a "petting zoo"?

Equipment

96. Have ample opportunities been provided for climbing, sliding, and swinging?

97. Has some more popular traditional equipment been included (or at least been seriously considered), such as swing sets and merry-go-rounds?

98. Are swings all sling or tire types, to avoid injury?

99. Is there a variety of things to climb on, including natural elements such as boulders or stumps?

100. Does the play structure have a variety of detachable accessories, for a periodic change of opportunities?

101. Have several different pieces of equipment been provided instead of a single, massive, "all-in-one" structure?

102. If there is space and opportunity, has a real vehicle been provided as a play element, stripped of engine, doors, and dangerous features?

Loose Parts

103. Have a variety of "loose parts" building materials been provided—planks, blocks, barrels, ladders?

104. Is there adequate storage at each play location for likely play equipment or props?

Wheeled Toys

105. Is there a path or paved area for wheeled toys and roller skates that does not infringe on quieter play areas?

106. Is the paved area designed to minimize "traffic" accidents, possibly incorporating a specific route and avoiding right-angle turns?

107. Are pedal-less riding toys provided if there are younger children in the program?

108. Are cooperative riding toys, such as wagons, provided?

109. Do wheeled-toy paths allow passing (five feet wide)?

Infant Spaces

110. Is there a separate area for nonmobile babies?

111. Can the older children be seen by the babies? Visit at the teacher's discretion?

112. Are there many sensory stimuli—mobiles, prisms, wind chimes?

113. Are bright and interesting plants visible but out of reach?

114. Is there a soft area (grass, mats) in the sun for sunbathing and curing diaper rash?

115. Are there dishpans or pools for water play by crawling babies?

116. Are there baby swings?

117. Are there railings, planters, and the like for babies to pull themselves up on?

118. Do toddlers have settings and props for fantasy play?

119. Are there slides, teeter-totters or rocking boats, and low sling or tire swings for toddlers?

120. Is a toddler's play area more a scaled-down version of a preschool yard than an infant space, to offer adequate challenge and stimulation?

121. Are there wheeled toys?

122. Has developmental grading been considered to differentiate among areas of the yard and provide age-appropriate experiences?

SOCIAL ISSUES

123. Is there adequate provision for watching others play—places to hang out and observe?

124. Are watching places located near most activity areas?

125. Can a tricycle rider drive up to many of the activity areas and casually join the group? Do paths pass near most activity areas and include "pull-off" nodes?

126. Are loose parts and props available to use as "offerings" in joining play?

127. Are structures and equipment designed with several options to facilitate "backing out" with dignity?

128. Are there several cozy and private spaces for children who feel the need to retreat?

129. Have the plantings been planned to allow little "hideouts" to be created?

ALTERNATIVES TO GROUND-LEVEL PLAY YARDS

130. Have all possible ground-level options been considered?

131. Is the roof capable of carrying the added load and remaining watertight?

132. Can a full range of developmentally appropriate play be provided in a roof location?

133. Has the creation of an "indoor street" or "outdoor room" been considered?

USER HANDBOOK

134. Has the designer created a handbook detailing the possibilities and considerations addressed by the design, for current and future users?

7

HOSPITAL OUTDOOR SPACES

Robert Paine and Carolyn Francis

After a long period of hospital design centered on the housing of technology and, perhaps, administrative efficiency, we are now entering a more humanistic phase. The public is becoming more interested in being involved in their medical care, more informed, and less willing to follow standard practices. Hospitals recognize these trends and, in response to consumer awareness in choosing health care, have begun to reexamine both their facilities and their services. Of equal importance to this concern in the business realm is the growing body of medical knowledge that supports the importance of both the patient's involvement and the environment in health care.

Something that may be overlooked in the hospital environment in a strictly functional analysis, yet is perhaps a fundamental aspect of patient support, is the provision of outdoor spaces. Few older hospitals were designed with outdoor spaces, but new hospital construction generally has one or more for patient and employee use, and renovations of older facilities may include the creation of a courtyard or garden. Little is known, however, about the effects of these spaces on hospital life. This chapter will look at the evolution of hospital design, including outdoor spaces, will review what is known about the use and elements of such spaces, and will present design recommendations and three case studies.

THE EVOLUTION OF HOSPITAL DESIGN AND MEDICAL THEORY

Why do so few hospitals currently have outdoor spaces? Cost is an obvious reason, but not the only one. The relationship between medical theory and hospital design created the present situation, and it is this same

relationship that is currently forcing hospital designers and administrators to reevaluate this absence of outdoor spaces and make provisions for them.

Before the 1850s, home patient care was emphasized and believed (quite correctly) to offer a patient the best chance of recovery. Only the deathly ill or the very poor, unable to afford home care, went to the hospital, where they most often died. Because the treatments for and causes of disease were not understood, the hospital could only offer a substandard version of personal patient care. The hospital's physical structure was seldom suited to patient care, and poor sanitation and space planning were common. Indeed, the concept of designing a hospital for patient treatment and recovery did not exist (Lindheim 1979–1980, pp. 237–241).

The perception of the hospital as an environment where the sick and injured are returned to a normal state of health was a radical change supported by the work of Florence Nightingale and the germ theory of disease. Nightingale promoted fresh air, individual nursing care, and rigorously maintained sanitation for all hospitals. Her spectacular nursing success during the Crimean War in the army hospitals where she instituted her ideas—patient mortality rates fell from 49 percent to 3 percent—dramatically demonstrated the importance of cleanliness in the treatment and prevention of disease.

The germ theory of disease was announced shortly after Nightingale published her findings regarding sanitary reforms. This theory—that disease occurs as a result of pathogenic agents and that the host's resistance and the germ's virulence determine the disease's severity—gave medicine a systematic, organized, and amazingly successful way to treat and research disease

Being able to sit outside in the sun and fresh air in a hospital setting, such as the Samuel Merritt Hospital in Oakland, California, may be a more important part of the recovery process than traditionally recognized. (Architect: Stone, Marracini, and Patterson; Landscape Architect: Carter, Hill, Nishita, McCulley Associates. Photo: Jane Lidz Photography, San Francisco)

(Lindheim and Syme 1983, p. 335). Nightingale's reforms and the germ theory of disease also gave the hospital a purpose and role in health care as the center for disease research, diagnosis, and treatment. Instead of care for the patient, the hospital offered treatment for disease, an important shift in the emphasis on and role of the patient. In addition, the hospital's physical structure became an important focus for conflict and discussion: How can the hospital best be designed as a treatment center? This emphasis in the United States was first achieved at the Johns Hopkins Hospital, Baltimore, Maryland. Although the final physical design was not particularly influential, the public debate and circulation of design proposals were. Theories about health and disease treatment, not patient care, were applied to the physical design of the hospital.

New engineering advances gave hospitals more treatment space. The hospital skyscraper became possible in 1900 with the introduction of the elevator and the steel skeleton building (Thompson and Golden 1975, pp. 190–192). Inside the building, the design determi-

nants were the new discoveries in medicine and medical technology. Laboratories, x-ray departments, and operating rooms with their fixed spatial requirements determined the availability of patient space. The design of the patients' wards was not necessarily based on the patients' comfort and care needs, and the spaces in these structures could not be easily changed (Thompson and Golden 1975, pp. 192–197). However, these early complaints were insignificant compared with the dramatically improved patient recovery rates in the more effective and efficient hospitals.

The Hill Burton Act of 1946, conceived as an alternative to the growing demand in the 1940s for national health insurance, was the next most significant event in the evolution of U.S. hospital design. The act shifted attention from the need for more widespread health care to the provision of more hospital facilities. Indeed, an important argument was the need for massive hospital building construction to replace the overcrowded, understaffed, and generally obsolete facilities left after the Depression and World War II (Feschbach 1979, p. 317). These new structures incorporated engineering advances: Air conditioning made possible windowless interior spaces and artificial ventilation; stronger building materials enabled higher and wider structures; and modern telecommunications led to decentralized planning.

The goals of the Hill Burton Act (HBA) succeeded beyond expectations. HBA hospitals offered better medical care and improved medical technology, but because all hospitals began to offer the same services, facilities and technology in the same area were duplicated, and the cost of medical care began to increase rapidly. However, this improved medical care and technology was at the same time made available to a wider population.

The most vocal criticism of the current technological emphasis in health care comes from those concerned with the cost of this care—the government, the insurance companies, and, to a less influential degree, the patients. Concurrent with this reaction has been criticism of hospitals as the focus of the "medical model," or a place organized for the treatment of illness. Such a model discourages intervention in illness before symptoms appear, treats the disease rather than the person, and makes the physician responsible for healing the patient, without encouraging or allowing the patient to participate in staying healthy. The medical profession does not share control and responsibility with society for health care, and the patient tends to see medicine as a technological "quick fix." Not only do patients and professionals generally not consider what patients can do to improve their health, but they also fail to consider the contribution of the physical environment to their recovery.

In a health care system to which disease treatment and disease technology is most important, the patients

These raised planters create a sense of separation between the outdoor courtyard and the indoor areas; allow opportunities to touch and smell grass by patients who might be unable to sit on the ground; and create a series of claimable subareas through articulation. (Walter Reed Army Medical Center, Washington, D.C. Architect: Stone, Marracini and Patterson; Landscape Architect: SWA Group. Photo: © Robert Lautman, Lautman Photography, Washington, D.C.)

are passive participants in their recovery. Their environment is not perceived as directly affecting disease treatment, and anything not directly affecting it has a lower priority in the costly business of the design, construction, and management of hospitals. Because technological space usually is viewed as a fixed quantity, it takes precedence over space for patient care. Space and strength requirements for new equipment increase construction costs, further encroaching on funds available for patient space. In fact, there is little need for outdoor spaces, according to the medical model, except as advertising and marketing tools.

Current medical practices and theories, however, have weakened this reasoning. Many studies have linked the effects of the social and physical environment to the frequency and severity of disease (see, for example, Syme and Berkman 1976). For example, the incidence of heart disease in "traditional" Japanese is

lower than in "Westernized" Japanese (Marmot 1976). And the death rates of the recently widowed, when compared with those of a corresponding married group, are significantly higher (Jacobs and Ostfeld 1977, Parks et al. 1969). Others have found that divorce, change of residence or job, and many other common life events can affect an individual's health (Boyce et al. 1977, Holmes and Masuda 1973, Holmes and Rahe 1967). Individuals ranked higher on a scale of socioeconomic status have lower disease rates than do those in lower-ranked positions (Lindheim and Syme 1983, p. 336). People with more meaningful social contacts have lower death rates than do those of the same age without such meaningful social contacts (Berkman and Syme 1979). A study that compared two intensive care units found higher rates of delirium in the unit without windows (40 percent versus 18 percent). This study concluded that views out of windows offer an important psychological "escape" for recovering surgical patients and that the stress of "windowlessness" is sufficient to tip the balance toward a "brief psychotic episode" for a significant number of patients (Wilson 1972). A study of six rehabilitation units in Chicago hospitals varying in levels of "windowness" showed that staff are better able to cope with windowlessness than patients are and that "meaningful involvement with windows and views is therapeutic for patients" (Verderber 1982, p. 428). All of these conclusions (and our own common sense) suggest that disease is not just a function of virulent pathogens, that many factors in the social and physical environment stress the body and help determine the prevalence of disease or changes in the health of any community's members (Cassel 1976, p. 121, Lindheim and Syme 1983, p. 336, Powels 1973).

Allowing patients to participate in their own health care and maintenance is an idea slowly being incorporated into modern health care and affecting the way in which patients use the hospital environment. A "return to normalcy"—physical stimulation, early discharge, and greater activity levels following medical treatment—are now routine. Walking in corridors, dangling legs over beds, or any other physical activity reduces the pooling of blood in the extremities, drains the bladder, decreases fluid collection in the lungs, and improves muscle tone, all leading to a swifter and more successful recovery. Both maternity and coronary care patients, with typical stays cut from two weeks to twelve hours and from six weeks to two weeks, respectively, illustrate the dramatically shorter hospitalizations resulting from stimulating the patient. Unfortunately, such stimulation must often occur in areas ill suited to the task—hallways, cramped rooms, or waiting rooms and lobby areas open to the general public.

Finally, the interior hospital environment is beginning to be recognized (if not quantified) as affecting patient recovery rates and staff morale, which indirectly affects patient care. Alternative birth centers and hospices, with their heightened emphasis on patient comfort, participation, control, and choice, have forced hospitals to offer similar services so as to fill unoccupied beds. An article by an architect, addressed to hospital administrators, warns: "As other hospitals upgrade their environment, the public will find it harder and harder to understand that an outdated, ugly, but well-equipped and well-staffed hospital might represent the better institution" (Falick 1981, p. 68). Same-day surgeries also appeal to medical consumers, as they can choose, in a limited way, the type of hospitalization they desire. The medical model is also changing to accommodate this improved, less costly medical care and is recognizing that the physical setting is directly related to the patients' comfort and recovery. As Olds and her colleagues reported, "Research in the behavioral sciences has confirmed that health care settings may in themselves slow recovery and induce emotional problems" (Olds, Lewis, and Joroff 1985, p. 445).

This changing medical paradigm is as important as some of the new technology and therefore is both challenging and difficult to design for. Decisions must be made about benefits of the environment and technology that cannot be compared. A common reaction encountered by Paine in his case studies of three California hospitals was: "I know that outdoor spaces affect the patients positively. I can't prove it. But I do know also that there are excellent patient recovery rates in hospitals without such spaces. Having one simply adds an extra dimension." This qualification—an unwillingness to accept the necessity of, and to allocate funds for, unquantified benefits to patient recovery —in a system based on quantifiable benefits—limits the provision of such spaces, even as the importance of a more normal and aesthetic environment is recognized. Obviously, outdoor spaces offer areas for stimulation and a much more normal environment for the patient. Consequently, such an environment can be hypothesized to have positive medical benefits, although it has not been traditionally used for patient care.

Within the medical profession, the debate continues over this possibility. *Environments for Humanized Health Care* (Lindheim 1979), a collection of articles on the effects of improved or different environments on the health and care of patients, illustrates the importance of the hospital environment. It is just this shift in thinking that requires hospital designers to reexamine the hospital environment in the same way that designers of playgrounds, mental health facilities, or housing for the elderly might do. How can these spaces be designed and managed so as to maximize benefits to the intended users?

THE LITERATURE

Whereas the other chapters in this book have had considerable bodies of literature on which to draw, the particular case of hospital outdoor space has as yet received little attention, and empirical studies of use are especially lacking.

Several writers have addressed the importance of windows and views, which may take advantage of an outdoor space as a visual amenity. There are both psychological and physiological benefits to providing views, as discussed in the work of Verderber, Ulrich, and Wilson.

Two books dealing with health care facilities for children—*Changing Hospital Environments for Children* by Lindheim, Glaser, and Coffin; and *Child Health Care Facilities* by Olds and Daniel—discuss outdoor spaces and design considerations in providing outdoor play areas for pediatric patients.

Design That Cares: Planning Health Facilities for Patients and Visitors, by Carpman, Grant, and Simmons, is quite an exhaustive volume developing out of the five-year Patient and Visitor Participation Project at the University of Michigan Hospitals at Ann Arbor. This book discusses and describes projects and design guidelines for creating supportive hospital environments, including outdoor spaces and views.

Unfortunately, even though many hospitals now provide outdoor spaces, there is little guidance available for their development, notwithstanding the exceptions listed here. *Hospital: The Planning and Design Process* (Hardy and Lammers 1986) does present as a principle of site design that "view for inpatients must be considered in determining building location" (p. 203) and points out that "site aesthetics are highly important and should be protected and enhanced to the extent possible . . . green space and objects of beautification must be carefully planned to avoid objectionable, harsh, or uninteresting appearances" (p. 201). Unfortunately, they offer no suggestions on how to preserve this green space or what it might be used for. Likewise, there is no specific discussion of the need, provision, or potential use of outdoor spaces in *British Hospital and Health-Care Buildings* (Stone 1980), *Design for Health Care* (Cox and Groves 1981), or *The Design of Medical and Dental Facilities* (Malkin 1982), even though all are comprehensive and thoughtful books. *Hospitals: Design and Development* (James and Tatton-Brown 1986) presents over sixty examples of hospital design. The only mention of outdoor areas, however, is photo captions explaining that a courtyard is beyond a particular room. In discussing early ambulation, the authors suggest that "early ambulation has led to the provision of dayrooms and additional toilets, because it is thought that a patient is more likely to be tempted to get out of bed if there is somewhere to go" (p. 69). Surely a pleasant outdoor space is more incentive than a toilet, unless that is the immediate need. In fact, Carpman, Grant, and Simmons (1986) reported that "in one study, 91 percent of the inpatients sampled at a tertiary care hospital said that they would like to use an outdoor space planned for walking or sitting. Because more than two-thirds of these patients reported walking to at least one place—from 25 feet to well over 1,000 feet from their rooms—their use of an outdoor space seems likely" (p. 198). This desire to use an outdoor area is equally evident in patients who are not able to walk: "The desire to use a courtyard is not limited to ambulatory patients. At one hospital, for example, patients on gurneys and in wheelchairs have such a strong desire to be outside that they are frequently seen on the front entrance sidewalk during warm months,

quite close to passing traffic" (Carpman, Grant, and Simmons 1986, p. 199).

A park built by Bellevue Hospital in New York City, enclosed by an earth berm and including walkways, benches, a fountain, and amphitheater, was found to be overwhelmingly popular. Interviews with patients, staff, and visitors indicate repeated use, appreciation of a comfortable and relaxing atmosphere in which to "re-energize," and a belief that the park stood for a caring attitude on the part of the hospital. When given a choice from a list of amenities, 98 percent of those interviewed preferred the park (Carpman, Grant, and Simmons 1986, Olds and Daniel 1987).

Such findings do indicate the importance of hospital outdoor space, despite the lack of discussion or recommendations found in the general literature on hospital design.

GENERAL FINDINGS

This section presents general findings from case studies of outdoor spaces at three different hospitals: Casa Colina Hospital, Pomona, California; Kaiser Permanente Hospital, Martinez, California; and Alta Bates Hospital, Berkeley, California, which were studied extensively in 1983 for a master's thesis (Paine 1984). These hospitals were chosen because they represent a range of hospital and patient types and because they have successfully integrated outdoor spaces into the routines of the patients, staff, and visitors. Where possible, the findings of the case studies are confirmed and/or augmented by relevant literature.

Users of Hospital Outdoor Spaces

There are three distinct types of users of hospital outdoor space—the patients, visitors, and employees—each with its own requirements and patterns of use. Observations from the case studies show the greatest use of outdoor spaces by the staff, either alone or in groups, followed by visitors with patients and patients alone.

Patients

Generally, the patients' health determines their ability to go outdoors. Patients who are not attached to monitoring equipment, have physical mobility independent of staff assistance, and/or are long-term care patients are the most likely to use outdoor spaces. Examples include

- Orthopedic patients: Those with broken legs or other broken bones who are basically healthy but recuperating.

This courtyard at Walter Reed Army Medical Center, Washington, D.C., offers places to sit (fountain edge, round seating platforms) and to lean (tall planter edges), as well as visual interest and the opportunity to walk through. (Architect: Stone, Marracini, and Patterson; Landscape Architect: SWA Group. Photo: © Robert Lautman, Lautman Photography, Washington, D.C.)

- Maternity care patients: Either pre- or postpartum.
- Rehabilitation patients: Those who are relearning to use their body and for whom outdoor spaces are an important part of the learning process.
- Alcohol and drug care patients.
- Psychiatric patients.

Generally, each of these patient types is physically healthy. They are capable of moving independently to some degree, and their condition generally need not be constantly monitored. It is important to note that this does not mean that acute care patients will not use outdoor spaces, only that current medical practice allows fewer opportunities for the independent use of such space. In the case studies, acute care—cancer, coronary, burn, and postsurgery—patients were observed outdoors. Typically, those with respiratory problems, those attached to monitoring devices, or those especially susceptible to infection were not. For almost any other patient, the ability to go outdoors is determined by the ability of staff or visitors to assist them. Different factors, such as distance from the outdoor space, time of day, staff attitude, or the visitors' willingness to assist, affected the patient's ability to move outdoors.

Disease reduces the body's ability to adjust to temperature. Consequently, sick persons are more susceptible to the effects of temperature and wind outdoors and are more sensitive overall to conditions that healthy individuals tolerate with ease. Examples include

- Pregnant women, whose body temperature control is affected, often leading to overheating.
- Patients on medication that causes sensitivity to the sun's rays.
- Burn patients, who are sensitive to heat and sun.

Patients need options when using outdoor space, including a choice of sun and shade, cool and warm; they also need ease of access to and ease of mobility within the space; access to restrooms and water; comfortable seating; and, in special cases, plants with little pollen or attraction to bees.

Another type of sensitivity, which is beyond the scope of this chapter to discuss in detail, is cognitive or perceptual dysfunction, which might be seen in either psychiatric or substance abuse patients. Although the findings and guidelines presented here reflect physical needs and general human perceptual and affective responses, we suggest that designers dealing with cognitive or perceptual dysfunction patients seek out the relevant literature or expert medical guidance in addition.

Child Patients

A special type of patient, yet one found in many hospitals, is the pediatric patient. Although most of the is-

sues concerning hospital outdoor spaces for adults are equally relevant to this group, the hospitalized child must also be allowed the opportunity to play. As Lindheim, Glaser, and Coffin discovered,

Grade school children show an astonishing amount of energy. When healthy they bound from one activity to the next and sleep soundly at night. In the hospital, activity is restricted, and children do not always find it possible to get really tired —tired enough to sleep well. Yet many hospitalized children could engage in a variety of vigorous activities without danger. (1972, p. 64)

These authors emphasize providing a variety of settings for creative and imaginative play, as well as for more physical play. Although school-aged children may be the most active, carefully designed outdoor areas are also important for infants and toddlers, preschoolers, and adolescents.

Play areas for hospitalized children may be similar to those for healthy children, "with the obvious exception that (they) must also provide specialized opportunities for play by children on gurneys, in wheelchairs, and in casts" (Lindheim, Glaser, and Coffin 1972, p. 50). Also, hospitalized children usually have less stamina than do healthy children. Many of the features discussed in Chapter 6 are equally appropriate to the hospital outdoor play area, although perhaps with modification. For example, for children on gurneys or in wheelchairs, sand and water play and gardening opportunities need to be provided at an appropriate height. Climbing structures or tree houses (as at the Stanford Children's Hospital) can be designed to be scaled by children of differing abilities, by ropes, ladders, stairs, or ramps. As Olds and Daniel found,

Children of all ages and all degrees of physical ability and disability need the opportunity to play. Proper facilities and landscaping help to encourage a child to touch, run, hide, or otherwise become engaged in the environment. Wherever there are children with handicapping conditions, the design challenge is to stimulate use of those faculties which are weak, as well as to challenge and strengthen those which are strong. Every opportunity for movement should be capitalized upon.

Play, whether planned or spontaneous, is in fact therapy for hospitalized children. Accordingly, concerns regarding surfaces and path width should be similar to those for any hospital outdoor space, but changes in elevation that might be taxing to recuperating adult patients should be incorporated into the design of play areas, for variation, rolling opportunities, and enclosure. Olds and Daniel made a case for architectural diversity, "with inclines, trees, winding paths, flowers, ponds, and even small animals . . . the terrain, vegetation, and landscaping are all critical aspects of the play and therapeutic experience of being outdoors" (1987, p. 105).

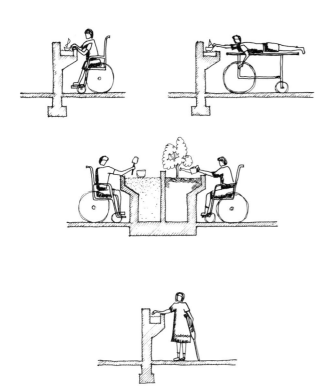

Sand and water play, as well as opportunities for gardening, can be provided for children in wheelchairs, on gurneys, or on crutches. (Based on an illustration from Lindheim, Glaser, and Coffin 1972)

Supervision is especially important in an outdoor setting for child patients. The outdoor space should open directly from the pediatric unit, perhaps from an indoor playroom, and be easily overseen from inside. The most desirable situation is one in which the pediatric facility is entirely on the ground floor, with a covered "porch" area connecting the interior to the outdoor play area. If urban density precludes this arrangement, the pediatric unit should be located next to a rooftop play area. Such a space has inherent limitations, however, particularly wind problems (see Chapter 6), and is definitely a less desirable option than a ground-level space. However, if this is the only way to have the outdoor space open directly from the unit, it is preferable to a play area in a remote location.

Seating should also take into account the issue of supervision. Staff or visitors should have comfortable places to sit, to oversee the children playing, so that they will enjoy accompanying the children outdoors. Seating should also permit weak or confined children to be next to children playing at various locations in the space, to allow for vicarious participation. Likewise, there should be areas for wheelchairs or gurneys to be parked out of the circulation path, next to seated friends or visitors or playing children.

It has been suggested that the qualities of an Adventure Playground may in fact be especially suitable for a hospital outdoor play space (Olds and Daniel 1987). The sense of control and mastery and the ability to act

on one's environment that are characteristic of children's experience in such a playground are clearly meaningful for those whose lives are largely beyond their own control in a hospital setting. Giving children construction materials and tools, together with movable "loose parts" and props, encourages greater exploration, creative imagination, and active involvement with the environment.

At the Handicapped Adventure Playground in London, children with a variety of conditions (physical, emotional, and developmental) come regularly to "explore the limits of their individual capabilities and initiative within the boundaries of safe practice" (Wolff 1979, p. 99). Although this playground was developed to serve children with permanent disabilities, such a setting is equally valuable for children temporarily disabled during hospitalization. Wolff reported:

Spastic and physically disabled children were seen to be motivated to use muscles that had long been considered inoperative. The mentally handicapped, who often found the adjustment from school to playground more difficult, were shown to be learning more from direct physical participation . . . than through other more formal teaching techniques. The maladjusted and emotionally disturbed were observed in more positive social interactions through involvement in cooperative projects. (1979, p. 112)

Finally, teenaged patients might fare best in a special area just for them. Teenagers are likely—as they are at home—to want to spend some time away from adults. An outdoor area may allow for casual socializing, perhaps playing popular music away from those who would find it irritating, or engaging in some sport—table tennis, shooting baskets, and so on. Lindheim, Glaser, and Coffin (1972) noted that teen patients are more likely to become bored than other patients are, and they also are especially concerned with any effects of illness or injury on their physical appearance and body functions. Concerns about physical attractiveness and future athletic ability might be ameliorated by provision of an outdoor "hangout" space where teens could relate and behave as though they were not in an institutional setting.

Visitors

The opportunity to visit with family or friends is extremely important to most patients. Such visits provide contact and continuity with a patient's normal life and a chance for mutual reassurance between patient and visitor. Visits may be emotionally intense, may focus on confidential issues, or may be a limited time in which to reestablish family dynamics. Clearly, such interactions require a supportive environment; yet most hospitals are not designed for visiting: The patients' rooms are too small for visitors to gather there comfortably; hallways are not private; and it may be inconven-

In their work at Children's Hospital, Stanford University, Palo Alto, California, the architects organized the building around a central courtyard/garden, directly on axis to the entry and open to all levels; developed a series of outdoor play courtyards opening off the clinics; and created a meandering walkway at roof level. (Photo of model courtesy of architects Anshen and Allen)

ient to move the patient to a cafeteria or lounge. Where the climate is obliging, outdoor spaces may thus become good places for patient/visitor interaction. Groups of visitors with a patient were commonly observed to number five or six people, and an extended family visit could bring as many as ten people to see one patient. This means that the outdoor space must be flexible, so as to accommodate varying group sizes and overall numbers of people.

Visitors often bring children to visit a patient. Children are still an anomaly in the hospital setting, having been permitted in many hospital areas only since the 1970s. They must be quiet and not touch anything or disturb the adult patients, visitors, or staff. This does not mean that patients do not want to see children, only that children do not usually fare well on long visits in a hospital room or ward. Outdoor spaces, however, can be more suitable for children's energies. If there were some things to do in the space, children could entertain themselves while the adults visit. For example, flower beds can be edged with logs of varying heights set into the ground, which children will enjoy walking on. A fish pond is quite engaging, especially if it is spanned by an observation bridge, or a telescope could be installed in a rooftop garden to survey the surroundings. Perhaps a simple playhouse or climbing structure can be included if children are expected to visit frequently.

Staff

Hospital staff are the most critical users of outdoor spaces, which is perhaps not surprising, as they spend every working day in the hospital environment. Interviews revealed that administrative staff are the most likely to have enough free time to use outdoor spaces, with usually a sixty-minute lunch period and regular break times. Physicians are the least likely to use outdoor spaces, as they send most of their time on patient rounds or in the office. Many physicians only consult at the hospital and have their offices at other locations. However, the physicians' awareness of the use of outdoor space is important because it is often they who decide whether a patient may go outdoors.

The nursing staff involved in daily patient care seldom have time to use outdoor space unless it is right next to the nursing unit. Nurses have the major daily responsibility for patient care and must be accessible at all times. Furthermore, their free time is often limited, and they frequently take their lunch period when time allows. At the three hospitals Paine observed, the nurses had a thirty-minute lunch break, and many stated that this was not long enough to use the cafeteria and to go outdoors, unless the space was next to either the cafeteria or the nursing unit.

Nurses are those most likely to help the patients go outdoors. If they cannot see the patients from the nursing station or unit, then they cannot leave them alone outside; and in most situations the nurses will not be able to take the time to stay with the patients outdoors. Thus the distance between outdoor space and the nursing station, and the nurses' responsibilities, negatively affect the use of outdoor space by both patients and nurses. In interviews the nurses stated that they were the ones among the staff most likely to recommend that a patient go outdoors. The nurses at all three hospitals reported moving patients outdoors to make them less conscious of their condition, believing that time spent sitting alone outdoors was more stimulating and health promoting than being in a room.

Privacy in hospitals for each user group is important. Staff do not want to be overheard or viewed by patients. Visitors want privacy to talk with the patient. Case study findings supported the general observations that each group in a hospital outdoor space tends to respect one another's privacy and territorial rights. There was little casual conversation among them; rather, each group would orient itself to promote privacy.

Activities in Hospital Outdoor Spaces

Although patients might be expected to use outdoor spaces the most often and to receive the greatest benefit from them, this expectation was disproved in the three hospitals observed. Outdoor space can be impor-

This lushly planted, naturalistic courtyard at Jerry L. Pettis Memorial Veterans Hospital in Loma Linda, California, offers a range of shapes and textures not encountered indoors. While the sitting rocks and gravel path add to the feeling of being "in nature," such elements are suited for use only by quite physically able patients, visitors, and staff. If less able patients were to use such a courtyard, it would be important to include some paved pathways and a wider range of seating options. (Architect: Stone, Marracini, and Patterson; Landscape Architect: AKA Inc. Photo: Gerald Ratto Photography, San Francisco)

tant to anyone in a hospital—patients, staff, and visitors. In fact, the amount of actual use does not necessarily determine the importance of these spaces. Interviews revealed that people also used the spaces by viewing them through windows, opening the windows for fresh air, or by simply being aware of their existence, adding to the quality of the hospital environment.

The social activity in any successful public outdoor space is similar to that in hospital outdoor spaces. The principal activities at the three hospitals Paine studied were socializing and eating, similar to those in urban plazas. Outdoor spaces also frequently provided a setting for therapy, staff meetings, team games such as volleyball, and children's play.

There are two distinct periods when outdoor spaces are used—weekdays and weekends—each characterized by a difference in use.

On weekdays, there is generally little activity outdoors until around 11:00 A.M., the beginning of the lunch hour. This is because morning is usually the busiest time for a hospital. Physicians are making early morning rounds to check patients and order tests. Nurses are readying the ward for the patients and the doctors and are making arrangements for the new incoming patients and the day's outgoing patients. Patients are being examined and tested and bathed for the coming day. Thus the lunch hour is the first time when a significant number of people have any free time.

The lunch hour is therefore the busiest time for outdoor use and is when staff are most likely to use the space. The patients, unless they are physically independent, are the group least likely to be outdoors for lunch, as hospitals normally deliver food to the patients' rooms. This lunch-hour peak use continues until about 2:00 P.M.; then the space is used sporadically throughout the afternoon.

Weekend activities do not usually begin until lunchtime, with use then remaining heavy throughout the afternoon. Visitors, least common on weekdays, are the largest user group during weekend afternoons. Hospital staff are not as significant a user population then because administrative staff do not come to work on weekends.

DESIGN RECOMMENDATIONS

The initial planning of a hospital building will do much to help make the outdoor spaces worthwhile. Too often, these spaces are leftover areas where no rooms could be built; where setbacks from streets, buildings, or parking were needed; where the hospital

had future plans to build another wing; or where lightwells into the interior of the building were needed. There is often little thought regarding the relationship between what is happening inside the hospital and what is to happen outdoors. Planning for outdoor space in the initial organization of the building thus allows its use to be integrated into the hospital's routine.

The needs that must be addressed in the design of an urban plaza also apply to hospital outdoor space: seating, visual interest, access, and amenities, including sun, trees, water, shade, temperature, food, and anything of interest that will draw people to a space. The following recommendations focus on what makes a hospital an exceptional case for its users and requires extra attention to planning and detailing.

Location of Hospital Outdoor Spaces

Outdoor space use patterns are determined in part by the adjacent building or room use and by the distance that a potential user may have to travel.

Recommendations

- *Locate an outdoor space next to the dining area.* Except for the front lobby, more people use the dining area than any other hospital space, and so here there is a constant supply of potential outdoor space users. Since interviews revealed that the lunch hour is also the only "approved" working time during which medical staff are comfortable relaxing outdoors, this is an especially suitable location.
- *Locate patients and staff who are to be encouraged to use the outdoor space closest to the access points.* Conversely, locate those patients and staff who should not or cannot use the outdoor spaces farthest from physical access. The distance away from an out-

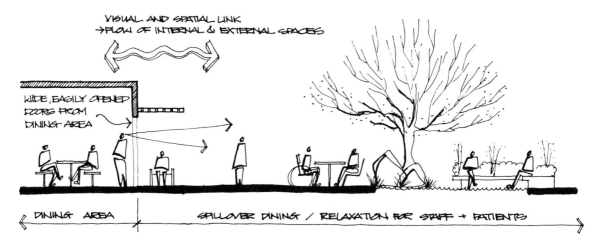

An outdoor space adjacent to the dining area will be heavily used.

door space affects the user's probability of using that space. The nurses who were interviewed felt that they must remain on call at all times for their patients. Unless outdoor spaces were near the unit, therefore, they did not feel that they could use them. The patients' physical condition determines how often they can independently (without staff or visitor assistance) use the outdoor space. Patients whose condition, such as respiratory problems, precludes using the outdoor space, should be assigned to those rooms farthest away from the access point. However, if a patient is unable to visit the outdoor space or is likely to do so infrequently, the importance of providing a view to the outdoors increases. For those patients who are equally able to use the outdoor space, put the most physically mobile farthest from the access point. Administrative staff are the least likely to be affected by distance, as they have longer lunch hours and greater flexibility.

- *Create outdoor spaces at least twenty feet wide where windows are directly across from each other.* Users of any outdoor space are very conscious of its "fishbowl" effect, of being stared at by people inside. A space at least twenty feet wide provides enough area for a table, gathering area, and planting (or other visual screens) against the windows. Twenty feet is also the approximate distance at which views from one window across the outdoor space into another window become unclear. This distance gives sufficient privacy to all concerned and is especially important where a hallway with windows looks across the outdoor space into patients' rooms or staff offices.
- *Give the hospital staff an outdoor space that the patients cannot easily see.* Nursing staff reported the desire to get away at times from the stress and tension of dealing with patients. Many of the activities that staff do to relax—smoke, talk in groups,

eat—may conflict with the patients' need for rest outdoors or are something that the patients are prohibited from doing. One hospital prohibited any of these activities in the outdoor spaces because they disturbed the patients. This does not mean, however, that a "staff only" outdoor space is needed or even desired. Instead, judicious screening or space planning can create a number of semiprivate spaces within an overall public outdoor space.

- *Plan the outdoor spaces with a protected or a southwest exposure.* This allows more use of the outdoor space in the cool early spring and late fall and enables winter use on warm days. In some climates, a shady location may be desirable for protection from harsh sun or extreme heat, but the goal should always be to maximize the amount of time the space can be used.

Physical Access to Outdoor Spaces

The entry to an outdoor space should be easily accessible in order to maximize the number of people who will use it. Physical access deals with door type, location and design of entrances, and surfacing materials.

- *Do not create an outdoor space solely for visual use if it can also be used in other ways.* A space that can be used to sit or walk in but is presented only as a visual amenity is often seen by staff members as a waste of space. At the hospitals Paine studied, the most common staff reaction to a space just for viewing was "What good is it?" On the other hand, an outdoor space that is located or dimensioned so as to be physically unusable should still be given considerable attention for the views it may provide.
- *Locate the main entry to an outdoor space to be most accessible to those most likely to use it.* If the space is

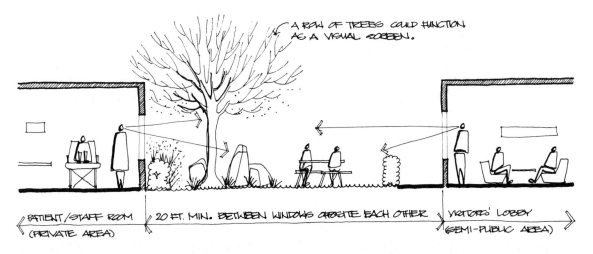

Screening and adequate dimensions prevent those outside from feeling "on display."

Corridor windows (left) and staff offices (right) overlook this therapy garden at the Kaiser Permanente Hospital, Martinez, California. The lack of screening in a relatively narrow space leads to office curtains' consistently being closed for privacy. (Photo: Robert Paine)

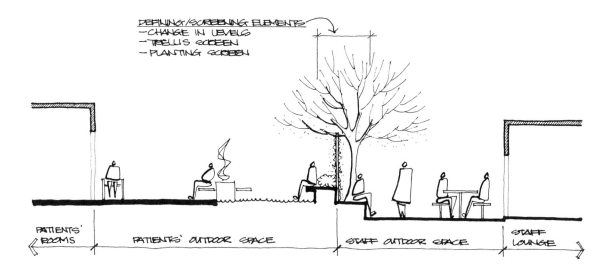

A staff area may be adjacent to, but screened from, the main outdoor space.

intended for general use, place the entry in a public area easily reached from corridors and elevators throughout the hospital. On the other hand, if it is a more specialized outdoor space, the easiest way to limit the number of people who use it is to install the entry in a seldom-traveled area, such as a staff corridor, or within a patient ward. Hospital staff, patients, and visitors are reluctant to walk through areas of the hospital beyond their assigned ward or visiting area, and so only those with immediate access to it will use such an outdoor space.

- *Install doors that are self-propping and easy to open and do not automatically lock when closed.* This is an

ideal door to an outdoor space. The following was learned from observing the use of common hospital doors and applies primarily to users with mobility problems: *Automatically opening doors:* An automatically opening door provides the easiest access, as any patient can use it. There are few difficulties coordinating accessory medical equipment attached to the patient while going through this door. However, staff may worry about patients wandering outdoors unsupervised. The patients' security, especially that of cognitive dysfunction patients, is an important concern. This type of door, therefore, is best for areas where there is supervision or where the patients' conditions do not require it. *Sliding glass doors:* A sliding glass door, assuming there is no threshold, is the second easiest door for patients to use, as no pushing or bracing is required. It also provides visual access to the space. *Push-bar doors:* A push-bar door is heavy and requires pushing and bracing; and thus patients in a weakened condition or in wheelchairs cannot open them unassisted. Coordinating medical equipment attached to the patient is difficult through these kinds of doors. *Self-locking doors:* Self-locking doors inconvenience the people using the outdoor spaces. Staff at all the hospitals with such doors were observed circumventing the doors by propping them open with trash containers or wood wedges or by taping the bolt shut.

- *Providing paving that does not inhibit movement.* Paving with deep grooves, heavy aggregates, or large joints such as mortared stone or large aggregate concrete blocks should be avoided, as they are difficult for people using wheelchairs, gurneys, walkers, or attached medical equipment such as IV units.

- *Provide handrails to support weakened and recovering patients.* Patients may want to use, and may benefit from using, the outdoor space, even if they have limited strength or stamina. A combination of handrails (coated so as not to be slippery when wet) and judiciously placed benches enable such use.

- *Make major walkways wide enough for two gurneys to pass (at least five feet).* The outdoor space will be used more often if it is easy to move into and out of it. If lots of maneuvering is required, patients and staff may not want to bother.

- *Limit grade changes in the main outdoor area.* For people whose mobility is impaired in any way, even a slight grade change may prove difficult. The best situation is to offer routes of varying incline, for patients to choose an appropriate challenge or to work on gradually building up their strength.

- *Enable the outdoor area to be used during as much of the year as possible.* Where snow or ice is likely to make walkways slippery, install melting devices to clear the walkway. Being able to go outdoors in the winter, even for a few moments, can be an important respite from "cabin fever."

- *Design the entry way to the outdoor space to be free of ramps or steps, and provide maneuvering space around the door.* Ramps near doors inhibit the patients' use of a space. Patients new to a wheelchair or gurney cannot independently maneuver up a ramp. Also it is difficult to coordinate a patient and accessory medical equipment such as an IV up or down a ramp, to stop at the door, and then to move through the door. A large area around the door offers maneuvering space for bringing people and their things (food tray, medical equipment) outdoors.

NEGATIVE

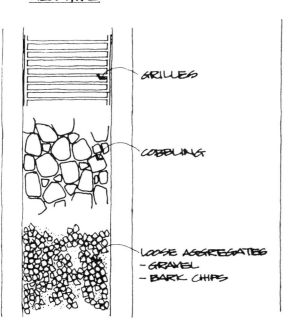

GRILLES

COBBLING

LOOSE AGGREGATES
- GRAVEL
- BARK CHIPS

POSITIVE*

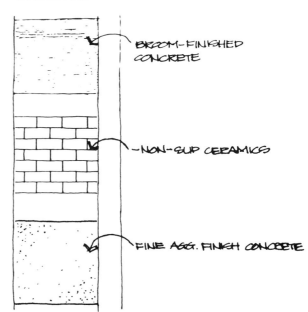

BROOM-FINISHED CONCRETE

NON-SLIP CERAMICS

FINE AGG. FINISH CONCRETE

* COLOR TO ALTER FROM INTERNAL TO EXTERNAL → DEFINE TRANSITION.

Paving surfaces should be used that are neither slippery nor uneven.

Views to Outdoors

A view of outdoor space can effectively "advertise" its presence, leading to more use of it. If it is possible to see a courtyard or garden from a lobby, cafeteria, or major corridor, many people will be made aware of it, leading either to spontaneous use or a decision to visit the space later.

Views are also important in their own right. Planning for outdoor space should certainly include consideration of the views created for inside rooms.

A number of studies have begun to supply empirical evidence for what most people would assume from common sense to be fact, notably, that windowlessness in hospitals is a significant form of sensory deprivation (Ulrich 1984; Verderber 1982; Wilson 1972). Studies of hospitals have joined those of windowless offices (Cooper, Wiltshire, and Hardy 1973; Ne'eman 1974), schools (Larson 1965), and factories (Manning 1963) to reinforce the psychological importance of windows to the building's occupants:

The window aperture symbolizes openness and freedom. For the hospital patient, windows are considerably more than panes and frames. They are a break in the walls which symbolize isolation from the environment outside the hospital. Through them, patients and staff may perceive the serenity of nature, the intensity of urban life, the transformation of one season to the next, the diurnal pattern of day becoming night, observe people and activity and, likewise, be observed by the passing world and experience an active involvement in it. (Verderber 1982, pp. 476–477)

Clearly, if the purpose of rehabilitation is to reintegrate the patient into society, then a view out to the real world of nature, city, pedestrians, animals, birds, and clouds is bound to have some therapeutic effect.

In fact, Roger Ulrich (1979, 1984; Ulrich and Simmons 1986) studied the psychological and physiological effects of views and found that "natural" scenes (characterized by vegetation and/or water) appear to decrease stress in the viewer, whereas urban scenes of buildings and/or traffic increase stress. In a comparative study of recovering gall bladder surgery patients, those whose hospital room windows overlooked trees were released earlier, had fewer negative chart notes, and took less pain medication than did patients whose view was of a brick wall (Ulrich 1984). In a highly quantified, physiological study of stress response to environment, "the findings clearly showed that subjects recovered faster and much more completely from stress when they were exposed to nature as opposed to either the pedestrian mall or traffic settings" (Ulrich and Simmons 1986, p. 118). All these studies support Ulrich's earlier suggestion that "location and design decisions for some activities and institutions—such as high stress workplaces and hospitals—should assign considerable importance to providing 'through the window' contact with nature" (Ulrich 1979, p. 22). Apparently, then, designers should consider the available alternatives when determining views. The importance of providing windows and views with some interest value can hardly be questioned. However if the patients' rooms can be arranged to look onto either a hospital courtyard or a park, hills, or water lying beyond the hospital, the latter may be preferable. In such a case, a (less-favored) view of the courtyard may be more valuable from a lounge.

Recommendations

- *Locate the windows to the outdoor space next to elevator lobbies, front entries, lounges, cafeterias, and patients' rooms.* More patients and visitors pass through these areas than any other hospital spaces, and so it is an excellent opportunity to advertise an outdoor space.
- *Locate some windows adjacent to the entry to the outdoor space.* This allows a user to examine the space

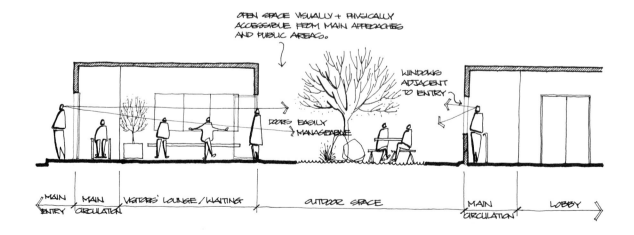

The outdoor space should be easily accessible, with views into it to advertise its presence.

before going outdoors, to determine who is present, whether a comfortable place to sit is available, or how the weather looks. Being able to "size up" a public place before entering it frequently contributes to its use.

- *Provide windows in patients' rooms, therapeutic settings, and staff offices.* We already discussed the research indicating the importance of views. The therapeutic effect of natural views on recovering patients, coupled with the recognition that those most impaired by windowlessness are the chronically ill, the paralyzed, and visually impaired patients, indicates that views from patients' rooms onto natural settings, trees, greenery, or water should receive the highest priority. Depending on the circumstances, the staff may also benefit from the stress-reducing quality of such views. Ideally, a window should allow views of close-in details (a tree or street scene), middle-distance settings (hills, the outlying urban area), and open sky.

- *Provide windows that ensure the patient's ability to see out while at the same time preventing others from seeing in.* Windows should have a sill height of between twenty and thirty inches, to allow bedridden patients and those in wheelchairs to see out. However, care must be taken to avoid the patients' feeling "on stage," owing to people looking in. Windows should not directly overlook public areas and should be screened. This can often be accomplished through planting, which allows a filtered view while maintaining privacy.

- *Provide vertical, as opposed to horizontal apertures.* Rooms with narrow, small, or horizontal windows tend to be disliked as much, if not more, than windowless rooms are. Rooms with too few windows create needless perceptual barriers, especially for those confined or bedridden for long periods of

time. Where possible, design vertical windows, but do not make them too narrow; also allow distant, middle-ground, and close-up views to be taken in simultaneously (Verderber 1982). If screens or curtains are used, the patients should be able to adjust them.

- *Provide shelves for indoor plants.* It is therapeutic for hospital patients to care for indoor plants and to be able to see them from their beds. When possible, provide shelves or table space for plants near the windows, yet make sure that the plants will not block the view outdoors for patients in bed or in wheelchairs and will not interfere with blinds or curtains.

Awareness of Outdoor Spaces

All patients and visitors should be made aware upon their entry to the hospital that outdoor spaces are available for them to use during their visit. This will encourage visitors to take patients outdoors, thereby freeing staff from having to do so.

Recommendations

- *Provide maps in the hospital, especially at elevator lobbies and front entries, to direct people to the outdoor spaces.*

- *Provide a map in the patient's information packet.* This will inform the patients of their location in the hospital, the proximity of outdoor spaces, and the routes to such spaces.

- *Offer a tour of the outdoor spaces for patients who preplan their hospitalization, for example, for elective surgery or maternity care.* These tours are effective marketing and advertising strategies for hospitals wishing to tell patients about features that differ-

Patients' rooms are screened by shrubbery. Bright flowers are planted between the windows and the shrubs for patients to look at, with a distant view over the shrubs, from the Alta Bates Hospital, Berkeley, California. (Photo: Carolyn Francis)

entiate a particular hospital from others. At one of the case study hospitals the outdoor space was included as part of the introductory tour of the maternity ward, and it always impressed prospective users.

Planting

Planting should provide sensory interest and relieve the hospital's institutional aspects. Plants provide a more normal homelike environment and may help relax patients. Planting to create natural views is also important from a therapeutic viewpoint.

Another possibility in hospital outdoor spaces is to set aside an area for limited gardening. As Charles Lewis noted, "The beneficial qualities of plants and gardening are also being used to heal and rehabilitate individuals in mental hospitals, physical rehabilitation centers, drug centers, prisons, and geriatric centers" (1979, p. 335). A professional discipline known as *horticultural therapy* has shown that one of the greatest benefits to hospital patients may be that

plants take away some of the anxiety and tension of the immediate now by showing us that there are long, enduring patterns in life. In a world of constant judgement, plants are non-threatening and non-discriminating. They respond to the care that is given them, not to the race or the intellectual or physical capacities of the gardener. It doesn't matter if one is black or white, has been to kindergarten or college, is poor or wealthy, healthy or handicapped, plants will grow if one gives proper care. They provide a benevolent setting in which a person can take first steps toward confidence. (Lewis 1979, p. 334)

Recommendations

- *Install a lawn area where feasible.* Case study interviews found that people in hospitals respond very positively to the sight of lush green grass. It has a powerful visual image; it is a versatile surface for children, patients, visitors, and staff; and the smell of newly mown or watered grass is particularly evocative.
- *Provide color variation in the planting.* People respond to color. In the case studies of existing spaces, color was often mentioned as lacking in the plantings. "You can hardly have enough flowers" was a typical response.
- *When planting trees, use the largest size possible.* Mature trees provide immediate visual interest; they also create shade and a sense of space. For most people, trees evoke a sense of permanence, which is especially important in a hospital setting where patients and visitors experience little sense of permanence and often high levels of anxiety.
- *Offer a variety of sunny and shady areas.* Patients are extremely sensitive to temperature and so must have many options from which to choose in order to be comfortable. If the outdoor space has been situated to maximize sun exposure, the designer should add features that will supply varying degrees of shade. Unless the climate is especially hot and bright, people usually prefer a "dappled" shade, such as that provided by a small-leafed tree or a trellis.
- *Plant densely, rather than sparsely, with many varieties of trees, shrubs, and flowers.* Carpman, Grant, and Simmons reported:

A lawn is a visual, tactile, and olfactory antidote to the typical antiseptic hospital atmosphere of Alta Bates Hospital, Berkeley, California and a great place for visiting children. (Photo: Carolyn Francis)

When people look at a scene, they seek a sense of involvement and a richness that gives them reason to continue viewing. For instance, a densely planted area provides greater visual interest than a sparsely planted one. In one (hospital based) study, scenes with a greater number of trees were consistently rated higher than those with fewer trees. The ratings increased in a linear fashion as the number of trees increased. Trees were seen as a source of visual interest as well as a source of beauty, shade, and color. Absence of planting was characterized as "bare" and "boring" by some respondents. (1986, p. 220)

- *Choose plants with strong fragrances.* Hospitals have an immediately noticeable odor that may evoke fear or apprehension in some patients and visitors, recalling childhood or other traumatic hospital experiences. People interviewed in hospital courtyards and roof gardens often remarked how good it felt to smell trees, grass, shrubbery, and flowers as a respite from the prevailing antiseptic odor in the hospital building.
- *Install "pop-up" sprinklers in any area where people gather.* Pop-up sprinklers reduce the possibility of people's tripping over a sprinkler head.
- *Provide a raised bed for gardening.* This is important when patients will be in residence for some time. But when patients stay only a few days, it may be unnecessary unless the staff would enjoy it.

Site Furniture

Site furniture makes the space usable. Without it, people's choices are limited, and they are likely only to look around or walk through a space and then leave. Site furniture should enable the space to be used by as many people as possible throughout the year.

Recommendations

- *Offer seating of as many types and forms as possible.* Without adequate seating, people cannot stay outside. Most people using the outdoor spaces are alone or in small groups of one to four. Some seating should consist of movable chairs which people can adjust for group size, sun, shade, wind, or desired views. In a comprehensive study carried out at the University of Michigan Hospitals, two hundred randomly sampled patients and visitors indicated a strong desire to be able to choose from a range of seating options (Carpman, Grant, and Simmons 1986, p. 203). This study also found a preference for chairs and benches made of wood, rather than wire or concrete, and for seats with backs and armrests for support. Carpman suggested that any seating provided should be comfortable for an hour or more if it is truly to support the activity potential of an outdoor space. Another seating arrangement, which might be provided by articulation of the perimeter, is "right-angle" seating. This configuration allows a comfortable distance and orientation for conversation. Fixed linear seating, by requiring companions to angle their heads or bodies toward one another, may cause discomfort. Certainly, it makes larger-group (even three or four) interaction virtually impossible. Fixed opposite seating in which companions directly face one another, or circular inward-facing seating, creates a "room" effect that may deter users who arrive after the space has been appropriated. Thus, a combination of right-angle seating and movable chairs may be best.
- *Design the fixed seating so that not all of it is arranged for groups.* People in hospitals, as in other semi-public places, do not necessarily want to interact with strangers or intrude on others' privacy. Therefore, designing a number of small seating areas for privacy may have the effect of limiting the number of people who can use them, because nobody wants to intrude on an unknown group or individual who has claimed that space. For example, six seating areas may limit their use to six groups (even six individuals). Although some semiprivate

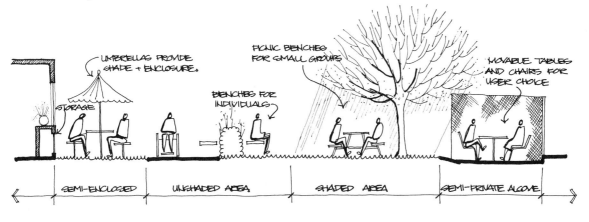

A variety of seating options and climatic conditions enables greater use of the outdoor space.

areas are desirable, it is good also to have a series of benches facing a view or circulation area rather than arranged in a group. Carpman, Grant, and Simmons (1986) described a study that found that benches designed to accommodate three to five people were preferred over either shorter (perceived as too short) or longer (too long) benches.

- *Provide some bench and table arrangements.* Tables allow more activities, including eating, reading, and writing, to occur in a space. They may also function as markers to establish territory, as people will seldom intrude on a table in use. Because the average group tends to contain four or fewer people, long tables such as eight-foot picnic tables are not as useful as are four-foot tables. Wood tables have the advantage of having a surface that does not have to look clean; however, the uneven surface may cause difficulties for people trying to write. People expect metal tables to be free of grease or soot and may not use tables they perceive as unclean. Umbrella tables with chairs are another popular option, providing shade and a semi-private grouping.

- *Place trash containers near all doors and social and pedestrian areas.* Trash containers permit easy disposal of food and paper products outdoors. The only litter of consequence at any of the hospitals observed was cigarette butts, eliciting complaints from maintenance workers. Smoking is not allowed inside the hospitals, and so it is done outdoors. Cheap, replaceable ash trays could be provided to reduce remains around tables or benches.

- *Orient all fixed seating to the views and sun.* This was the only constant found in the case studies. People

sit to observe the views. Orientation to the sun also is important, especially to patients.

- *Around some of the seating, use planting to create a sense of enclosure.* People gain a sense of security from sitting with something at their back, and in some type of enclosure. In the University of Michigan Hospitals study cited earlier, people preferred seating surrounded by a combination of shrubs and trees. Such seating will be enjoyed if oriented to a view of activity in such a way that one can observe without feeling observed in return.

- *Provide unusual or memorable items in the outdoor spaces.* Basic site furniture makes the space usable; unusual items make it memorable. Such things as water fountains, aviaries, extraordinary views, and artwork, are popular with patients and staff, offer a contrast with the hospital environment, and can lead to spontaneous conversation between strangers. Unusual items attract patients to a space, and they often show these features to visitors. For example, one year after an aviary was removed from a courtyard at a hospital, the staff still remembered it and felt that it had given a great deal of enjoyment to the patients.

- *Provide a drinking fountain outside and a bathroom within or next to the outdoor space.* These are basic amenities for any outdoor space and are necessary except for a short visit. They are particularly important to patients who have difficulty in changing location, or to visiting children, who might be discouraged from using indoor facilities for fear of disturbing the staff or patients. Make sure that the drinking fountain can be used by children and people in wheelchairs as well as standing adults, possibly on crutches, and that the water control is

At Casa Colina Hospital, Pomona, California, table and bench combinations can accommodate a wheelchair or gurney. Seating is supplemented by movable chairs and planter seats. This space opens directly from the dining room, with good visual and physical access, and offers a choice of sun and shade. (Photo: Robert Paine)

simple (requiring minimal manipulation and strength).

- *Consider putting an information kiosk or bulletin board in the outdoor space.* This could inform the patients of activities or opportunities in the hospital and services that might be needed or desired after discharge. It could also allow informal communication such as wanted or for sale notices (for example, someone selling a wheelchair or hospital bed for home use).

Storage and Equipment Areas

Make sure that both the use and the maintenance of the outdoor space are as simple as possible. Outdoor areas where the staff organize activities or therapy for patients should have storage space for any necessary equipment.

Recommendations

- *Supply a general storage room either adjacent to the outdoor space or with access immediately from the outdoor space.* Movable chairs, small tools, holiday decorations, maintenance tools, or therapy equipment can be stored here. At one hospital, the lack of such a storage area made it virtually impossible to perform therapeutic activities outdoors.
- *Provide electrical outlets in all outdoor spaces.* These are necessary not only for emergency care but also for any other special activities outdoors. Examples are power for listening to a radio and for hot plates at special functions.

A Supervisor for the Largest Spaces

The outdoor space should be as accessible as possible to the patients, but many inevitably will be far from the outdoor space. Some patients cannot physically move to the space by themselves, nor does the hospital staff want them left there unattended. Having a trained supervisor in the outdoor space thus may enable patients to use it freely without a regular medical staff member being present. A part-time supervisor could be hired to be on duty during those times when patients are not likely to use the space. The supervisor should have a comfortable location from which he or she can easily see the patients, with a connection to the hospital communications system for emergencies. In fact, even if an outdoor space is not supervised, it should have an emergency phone to summon assistance for patients and visitors.

This chapter has attempted to identify some common characteristics of hospital outdoor open spaces, their users, and the ways in which they are used. The findings of three case studies, together with the limited amount of literature available on hospital outdoor spaces, were drawn upon to create design recommendations.

It should be noted that the case studies were limited in sample time, respondents, geographic region, and climate. Certainly more studies are needed to verify the generalizations of documented patterns. Perhaps a comparative study similar to William Whyte's work on urban plazas might be undertaken. Guidelines for doors, seating arrangements, and pavings may apply equally in all regions; but those concerned with climate —sun, wind, rain—will clearly generate a range of responses. Another useful area of inquiry may be *indoor* social spaces: lounges, cafeterias, atriums, solariums, which interviews suggest are useful throughout the year.

Interviews from all three case-study hospitals revealed widespread belief that the physical environment *does* affect the patient. However, despite this belief,

The roof-garden at Alta Bates Hospital, Berkeley, California, where patients, staff, and visitors can find a comfortable place to sit in the sun, visit, or eat lunch. An extensive, highly articulated seating ledge creates long and short sitting areas, at both the center and the periphery of the garden, which can be used in conjunction with movable tables and chairs.

and the newly emerging research findings such as those of Verderber and Ulrich which indicate substantial benefits from natural and outdoor settings, the interviewees often added that a "pleasant" environment is not "really necessary" to recovery. This reveals the sketchy level of knowledge regarding the significance of outdoor use in hospitals. It suggests an important research question, which could be looked at from a variety of perspectives: does having a more pleasant environment directly affect patients' recovery rates or other aspects of recovery? This question is directly related to the justification for funding particular amenities, such as outdoor spaces, in the design of hospitals. Too often, elements are left out of a design as "not necessary," yet many people in the health profession are questioning that judgment as it relates to outdoor spaces. The therapeutic benefits of outdoor space for patients should be considered in conjunction with the benefits of such space for hospital staff. In making a case for the inclusion of hospital outdoor space to cost-conscious administrators, the prospect of more satisfied employees may tip the balance.

Finally, just as the development of medical technology has shaped the design of hospitals, and their outdoor spaces should they exist, further advances in both medical practice and technology will likely continue to influence design. In the more holistic and patient-oriented medical setting, outdoor space may reach its greatest potential. Carpman, Grant, and Simmons summarize the issue well: "Providing access to nature is not only beneficial, it is necessary. It is not a luxury or an optional 'add-on' feature. It is an integral part of a humane and caring environment" (1986, p. 212).

CASE STUDIES

Casa Colina Hospital, Pomona, California

Location and Context

Casa Colina Hospital is a sixty-patient rehabilitation hospital with four outdoor spaces. This hospital serves long-term patients with limited mobility (spinal injuries, brain dysfunction, and heart and stroke problems), and the staff actively use the outdoors for the

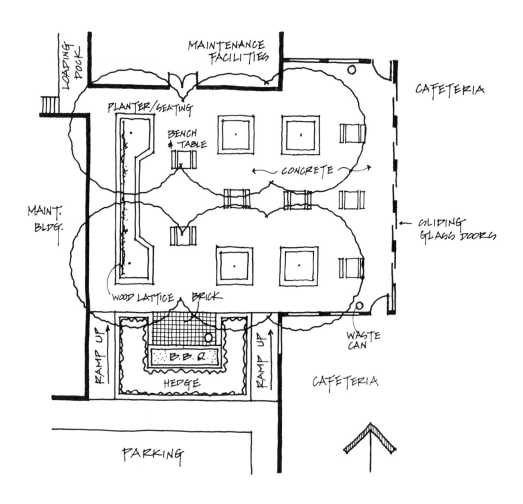

The Cafeteria Courtyard at Casa Colina Hospital, Pomona, California.

The Cafeteria Courtyard opens directly from the dining room, offers seating options (more movable chairs are often used), and good shading from the tree canopy.

patients' therapy. Most of the patients are in wheelchairs; some use walkers or are on gurneys. Spinal injury patients, because of their unimpaired cognitive abilities, are the most social. Staff include medical, therapeutic, and administrative persons. This hospital was the only one studied that had an outdoor space adjacent to a dining area, and so this was the outdoor space looked at most closely.

Description

The courtyard is approximately 60 by 65 feet. Access to the Cafeteria Courtyard is from a parking lot and from the dining room's sliding glass and heavy, push-bar doors. The courtyard has an adjustable barbecue and grill, wide aisles, and tables, all of which were chosen for disabled people's accessibility and use. Movable chairs and stuccoed block walls around the trees provide additional seating. The courtyard was renovated in 1981, two years before these observations.

Major Uses and Users

All staff may use the space. Hospital rules require that patients eat in their room unless they can eat (not necessarily travel to the dining room) unassisted by staff. This policy limits use of the dining room and Cafeteria Courtyard during mealtimes primarily to spinal injury and some stroke patients. The courtyard is the most frequently used outdoor space at the hospital, owing to its location near the dining room, where almost everybody in the hospital gathers sometime during the day. Consequently, the courtyard is well advertised. Weekday use is heaviest during lunch (11 A.M. to 2 P.M.) and in the afternoon by staff who eat and socialize here. Sometimes there was a problem with the patients' food trays being left outside—the staff did not feel that

it was up to them to remove the trays, and it was not part of the cafeteria's responsibility. However, after the renovation in 1981, things had been much better, and a dietician suggested that there was a sense of pride in the way the place looked that motivated people to clean up more carefully. Since the renovation, the courtyard was used for lunch by more staff and more visitors, with one therapist remarking on the difficulty of finding a table there at lunchtime.

On weekends, visitors use the courtyard most often during the midafternoon, socializing with patients. Patients most often use the space with visitors. Large groups of visitors and patients (one group of nine people was observed) were easily accommodated. Patients in wheelchairs and gurneys had no trouble operating the sliding glass doors. A second push-bar door can be opened by visitors and staff, but not by patients. Seating walls are occasionally used during the lunch hour as overflow areas or by children playing on them. The staff use the movable chairs at the sides of the tables where there is no bench available. The chairs are also used as footrests and shelves.

Successful Features

• The adjacent building space is well known and frequently used. The Cafeteria Courtyard acts as a spillover space from the dining room. Because the dining room is popular, the number of courtyard users is high.
• The disabled have been taken into account in all aspects.
• Movable chairs are available for additional seating around the tables.
• Dining room furniture arrangement provides easy access to sliding doors.

• Raised seating walls provide additional places to sit during crowded lunch hours.
• Abundant trash containers are close to tables and all doors.
• Windows from dining room advertise courtyard.
• Staff encourage patients to use the courtyard.
• Night lighting is supplied for use on warm evenings.

Unsuccessful Features

• Large planters reduce the room available for tables.
• Trees are not yet large enough to shade tables.
• Brick paving in front of the barbecue is a slight impediment to wheelchair use, but apparently no real problem.
• Push-bar doors are heavy and hard to open.

Kaiser Permanente Hospital, Martinez, California

Location and Context

Kaiser Permanente Hospital is a 204-patient-capacity facility, but as of 1983, only ninety-plus beds were occupied. The extra rooms were used for administrative and medical offices. This facility is primarily a medical and surgical hospital, although it does house the Kaiser system's regional inpatient psychiatric unit (approximately twenty-six patients). The psychiatric patients are treated for depression, trauma, alcohol, and drug

abuse. No psychiatric patient is admitted to the unit if considered dangerous to self or others.

The Therapy Garden is located in the psychiatric unit, enclosed by psychiatric offices and hallways. The garden was built by the staff and patients, who also maintain it. The psychiatric patients are physically healthy and mobile, and as part of their therapy, they are encouraged to socialize with other patients. There is another larger outdoor space next to the unit for recreation and games and also five other courtyards, similar in size, but they have not yet been developed.

Description

The garden is 75 by 20 feet, or 1,500 square feet. Sliding glass doors from the hallways open out onto the garden, but the sliding glass doors from the psychiatric offices are seldom used. There is a small lawn area and six raised planting beds with vegetables and flowers. The flowers were praised in a number of interviews. Seating is provided on a bench next to the sliding door, on two lawn chairs, or on the edges of the planters (a two-by-six turned sideways). There is a tool rack and storage shelves under the eaves, and a maintenance room adjacent to the lawn. The garden is surrounded by psychiatric medical offices.

Major Uses and Users

The psychiatric patients, performing prescribed tasks assigned by the therapists, use this space the most often. Such tasks are designed to help the patients engage in work that occupies them and directs them away from depressed introspection. Garden tasks are specifically designed to relate to the patient's acuity level. Some patients also use this space to sit on the bench and smoke or talk to another patient or a staff member.

This is also an important visual space for the unit, as the unit's main hallway runs along the garden's east side. The patients' telephone, constantly used, also overlooks the space.

Successful Features

• Maintenance, storage, and tool space are immediately adjacent and accessible to the space.
• The garden is not dependent on any other hospital department. Actual maintenance is by the patients and is part of the patients' therapy.
• The garden was conceived as part of the unit and the therapy program, and its central location promotes its use by the unit.
• Corridor windows advertise the garden's presence, and so people are always aware it is there.

Unsuccessful Features

• The garden has an identity problem, as the staff consider it the patients' space. But the patients use it

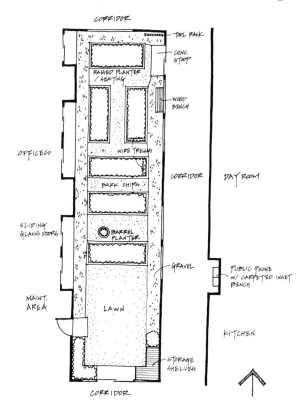

The therapy garden at Kaiser Permanente Hospital, Martinez, California.

primarily for assigned tasks. Its potential for socializing has not been fully developed.

• The garden needs a better socializing area. Seating is limited. Planter edges are useful only when working on the garden. Even an area conceived as a therapy and task space should have spaces for socializing, either during the task period or times when the space is unscheduled.

Alta Bates Hospital, Berkeley, California

Location and Context

Alta Bates Hospital is a six-story acute care hospital for three hundred patients. The average patient's stay is

6.4 days, but this can vary from twelve hours (maternity patient) to six weeks (chemical dependency patient) and beyond. Staff and patient type vary tremendously.

The hospital has four rooftop gardens and a ground-level street mall in front. The third-floor rooftop garden is next to the maternity ward and is the hospital's only garden with easy public access for staff, patients, and visitors. The maternity ward's nursing station overlooks the garden's entry from the building.

Description

The garden is 60 by 120 feet, or 7,200 square feet. It is on the southwest side of the building, with three sides

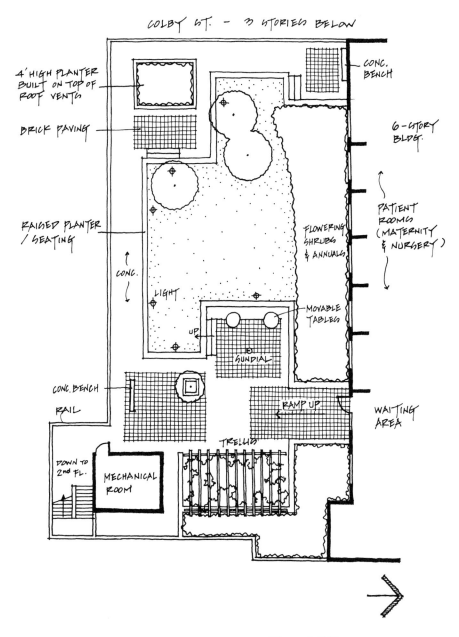

Third-floor rooftop garden at Alta Bates Hospital, Berkeley, California, in 1983. The south (left) boundary has been extended to create a much larger outdoor area, seen in the next figure.

286

Alta Bates Hospital rooftop garden in 1989. The area beyond the stairwell was added after the case study, incorporating many nooks and crannies, a variety of sitting spaces, and attractive, colorful planting.

open to the views and the street below, which changed in 1986 when a new building was built on the south side at the same level as the courtyard. There are three major seating areas: under the trellis, in the central paved area where there are two tables, and behind the planting bed at the far west side. Movable chairs are available except during the winter rainy season. There are two small trash containers by the trellis posts.

Major Uses and Users

On weekdays, this space is used primarily by staff, alone or in small groups, during lunchtime (11 A.M. to 2 P.M.) and again in the late afternoon to eat, talk, or smoke. On weekends, primarily visitors with patients use it for similar activities. Staff use decreases on the weekends because most of the administrative staff do not work then. The patients' use does not vary greatly between weekday and weekend. Most patient users were from the adjacent maternity ward (since moved to another location within the hospital), although the ease of access to this space from other floors allows more of the other patients to visit. This is the only garden at Alta Bates that has such easy access. Chil-

dren play on the grass, and a nurse noted that many younger patients and staff prefer to sit on the grass. The seating walls are extensively used, with people forming private groups on the walls by half-turning their backs to other users. A hospital consultant interviewed in the garden remarked on a food tray–litter problem similar to that at Casa Colina, which in this case was resolved by using disposable trays and providing trash containers. (*Note:* Since the case study was completed, new construction has essentially doubled the size of the rooftop garden, and some features have been changed. However, no new use information was available to update this study.)

Successful Features

• The hospital elevator to other floors is next to this garden's entry.
• Visiting children have room to play.
• Location on the southwest side of the building provides the most possible sun and heat for a cool coastal climate and so enables its use during the winter.
• Staff advertise the space, telling the patients about the garden.
• A large walking area is provided for exercise and stimulation of patients.
• Grass provides a pleasant smell, in contrast with regular hospital odors.
• Adjacent nursing station provides some control of the space.
• There are some private spaces behind the planter and shrub bed.
• Planting against the windows screens patients from people looking in. The hospital plants flowers between the shrubs and the windows for the patients inside to view.
• There is a variety of seating areas—public, private, open, enclosed, sunny, shaded. The linear permanent seating (the concrete seating walls) can be augmented by movable chairs for large- and small-group gatherings.
• Concrete seating walls provide places to sit during the wintertime when the chairs are stored.

Unsuccessful Features

• Brick ramp at the doors creates problems for wheelchairs and any attached IV units. It is difficult to coordinate movements over the mortar joints while going through the door
• There are few trash containers, though the maintenance is excellent
• There is no formal advertising of the space, no maps or notices of this garden. This is especially important to rooftop gardens where access requires changing floors
• The viewing area from the access door is too narrow. It is difficult to see the space from the access point,

which is through a narrow waiting area
• The door is not easily opened by wheelchair patients or anyone else in a weakened state

REFERENCES

Berkman, Lisa, and S. L. Syme. 1979. Social Networks, host resistance, and mortality: A 9 year follow-up study of Alameda County residents. *American Journal of Epidemiology* 109 (2): 186–204.

Boyce, W. Thomas, Eric Jensen, John G. Cassel, Albert Collier, Allan Smith, and Craig T. Ramey. 1977. Influence of life events and family routines on childhood respiratory tract illness. *Pediatrics* 60 (4), pt. 2: 609–615.

Canter, Sandra, and David Canter, eds. 1979. *Designing for therapeutic environments, a review of research.* New York: Wiley.

Carpman, Janet R., Myron Grant, and Deborah Simmons. 1986. *Design that cares: Planning health facilities for patients and visitors.* Chicago: American Hospital Association.

Cassel, John. 1976. The contribution of the social environment to host resistance. *American Journal of Epidemiology* 104 (2): 107–123.

Cooper, V. R., T. Wiltshire, and A. C. Hardy. 1973. Attitudes towards the use of heat-rejecting low light transmission glasses in office buildings. *Proceedings of CIE Conference*, Istanbul, October.

Cox, Anthony, and Philip Groves. 1981. *Design for health care.* London: Butterworth.

Dubos, Rene. 1959. *Mirage of health.* Garden City, N.Y.: Anchor Books.

————. 1968. *So human an animal.* New York: Scribner.

Falick, James. 1981. Humanistic design sells your hospital. *Hospitals*, February 16, pp. 68–74.

Feschbach, Dan. 1975. The dynamics of hospital expansion: A case study of "non-profit capitalism." *Health/PAC Bulletin*, May–June, pp. 16–20.

————. 1979. What's inside the black box: A case study of allocative politics in the Hill–Burton program. *International Journal of Health Services* 9 (2): 312–339.

Gruffydd, Bodfan. 1967. *Landscape architecture for new hospitals.* London: King Edwards Hospital Fund for London.

Hagedorn, Rosemary. 1981. Gardening and rehabilitation. In *Gardens and grounds for disabled and elderly people,* ed. Penny Smith, pp. 12–14. London: Centre on Environment for the Handicapped.

Hardy, Owen B., and Lawrence P. Lammers. 1986. *Hospitals: The planning and design process.* Rockville, Md.: Aspen.

Holmes, Thomas, and Minoru Masuda. 1973. Life change and illness susceptibility. In *Separation and depression: Clinical and research aspects,* ed. John Paul Scott and Edward C. Senay, pp. 161–186. Washington, D.C.: American Association for the Advancement of Science.

Holmes, Thomas, and R. H. Rahe. 1967. The Social Readjustment Rating Scale. *Journal of Psychosomatic Research* 11:213–218.

Jacobs, Selby, and Adrian Ostfeld. 1977. An epidemiological review of the mortality of bereavement. *Psychosomatic Medicine* 39 (5): 344–357.

James, W. Paul, and William Tatton-Brown. 1986. *Hospitals: Design and development.* London: Architectural Press.

Larson, C. T., ed. 1965. The effect of windowless classrooms on elementary school children. Ann Arbor: University of Michigan Architectural Research Laboratory.

Lewis, Charles A. 1979. Comment: Healing in the urban environment. A person/plant viewpoint. *APA Journal*, July, pp. 330–338.

Lindheim, Roslyn, ed. 1979. *Environments for humanized health care: Proceedings of the symposium.* Berkeley and Los Angeles: University of California Press.

————. 1979–1980. How modern hospitals got that way. *The CoEvolution Quarterly*, Winter, pp. 335–339.

————. 1981. Birthing centers and hospices: Reclaiming birth and death. *American Review of Public Health* 2: 1–29.

Lindheim, Roslyn, H. Glaser, and C. Coffin. 1972. *Changing hospital environments for children.* Cambridge, Mass.: Harvard University Press.

Lindheim, Roslyn, and S. L. Syme. 1983. Environments, people, and health. *Annual Review of Public Health* 4: 335–339.

Malkin, Jain. 1982. *The design of medical and dental facilities.* New York: Van Nostrand Reinhold.

Manning, P. 1963. Daylighted or windowless design for single-story factories? *Light and Lighting* 56: 188–192.

Marmot, Michael. 1976. Affluence, urbanization, and coronary heart disease in Japanese Americans. *American Journal of Epidemiology* 104: 225–247.

National Institute of Mental Health. Spring 1966. *The community mental health center, a three volume series: Planning, programming, and design for the community mental health center.* New York: Mental Health Materials Center.

Ne'eman, E. 1974. Visual aspects of sunlight in buildings. *Lighting Research and Technology* 6: 159–164.

Olds, Anita, and Patricia Daniel. 1987. *Child health care facilities: Design guidelines and literature outline.* Washington, D.C.: Association for the Care of Children's Health.

Olds, Anita, Beatrice Lewis, and Michael Joroff. 1985. Environmental design of child health care facilities. In *Research and design 85: Architectural applications of design and technology research.* General Proceedings. Washington, D.C.: American Institute of Architects Foundation.

Olsen, R. V. n.d. A user evaluation of a hospital park. Report. Bellevue Hospital Center, New York: Environmental Design Program.

Paine, Robert. 1984. Design guidelines for hospital outdoor spaces: Case studies of three hospitals. Master's thesis, University of California at Berkeley.

Parkes, C. Murray, B. Benjamin, and R. G. Fitzgerald. 1969. Broken heart: A statistical study of increased mortality among widowers. *British Medical Journal* 1(5646): 740–743.

Powels, John. 1973. On the limitations of modern medicine. *Science, Medicine and Man* 1: 1–30.

Stone, Peter, ed. 1980. *British hospital and health-care buildings: Designs and appraisals.* London: Architectural Press.

Syme, S. L., and Lisa Berkman. 1976. Social class, susceptibility, and sickness. *American Journal of Epidemiology* 104 (1): 1–8.

Thompson, John D., and Grace Golden. 1975. *The hospital: A social and architectural history.* New Haven, Conn.: Yale University Press.

Ulrich, Roger S. 1979. Visual landscapes and psychological well-being. *Landscape Research* 4: 17–19.

———. 1984. View through a window may influence recovery from surgery. *Science* 224: 420–21.

Ulrich, Roger S., and Robert P. Simons. 1986. Recovery from stress during exposure to everyday outdoor environments. In *The costs of not knowing*, ed. J. Wineman, R. Barnes, and C. Zimring, pp. 115–122. *Proceedings of the Seventeenth Annual Conference of the Environmental Research Association* (EDRA). Washington, D.C.: EDRA.

Verderber, Stephen F. 1982. Designing for the therapeutic functions of windows in the hospital rehabilitation environment. In *Knowledge for design*, ed P. Bart et al., pp. 476–492. College Park, Md.: Environmental Design Research Association.

———. 1986. Dimensions of person–window transactions in the hospital environment. *Environment and Behavior* 18: 450–466.

Whyte, William H. 1980. *The social life of small urban spaces.* Washington, D.C.: Conservation Foundation.

Wilson, Larkin. August 1972. Intensive care delirium, the effect of outside deprivation in a windowless unit. *Archives of Internal Medicine* 130: 225–226.

Wolff, Paul. 1979. The Adventure Playground as a therapeutic environment. In *Designing for therapeutic environments: A review of research*, ed. David Canter and Sandra Canter, pp. 87–117. Chichester, England: Wiley.

DESIGN REVIEW CHECKLIST

TYPES OF USERS

Adult Patients

1. Will the space be used primarily by a particular type of patient—orthopedic, maternity, psychiatric? If so, have the particular needs and abilities of that type of patient been determined and been used to inform the design?

2. Have patients' generally greater sensitivity to environmental conditions been taken into account, by providing protection from wind and a range of seating choices, from sunny to shady?

3. Is there easy access to restrooms and drinking fountains?

Child Patients

4. Does the outdoor play area open directly from the pediatric unit and offer good visibility from indoors?

5. Has every effort been made to locate the combined indoor and outdoor pediatric facilities on the ground floor? If this is impossible, has a rooftop location been chosen in preference to a play area separate from the unit?

6. Does a transitional "porch" area connect the indoors to the outdoor play area?

7. Has provision been made for creative and imaginative play, as well as physical play?

8. Have water, sand, and gardening areas been created that a child on a gurney or in a wheelchair can use? An ambulatory child?

9. Do climbing structures or tree houses offer various means of access—ramps, stairs, ladders, ropes to support different levels of ability?

10. Have any changes in elevation been used to create variation, challenge, opportunities to roll or slide, or enclosure?

11. Is the space interesting and sensorially rich—with a variety of trees, shrubs, and flowers; winding paths; and water features—elements offering different colors, shapes, textures, sounds, and smells?

12. Are there comfortable places for staff or visitors to sit while overseeing children at play?

13. Can most of the seating accommodate a wheelchair or gurney next to those seated, without blocking circulation? Do some of these arrangements include tables, where children can draw or play games with visitors or other patients or staff?

14. Does the seating at play opportunities allow for the participation (either actual or vicarious) of a weak child? Likewise, are there "parking nodes" out of the circulation path at these places for children using wheelchairs or gurneys?

15. Have the concepts of an Adventure Playground been considered, to allow children some control and to become actively involved with the environment?

16. If they are to be incorporated, is there adequate storage for "loose parts" and tools and an area for construction materials?

17. If teenaged patients are expected, has a separate, casual outdoor "hangout" area been considered, where patients can play music or engage in some types of sport?

Visitors

18. Are there outdoor spaces to support important and often emotional interactions between patients and visitors? Is the seating screened and oriented to create a sense of privacy, and have comfortable, residential—rather than institutional—materials been used?

19. Can outdoor spaces support groups of varying size, from two to five or six, or even ten? Are there subspaces of varying size, as well as movable furniture, to allow for flexibility?

20. Are there some elements or features that appeal to child visitors, as well as giving them an acceptable outlet for pent-up energy or anxiety?

Staff

21. Is there outdoor space immediately adjacent to various nursing units, to allow use by both the nurses themselves and the patients they oversee?

22. Are there spaces outdoors where staff members can spend time away from patients and visitors? Perhaps by temporarily claiming a subarea?

Location

23. Is there an outdoor space next to the dining area and opening directly from it?

24. Are access points to outdoor spaces nearest to those patients and staff who are most encouraged to use the spaces?

25. In a group of patients equally able (medically) to use the outdoor space, is the access point closest to those who are the least mobile?

26. In determining proximity to an outdoor space, have administrative staff been located farther away, in light of their longer lunch hours?

27. Do patients or staff unlikely to be able to visit an outdoor space have a view of the outdoors?

28. If windows face each other directly across an open space, is the space at least twenty feet wide, to avoid the "fishbowl" effect and maintain privacy?

29. Are outdoor spaces located to maximize their use throughout the year? Generally in a protected, southwest location?

PHYSICAL ACCESS

30. If at all possible, have outdoor spaces been made physically accessible, as opposed to just viewable?

31. Is the main entry to each outdoor space located appropriately for the intended users? That is, if the space is for general use, is the entry from a public area; or if it is for a specific group, is the entry in a ward or from a staff corridor?

32. Are the entry doors self-propping, easy to open, and not set to lock automatically upon closing?

33. Where possible, have automatic opening doors—which provide the easiest access—been chosen? Have sliding glass doors, without thresholds, been given the next highest preference?

34. Has smooth yet nonslippery paving been used?

35. Have nonslip coated railings been provided?

36. Are major walkways wide enough for two gurneys to pass (at least five feet)?

37. Where possible, have grade changes been used to create routes of varying difficulty within the outdoor space, including level routes? Have abrupt or extreme grade changes been avoided?

38. Where the climate permits, have melting devices been installed to allow use of walkways that might otherwise be made slippery by snow or ice?

39. Have entryways been designed to be free of ramps or steps and to allow maneuvering space around the door?

VIEWS TO OUTDOORS

40. Have windows onto outdoor spaces been located adjacent to elevator lobbies, front entries, lounges, cafeterias, and patients' rooms, to advertise the existence of the spaces?

41. Are there windows next to the entries to outdoor spaces —unless the doors themselves are an expanse of glass—to allow prospective users to "size up" the space before entering it?

42. Are there windows in the patients' rooms, therapeutic settings, and staff offices, with sill heights of twenty to thirty inches and preferably a "three-layer" view of the outdoors?

43. Have views been provided for patients who are chronically ill, paralyzed, or visually impaired?

44. Have vertical rather than horizontal window apertures been chosen, though with care not to create overnarrow "slits"?

45. Can any screens or curtains on the windows in the patients' rooms be easily operated by the patients themselves?

46. Is there a shelf or table near the window where a patient could tend indoor plants?

47. When a choice of views is possible, especially for patients' rooms, have natural elements such as vegetation or water been given preference over built or populated settings?

AWARENESS OF OUTDOOR SPACES

48. Are there maps of the hospital at the front entry and by elevators, clearly marking the location of outdoor spaces?

49. Is a map included in the patients' information packet, showing the location of outdoor spaces and the routes to them?

50. Is a tour of hospital facilities, including the outdoor spaces, available to patients who preplan their hospitalization?

PLANTING

51. If possible, has a lawn area been included in at least one outdoor space?

52. Does the planting offer a variety of color?

53. Have the largest possible tree specimens been used, to achieve mature trees as quickly as possible?

54. Does the planting create a variety of sunny to shady areas, including "dappled" shade?

55. Is planting dense rather than sparse, and does it use many varieties of trees, shrubs, and flowers?

56. Have plants with strong fragrances been introduced to contrast with the antiseptic odor common in hospitals?

57. Have "pop-up" sprinklers been used where people may walk, to avoid their tripping?

58. Have raised beds been considered for gardening, especially in settings where patients will be in residence for some time?

SITE FURNITURE

59. Is there a variety of seating, including movable chairs and right-angle configurations, emphasizing wood rather than wire or concrete, and supplied with backs and armrests?

60. Is the seating comfortable for stays of an hour or more?

61. Is there some bench seating that faces a view or circulation path, rather than being arranged in a group?

62. Are there some bench and table arrangements or umbrella tables with movable chairs?

63. Are there trash containers near all doors and social and pedestrian areas?

64. Is the fixed seating oriented to views and to sun?

65. Does the planting create a sense of enclosure around some of the seating?

66. Is there an unusual or memorable feature in the outdoor space, such as a fountain, aviary, or exceptional view?

67. Is there a drinking fountain and access to a bathroom within or near the outdoor space?

68. Has an information kiosk or bulletin board been considered?

STORAGE AND EQUIPMENT

69. Is there a general storage area either next to, or preferably opening directly from, the outdoor space? With provision for storing movable chairs, small tools, holiday decorations, maintenance equipment, therapy equipment, and the like?

70. Are there electrical outlets in all outdoor spaces, both for emergency care and for hot plates, record players, and so forth?

SUPERVISION/SAFETY

71. Has consideration been given to hiring a trained supervisor to staff a larger outdoor space, to allow more patients to use it without requiring the presence of a regular medical staff member?

72. Is there an emergency phone to summon assistance for patients or visitors?

INDEX

Adventure Playgrounds, 226, 269
Alcoa Plaza, San Francisco, 30, 39, 40
Alioto, Joseph, 120
Allendale Nursing Home, Allendale,
    New Jersey (case study), 201–203
Alta Bates Hospital, Berkeley, Calif.
    (case study), 285–287
American parks, history of, 69–70
AT&T Building, New York, 35
Automobile, pedestrians squeezed out
    by, 13

Berkeley BART Plaza, Berkeley, Calif.,
    57–59
Berkeley Totland, Berkeley, Calif. (case
    study), 138–139
Berkeley Way Minipark, Berkeley,
    Calif. (case study), 135–136
Blacksburg Christian Church Day Care
    Center, Blacksburg, Va. (case
    study), 249–250
Boeddeker Park, San Francisco, 87–88
    case study, 104–106
Bonus legislation, 13, 14
Bosselmann, Peter, 27
Boundaries
    of miniparks, 126–127
    of plazas, 27–29
Breuer, Marcel, 13, 46

Campus outdoor spaces, 143–167
    backdoor, 151–153
    backyard, 150–151
    campus entrances, 153–154
    campus spaces used by everyone, 153
    campus wear and tear, 162
    case studies, 163–167

common turf, campus spaces used by
    everyone, 153
crime and fear of crime, 158, 161
criterion for evaluating, 143
design recommendations, 144–163
design review questions, 169–170
favorite outdoor spaces, 156–158,
    159
finding one's way, 162
front porch, 145–146
front yard, 147–149
home base, spaces adjacent to specific
    buildings, 144–153
impromptu meetings, 143
literature on, 143–144
major plaza spaces, 154–156
outdoor study areas, 158–160
references, 167–168
spatial attributes, 155–156
traffic, 161–162
wear and tear, 162
Canada Mortgage and Housing
    Corporation, 246
Carpman, Janet R., 279, 280, 282
Casa Colina Hospital, Pomona, Calif.
    (case study), 282–284
Cashdan, Lisa, 120
CBS Building Plaza, New York City,
    20, 21
Central plaza, in campus outdoor
    spaces, 154–156
Central Plaza, Laney College, Oakland,
    Calif. (case study), 165–167
Charlie Dorr Minipark, Berkeley, Calif.
    (case study), 136–138
Chase Manhattan Plaza, New York, 33
Chevron Garden Plaza, San Francisco,

38
Chicago, First National Bank Plaza, 23,
    39–40, 44
Children. See also Day care outdoor
    spaces
    backing out, 244
    cognitive or perceptual development,
        219
    destructive needs of, 226
    as hospital patients, 268–269
    infants, spaces for, 242–243
    joining, 243–244, 248
    manipulation of environment by,
        226, 236, 239
    minipark use by, 123–134
    park use by, 77–80
    physical development, 219, 239, 242,
        250
    play areas for, at housing for elderly,
        194
    retreat, 244
    social development, 219
    watching, 243
Circulation
    in campus outdoor spaces, 146, 148,
        150, 153–155, 158
    in day care outdoor spaces, 232, 233,
        240
    in elderly housing outdoor spaces,
        179, 183, 188, 193–194
    in neighborhood parks, 72, 73, 74,
        76, 77, 88
    in plazas, 30–31
City Hall Square, Sacramento, 86
Coffin, C., 268
Congregate housing for Seniors,
    Aurora, Ill. (case study), 203–204

Corporate plazas, 9, 13–15, 16, 47–48, 51–55
Courthouse Square, Vancouver, 42
Covert socializing, in parks, 74
Cranz, Galen, 24–25, 69–70, 71
Crime and fear of crime, on campuses, 158, 161
Crocker Plaza, San Francisco, 2, 20, 22, 37, 47–49
Crowhurst-Lennard and Lennard, 12, 40, 42
Cudrohufsky, Walt, 144

Day care, demand for, 215
Day care outdoor spaces, 4, 215–256.
    See also Children
    activity areas and paths, 232, 237, 240, 244, 252
    adjacent uses, 229–230
    alternatives to ground-level playgrounds, 246
    ambiguity in play structure design, 219
    amount of space, 229, 252
    animals, 228, 231, 238–239, 255
    backing out, 244
    building and yard, 223, 231–232
    case studies, 246–256
    children served, numbers and ages of, 222–223
    climbing, sliding, and swinging, 239
    cognitive development, 219
    connection to neighborhood, 229–230, 253
    design review checklist, 259–261
    entry, 230–231
    gardening, 217, 227–228
    goals of, 222
    high places, 224, 253
    importance of environment, 216–218
    infants, spaces for, 242–243
    joining, 243, 248
    learning opportunities, 225, 226, 227, 228
    literature on, 218–219
    loose parts, 219, 239–240, 244, 248, 255
    manipulable elements, 226, 236, 239
    microclimate, 233–234, 246
    natural areas, 231, 250
    outdoor activities, 226–228
    outdoor eating, 227
    physical development, 219, 239, 242, 250
    planting guide, 235–237
    play and development in, 219–221, 232, 239, 242, 243
    play equipment 239, 244, 248, 255
    play units, 224
    porch, 232, 234, 252, 253
    real vehicles, 240–242
    real work, 227–228, 235, 256
    relationship of program to environment, 221–222
    retreat, 221, 244, 250
    safety, 223, 236–237, 242, 246
    scale, children's, 223–224, 252
    sensory stimulation, 225, 242
    site characteristics, 223, 228–229
    social development or role play, 219, 224, 243, 250
    social issues, 243–244
    storage, 222, 234–235, 240, 256
    subdividing the outdoor space, 223, 252, 253
    supervision, 217
    topography, 231
    user's handbook, 246
    variety and opportunity, 224–225
    watching, 243, 248
    water, sand, and dirt, 236–237
    wheeled toys, 240, 243, 244, 256
DeMars, Vernon, 163
de Moncheaux, Suzanne, 225, 226
Design guidelines, 5–6
Disabled park users, 77, 128
Disease, germ theory of, and hospital design, 263–264
Dog walking, in parks, 85
Dornbusch, David M., 14, 25
Downtown plaza designs, 2
    places to sit in, 3 *(fig)*
Duncaster Life Care Center, Bloomfield, Conn. (case study), 206–208

Eating outdoors. *See also* Picnicking
    in campus outdoor spaces, 145, 150, 155, 156, 157, 164
    in day care outdoor spaces, 227
    in elderly housing outdoor spaces, 182
    in miniparks, 134
    in parks, 83–84
    in plazas, 9, 43–44
Elderly. *See also* Housing for elderly
    design and aging process, 171–172
    housing alternatives for overlapping groups of, 173 *(tab)*
    increasing number of, 171
    literature on design and aging, 173–174
    minipark use by, 123–124, 133
    use of outdoor spaces by, 171
    use of parks by, 74–76
    use of public spaces by, 3
Ellis, Havelock, 43
Embarcadero Center, San Francisco, 35
Entry, design
    of campus, 144–146, 150–154
    of day care center, 230–231
    of elderly housing, 185–187
    of hospital outdoor space, 274–275
    of minipark, 125–126
    of neighborhood park, 75, 81
    of plaza, 20
Exxon Building, New York, 43–44

Faculty Glade, University of California at Berkeley (case study), 164–165
Faneuil Hall, Boston, 44
Farmers' markets, 46
Federal Office Building Plaza, Seattle, 17, 29, 33, 44, 45
Festival market places, 2
Fields, Keila, 223
50 Fremont Street Plaza, San Francisco, 28
First Interstate Bank Center, Seattle, 41
First National Bank Plaza, Chicago, 23, 39–40, 44
Fountains, 42–43
Francis, Mark, 71, 120
Free Speech Movement, 163
Freeway Park, Seattle, 6, 89
Front porch, in campus outdoor spaces, 145–146
Front yard, in campus outdoor spaces, 147–149
Fruin, John J., 14, 15, 63

Gardening
    in day care outdoor spaces, 217, 227–228
    in elderly housing outdoor spaces, 177, 182, 184, 190, 191–193, 204, 206
    in hospital outdoor spaces, 278, 284
Gehl, Jan, 10, 11, 12
General Services Administration, Public Building Service of, 12
Ghirardelli Square, San Francisco, 44
Giannini Plaza, Bank of America Building, San Francisco, 26, 29, 39, 40, 43, (case study), 52–55
Gold, Seymour, 70, 71
Goldberger, Paul, 15
Golden Gate Heights Park, San Francisco (case study), 101–102
Granville Square, Vancouver, 36
Gray, David, 76

Hacienda Child Development Center, Pleasanton, Calif. (case study), 250–253
Hallidie Plaza, San Francisco, 38, 39, 40
Halprin, Lawrence, 42, 72, 163
Handicapped Adventure Playground, London, 269
Harold B. Jones Child Study Center, Berkeley, Calif. (case study), 246–249
Hester, Rudolph, 71
Hill Burton Act (HBA) of 1946, 264
Homeless users of public space, 3–4, 97
Horticultural therapy, 278

Hospital outdoor spaces, 4–5, 263–286
  activities in, 271–272
  awareness of, 277–278
  case studies, 282–286
  child patients as users of, 268–269
  design review checklist, 289–290
  desire for, 267
  disease, relationship to social and
    physical environment, 265, 276,
    278, 282
  doors to, 274–275, 283
  evolution of hospital design and
    medical theory, 263–266
  gardening, 278, 284
  history of hospital design, 263–265
  hospital staff as users of, 271, 273,
    282
  importance of environment, 266
  literature on, 266–267
  location of, 269, 271, 272–273, 283,
    286
  patients as users of, 267–268
  paving and surfaces, 275
  physical access to, 273–275
  planting, 278–279
  play areas, 268–269, 270
  privacy in, 271, 273, 286
  site furniture and seating areas, 269,
    279–281, 283, 286
  size and dimensions of, 270, 273
  storage and equipment areas, 281,
    284
  supervisor for largest spaces, 281–282
  teenaged patients as users of, 269
  views to outdoors, 265, 266, 276–
    277, 283, 284
  visitors as users of, 269–271
  walkways, 275
  weekday/weekend use of, 272
  windows, 276–277
Housing, and outdoor spaces for the
    elderly, 171–208. See also Elderly
  age-related sensory losses, 179–180,
    188
  case studies, 197–208
  congregate housing for seniors, 203–
    204
  designing for autonomy of elderly,
    177, 187, 190, 192
  design recommendations, 174–197
  design review checklist, 210–214
  different levels of care on same site,
    174–176
  entry drive, 186–187
  exercise areas, 182–184, 194, 207
  finding one's way outdoors, 179
  gardening areas, 177, 182, 184, 190,
    191–193, 204, 206
  general layout and clustering, 174
  handrails, 177, 196–197
  lawn areas, 190
  literature review of design and aging,

  173–174
  location of, 177, 181, 188, 190, 194
  main entry/arrival court, 187
  management role, 172, 193, 201, 202
  microclimate, 176, 188, 190, 201,
    202
  outdoor lighting, 185, 187, 188, 189,
    197
  outdoor spaces, desire for, 171
  outdoor spaces for enjoying nature,
    184, 190, 206–207
  parking and secondary building
    access, 186–188, 198–199, 207
  physical therapy area, 182–183
  play areas for visiting children, 194
  private patios and balconies, 177,
    190–191, 204
  "prosthetic environment" for, 177
  ramps and stairs, 196
  safety and security in outdoor spaces,
    177–178, 185, 189, 190, 195–197,
    203–204
  seating, 178, 181, 185, 187, 188,
    194–195, 201
  shared patios and terraces, 188–189
  signage, 185, 187
  site entry, 178, 185
  spaces for social interaction, 180–182
  storage, 193
  subspaces for differing social needs,
    178–179, 188, 200
  tables, 195
  transition zone between indoor and
    outdoor areas, 178, 187, 189, 198–
    199, 204
  viewing outdoor areas from within
    building, 184–185, 202, 207
  walking surfaces, 189, 195–196
  walkways, 179, 183, 188, 193–194,
    207
HUD Building, Washington, D.C., 13,
    37, 46

Independent Apartments for Seniors,
    Lakewood, Calif. (case study),
    197–199
Independent Apartments for Seniors,
    San Rafael Commons, San Rafael,
    Calif., 199–201
Indoor street, 246
Infants, spaces for, 242–243
Information and signs
  in campus outdoor spaces, 146, 154,
    156
  in day care outdoor spaces, 231
  in elderly housing outdoor spaces,
    185, 197
  in miniparks, 125
  in neighborhood parks, 90
  in plazas, 46

Jackson, J.B., 10

Jacobs, Jane, 71
Jensen, Robert, 9
Joardar, S.D., 19, 21, 37
John Muir School Park, Berkeley, Calif.
    (case study), 111–112
Johns Hopkins Hospital, Baltimore, 264
Justin Herman Plaza, San Francisco, 18,
    19, 24, 25, (case study) 59–60

Kaiser Permanente Hospital, Martinez,
    Calif. (case study), 284–285
Kerline, George, 88
Krier, Rob and Leon, 11
Kritchevsky, Sybil, 217, 218, 224, 232,
    233, 239

LaFayette Square, Oakland, Calif., 3
Larkey Park, Walnut Creek, Calif. (case
    study), 91–93
Laurie, Michael, 70, 71
Leconte School Park, Berkeley, Calif.
    (case study), 112–113
Level changes, in plazas, 39–40
Lever House, New York City, 20
Lewis, Charles, 278
Lieberman, Eva, 26
Lighting
  in campus outdoor spaces, 161
  in housing for elderly, 185, 187, 188,
    189, 197
  in miniparks, 134
Lindheim, Roslyn, 268
Linn, Karl, 119
Literature review, design
  of campus outdoor spaces, 143–144
  of day care outdoor spaces, 218–219
  of elderly housing outdoor spaces,
    173–174
  of hospital outdoor spaces, 266–267
  of neighborhood parks, 71
  of plazas, 11–12
Live Oak Park, Berkeley, Calif. (case
    study), 97–99
Los Angeles, MacArthur Park, 74
London, St. James Park, 72
Lynch, Kevin, 10, 19, 132, 225

MacArthur Park, Los Angeles, 3, 74
Maintenance
  of elderly housing outdoor space,
    192–193
  of miniparks, 134–135
  of neighborhood parks, 90
  of plazas, 46
Maple Terrace, Aurora, Ill. (case
    study), 203–204
Martinelli House, San Rafael, 199
Martin Luther King Park, Berkeley, 82
Mechanics Plaza, San Francisco (case
    study), 49–51
Men
  seating location and, 155

Men (*Continued*)
  use of campus outdoor spaces by, 155, 161, 164
  use of parks by, 71, 74, 76, 86, 88, 95, 97, 100, 104
  use of plazas by, 21–22
Microclimate
  in campus outdoor spaces, 146
  in day care outdoor spaces, 233–234, 246
  in elderly housing outdoor spaces, 176, 188, 190, 201, 202
  in miniparks, 122
  in neighborhood parks, 73
  in plazas, 25–27
Milchert, Jurgen, 71–72
Miniparks, 119–139
  boundaries, 126–127
  case studies, 135–139
  design program, 123–125
  design recommendations, 120–135
  design review questions, 141–142
  entrance, 125–126
  functional areas, 127–128
  history of, 119–120
  location and size, 122–123
  maintenance, 134–135
  personnel and funding, 135
  plant materials, 132–133
  play areas, 128–131
  purpose of, 119–120
  references, 140
  site furniture, 133–135
  site selection, 121–122
  surfaces, 133
  usual design features, 120
Mission Dolores Park, San Francisco (case study), 99–101
Montgomery, Robert, 163
Moore, Gary, 217, 218, 221, 222, 225, 226
Moore, Robin, 109, 231
Mozingo, Louise, 22, 64

Neighborhood Commons, 119
Neighborhood parks, 4. *See also* Parks
Neill, J.W., 19, 27
New York, N.Y., 1961 zoning law, 13
Nightingale, Florence, 263
Noguchi, Isamu, 43

Ohlone Dog Park Association, 85
Ohlone Park, Berkeley, 85
Olds, Anita, 266, 268
Orinda Community Park, Orinda, Calif. (case study), 95–97
Osman, Fred Linn, 218

Pacific Oaks College Children's School, Pasadena, Calif., 223, (case study) 253–256
Parks. *See also* Miniparks

case studies, 91–113
children aged six to twelve, 78–80
coming to meet others, 74
coming with others, 73–74
court games, 82–83
covert socializing, 74
cycling, skateboarding, and roller skating, 85
design recommendations, 71–74
design review checklist, 115–118
disabled park users, 76
dog walking in, 85
future of neighborhood parks, 70–71
in high density, low- to medium-income neighborhoods, 102–107
in high density, medium- to high-income neighborhoods, 107–108
history of, 69–70
housing density and income levels of neighborhood, 90 *(tab)*
informal recreation, 83
jogging, 83
lawn games, 83
lights, 90
literature on urban parks, 71
in low density, low- to medium-income neighborhoods, 90–95
in low density, medium- to high-income neighborhoods, 95–97
lunchtime use by teenagers, 82
management and activity programming, 90
in medium density, low- to medium-income neighborhoods, 97–101
in medium density, medium- to high-income neighborhoods, 101–102
need for human contact, 73
need for natural setting, 71–73
overt socializing, 73–74
picnicking, 83–84
planting, 90
preschool users, 77–78
references, 113–114
retired and elderly users, 74–76
school parks, 108–113
signs, 90
skating, 83
sledding, 83
sunbathing, 83
tables and benches, 90
teenage users, 80–82
trash cans, 90
typical activities, 82–90
typology of, 90–91
vagrancy, 86–88
vandalism, 88–90
walls and fences, 90
Participation, by public in design process, 6, 71, 124, 171, 183, 221, 253
Paving and surfaces, 43
  in elderly housing outdoor spaces,

189, 190, 195–196
  in hospital outdoor spaces, 275
  in miniparks, 133
  in neighborhood parks, 77–78
  in plazas, 43
Paxson, Lynn, 120
Pedestrians in plazas
  behavior of, 21 *(tab)*
  effect of wind on, 26 *(tab)*
  flow of, 30–31
  squeezed out by automobiles, 13
People places, overall criteria for success in, 6
People's Park, Berkeley, Calif., 3
Pershing Square, Los Angeles, 3
Piazza, as term, 9
Picnicking
  by children, 227
  in public parks, 83–84
Place, as term, 9
Planting, 36–39
  in campus outdoor spaces, 156–158, 161
  in day care outdoor spaces, 235–236
  in hospital outdoor spaces, 278–279
  in miniparks, 132–133
  in neighborhood parks, 71–73, 79, 80
  in plazas, 36–39
Plazas
  boundaries and transitions, 27–29
  case studies, 47–62
  circulation, 30–31
  in contemporary U.S. scene, 12–15
  current use of, 9–10
  definition, 10
  design recommendations, 18–46
  design review checklist, 65–68
  discouraging use of, 3, 12
  in downtown office districts, 2
  food in, 43–44
  fountains, 42–43
  glare, 26
  information and signs, 46
  lawn areas, 38
  level changes, 39–40
  literature on, 10–12
  location, 18–19
  maintenance and amenities, 46
  male users, 21–22
  microclimate, 25–27
  overall comfort, 27
  passers through and lingerers, 20–21
  paving, 43
  pedestrian flow, 30–31
  pedestrian planning and health, 30
  pedestrians' behavior in, 21
  people watching, 33
  planting, 36–39
  primary and secondary seating, 33
  programs, 44–45
  public art, 40–43

references, 63–64
seating, 31–36
service area, 25
sitting alone and in groups, 35–36
size, 19
styles of seating, 33–35
subspaces, 29–30
sunlight, 25–26
temperature, 26
as term, 9
typical behavior in, 23–25
typology of downtown plazas, 15–18
uses and activities, 20–25, 30–36
vandalism and undesirables, 25, 32
vending, 45–46
visual complexity, 19–20
wind, 26
women users, 21–23
Portsmouth Square, San Francisco (case study), 103–104
Prescott, Elizabeth, 232, 233, 239
Privatization of public space, 2–3
Programs
    in miniparks, 135
    in neighborhood parks, 76, 81
    in plazas, 44–45
Project for Public Spaces Inc., 12, 44, 45, 46
Public art, 40–43
Public Building Service, General Services Administration, 12
Public events, location of, 1–2
Public life, need for, 1
Pushkarev, Boris, 12, 14, 20, 31, 39, 64

Regnier, Victor, 174, 175
Retired, use of parks by, 74–76
Rooftop play spaces, 246
Rosa Parks Towers, San Francisco (case study), 204–206
Rossi, Aldo, 11
Rudofsky, Bernard, 9, 43, 64
Rutledge, Albert J., 71

St. James Park, London, 72
St. Mary's Square, San Francisco, 37, 38, 40
Sacramento, City Hall Square in, 86
San Francisco, Downtown Plan, 15, 27, 29
San Pablo Park, Berkeley, Calif. (case study) 93–95
San Rafael Commons, San Rafael, Calif. (case study) 199–201

School parks, 108–112
    case studies, 111–113
    design guidelines, 110–111
Seating
    in campus outdoor spaces, 145–146, 149, 151, 155, 157, 159–160
    in elderly housing outdoor spaces, 178, 181, 185, 187, 188, 194–195, 201, 203–204
    in hospital outdoor spaces, 269, 279–281, 283, 286
    in miniparks, 133–134
    in neighborhood parks, 72–76, 78, 81, 90
    in plazas, 31–36
Serra, Richard, 42
Seating, 31–36
    amount of, 36
    materials used for, 36
    orientation of, 36
    primary and secondary, 33
    sitting alone and in groups, 35–36
    styles of, 33–35
Service area
    of miniparks, 121, 123
    of plazas, 25
Sidney Walton Square, San Francisco (case study), 107–108
Simmons, Maureen, 235, 280, 282
Sitte, Camillo, 10, 42
Sproul Plaza, University of California at Berkeley (case study), 163–164
Stirnberg, Bonafatius, 42
Street Life Project, 12, 43
Students, favorite places of, 157
Subspaces
    in elderly housing outdoor spaces, 178, 188–189
    in hospital outdoor spaces, 271, 273
    in miniparks, 127–128
    in plazas, 29–30
Sunbathing, in parks, 83

Teenagers
    favorite spaces of, 157
    as hospital patients, 269
    minipark use by, 123, 124, 128
    park use by, 80–82
Time-Life Plaza, New York City, 20
Toilets, for minipark, 134
Traffic, on campuses, 161–162
TransAmerica Redwood Park, San Francisco, 24–25, 38, 39, 43, 55–57, 87

Triangulation, 40
Trust for Public Land, 120

Ulrich, Roger, 276, 282
Union Square, San Francisco (case study), 10, 61–63
United Community Day Care Center, Brooklyn, 246
United Nations Plaza, San Francisco, 46
University of California at Santa Cruz, 162
University of Illinois at Champaign-Urbana, 154
    safety on campus, 161
University of Michigan Hospitals, 279, 280
University of New Mexico
    duck pond, 157
    safety on campus, 161
    Scholes Park, 157
    Smith Plaza, 154
University of Southern California, 162
University of Virginia, 154

Vagrancy, 86–88
Vandalism, 25, 88–90
    categories of damage, 89
    teenagers as cause of, 81
Vending, in plazas, 45–46
Verderber, Stephen F., 282

Washington Environmental Yard, Berkeley, Calif., 109, 231
Watkins Buchanan School Park, Washington, D.C., 109
Whyte, William, 9, 12, 13, 14, 21, 22, 32, 40, 43, 44, 87, 281
Wise, James, 89
Wolff, Paul, 269
Women
    fear of crime on campuses, 161
    seating location and, 155
    use of parks by, 71, 74, 76, 96, 104
    use of plazas by, 21–23
Workshop on Urban Open Space, 120
World Trade Center plaza, 13
Wright, "Mother," 3

Yamasaki, Minoru, 13

Zellerbach Plaza, San Francisco, 14, 51–52
Zimbardo, Phillip, 88
Zupan, Jeffrey, 13, 14, 20, 31, 39, 64